An Illustrated
OUTLINE HISTORY
OF MANKIND

An
Outline History

IN COLLABORATION WITH

✳

HAROLD LEE HITCHENS, M.A.
*Associate Editor, American Peoples
Encyclopedia*

✳

ALFRED DeGRAZIA, PH.D.
*Executive Officer, Committee for Research
in Social Sciences, Stanford University*

✳

FRANK L. ESTERQUEST, PH.D.
*Chairman, Department of History
Western College*

✳

CHARLES W. PAAPE, PH.D.
*Associate Professor of History, Carnegie
Institute of Technology*

Illustrated
of MANKIND

EDITED BY

Fay-Cooper Cole, Ph.D., Sc.D., LL.D.
Former Chairman, Department of Anthropology, The University of Chicago

AND

Harris Gaylord Warren, Ph.D.
Professor of History, University of Mississippi

WITH AN INTRODUCTION BY

Harry Elmer Barnes, Ph.D.
AUTHOR OF: The History of Western Civilization; An Intellectual
and Cultural History of the Western World; A History of
Historical Writing; Social Institutions;
Society in Transition

Chicago

SPENCER PRESS, Inc.

PRINTED IN THE UNITED STATES OF AMERICA

Part VII: EXPANSION OF THE EUROPEAN WORLD

42. An All-Water Route to India

EUROPE LOOKS BEYOND

SINCE THE BEGINNING OF recorded history, civilization has been moving westward. As the peoples of the Tigris and Euphrates valleys reached the height of their cultures, they lived to see their western neighbors of the "fertile crescent" region adopt their civilization and adapt it to the new and different requirements of their environment. Later the Greeks took the torch of civilization, then the Romans. Each time culture traveled, some of its characteristics were retained; but the acquirement of the new frontier caused changes and variations in the old order. This influence of the frontier has been one of the most important factors in the development of civilization.

This process of movement and change was about to make its most spectacular westward leap at the opening of the modern era. At the same time that kings were centralizing their power and modern nations were making their appearance, Europe was looking beyond its borders.

Part of this enlarged point of view was a result of the Crusades. Knights, on returning from the Holy Land, brought with them strange tales of stranger lands. They aroused interest and curiosity about what existed beyond the knowledge of those who stayed at home. Their awakened imagination demanded more information of the East.

The returning Crusaders brought with them something of even greater importance—spices! The value of this eastern product was obvious to a Europe which had no refrigeration, and was accustomed to food of uncertain age. With this oriental luxury, dining became more enjoyable; in fact, so accustomed did the noble and middle-class families become to these condiments that, lacking spices, the food formerly eaten without question became almost inedible. Spices from the East had become necessities.

IMPORTANCE OF THE RENAISSANCE

Two centuries earlier this interest in the East and the demand for an eastern product would have gone largely unsatisfied. Now, however, there were those who were ready to meet the need. This was a result of the great change, known as the Renaissance, which had swept over southern Europe by the middle of the fifteenth century.

No longer were the most intelligent and best educated minds restricted to supernatural matters. An interest in things worldly was no longer condemned. The attitude of the church toward business and commerce was relaxed, as can be seen in the Catholic theologians' arguments that the taking of interest on money loaned was no longer a sin, and in the beginnings of the Medici banking facilities in Italy. Throughout Europe trade was awakening and commerce was developing under a crude capitalistic system. This commercial revolution, which has been described in a previous section, was part of the general awakening which was affecting every phase of European life.

Marco Polo and his father and uncle on their arrival at the court of Kublai Khan

The Renaissance, however, did not change the attitude of Europe merely toward trade and commerce. The new interest in history, literature, and the humanities seemed to increase the thirst for knowledge of things beyond the limited confines of the European world. An appreciative audience was found by travelers and merchants who told of their visits to India, China, or Japan.

MARCO POLO

The most famous of the men who recounted what had been seen in the East was Marco

Marco Polo (1254?–?1324)

Polo, a Venetian merchant. His father, Nicolo Polo, and his uncle, Maffeo Polo, had made extensive travels through the Far East in the course of their trading ventures, and had visited the magnificent court of the Tartar emperor, Kublai Khan. In 1271 Marco Polo accompanied them on another long trading journey, and in 1275 they arrived in Peking. Marco quickly became a favorite of the Khan, and was entrusted with several official missions for the government. Wherever he went, Marco Polo was impressed by the splendor and riches of the Orient. This wealth, accumulated over centuries by Oriental despots, was a source of amazement to a man of 13th-century Europe, where there was no over-all ruler, and conflicts among small states and feudal principalities had helped prevent such great magnificence and display of riches. The Venetian travelers remained in China for 17 years. Finally given permission to leave, they sailed along the Chinese, Malayan, and Indian coasts to Persia, and then traveled overland to the Mediterranean. They arrived in Venice in 1295.

A few years later, while he was fighting for the Venetians in one of the numerous wars between Italian city-states, Marco Polo was captured in a naval encounter with the Genoese, and was thrown into prison. There he dictated an account of his travels to a fellow captive. Published as *The Book of Marco Polo*, his book showed him to be a keen, entertaining observer. Its descriptions of Oriental wealth and magnificence stirred European interest in the Far East and encouraged attempts to find a more direct route to it. It undoubtedly had a great influence on subsequent European exploration.

NEW INVENTIONS

Great inventions and discoveries in the field of science made it possible to spread information about lands beyond Europe. To Johann Gutenberg of Mainz is usually given the credit for the invention, about 1447, of printing by means of movable type although the use of movable initial letters, certainly a forerunner of the invention, was in use previously. This epoch-making invention's effect on the spread of knowledge can hardly be over-emphasized. Information regarding dis-

Map of the World, made by Battista Agnese in the 16th century. Agnese, a Genoese, is supposed to have made his maps in Venice, about 1536–64

coveries or explorations would henceforth be rapidly diffused over broad areas. As each new seeker of knowledge set out, he had at hand the combined information gained by all of his predecessors.

About the same time more accurate maps and charts were introduced. Earlier, the compass and astrolabe had come into use. These new aids permitted the navigator to make longer voyages. No more must the mariner hug the coast and follow each irregularity of the shore line. Finally the invention of the telescope, though it occurred much later (1609), freed the sailor from much of the uncertainty of sea travel.

TRADE ROUTES OF VENICE AND GENOA

The first European traders to profit as a result of the demand for products of the East were those of the Italian city-states. Making their way through the Mediterranean to Asia, these Italians were met by Arab traders, who had carried goods from such centers as Calicut and Malacca. These products were then distributed in Europe by the Italians themselves or passed on to merchants from the countries of northern Europe. The Asiatic routes were either overland, across deserts and mountains, or else by a long sea route around the eastern and southern coasts,

then through the Red Sea or Persian Gulf, and finally by land to the cities of the Black and Mediterranean seas.

Either by land or by sea, this means of transporting goods was uncertain and very expensive. Not only was the route long, and the mountains, deserts, and seas dangerous, but the threat of bandits and pirates was always present.

In spite of the tremendous risks involved, Venice, Genoa, and the other Italian cities profited because of their geographical position. The position of Italy made it the logical center of Mediterranean shipping, and trade bound for the German rivers of northern Europe found it convenient to use Venice or Genoa as southern terminals. It was partly an accident of geography that gave Italy a virtual monopoly of intercontinental trade.

This monopoly depended upon two conditions: the eastern end of the Mediterranean, the gateway to the Orient, must remain open; and this gateway must be the only one into Asia. The Portuguese and the Ottoman Turks threatened to remove these requirements for monopoly. Portuguese navigators, directed by Prince Henry, began cautiously to advance along the unknown African coast in an attempt to find an all-water route to India. If they succeeded, not only would transportation costs be lowered significantly, but also

Levant Traders, from a 15th-century MS. The Levant was the eastern Mediterranean region

the bulk of the trade from the Orient would avoid the Mediterranean and Italy entirely by following the Atlantic coast to the northern European market.

The idea that the Turks closed the trade routes, and so caused the discovery of America and the all-water route to India, persists in spite of revelations which modify that interpretation. Traders from Italian city-states enjoyed favored positions in important Near Eastern cities. Their privileges were threatened by the expansion of the Ottoman Turks, and considerable friction resulted. Mohammed II began in 1452 to levy tariff duties, or tribute, on trading vessels passing through the Bosporous. Constantinople fell in 1453, and ten years later the Turks and the Venetians began a war which lasted until 1479. During this period there were clashes in Syria, Asia Minor, Greece, and the Mediterranean islands. By 1500, Genoa as well as Venice lost important colonies in the Near East.

The northern trade route from the Orient was threatened by warfare between the Turks; but Damascus, Beirut, Aleppo, and Alexandria grew in importance while the middle and northern routes were practically closed. The Turks continued their advance. Damascus fell in 1516, and in the following year Cairo was added to the Ottoman possessions. So it was that by 1520 the old routes between Orient and Occident were under Ottoman control.

PRINCE HENRY THE NAVIGATOR

Significant events were happening in the West while the Ottoman Turks were successfully challenging Italian preeminence in the Near East. Prince Henry, a younger son of King John I of Portugal, was directing the Portuguese search for an all-water route to India. The Navigator, as he is known to history, had taken part in the conquest of Ceuta and was inspired with the hope of finding the rumored kingdom of Prester John. Henry possessed an independent income and was keenly interested in geography and navigation. The astronomical laboratory which he built on the promontory of Sagres in south-

Prince Henry the Navigator (1394–1460)

western Portugal, became the gathering place of those daring navigators who were advancing down the African coast. As these voyages continued, Henry apparently lost much of his desire to effect an alliance with Prester John to attack the Ottomans from the rear, and concentrated his attention on discovery.

Trained in the school conducted at the laboratory, financed by the prince, encouraged and aided by new charts and maps, daring mariners made important progress. The Madeira Islands were reached by 1420, and then in time the whole western coast of Africa became known to Europeans. Cape Verde was reached in 1445, the mouth of the Gambia River in 1455, and, when Henry died in 1462, his navigators had advanced to a point within twelve degrees of the equator.

Tracing the African coast line was only one of the contributions made by Prince Henry and his associates. An even more important result was the training given to navigators and the development of navigation. It can be said that the science of navigation originated with Prince Henry, since it scarcely existed before his day. A large number of the early explorers and discoverers of the New World were trained by Henry, and they all profited from his efforts.

DOWN AND AROUND AFRICA

Moreover, the attempts to encircle Africa did not die with the prince. Portuguese captains continued their efforts. When Cape Palmas was discovered and it was found that the coast bent eastward, there was great rejoicing. Now the sea route to India had been found! The southern coast of Africa had been reached! Hopes were dashed the following year when they discovered that, after twelve hundred miles, the coast again swung southward. The slow, progressive, stage-by-stage following of the coast line had to be continued. In 1471 the equator was crossed, and thereafter progress was more rapid.

Vasco da Gama (1469?–1524)

Bartholomew Diaz (1450?–1500), Portuguese mariner who discovered the Cape of Good Hope

In 1486, Diaz encountered a storm off the coast and for thirteen days was blown southward, out of sight of shore. When he saw land again, he found he was two hundred miles east of the southern tip of Africa. Upon his return, Diaz named this point the Cape of Storms; but soon afterward King John II changed the name to Cape of Good Hope, because it gave promise of a sea route to India and great profits.

Both of these hopes were realized in 1498 when Vasco da Gama reached India and on his return brought back a cargo worth sixty times the cost of his expedition. This discovery of a sea route to India was the finishing blow to Italian trade supremacy. The Asiatic land routes were almost wholly discarded and the Atlantic superseded the Mediterranean as the center of European sea trade. World economic leadership moved westward from Italy to Portugal and her neighbor in the Iberian peninsula, Spain.

Christopher Columbus at the Royal Court of Spain

Departure of Columbus' Expedition from Palos, Spain, in August, 1492

Columbus' Landing on San Salvador, from a copper engraving by Theodore de Bry, 1590

Columbus in Cuba, left; center, discovery of San Domingo, from a sketch attributed to Columbus, in "Epistola Christofori Colom", published about 1494; right, one of Columbus' vessels, from the same book

43. The Search for "El Dorado"

COLUMBUS

THE ENTERPRISING Spanish monarchs, having expelled the Moors from Spain, were free to turn their attention to the pleas of Columbus, a Genoese seafarer, who had lived for several years in the Madeira Islands. Here he had listened eagerly to his fellow sailors discussing stories and legends of the uncharted lands to the west. He had early accepted the views of the new scientific school: that the world was spherical in shape and that but a short stretch of water lay between western Europe and the Orient. He was fired with the desire to be the first to find a western route to the rich spice markets.

Repeated discouragement and failure met his efforts to gain royal aid in both Portugal and England. Queen Isabella of Spain, however, was finally won over by his enthusiasm and persistence. Thus, but for the shortsightedness of John II of Portugal and Henry VII of England, those countries might have had the honor of discovering the new world.

Three small vessels, well fitted out and manned by crews of capable young sailors, set sail from Palos on August 3, 1492. The little fleet first made the Canary Islands, and then sailed westward September 6 on the real voyage of discovery. After five weeks, Columbus' expedition sighted land on October 12, 1492. It was probably the island known now as Watling Island in the Bahama group. The natives found there were called "Indians" by Columbus, because he believed he had reached a part of the Indies.

After sailing along the coast of Cuba and exploring the island of Haiti in a fruitless search for gold and spices, Columbus left for Spain with two vessels of the fleet. The wreckage of the third, which had run aground on the shores of the island of Haiti, was used to construct a fort for the forty-four Spaniards who remained and founded the first colony in the New World.

Columbus was received by Ferdinand and Isabella with great honor and was granted the titles of admiral, and viceroy of all the lands he had discovered. He made three other western voyages, in which he touched various islands of the Caribbean, the northern coast of South America, and what is now British Honduras. He died in 1506, probably not knowing that instead of discovering a new route to the Indies, he had found a New World.

There is fairly valid evidence to show that Leif Ericsson discovered America in the year 1000, and gave the name Vinland to the

Landing of Lief Ericsson in the New World, from an original painting by Edward Moran

Americus Vespucius

region he visited. No permanent results came from this discovery, and so far as the European world is concerned, Columbus was the discoverer of America. Although Columbus made one of the greatest discoveries in history, the New World was named for Americus Vespucius. Without any basis of fact, Vespucius claimed to have made a voyage to the New World before Columbus' voyage of 1498, and geographers called the new lands America.

Spain and Portugal divided the newly discovered lands between them by the Treaty of Tordesillas in 1494. This treaty took the place of the papal bull of 1493, and gave to Portugal those areas which lay east of a line drawn 370 leagues west of the Cape Verde Islands, while Spain was to have those areas which lay west of the line.

MAGELLAN

Various Spanish expeditions between 1493 and about 1530, traced the American coast line from what became New England to the Straits of Magellan. Greatest of all Spanish explorers was Magellan, a native of Portugal who entered Spanish service.

On September 10, 1519, Magellan's little fleet of five vessels and some 250 men set sail from Spain. Only one of the five was to complete the first voyage around the world.

Ferdinand Magellan

After spending the winter on the shores of Patagonia in southern Argentina, quelling innumerable mutinies among his crew, and suffering terrible physical hardships, Magellan reached the Philippine Islands early in the

spring of 1521. Here he lost his life in a native uprising. In spite of the loss of leader, vessels, and crew, one ship of the original fleet, the *Victoria*, persevered and cast anchor in Seville on September 8, 1522, just three years after it had left Spain.

This voyage, supplemented by earlier ones, gave the Spaniards a limited idea, at least, of the Atlantic coast line of the New World and definitely proved that the Spice Islands could be reached by sailing west. Spanish interest in the lucrative spice trade was reawakened, and stately galleons soon appeared in the regions visited by Magellan and his companions.

CORTÉS—GREATEST OF THE CONQUISTADORES

Balboa, a bankrupt stowaway on an expedition to Central America, led an expedition across the Isthmus of Panama in 1513 and discovered the Pacific Ocean, which he called the South Sea. Unfortunately, Balboa was executed by the treacherous Pedrarias Dávila, the governor who was sent by Charles V to take charge of affairs on the Isthmus.

Great as were the achievements of Balboa, another explorer was to surpass them within a few years. This man was Hernando Cortés, who possessed remarkable military and executive ability. After distinguishing himself in the conquest of Cuba, Cortés won greater glory in Mexico. The governor of Cuba gave him command of an expedition to Mexico in

Balboa claiming the Pacific Ocean for Spain

1519, a command which Cortés retained in spite of later efforts to remove him. Equipped with eleven vessels, four hundred soldiers, two hundred Indians, thirty-two horses, and ten cannon, Cortés set out for the mainland and disembarked at what is now Vera Cruz.

In Mexico he found the Aztecs, a powerful and highly civilized people who had migrated from the north early in the fourteenth century. They had quickly conquered the natives and set up a harsh rule over them. The subjugated tribes saw in Cortés and his army a way to avenge themselves and were eager to join forces against their hated rulers. Montezuma, the Aztec king, feared that these white strangers were the supernatural beings for whom his subject people had been waiting to free them from oppression. He hastened to send gifts to the Spaniards rather than attacking them. Cortés, fired with the zeal of conquest, proceeded on his way to the Aztec capital, Mexico City, or Tenochtitlán, as it was then called.

The magnificence of this city, with its great stone buildings and its vast stores of precious metals, exceeded even the most extravagant hopes of Cortés and his followers. The daring Spanish leader immediately strengthened his position by seizing the person of Montezuma and assuming virtual charge of the government. His successful conquest, however, was interrupted by a recall expedition sent out by Velásquez, governor of Cuba. Cortés ignored the governor's command, defeated his forces, and incorporated them into his own troops.

Upon returning to the Aztec capital, the Spanish conqueror found the city and countryside in a state of insurrection. He released Montezuma, hoping that his influence would quiet the frenzied condition of the Aztecs. This stratagem was of no avail, for the native ruler was fatally wounded by one of his own race when he urged obedience to the Spaniards.

Attacked by Indian hordes, Cortés' army suffered severely, losing most of its horses, cannon, and treasure, although a few soldiers survived and escaped to friendly near-by tribes. Sufficient reinforcements arrived from Cuba late in 1520, however, so that by the summer of the next year, Cortés recaptured Mexico City and proceeded to consolidate the conquest of the rest of Mexico. Not content with this, he organized new expeditions to explore the territory south of Mexico, and to voyage along the Pacific coast in an attempt to find a strait through the continent.

CONQUEST OF THE INCAS

Similar activity was going on in South America with Panama as a base. The most spectacular of these expeditions and conquests was that of Pizarro in Peru, which parallels the earlier Mexican conquest in many instances. The natives of Peru, the Incas, were as far advanced in government and civilization as the Aztecs in Mexico. By conquest and amalgamation, the Inca

Cortés and Montezuma

Execution of the Inca by Pizarro

An Inca Dwelling

empire had acquired great wealth and political efficiency.

Pizarro, the Spanish conqueror of Peru, was of humble origin. His was a striking military character, with tremendous capacity for work, and indomitable perseverance. Though less brilliant and attractive than Cortés, Pizarro gained the confidence and obedience of his subordinates. Associated with him were an adventurous soldier named Almagro and a renegade priest known as De Luque. This priest had gained a considerable fortune and served as financier of the Pizarro expeditions.

After several perilous attempts, Pizarro sailed for Peru in January, 1531, with an army of less than two hundred men, and twenty-seven horses. He established his headquarters near the present Tumbez. Here he learned of civil war caused by the jealousy of two Inca brothers, Huascar and Atahualpa. The latter had succeeded in establishing his authority in Cuzco, and like Montezuma, was inclined to believe the white intruders were supernatural beings and sought to placate them with gifts.

The Spaniards, in the meantime, moved into the interior toward Caxamarca, which they found deserted. Outside the city, Atahualpa and the Inca army of forty thousand drew up ready to annihilate the tiny Spanish force. Pizarro stationed his forces in strategic positions, seized the Inca, and slaughtered great numbers of the over-confident natives. Atahualpa hoped to secure his release by assembling a dazzling store of treasure; but the Spaniards took the treasure and then executed the Inca because of his complicity in the death of Huascar.

Pizarro entered Cuzco in November, 1533, and began to consolidate his victories. Details of government, allotment of lands and Indian laborers, management of mines, and the organization of new expeditions occupied the efforts of Pizarro for the next few years. Civil wars and rebellion disturbed the peace of Peru until the Pizarros and the Almagros were eliminated, but the conquest of South America continued.

EXTENSION OF SPANISH CONTROL

Tales of mines of fabulous wealth, rich cities, and incredible buried treasure kept these eager conquerors in constant search of "El Dorado." Hostile natives, swamps, rivers, pathless mountains, deserts, disease, and jealousy did not daunt them. Always just beyond, they expected to find the veritable pot of gold. Although Cortés and Pizarro present the most fascinating and picturesque figures among them, many others in a lesser degree carried on similar conquests in Ecuador, Colombia, the Amazon basin, and Chile.

Spanish conquest of the central portion of the continent, now occupied largely by Argentina and Paraguay, began with the expedition of Mendoza to the Plata basin in 1536. An early attempt to found Buenos Aires failed, but control over the great river system which converges into the estuary known as La Plata, was secured after 1537. In that year a fort was built at the site of Asunción, now the capital of Paraguay. Martínez de Irala governed Asunción with more than usual skill, and sent exploring expeditions into the Gran Chaco west of the Paraguay River. Buenos Aires was finally founded in 1580 by Garay; but by that time the western portion of modern Argentina was being settled from Chile and Peru.

SPANISH CONQUESTS NORTH OF THE GULF AND THE RIO GRANDE

Spanish efforts in the New World were by no means confined to Mexico and South America during the era of the *conquistadores*. Florida, the northern Gulf coast, and the

De Soto's Discovery of the Mississippi in 1541, from a painting by W. H. Powell. (Three Lions)

great southwest were traversed by Spanish forces before 1550.

The first Spanish adventurer to visit what is now the United States, was Juan Ponce de León who sought in vain for the Fountain of Youth in Florida. Many attempts to colonize Florida failed. An expedition led by Narvaez in 1528 was almost completely destroyed. Hernando de Soto landed at Tampa Bay in 1539 with more than five hundred men. For three years De Soto led his men through the wilderness in an irregular march which crossed most of what is now the southern part of the United States east of the Mississippi River. De Soto himself was buried in the Mississippi when he died in 1542, and the remnants of the expedition returned to Mexico.

Ponce de León

Francisco Vásquez de Coronado led another expedition into the great southwest while De Soto was on his odyssey. Coronado was seeking the Seven Cities of Cibola, supposedly rich in gold and other treasures. The exploration took Coronado as far as modern Kansas, but no wealthy cities were found. A party from this expedition discovered the Grand Canyon of the Colorado and added much to knowledge of the regions visited.

In the same year that Coronado returned to Mexico, 1542, explorations were made by sea northward along the California coast by Cabrillo and Ferrelo. Sixty years later Vizcaíno sailed along the same route.

Successful Spanish colonies were established by 1609 at two points in what is now the United States. The first was that of St. Augustine, Florida, which Menéndez de Avilés founded in 1565 to defeat French efforts to gain a foothold. The second was Santa Fe, New Mexico, which Juan de Oñate placed on a permanent basis between 1598 and 1609. It has been a capital ever since.

Coronado leading his men across New Mexico in their search for the Seven Cities of Cibola

Spain was less successful in her colonizing efforts in continental North America than in the southern continent. This situation is partially explained by the wide area over which Spanish efforts were scattered, and by the small population of Spain itself. Then, too, the northern wilderness was far less attractive than the more southern regions where Indian tribes were usually more docile, and where there were rich civilizations to conquer.

POLITICAL ADMINISTRATION IN SPANISH COLONIES

The whole Spanish colonial policy was dictated by royal authority. The Spanish possessions in the New World were considered as belonging personally to the sovereigns of Castile. With the rapid growth of colonial territory, it was necessary in 1524 to organize a special advisory committee. This royal body, the Council of the Indies, was the final legislative and judicial authority of Spanish America. It organized territorial units, and filled political and religious offices.

At first the king had allowed private adventurers to organize and subsidize their own expeditions, and rule and dispose of the territory they had conquered, with certain royal restrictions. It was found, however, that frequently the "conqueror" was tempted to ignore superior authority. Thus the king decided to send a royal appointee, known as a viceroy, to represent him personally in the New World. The territory over which he had charge was known as a viceroyalty.

The *audiencia*, in reality an administrative court system, grew up as a check on the viceroy. This body acted as the supreme judicial authority in the colonies, and had original jurisdiction over matters concerning the crown and the Indians. It came to act in a supervisory capacity over trade and finance, as well as over general preservation of law and order.

In the colonial towns, some degree of self-government manifested itself. The function of the *cabildo*, or municipal council, was similar to that of the New England town meeting. The tendency in Spanish America, however, was

Latin America about 1700

away from municipal democratic political organization, due largely to royal hostility and local corruption. Spain made an effort to maintain an honest and efficient colonial administration, which resulted in a system of checks on all officials. The viceroy was watched by the *audiencia*, which in turn was spied upon by the lower officials. Later on, a *residencia*, or royal visitor, was sent over to look into the conduct of all the officials, large and small, in a given political unit.

Since corruption, however, was a chronic malady in Spanish America, the wonder is not that the governmental structure finally weakened, but that it survived as long as it did.

ECONOMIC ORGANIZATION IN SOUTH AMERICA

The economic life of the Spanish colonies was also closely supervised by government officials. Spain, as well as the other nations, held mercantilist views of commerce. The welfare of the state, so the theory proposed, required a full treasury of gold, a large consuming and producing population, and an extensive merchant marine. A favorable balance of trade must be always maintained; therefore, exports must exceed imports so that specie may come into the country. To accomplish this, raw materials must be brought in, manufactured, exported, and sold.

Colonies, it was held, should furnish raw materials and markets for the mother country, but must not be competitors. It was the policy of each European state to monopolize and control the trade of its colonies.

As early as 1503, Spain organized the *Casa de Contratación* or House of Trade, for the purpose of controlling colonial commerce. Certain ports, such as Seville in Spain and Vera Cruz and Porto Bello in America, were opened for colonial trade. To protect and supervise this commerce, a fleet system was established. Land commerce in America had to be carried on by pack trains and river boats, while wholesale and retail trade was conducted in markets and fairs, the most famous of which was held in Porto Bello in Panama.

In spite of her efforts, Spain was not able to maintain her trade monopoly, for Dutch, English, and French freebooters and pirates captured her treasure fleets, and smuggled great quantities of goods into Spanish colonial ports.

The labor supply in Spanish America came largely from the native population. The first "conquerors" were given the right to the labor of the Indians living within their royal grant. This plan was known as the *encomienda* system and aimed to protect and civilize the native, as

Mission San Diego de Alcala

well as to exploit him. Among those who early opposed this virtual enslavement of the Indian population was Father Las Casas. He used his influence against the continuance of this system, but, strange to say, favored Negro slavery in its place.

The principal occupations in Spanish America were agriculture and stock raising, although mining attracted the attention of the more adventurous and was heavily subsidized by the home government.

SOCIAL LIFE IN THE SPANISH COLONIES

Spanish American civilization became a composite of Spanish and native culture, based on a fairly rigid caste system. Most of the high political offices were held by native born Spaniards, while next in the social scale were the Creoles, who were American born. Below them came the *mestizo*, half Spanish and half Indian, who made up the larger part of the army. The two lowest classes, the Indians and the Negroes, had no social or political privileges and were held in slavery.

Education was by no means neglected, but it too was based on the caste system. Only the sons of government officials, wealthy merchants, and professional men attended the colonial universities. The scholarly qualities of the universities of Mexico and Lima, established by royal decree in 1553, were recognized by contemporary European institutions of higher learning. Many of the clergy were devotees of intellectual pursuits, and books were written on scholarly and popular subjects.

Las Casas protecting Indians from soldiers

393

Instruction and curriculum in the universities, as well as in the mission school, were supervised closely by the Church. Only the most elementary educational institutions were opened to the *mestizos*.

The influence of the Church, however, was perhaps felt most in the frontier Indian mission, where the *encomienda* system failed or proved unprofitable. Members of the Jesuit, Dominican, and Franciscan orders were especially zealous in carrying Christianity and European civilization to the frontier natives. The aim of these missionaries was not only to gain religious converts, but to give industrial and agricultural training.

Each mission had its grain fields, ranges, vegetable gardens, orchards, and vineyards, which were cared for by the Indians. The men were given instruction in carpentry and wine-making, while the native women learned spinning, weaving, sewing, and cooking. The intention was to train the natives to support themselves, and eventually to give them the mission lands and transfer their religious care to the parish priest.

By continuing this process, the Spanish missionaries gradually carried Christianity north of the Rio Grande into Texas, and by 1776 they had gone as far north as the present San Francisco. Prominent among these zealous *padres* were Kino and Serra who planted missions in the southwest and in California.

Frequently military posts, *presidios*, were found necessary to protect the mission outposts. Thus the *padre* and the soldier became the two civilizing forces on the frontier. In spite of these military and religious efforts, however, the Spaniards were unable to gain more than a feeble political hold on what is now southwestern United States.

Whatever the shortcomings of the Spanish treatment of the native population, it does not compare unfavorably with that of other European powers. Spain aimed at racial, religious, and cultural assimilation rather than annihilation as England did. This practice resulted in a large population of mixed blood and the removal of racial antipathies. Today there are in Spanish America relatively few families of pure European blood.

CONTRIBUTION OF SPAIN TO THE AMERICAS

Historians in the past have unjustly minimized Spanish contributions to the Americas. The "conquerors" bore not only the sword, but also Christianity to the New World. They brought with them such plants as the citrus fruits, sugar and cotton; and such animals as cattle, sheep, horses, and mules.

From Mexico to Chile, the Spanish language and institutions are still dominant. Some of the United States have Spanish names, namely, California, Florida, Colorado, and Nevada. Innumerable rivers, mountains, towns, and cities north of the Río Grande bear Spanish names, while the southwestern Indian tribes in the United States still speak Spanish in preference to English. In many of the cities in the same region, there is a Spanish quarter in which life goes on much as it has done for generations past. Spanish architecture is still popular, and in Florida and the southwestern states are interesting old missions and government buildings erected by the early Spaniards.

The southern and western festival, rodeo, and mission plays are carried over from colonial days. Even the American cowboy has inherited his trade, his horse, his outfit, vocabulary, and methods from his earlier Spanish prototype. Bells in numerous belfries of mission churches and cathedrals from Florida to California bear the Spanish royal coat of arms; while land surveys in many of the southwestern states still rest on early Spanish grants, whose original records are now in Mexico City or Madrid. In fact, the literature, history, and life of this whole region of the United States is distinctly colored by its early background. Thus in spite of the fact that Spain was eventually pushed out of the limits of the United States, she has left us a rich heritage.

Her greatest contribution, however, was made to the present Latin-American nations. Today the Spanish blood, language, religion, and culture are the dominant forces in the republics to the south. Spain no longer controls the political destiny of any area of the New World, but she still wields immeasurable influence in her gift of Hispanic civilization.

44. French Exploration and Settlement in the New World

EARLY EXPLORATIONS AND SETTLEMENTS

EARLY IN THE SIXTEENTH CENTURY, France began to contest the exclusive claim of Spain and Portugal to the New World. Her ambitious young monarch, Francis I, actively encouraged exploration. Verrazano, a Florentine, was the first explorer authorized to sail to America under the French flag. He was to seek a northwestern route to the Orient. Although the voyage failed in this objective, Verrazano sailed along the North American coast from Cape Fear to Newfoundland. To the St. Lawrence area, he gave the significant name of New France. Cartier's voyages (1534-1541) continued these explorations. He established French territorial claims to Newfoundland, the gulf area of the St. Lawrence River, and sailed as far inland as the present Montreal.

The first attempt at a permanent French settlement in North America was made by Ribaut on Port Royal Sound in the Carolinas in 1562. Composed entirely of men, ill-adapted to an agricultural life, and surrounded by hostile Indians, the colony was soon abandoned. Two years later, the Huguenot, Laudonnière, led an expedition to the St. Johns River in Florida. Here the active opposition of the Spaniards to the French Protestants prevented a permanent settlement.

FRENCH IN CANADA

French fishermen had long been among those Europeans who frequented the Newfoundland fisheries. Except for this contact, France for over fifty years after Cartier, turned her back on the New World and consolidated her position on the Continent. There were several attempts at settlement in the early seventeenth century. The first was made on the island of St. Croix in 1604. The severe winter nearly destroyed the colony, and the survivors moved across the Bay of Fundy, locating at present day Annapolis Royal, Nova Scotia.

Samuel de Champlain

The founding of Quebec by the intrepid Champlain in 1608, marked the beginning of the active French regime in Canada. His earlier experiences in the Caribbean area had fitted him for strenuous explorations in the north. He coasted along the New England shore to below Cape Cod. Later he explored the interior south of Quebec, discovering the lake that now bears his name. Champlain's most important exploring expeditions, however, were those which took him on fur-trading ventures and on elusive quests for a northwest passage. He ascended the Ottawa River in 1613 and reached the shores of Lake Huron two years later. Nicolet, his agent, entered the Lake Michigan area in 1634. Shortly thereafter, the explorer-traders, Radisson and Groseilliers, entered the region west and north of Lake Superior.

Champlain, with his vision of empire, found the French court indifferent to his plans. His settlement at Quebec seemed feeble when compared with the thriving English colonies, but by 1650 it was the center from which all French activities in North America radiated. The "city on the rock" was also the center of the Jesuit missionary operations. This religious order proved invaluable to France in winning Indian allies and exploring the interior. Unfortunately for the French, their friendship for

Giovanni da Verrazano, who explored the coast of North America northward from Cape Fear. (Three Lions)

the Algonquins, dating from Champlain's aid to them in 1609, had won the implacable hatred of the Iroquois. This hostility was to drive the latter into an alliance with the British that continuously threatened the French fur trade. In venting their enmity, the Iroquois made no distinction between adventurers and missionaries. Martyrdom came to Father Jean de Brébeuf and many of his contemporaries during these years.

GOVERNORS OF NEW FRANCE

After a period of inactivity, New France became a royal province in 1663. Among the new personnel sent out to administer the government, were men whose names were to rank with Champlain's. Authority in the colony

was vested in three officials: governor, bishop, and *intendant.* Bishop and governor repeated overseas the familiar European struggle between civil and religious groups for supremacy. The *intendant* was often left to execute the actual tasks of government. The first of these, Jean Talon, was appointed in 1665. He directed the administration of justice and audited financial and military records. He took advantage of his wide supervisory power and sent agents into the interior. The expansion of agriculture, fishing, and the production of naval stores, were encouraged.

Among the colonial governors, the Count de Frontenac was perhaps the greatest figure. He possessed unusual insight into the ultimate importance of the interior in relation to the impending Anglo-French duel. Frontenac planned a chain of forts to extend southwestward along the Great Lakes and Mississippi. He appreciated the importance of Indian allies, and whooped and danced around camp fires with the Indian braves when good policy demanded it. Bitter quarrels with the bishop and the *intendant* brought about his recall in 1682. Seven years later he was reappointed to secure New France against English attack.

FRANCE IN THE CARIBBEAN

While interest in Canada had lagged, France sought tropical islands. She was no more immune to the lure of the Caribbean than were the other nations. Her belated entrance into competition with the English, Dutch, and Spanish put her at some disadvantage, but by 1664 France held fourteen of the lesser islands. The early trading companies had sold out to proprietors who were prospering on the sugar

Jacques Cartier landing in 1534 on the Gaspe Peninsula, Canada. (Three Lions)

Jean Nicolet in Wisconsin, 1634. Nicolet was the first white man to explore the Wisconsin area

Marquette and Jolliet descending the Mississippi in 1673

business, made possible by a plantation and slave economy. When Colbert became finance minister in 1662, he sent agents to curtail these private powers and to re-establish royal authority. Two years later, Louis XIV chartered the West India Company, granting it a forty-year monopoly of trade and colonization. Despite royal patronage, the company could not defend its holdings against England and Holland, and dissolved in 1674.

FRENCH IN THE MISSISSIPPI VALLEY

Several of the early Jesuits had ventured to the Great Lakes and entered some of their tributaries. French influence on the Mississippi, which began with Marquette and Jolliet in 1673, was extended by one of the greatest of explorers. This man was La Salle, member of a wealthy bourgeois family, who bore a royal patent to build forts and engage in the fur trade. He was fortunate to have the complete sympathy of Governor Frontenac, who encouraged him to undertake more explorations. In 1677 LaSalle was given a monopoly of the

Count Frontenac meeting Iroquois chiefs in 1673. The Iroquois were usually hostile to France. (Three Lions)

fur trade in the Mississippi region. Two years later, on Lake Erie, he built the *Griffon*, the first sailing vessel on the upper Great Lakes. Later he made several journeys into the interior. In 1680 La Salle left his faithful lieutenant, Tonty, at Fort Crevecouer in Illinois, while he returned for supplies. Meanwhile, Michel Aco and Father Hennepin explored the upper Mississippi. Mutiny and Indian attacks forced Tonti to retire to Green Bay. There La Salle met him, and in 1682 the two led an expedition which floated down the Mississippi from the Illinois country to its mouth. There, on April 9, La Salle took possession of the entire Mississippi Valley for his king, and named it Louisiana, after him.

La Salle at the mouth of the Mississippi, claiming the great valley for his king

With the French entrance upon the Gulf of Mexico, a Franco-Spanish frontier was formed. In 1684, La Salle returned from France to plant a colony at the mouth of the Mississippi. Insufficient geographical knowledge and faulty navigation caused the expedition to land at a lonely spot on the Texas coast. Spanish ships, like so many vultures, were dispatched at once from Vera Cruz to destroy the trespassers. Five expeditions sailed and returned, however, without having sighted them.

Throughout a weary three years, La Salle and his party tried to find the Mississippi, his original goal. It finally became evident that their only hope was to attempt to reach Canada overland. A small group, led by La Salle, undertook this journey in 1687. The daring leader, unfortunately, was assassinated by mutineers while they were still in Texas. Only a handful lived to reach Canada.

Spain had a dual reason for awakening to the necessity of defending the northern Gulf coast in the late seventeenth century. The English had firmly entrenched themselves in Carolina and were expanding westward through trade connections. The French, also, were becoming a menace in the Mississippi Valley. To meet this competition, Spanish officials decided on the occupation of Pensacola Bay. An expedition left Mexico in October, 1698, only a few days before a French fleet sailed from Europe, bound for the same destination.

The French government had bestowed La Salle's patent upon Iberville, distinguished in French service in the Hudson's Bay region. He put in at Pensacola for supplies. Beneath the elaborate exchange of Latin courtesies between the commanders, it was obvious that Spain had made good her claim. Iberville went on to the Bay of Biloxi, and from that port proceeded to re-discover the Mississippi River.

The French were anxious to prevent the Gulf from becoming a Spanish lake, and knew the miserable state of the Pensacola settlement. In turn, the Spanish were aware that the French Gulf colonies were intended ultimately to serve as bases for the conquest of the Mexican mines. The *entente* of the two royal houses in Europe, however, prevented open hostilities and kept unblemished the veneer of courtesy.

MOBILE BAY SETTLEMENT

Iberville moved his colony to a site on the Mobile River in 1702. When he returned to France, Bienville, his brother, replaced him. Under the latter's leadership, Mobile was founded in 1710, New Orleans in 1718, and numerous French posts appeared on the Red and Arkansas rivers. At the same time, Alarcón, the Spanish governor, established San Antonio across the narrowing frontier.

Under the cloak of exploration, plans were made to extend the French forts northward to cut into the trade with the prairie tribes and open a route to Mexico. Along what is now the Canadian-American frontier, the La Vérendrye family penetrated beyond Lake Superior to Lake Winnepeg in 1733. A few years later they reached to the Missouri River.

Frequent clashes occurred on the Louisiana-Texas frontier. It was evident that, despite orders from Europe, there were many New World issues which could be settled only in the areas concerned. The long period of Franco-Spanish rivalry in the Gulf region ended with Spain's alliance with France in 1761 against the traditional English enemy. Spain was rewarded for its support by the cession of part of Louisiana which lay west of the Mississippi. The problem of frontier maintenance now was vastly increased. For France, after 1763, the bitter struggle with England and Spain for the domination of the New World was a phase of the past. The wonder is not that France, like Spain, lost her colonial possessions, but that she held them so long.

FRENCH RULE IN AMERICA

The primary interest of France in her North American possessions lay in the development of fisheries and the fur trade. France, in common with the European economic policy of the seventeenth and eighteenth centuries, had built her colonial system upon the mercantilist theory. The increase of revenue was the goal of colonial administration and conditioned the methods of government. French overseas control soon came to be synonymous with trade monopoly and close unity of Church and state. Paternalism pervaded every phase of society—

The Old Courthouse at Cahokia, from a photograph made about 1890

from the royal governor to the half-savage *coureur-de-bois*. Private enterprise and individualism were completely smothered under such a system. Domination and supervision were the watchwords of every official, no matter how petty his rank.

Colonists did not come to New France with their families or with plans for permanent homes, as they did in the English provinces. Without the transplantation of ordinary family and municipal life, there was no demand for local political institutions. A sparse population spread over a huge wilderness area from Quebec to New Orleans. Tiny trading posts and missions, well armed forts, and diminutive villages dotted the lakes and rivers of the French western empire.

Missions were established at Cahokia and Kaskaskia in "the Illinois" by 1700. Fort Chartres and Prairie du Rocher, in the same area, were founded in the next four decades. Fort Detroit, built in 1701, was essential for the defense of the western water highways against the Iroquois; while Fort Vincennes, on the Wabash River, founded in 1732, became an important interior post. Fur trading and agriculture were the chief pursuits of these western settlements. A large quantity of produce was exported, to both Detroit and the French West Indies. The agricultural production of all New France, however, was insufficient for its own needs.

It was hoped that these settlements could hold and develop the rich fur-bearing region. The constant concern of French officials was defense against the Indians, the English, and, in the lower Mississippi Valley, the Spanish.

New France was then, generally speaking, more of an outpost than a colony.

COMPANY OF NEW FRANCE

The right to exploit French possessions and establish the necessary civil, religious, and military jurisdiction was granted by the king to companies or individuals. To these proprietors the fur trade was the great attraction, and the founding of permanent settlements lagged. In 1627, monopolistic powers were assigned to the Company of New France, patronized by Cardinal Richelieu. Continental entanglements, financial difficulties, and the constant hostility of the English and Iroquois were sufficient to cause its failure.

An organization of merchants in New France now took over the company's privileges and obligations. In 1647, the king allowed the new proprietors to set up the Council of Quebec. This consisted of the Jesuit superior and the commandant of the troops at Montreal, in association with the governor. Two citizens were added to that body the next year, but it bore no likeness to the representative institutions in Virginia or New England.

New France became a royal province in 1663. Slow economic development and a quarreling officialdom were the reasons for the cancellation of the company's charter. A Sovereign Council of Quebec was created by the Crown and remained a vital arm of the government until the end of the French regime. This body consisted of the governor, bishop, *intendant*, and certain councilors, the number being increased several times. The Council administered and enforced the laws, served as a court of appeal, and regulated trade.

The governor, as the representative of the Crown, acted as official head of the Council. His conduct, in turn, was checked by the *intendant* who had charge of expenditures, and exercised some judicial powers. This system of divided administrative responsibility resulted in bitter conflict and inefficient control.

THE CHURCH IN NEW FRANCE

After the early period of courageous missionary efforts, the Church became an influential temporal as well as spiritual enterprise.

François de Laval became the first bishop of the diocese of Quebec in 1658, and exercised ecclesiastical jurisdiction over all of New France. He used his influence in the Council to uphold the Church and to fight the liquor traffic with the Indians. His interest in education led to the establishment of an academy in Quebec, which later became Laval University.

The Church controlled about one-fourth of the lands granted for settlement and was the greatest single landholder. The parish was the unit for the administration of justice and the levying of the militia, as well as the basis for the social life of the community. The clergy had complete control over education, and censored the reading material which came into the colony. To the influence of the Church is due much of the picturesque charm and color of the Quebec of today.

LANDHOLDING IN NEW FRANCE

The landholding policy of New France was a system already growing antiquated in France when it was introduced into the New World. The custom of granting land titles and certain privileges and responsibilities to prominent persons was known as the "*seigneurial system*." In this feudal hierarchy, the *seigneur* guaranteed military aid to the Crown, in return for large grants usually along the St. Lawrence River. His feudal tenants, or *habitants*, occupied the subdivisions of the estate, rendering to the lord certain services and dues, such as produce and labor, at stated intervals. The *seigneuries*, large and small, were always apportioned in the form of long narrow strips, with river frontage to solve the important problems of transportation and communication. With a *habitant* house on each strip, the general impression was of a continuous line of buildings as one went down the St. Lawrence.

SOCIAL LIFE IN NEW FRANCE

The social cleavage between the lord and *habitant* was slight. Frequently the former spent the winter in Quebec, but during the summer months might be found in the field with his tenants. As a group, the latter lived a happy, carefree existence, and left political and economic problems to their officials in Quebec. Social life was relatively simple in the country communities, with the curè, the *seigneur*, and the two counselors of the parish taking the lead in their activities. Quebec and Montreal had some small degree of winter court life, but it was very informal and crude.

This feudal system, however, gradually fell into decay as the *habitants* deserted to become trappers. These *coureurs-de-bois* soon forgot their European heritage as they ranged the forests, often living as members of Indian tribes. This life not only furnished adventure, but also great returns on illicit trade. In fact, the commerce in furs was the only really profitable occupation of the colony, since industry was neglected and primitive agricultural methods produced insignificant results.

At the close of the French regime in 1763, the population of New France numbered only 65,000. Most of the people lived along the banks of the St. Lawrence, and but a few thousand were scattered throughout the Middle West. This population, spaced so thinly over such a vast area, could be only an outpost of French power, but it was a serious barrier to English expansion from the tidewater region east of the Alleghenies.

FRENCH CONTRIBUTIONS TO THE NEW WORLD

We are apt to conclude that French influence in America ended with its defeat by England in 1763. However, visitors in the province of Quebec today are amazed at the amount of French atmosphere and culture still in existence. This is not surprising, when one realizes that at least 80 per cent of the population is of French extraction. Beautiful churches, wayside shrines, lovely old châteaux, dog carts, and thatched roofs, all testify to an earlier French civilization. The names of innumerable rivers, lakes, villages, and cities throughout the eastern half of the North American continent bear witness to the exploring zeal of the French *voyageur*. Perhaps the most charming bit of New France left in the United States is in the city of New Orleans, where French colonial architecture, customs, and traditions still remain as living evidence of a delightful Old World existence.

45. English Colonies in the New World

ENGLISH SEA-DOGS

ENGLISH ACTIVITY in the New World parallels that of France. It took a century of warfare on the sea with Spain before England made definite steps to compete with the discoverers of America for its possession. The claim of the British Lion to the Western Hemisphere was based on the voyages of the Cabots, in particular that of John Cabot in 1497. These voyages extended along the coast of North America from about Cape Breton Island to South Carolina. Not

only did these voyages furnish England a claim to America, but they laid out an immediately used route to the Newfoundland fisheries. For these great services, the thrifty Henry VII gave Cabot the sum of ten pounds sterling and a pension of twenty pounds annually.

Sir John Hawkins

Sir Francis Drake

During the next century, the efforts of England in America were motivated almost entirely by the desire to injure Spain in her colonial empire "for the glory of God and King." Hawkins, one of the most relentless enemies of Catholic Spain, urged his Protestant seamen to read their Bibles and sing hymns in the intervals between attacks on Spanish treasure ships. He saw nothing irreligious, moreover, in kidnaping Negroes in Africa and selling them as slaves in the Spanish possessions.

Hawkins' most noted associate in "singeing the Spanish beard" was Francis Drake. He fearlessly preyed upon the Spanish ships conveying American gold and silver to the mother country. He even attacked the Spaniards in their own colonial ports, once sacking Panama, and climaxing his career by sailing through the Straits of Magellan and capturing the surprised Spanish treasure ships in the harbors of Peru.

Then, realizing that the Spaniards would be lying in wait for him on his eastward return, he turned his prow westward and continued around the world (1577).

Other English, as well as French and Dutch, "sea-dogs" made their headquarters in the many islands of the West Indies and on the northern coast of South America. From here they inflicted stinging blows on the Spaniards who regarded them as pirates. For almost three hundred years they made this region, known as "The Spanish Main," a fearsome place indeed.

NORTHWEST PASSAGE

To the north, other English captains were considering America as a barrier which must be penetrated before the more attractive India and China could be reached. Among those who searched for a northwest passage to Asia were Frobisher, who explored Labrador, Baffin Bay, and Frobisher Bay (1576); Davis, who explored the same region (1585); Hudson, who discovered the bay bearing his name (1610); and Baffin (1615-1616). Davis also discovered the Falkland Islands, east of the Straits of Magellan.

Hakluyt is also important in the story of early English exploration. His contribution consisted of collecting and publishing accounts

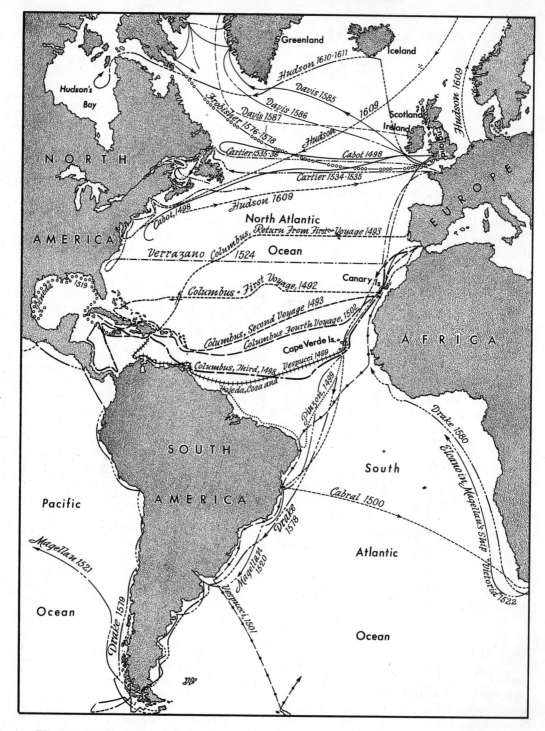

The Atlantic in the age of discovery—Important voyages by European navigators, 1492-1615

John Cabot and his son landing on Cape Breton Island in 1497. (Three Lions)

of these voyages, thus popularizing the new geographical knowledge.

EARLY COLONIZERS

England's first attempt to colonize America occurred in 1578, when Sir Humphrey Gilbert was given a charter which assigned land in

Sir Humphrey Gilbert reading the charter granting him rights to explore and colonize in America

Sir Walter Raleigh

Newfoundland to him. The group of settlers who went with him found this region unsuitable for colonization and returned to England. Gilbert died in a storm on the return voyage and efforts at colonizing were carried on by his half-brother, Raleigh, who made several attempts to found colonies along the Virginia and Carolina coast. None of these was permanent. Because England was so completely involved in fighting the Spanish Armada in 1588, no supplies were sent, nor any communications maintained with the settlements. When in 1591 an English ship finally did arrive on the Virginia coast, not a single trace could be found of the settlers except the single word "Croatoan" cut in the bark of a tree. Croatoan was the name of a friendly Indian tribe. No more has ever been learned about the fate of this "Lost Colony of Roanoke." Perhaps the settlers were killed by Indians or Spaniards, absorbed by an Indian tribe, or possibly they attempted to move their settlement and were

The "Lost Colony's" only trace was the word "Croatoan" carved on a tree trunk

lost at sea. Among those who disappeared was Virginia Dare, the first white child born in English America.

REASONS FOR COLONIZATION

The question arises as to why English colonization took place. Why was it that, within a period of seventy-five years (1607-1682), twelve English colonies were planted on the American continent? The general motives for expansion, found whenever peoples engage in such a movement, are curiosity, hope for trade, religious zeal, discontent with home conditions, desire to lessen the surplus home population, patriotism, and the military need to forestall rivals and to seize strategic points. Almost all of these reasons can be found behind English colonization.

In 1485, Henry VII, a Tudor, became king of England. He needed support in order to keep his throne and turned for aid to the middle class. Although prices were rising as a result of the inflation caused by the great imports of gold from America, Henry VII and his successors favored the merchant class by setting maximum wage regulations. Thus, with prices rising, wages were held static. Workers had to resort to charity as a necessary supplement to their meager incomes.

Until the middle of the sixteenth century the main, in fact the only, source of charity was the monasteries. These, however, were abolished about 1546 by Henry VIII as part of the English Reformation and because confiscation of their lands enriched the purse of the king. Thus the English poor were deprived of charity from the monasteries. This later may have led some of them to go to the New World.

At the same time, there were many who believed that the English Reformation had not gone far enough. These Dissenters, as they were called, were divided into two groups, the Puritans and the Separatists. The former sought to purify the Established Church, and the latter wished to separate entirely from it. These, together with Catholics, were persecuted by the English government which sought to establish conformity.

With the accession of the first Tudor, Henry VII, in 1485, national patriotism in England grew rapidly. This spirit culminated in the reign of Elizabeth when the feeling of national pride was expressed in almost every field—literature, finance, commerce, and colonization. With this patriotism was combined an intense hatred for Spain. This attitude was exemplified in the actions of Drake, Hawkins, and other "sea-dogs" on the Atlantic, while Shakespeare is generally thought of as expressing the greatest example of English nationalism in literature.

America, in the sixteenth century, was a magic word in Europe. Knowledge of the New World was scant and superficial. It was generally thought that gold and silver could be found throughout the continent; it was hoped that almonds, silk, and other tropical products could be grown in the Carolinas; and most early settlers spent much time exploring and searching for a passage through the land barrier for a route to India.

PROMOTERS OF ENGLISH COLONIES

These religious, political, and economic conditions all helped to encourage colonization. Individuals were willing to leave their homes and settle in the wilderness to avoid religious or political persecution, and to escape the hard times in England. They hoped to better themselves economically, and were lured on by the bait of free land. Many others, adventurers at heart, went to America imbued with a wanderlust spirit.

Since most of these malcontents had little or no money, their colonization of America would have been impossible if groups in England had not been willing to finance their transportation and underwrite the colonial enterprises during the first years. Several such groups could be found. There were the idealists who thought of America as a model place to try out Utopian schemes and social experiments. There were patriotic groups who hoped to hurt Spain, to establish English trade colonies and develop a mercantile organization, to provide a place for the supposedly surplus population of England, and to relieve England of undesirables. There were religious sects who were determined that the persecuted of their faith should have a place of refuge. Finally, there were groups of merchants who anticipated individual profit in trade resulting from colonial markets. These merchants were willing to invest sums of money in planting colonies if a monopoly of the resulting trade could be assured them and if their personal liability for losses could be limited in some manner.

A model for such a company was the joint-stock trading company. Several of these companies had received charters giving them monopoly rights to all trade in a specified region, to the exclusion of other Englishmen. In 1553, the Muscovy Company had been organized to trade with Russia and to find a northeast passage to China. The Baltic and Turkey Companies were chartered in 1579 and 1581, respectively. In 1600, the great East India Company was organized. Profits were unbelievable; dividends to the amount of 600 per cent per year, in the case of this company, were paid. Hope for such returns led to the formation of similar trade companies, which colonized Virginia, Massachusetts, and Delaware.

THE LANDED PROPRIETORS

During the feudal ages, favorites of the king, or those who had contributed something to the crown or nation, were often given vast tracts of land to be held in fief under the ruler. In the seventeenth century, a practice reminiscent of this earlier age developed. A proprietor or group of proprietors might receive from the king a charter that gave full economic and political control over a region. Usually these proprietors hoped for economic gain through the rental or sale of land and through customs duties. Penn advertised throughout Germany the liberal terms under which he would dispose

of his lands in Pennsylvania. Lord Baltimore, John Mason, William Berkeley, and James, duke of York, attempted to get purchasers for their land in Maryland, New Hampshire, New Jersey and New York, respectively. Eight men who helped Charles II gain the English throne were given a charter granting them the Carolinas. In the next century a board of trustees, headed by James Oglethorpe, was granted Georgia. Sometimes the hope of gain was tempered by a desire to create a place for the religiously persecuted, as in the case of Penn and Baltimore, or by humanitarian interests, as in the case of Oglethorpe.

Some of the settlers of Massachusetts were stockholders of the trading company and took their charter with them to America. Connecticut and Rhode Island were settled in part by malcontents from Massachusetts. They secured charters from the English king and kept them in America. These provinces, which thus held their own charters, were known as corporate colonies.

Another method of securing colonies in America was by conquest. The Dutch conquered the Swedish settlements in Delaware in 1655, as part of the expanding of Dutch influence from New York. In 1664, an English fleet sailed into New York harbor and at one stroke New York, New Jersey and Delaware were obtained for England.

VIRGINIA

Virginia was the first permanent English colony in America. It was established by the London Company, one of the trading companies described above. The first settlers were

The Old Church Tower at Jamestown, Virginia. On this site, on July 30, 1619, met the first legislative assembly in the New World

John Smith

considered as employees rather than as genuine colonists. The early years were tragic. Between one-half and two-thirds of each group of settlers died within a year after leaving England. Disease, hostile Indians, and lack of initiative played their parts in hindering the growth of the colony. John Smith's term as governor and his edict, "He who does not work shall not eat," started the colony on a more prosperous path.

About 1617 the discovery of an improved method of curing tobacco accelerated the growth and prosperity of the colony. The English government revoked the charter of the company in 1624, and Virginia came directly under the control of the British crown. Tobacco made the colony fairly prosperous, but, since that became the only crop raised, general prosperity depended almost entirely on the price of the leaf in London.

MASSACHUSETTS

A religious group which opposed the rituals of the established church of England sailed from Plymouth in 1620 on the little ship *Mayflower*. After a stormy voyage these "Pilgrims" landed at the tip of Cape Cod. An exploring group was sent to find a suitable place for settlement. On December 21, 1620, the site of Plymouth was selected. The plan of working and sharing in common was tried here

at first and proved to be as unsuccessful as it had been at Jamestown.

While the *Mayflower* had been anchored off Cape Cod, the Pilgrim fathers drew up a compact agreeing to draft fair and just laws and to live up to them. The Mayflower Compact, as this agreement came to be called, was the first instrument of government devised in America. It swore allegiance to James I and provided for the setting up of governmental machinery.

About ten years later, a trading company was organized to settle the region around modern Boston. These colonists were Puritans who took their charters with them from England. Within a short time thousands of Puritans migrated from England to America. The soil of New England was not suited to the production of a commercial crop like tobacco. Instead, farms developed around a great many small towns. Besides the raising of food crops, commerce and manufacturing were soon begun. Although most of the colonists had left England because of opposition to the Established Church, in Massachusetts a Puritan state church was soon established and the enjoyment of political rights was dependent upon church membership.

THE FOUNDING OF OTHER NEW ENGLAND COLONIES

General dissatisfaction in Massachusetts led to the establishment of separate colonies by discontented people. Thomas Hooker, in 1636, led a group southwestward to the vicinity of the valley of the Connecticut River. These colonists were impelled by economic and personal as well as by religious reasons. In

The Pilgrims signing the Compact on board the "Mayflower," November 11, 1620

Roger Williams landing at the place where he founded the colony of Providence

1662 the king gave them a charter, which incorporated the New Haven settlements made earlier under John Davenport.

Another group of radical opponents of the Puritan church settled in Rhode Island under the leadership of Roger Williams and Anne Hutchinson. Peaceful relations were maintained with the Indians. Here a colony started without a church establishment, tithes, or compulsory church attendance. Rhode Island, with its fugitives, exiles, and strong individualists, became the most democratic colony in America.

Other groups went north and northeastward from Massachusetts, mainly for economic reasons, and settled in New Hampshire and Maine. As was also true in regard to the other settlements, Massachusetts attempted to retain political control over these northern colonies. She was successful in regard to Maine, but New Hampshire was set up finally as a separate colony. Both regions had originally been given by charter to Gorges and Mason. Their colonies failed and for forty years Massachusetts governed these regions. New Hampshire was established as a royal colony, directly under the control of the king, in 1680.

THE CAROLINAS

While Massachusetts was thus expanding, the same process was taking place in Virginia. To the west and south, frontier settlements grew up. Those to the south, on the Albemarle River, were an especially unorthodox group of malcontents and individualistic colonists. In 1663, when Charles II decided to reward eight of those who helped him gain his throne by giving them land in America, these settlements were included in the grant.

The settlers had left Virginia because they had objected to what they considered excessive governmental regulation. When the proprietors attempted to install a theoretical type of feudal government, under a novel constitution drawn by John Locke, they were loud in their complaints. So much opposition was encountered by the governors in the northern section of the grant that the plan was never put into effect.

The first and main settlement made by the proprietors was at Charlestown, which had one of the finest harbors south of Baltimore. Charlestown progressed rapidly, especially after 1685 when groups of French Protestants began to arrive. In that year, Louis XIV revoked the Edict of Nantes, which for almost one hundred years had given the Protestants political, social, and religious rights. These Huguenots included members of the sturdy middle class in France, and made ideal colonists. Charlestown and the surrounding region prospered rapidly, and by 1685 it had a population of 2,500.

Although the backers of this colony hoped to raise tropical products such as silks and spices, a fair degree of prosperity resulted from the production of rice and indigo. The Carolinas were divided into North and South Carolina after the failure of attempts to establish a single government over the colony. Large plantations and something of an aristocratic population developed in the southern portion, while the farms of North Carolina remained relatively small and the population retained its large element of independent, quarrelsome, individualistic frontiersmen. It is not surprising that North Carolina was soon referred to as a "Valley of Humility between two peaks of Arrogance." Even today, this phrase has been used to indicate the relative position and attitudes of Virginia and South Carolina toward their mutual neighbor, North Carolina.

MARYLAND—A CATHOLIC REFUGE

The Carolinas were not the first of the proprietary colonies. As early as 1632, Cecilius Calvert, Lord Baltimore, received a charter granting him a strip of land to the north of Vir-

"Penn's Treaty with the Indians," a famous painting by Benjamin West. On Penn's arrival in America he immediately concluded a treaty with the Indians, purchasing their land "rights"

ginia and awarding him full political and economic rights. His father, George Calvert, had long sought such a grant.

George Calvert's main motive was the founding of a large family estate in America. A secondary consideration was his desire to establish a refuge for fellow Catholics who had been persecuted for nearly a hundred years in England. His son, how-ever, who sent out the colonists to Maryland, was impelled primarily by the religious motive; but he also was too good a business man to refuse Protestants who were willing to buy or lease land. In fact, seventy-five per cent of the first group were Protestants, and this proportion was maintained and even increased during the colonial period.

Cecil Calvert

Perhaps in fear lest the English government be offended, no attempt was made to grant specific rights to Catholics. Instead, a general toleration act was passed which gave political rights to all Christians except Quakers and Unitarians. Tobacco and wheat became the chief products of the colony. It was not a lack of prosperity, but the proprietor's attempts to collect quit-rents, or small annual payments for land, which caused most of the discontent. These fees amounted to only a penny per acre or even less, but they caused grumbling.

PENNSYLVANIA—AN EXPERIMENT IN BROTHERLY LOVE

To the north was another proprietary colony which belonged to William Penn. This most interesting individual, although a Quaker, was able to remain on friendly and even intimate terms with Puritan leaders of Parliament, Anglican Charles II, and Catholic James II. In 1681, he was given the territory north of Maryland in consideration of the royal debts due him.

Penn's primary intention was to found a colony for the persecuted Quakers, of whom ten thousand had been imprisoned and many of whom had died from cruel treatment in England. His hopes were realized, and immigration began on a grand scale. Within three years Philadelphia was the largest town in the colonies, with over four hundred houses. More than eight thousand colonists lived within the limits of Penn's grant. To the English population were added many Dutch and Germans who had responded to Penn's attractive advertisements. Germantown, near Philadelphia, and the large German and Dutch elements on the Susquehanna River even today are reminders that Penn used modern real estate methods in advertising his lands.

The story of friendship between Quakers and the Indians has been told many times. Although there was much quarreling between the governor and the assembly and about the collection of quit-rents, the colony made the most rapid progress of any in America.

Arrival of the Swedes in the Delaware Valley, 1638. This is an artist's conception; actually, the first women and children did not come until 1641. (American Swedish Historical Museum)

THE SWEDISH AND THE DUTCH

In the middle portion of the Atlantic seaboard, two other nations attempted to set up colonies. The first colony established by the Dutch on the North American continent was purely a commercial venture. In 1621 a branch of the Dutch East India Company was chartered for the purpose of exploiting the New World, as the parent company was successfully doing in the East. Earlier, a fort and trading post had been erected at Albany, one hundred and thirty-five miles up the Hudson River, which was a splendid gateway to the region of the Iroquois fur trade. Two settlements were made in 1623, one on the site of Camden, New Jersey, and the other at Albany. Three years later, Peter Minuit bought the island of Manhattan from the Indians for goods valued at twenty-five dollars. The third fort and most important settlement were located here.

The colony was based almost entirely on the fur trade, and the company attempted to lessen the cost of colonizing by awarding huge tracts of land to patroons, who contracted to bring over a number of tenants. To avoid the complexities of government, the company gave these patroons full political as well as economic control over their tenants. As a result, the internal history of the colony is replete with complaints and remonstrances.

In spite of this, the colonists prospered and expanded in every direction. Eastward they reached the Connecticut River, where they came into contact with the English. Southward they spread over New Jersey until they came in contact with the Swedes in Delaware.

New Sweden had been founded by the South Company of Sweden in 1638, when Fort Christina was built near the present site of Wilmington, Delaware. Although twelve expeditions were sent during the years in which

Peter Minuit purchasing the island of Manhattan from the Indians. Right, Governor Stuyvesant of New Netherland destroying the British summons to surrender, in 1664. He soon surrendered, however

Sweden maintained control, slight progress was made and by 1653 the population was only two hundred. With little effort the Dutch seized the colony in 1655, and New Sweden was erased from the map.

To the north the Dutch held Albany, which became the greatest fur trade center of the world. One single shipment from here in 1626 consisted of 7,246 beaver skins, almost a thousand otter skins and $25,000 worth of other furs. Soon all Europe was wearing beaver hats. New Netherland became increasingly prosperous. This prosperity, however, proved her undoing, for England saw in it the threat to her colonies of New England and Maryland as well as the enrichment of her commercial rival. In 1664 an English fleet sailed into the magnificent harbor of New Amsterdam, and old peg-legged Peter Stuyvesant could only fume and storm before hauling down the Dutch flag. Ten years later the Dutch regained the colony for a period of fifteen months, after which it was held by the English until the American Revolution.

ORGANIZING THE MIDDLE COLONIES

New York became a proprietary colony of the Duke of York, and, when he inherited the throne in 1685 as James II, it automatically became a royal colony. Fur trading was the main interest of the inhabitants, and the commercial advantages of New York's geographical position were not utilized until later, although its strategic location was early recognized.

New Jersey was included in the grant made to York, but he gave it to two friends. After several transfers the western half came into the possession of Penn, and the eastern half was purchased by a syndicate of Quakers headed by Penn. In 1685, an attempt was made to unite New Jersey to New York under Governor Edmund Andros, but the Glorious Revolution of 1688 resulted in the restoration of the two Jerseys to their proprietors, who in 1702 surrendered their patents, and the single royal colony of New Jersey was formed.

Possession of Delaware was long disputed by Penn and York. Penn felt his colony must have control of one shore of the Delaware to

Sir Edmund Andros walking down a Boston street. In 1688 he was deposed as governor of New England

the sea if the interests of Pennsylvania were to be protected. York granted him the territory in 1682 and Delaware and Pennsylvania were united, although separate assemblies were set up a short while later and Delaware was thought of as a separate colony.

GEORGIA—A HAVEN OF THE OPPRESSED

The last colony to be established by England on the North American continent was Georgia (1733). Several motives were behind the settling of this region. The English government wished to protect its Carolina settlements from Indian depredations encouraged by the Spaniard to the south. There was also the desire to forestall the Spanish occupation of the territory between South Carolina and Florida. Thus, James Oglethorpe, a philanthropist, found the government receptive when he advanced a plan to found a place of refuge for Protestants persecuted in Catholic countries, as well as for Englishmen in jail because of debt.

The character of the settlers and the military purpose of the colony led the organizers to provide for strict political regulations. The settlers were given no voice in their government, and slavery, intoxicants, and large landed estates were prohibited. These restraints, as well as fear of the near-by Spaniards, held back the growth of the colony until after it became a royal province in 1750, when the restrictions were removed.

46. The Development of the English Colonies

LANDHOLDING IN THE ENGLISH COLONIES

UP TO THIS POINT the development of the English colonies during the seventeenth century has been noted. Each of the colonies had to be considered individually, since the motives for settlement, the methods of colonization, and the early experiences were so diverse. However, by 1700 all but one of the thirteen colonies had been settled and these twelve had progressed to the point at which definite patterns can be seen in the various fields of development, such as industry, commerce, government, education, and labor. Thus it is possible and logical to discuss the colonies during the eighteenth century topically rather than geographically.

Since the beginning of history, free land has been a magnet which has drawn civilized people toward new frontiers. In the case of America, the hope of becoming a landowner was one of the most important influences causing the European to cross the Atlantic.

In New England, the township was the unit of landholding. The town proprietors usually assigned to each settler a small farm as well as a town lot. It was held in fee simple and generally divided among all the male heirs when the owner died. Thus small farms, rather than large estates, were typical in the New England colonies.

In the South, the culture of single commercial crops using slave labor led to the development of plantations. It became the practice to hold large areas and cultivate only a part each year. This system was followed because tobacco so exhausted the soil. In general, the system of primogeniture, or the passing of estates to the eldest son, was retained. Quitrents were supposed to be collected but in reality evasion was the rule rather than the exception.

Since the middle colonies were largely proprietary, a feudal system of land ownership was attempted, although the usual feudal obligations were often translated into terms of quit-rent. On the whole, farms were a little larger than in New England and smaller than in the South. Both forms of inheritance, primogeniture and division among male heirs, were in use.

In the eighteenth century, the fertile lands on the edge of the settlements attracted two types of individuals, the pioneers who wished to settle the land and put it under the plow, and the speculators who wished to hold it for an advance in value. Some individuals secured immense tracts in the West and consequently were hated and despised by the settlers, many of whom were squatters.

LABOR

It was difficult to keep servants and laborers when there was so much cheap land; consequently, forced labor appeared in different forms. The earliest type was the indentured servant or bondsman who was under contract to work for a trading company, colony, or individual for a specified number of years. Many of these servants bonded themselves willingly in return for passage and the promise of land after the period of service, which usually amounted to about seven years.

Others, however, were "shanghaied" by kidnapers in English ports, or were sentenced to indenture service by English courts for misdemeanors and crimes, as well as for religious and political offenses. In the colonies, where only 50 per cent of the English were able to pay their own transportation, these servants could hope to reach the highest social strata

Arrival of the First Slaves in Virginia, in 1619, from a painting by Howard Pyle

after becoming free. They were particularly numerous in the Middle Colonies, although a few also were to be found in the South.

Slave labor was widely used in the southern colonies, because tobacco and rice could be cultivated by an untrained, servile labor force. In 1619 slaves were introduced into Virginia, and, after the English merchants won an important share of the slave trade, a steady stream of Negroes came into the colonies.

THE PRODUCTS OF THE COLONIES

The main occupation in all the colonies was farming. Commercial crops of tobacco, rice, and indigo came from the South, which also raised a little grain and some fruits. The Middle Colonies were referred to as the "breadbasket" provinces because of their large crops of wheat, corn, and other grains. Other foodstuffs from this section included cattle, sheep, swine, fruits, and vegetables, which were also produced on the small New England farms.

Fishing, commerce, and shipbuilding were important in New England, and were limited mainly to that region. A basic export of the northern colonies was fish, and 10,000 men with about 360 vessels earned nearly $2,000,-000 annually in the third quarter of the eighteenth century. New England ships could be found throughout the world, and her mariners played an increasingly important role in international commerce.

The fur trade was most important in New York and the Middle Colonies. However, in the eighteenth century there were indications of a decline there, while Augusta in Georgia was doing a thriving business.

Naval stores—pitch, tar, and turpentine—for the British navy were obtained in the forests of the Carolinas, while the trees of Maine furnished masts. Lumber, staves, and other wood products were exported from almost all the colonies.

Colonial manufactures were discouraged by England, since it was feared that they would compete with English products, a situation contrary to the mercantile theory which guided English policy. Statesmen and merchants in England wanted the colonies to supply raw materials for home industries, and at the same time to be markets for manufactured goods. Regulations designed to place restrictions on colonial trade and manufactures met with only partial success. Smuggling became a customary practice for the evasion of trade regulations; but natural conditions, combined with English regulations, prevented the development of manufacturing to important proportions.

Domestic production and small scale handicraft industries did develop in the colonies. Some iron and textile manufacturing was carried on widely, and paper and glass were produced in the Middle Colonies. The southern plantations attempted, with only partial success, to make themselves entirely self-sufficient. The distillation of rum became one of the chief manufacturing industries in New England, and became an integral part of the triangular trade. This last term was used to describe the shipping of molasses from the sugar plantations of the West Indies to the distilleries of New England, whence it went as rum to Africa for the purchase of slaves. Negroes were sold in the West Indies in exchange for molasses, which was taken to New England and the process repeated.

RELIGION AND EDUCATION

In all the colonies, except Rhode Island and Pennsylvania, there were established churches at one time or another. Massachusetts and Connecticut supported the Congregational Church, while the Anglican Church was established in the other colonies. During the colonial period, however, the definite trend was toward toleration. Maryland, Rhode Island, and Pennsylvania all passed toleration acts, but in the other colonies dissenters encountered many barriers. Of these, the Quakers, perhaps, had the greatest difficulties, although the Baptists, Presbyterians, Methodists, and other lesser sects suffered some political discrimination.

With the exception of a period of religious fervor, known as the "Great Awakening," religion tended to play a progressively smaller part in the lives of the colonists as the century progressed.

Education was early made a part of the colonial life in New England. The ideal of an elementary school in every town was set up in Massachusetts in 1647. Those towns of fifty households which failed to provide schools were subject to fines. There were some public schools in the Middle Colonies; but here, as was the case almost entirely in the South, education depended upon religious and other private agencies. Few schools developed in the South, with its large plantations, great distances, and small centers of population. Perhaps half the population in the South was illiterate in the eighteenth century, in spite of the efforts of private tutors.

By the time of the Revolution there were nine colleges, eight religious and one private. There were Harvard (1636); William and Mary (1693); Yale (1701); College of New Jersey, now Princeton (1746); Benjamin Franklin's Philadelphia Academy, now University of Pennsylvania (1751); King's College, now Columbia (1754); Brown (1764); Rutgers (1766); and Dartmouth (1769). In addition, many wealthy Southerners sent their sons to English universities.

EARLY AMERICAN CULTURE

In studying various peoples, we have noted that every movement of population is accompanied by its culture which becomes adapted to the new environment. By the time of the American Revolution it was clear that a transformation had taken place in the European civilization which had been transplanted to the New World. The result was a new culture, based on that of England but truly American.

This culture was represented by more than fifty newspapers, large private libraries, many subscription libraries, and several learned groups. The American Philosophical Society, of which Franklin was the most prominent member, was a leading intellectual group. As yet, there was little of American painting, music, drama, or architecture, although such artists as Gilbert Stuart, John Singleton Copley, Benjamin West, and Charles Wilson Peale, gained both European and American renown.

COLONIAL GOVERNMENT

While the government of the individual colonies varied from time to time, as well as from one colony to another, three definite types of colonial government developed. When the Revolution began, Connecticut and Rhode Island were corporate colonies while Pennsylvania, Delaware, and Maryland remained proprietary. The remaining eight colonies were royal. In all the colonies there were legislative assemblies chosen by the people, but property and religious qualifications usually limited the suffrage; so the assemblies were less representative than might be supposed.

Sitting as an upper house was a council appointed by proprietor, royal governor, or king, or elected by the people. Usually, by the time of the Revolution, the members of this group were colonists, but this was by no means a requirement.

Governor's Palace at Williamsburg, Virginia

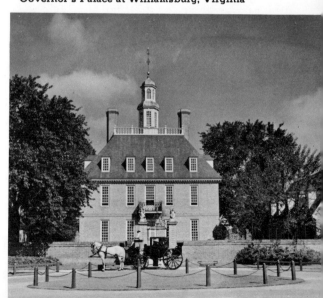

The governor in Pennsylvania, Delaware, and Maryland, was appointed by the proprietor with the approval of the king. Governors of royal colonies were appointed directly by the king, and in all colonies they exercised a veto power over all laws passed by their colonial legislatures. In addition, all colonial laws were subject to the approval of the proprietor and the king. Moreover, since the Privy Council had the right to hear appeals from provincial courts, it had a final right to declare colonial laws inconsistent with the laws of England, and hence null and void. The appointment of colonial judges was usually in the hands of the governor. The Crown appointed all customs collectors and the judges of the admiralty courts.

Local government varied greatly from colony to colony. In New England, the township was the unit of local government. Here the democratic town meeting developed a type of American political philosophy that was to influence materially the cause of the Revolution. The unity of government in the South was the county, patterned on the shire of England. Its chief officer was the justice of the peace, who, with other officers, was appointed by the colonial assembly and governor. People in the southern colonies had less voice in local government than those in New England.

AMERICA'S ENGLISH HERITAGE

In spite of the fact that the colonies were somewhat "Americanized" by the time of the Revolution, it must be kept in mind that they had built their culture on English foundations, adapted to life in the wilderness of a new world. This English heritage furnished the strongest common bond among the colonies and was a prominent factor in the movement for union and in the final creation of a single nation out of thirteen separate and distinct colonies.

This English influence enveloped all the colonies, for the largest single group of the colonists had come from England. They formed more than 50 per cent of the population, and the rest of the people represented such diverse nationalities and divided interests that English predominance was emphasized.

In the seventeenth and eighteenth centuries about 300,000 Scotch-Irish came to America. Most of them settled along the Susquehanna in Pennsylvania and in the back country of the Middle Colonies. About 200,000 Germans, seeking a haven from war and oppression, had settled on the frontiers from New York to the Carolinas by 1775. In addition there were German groups around Philadelphia and New York. A few Welsh, Scots, and Irish were scattered throughout the Atlantic seaboard by 1763. French Huguenots were numerous in the Carolinas and in the back country of Pennsylvania and Virginia. There were a few Swiss settlements in several colonies.

Except among the French Huguenots in South Carolina and the Germans on the Susquehanna in Pennsylvania, who were in more or less compact, isolated groups, the English language was generally spoken. Only in the latter section were there newspapers in a language other than English.

The literature of the colonies was the literature of England. The authors read in the colonies were English authors, and the books were, for the most part, printed in England. The colonial historical heroes, in general, were Englishmen who had "singed the beard" of the Spaniard or had fought the French or the Indian.

The government of the English colonies was copied after that of the mother country. The jury system, the organization of country courts, the legal processes, and the general court procedure rules were all used in this country with few changes or modifications.

The whole concept of the rights of man and the personal, civil, and political rights which had developed in England from the time of Magna Charta were taken over by the colonials who considered these rights as inalienable. In fact, the very ideas of the American Declaration of Independence are in large part the ideas of the English philosopher and political scientist, John Locke.

The American colonies were illustrative of the frontier theory of civilization. English culture had crossed the ocean, but it had been modified so as to produce an Anglo-American civilization.

47. Europe in Search of Spice, Land, and Souls

PORTUGUESE PIONEERS

WHILE SUCH LATINS as Vespucius and Columbus were being impeded by the American continent in their attempt to reach the East Indies, Vasco da Gama pushed around the tip of Africa and on to Calicut. Subsequent expansion by the Portuguese fully justified the title which Pope Alexander VI bestowed on the king of Portugal: "Lord of the navigation, conquests and trade of Ethiopia, Arabia, Persia, and India." In 1505 Almeida was commissioned as the first Portuguese viceroy of India; his successor, Alfonso d'Albuquerque, had been in office only a year when Goa, on the west coast, was captured and made the base of Portuguese operations (1510).

Portuguese expansion was not satiated, however, and control over Malacca was established in the same year. Portuguese merchants enjoyed a monopoly of the India trade during the sixteenth century. Their administration succeeded easily at first because the Indian states were quailing before the thrusts of the Moguls—an Indo-Scythian people. The purpose and organization of Portuguese jurisdiction was to exploit rather than to develop. However this may justify criticism, the maritime pioneers of Portugal deserve credit. They laid the foundation of modern trade between the Occident and Orient. Until the eighteenth century, Portuguese was the trade language in Far Eastern waters, and it is one component of that lingual hash, the business patois of the East, which today is called "pidgin English."

As early as 1517 the first Portuguese, Fernão Perez de Andrade, reached the town of Macao, not far from Canton. His brother Simon was also received in the following year,

but was expelled when he erected a fort and allowed violence to be employed against citizens of the Central Flowery Kingdom, as China was called. Nevertheless in 1533 Portuguese merchantmen sailed as far north as Foochow and Ningpo, flourishing ports which declined a few years later. Several embassies were sent from Goa intended to penetrate to the Manchu court in Peking, but none traveled beyond Canton. A fourth mission was sent in 1667, requesting legalized trade relations; the fifth came in 1727, and the sixth in 1753. These failed largely because the Portuguese did not conform to court etiquette. The Chinese and their Manchu rulers were accustomed to receive tribute from abroad, a characteristic of their foreign relations for more than three centuries.

A permanent Portuguese settlement on the peninsula of Macao was secured in 1557 by bribery and the payment of rent. Although Portuguese trade at Macao diminished, it was this city that became the center for China's trade with all foreigners. Even when the "barbarians" were permitted to establish trading centers (called "factories") at Canton, these posts were to be occupied during the business season only. At other times, the members of the European mercantile community were to reside at Macao. The trade was mostly in silk and tea for Europe and opium for China.

OCCIDENTALS REACH JAPAN AND THE PHILIPPINES

In 1542 or 1543, three Portuguese merchants were blown off their intended course from Siam to China and landed in southern Japan. This episode marked the beginning of European penetration into the island kingdom. They were followed by Francis Xavier, co-founder of the Jesuit Order, who, in 1549, arrived in the "Land of the Gods" and for twenty-seven months proclaimed a hitherto unknown deity. A generation later the number of nominal Christians in Japan was reported as 150,000. When Oda Nobunaga became *de facto* ruler of Japan by 1568, he saw fit to encourage Christianity as a counter force against rising, arrogant Buddhists.

Relations between natives and foreigners were satisfactory until the last quarter of the sixteenth century when Spanish missionary competition, largely Dominican, resulted in disorders between Christian sects. All foreign clergy were ordered out of the country in 1587, but Hideyoshi, the second of the great Japanese triumvirate, winked at lax enforcement of the decree. Trade and proselytizing continued apace.

The antagonism which the Portuguese encountered from the Spaniards in Japan emanated principally from the Philippines. The Spaniards, preoccupied with exploration in the New World and encouraged by the pope's bull of demarcation, were a half-century later than their nearest European neighbors in sending expeditions to the Far East. Although Magellan touched the southern part of the Philippines, the islands were not placed under Spanish rule until 1543. Only gradually did these Westerners explore and extend jurisdiction over the archipelago. Manila was founded in 1571, and four years later, upon invitation, an embassy was sent to China. It was not long until the Spaniards were allowed to transact business at Canton. Their merchantmen also visited Japan, where they met vessels from other European trading companies, mostly Portuguese, Dutch, and British. However, the Spaniards concentrated most of their trading efforts in the Far East in the Philippines.

NORTHERN EUROPEANS VENTURE TO THE EAST

English merchants, who had found the commercial company to be effective for business ventures, began to vie with the Portuguese in Indian waters early in the seventeenth century. The East India Company was chartered in 1600. For the next two hundred and thirty-four years this company was the principal agent of British expansion and, for over a century, a profitable enterprise for London shareholders.

Almost simultaneously the Dutch and the French also formed East India companies. It was entrenched Portuguese opposition, however, which the English first met, an antagonism which culminated in the battle of Swally. Portuguese defeat on this occasion made it possible for an English factory to be established at Surat in 1614. Although the British met with reverses in India, within a decade their administration in southern India assumed aspects of permanence, and Madras was founded in 1639.

The French also ventured into the remote Orient. In 1529 a French vessel reached Sumatra. Despite repeated grants of commercial monopolies to French companies, domestic conditions hindered activity, and it was not until 1699 that a French ship called at Canton. But France's primary concerns abroad were in North America. True, her nationals had begun to penetrate India, but they encountered there determined opposition from the English and Portuguese.

THE DUTCH TURN TO THE EAST

Holland joined the search for spices and silks early in the seventeenth century. Hitherto the Dutch had been the chief carriers of oriental products from Lisbon to northern Europe, but in 1594 the port of Lisbon was closed to them. Their ships engaged in this spice trade were soon sailing to the source of the supply. In 1604 and 1607, these ships applying at Canton were turned away by the exercise of influence from authorities at Macao. Fifteen ships, which Kornelis Rayerszoon led against the Portuguese at Macao in 1622 failed to dislodge them.

The agents of the Dutch East India Company settled in the Pescadores Islands, and then moved to Formosa in 1625.

Dutch missions failed repeatedly in their petitions for commercial intercourse with the Chinese Empire. A minor concession was obtained in 1655 when agents of the Dutch East India Company were allowed to send an embassy with four trading vessels every eight years. Europeans generally were required to observe servility and humility in their relations with governments of the Far East. The Dutch cooperated with Emperor K'ang-hsi to suppress the notorious pirate, Cheng Cheng-kung (Koxinga), who dislodged them from Formosa. The naval detachment was followed with petitions which the Chinese considered as coming from a tributary state. It was not until 1762 that a Dutch factory, or trading post, was erected in Canton, and by that time it was only one among many.

Operating from their base in India, the English in 1613 succeeded in establishing a factory at Hirado on the Japanese island of Honshu. The first Englishman to reach Japan was one Will Adams, who piloted a Dutch ship and suffered disaster on the rugged coast of Nippon in 1600. He became adviser to the Shogun, Ieyasu, who founded the Tokugawa line of military rulers three years later.

Adams not only instructed his hosts in mathematics, astronomy, and shipbuilding, but also confirmed their fears of Europeans. Ieyasu was suspicious of the feverish explorations in Japanese waters, and he feared the drain of metals from the empire. Christian sects periodically came into conflict, and the shogun anticipated an appeal for a foreign alliance against the *bakufu*, or military government. Another source of friction was commercial rivalry and consequent political scheming for the favor of the Yedo (modern Tokyo) government.

JAPAN BECOMES A HERMIT NATION

In 1615 a Japanese mission was sent to Europe, but, before its return, persecution of Christians was fully under way. Hidetada, son and successor of Ieyasu, forbade the entrance of Spaniards into his domains, and by 1638 all intercourse with Westerners was proscribed, with one exception. The Dutch, who were prepared to make any adjustment, were confined to the tiny island of Deshima in Nagasaki harbor; for two hundred and fourteen years this was the only permanent window which received rays of light from reawakened Europe.

Throughout the next two centuries, however, Europeans by no means forgot the Land of the Rising Sun. Russian, British, Spanish, French, Portuguese, as well as Dutch ships cruised or were wrecked off those shores. Within two years of the framing of the American Constitution, Yankees attempted to trade furs with the Nipponese, and during Napoleon's occupation of Holland the Dutch East India trade was conducted in American bottoms. For a few years Deshima was the sole spot on the globe to fly the Dutch flag.

Exclusion of the Portuguese from Japan occurred at approximately the same time as that at which their fatherland was freed from union under the crown of Spain. During this "imprisonment," which commenced in 1580, colonial control was centralized in Madrid, but the Portuguese successfully neutralized its effectiveness. Dutch pilots were introduced, and in one thirty-year period scarcely more than five ships completed the India circuit safely. This sealed the eventual doom of Portuguese commercial supremacy, especially in the Far East.

K'ang-hsi, emperor of China, 1662-1722

CHINA OPENED TO TRADE

Meanwhile the English East India Company had become eager to share in the lucrative trade with the Celestials of Kwangtung and Fukien provinces. Access to Canton was at first (1635-1637) refused, because of the connivance of the Portuguese who later secured a monopoly. It was not until 1685 that imperial decree opened the ports of China to traders of all nations. This decree did not evince a change of China's policy, but merely showed the Manchu fear of becoming solely dependent upon the Portuguese. Actually, European trade with China was for the most part restricted to Canton.

British attempts to open direct negotiations with the Manchu court at Peking met with no success. In 1793, Viscount Macartney failed to obtain commercial privileges, in part because he refused to perform the kowtow. Trade at Canton was, by the late eighteenth century, brisk but not large. Tea, spices, silks, lacquer ware, china, and small amounts of metals constituted, at first, the chief articles of trade. Chinese merchants grew wealthy from the traffic, and in 1720 they formed a guild or Cohong which by 1782 had become limited to twelve, and later to thirteen, merchants. These Chinese were responsible for all relations with the "barbarians." China, being economically self-sufficient, had little desire to trade abroad. If lesser peoples required intercourse with the Middle Kingdom, it must be on Chinese terms —which meant the Westerners were subject to severe exactions.

RUSSIA EXPANDS EASTWARD BY OVERLAND ROUTES

One other people, though not strictly European, expanded in this period toward the Far East by ancient overland routes. The first Russian embassy, which reached Peking in 1567, failed because it did not bear sufficient gifts. Russian movement into Siberia was started by Yermak in 1581. Utilizing Cossack frontiersmen, the Russians reached the Pacific in 1636. The Amur River furnished them a highway by mid-century, and forts were constructed to meet the requirements of frontier warfare along the ill-defined Chinese boundary. Hostilities were finally terminated when, on August 27, 1689, plenipotentiaries signed, at Nerchinsk, China's first treaty with a European government.

Repeated embassies were sent to the Manchu capital but none succeeded. In 1727, two conventions and two protocols signed at Kiakhta delimited the northwestern boundary of China and confirmed the existence of a Russian ecclesiastical mission to Peking. North of the Great Wall, the Russians expanded farther along the Amur until the Sea of Okhotsk was reached and Irkutsk founded. In 1728, Vitus Bering, a Danish captain in Russian employ, explored northern Pacific waters. Soon Russians were occupying the Kuriles, vainly attempting to rupture the cocoon in which Japan maintained her isolation, and sailing even to Alaska and Oregon. Two Russian ships succeeded in exchanging their cargoes at Canton in 1806, but immediate orders from Peking restrained Sino-Russian intercourse to land frontiers.

In reopening relations with the remotest Orient in the mid-sixteenth century, Europeans were completing a cultural cycle. The fundamental principles behind the very instruments which enabled ambitious navigators to sail from European shores had come from the East with the Moslems and Greeks as transmitters. Following the Crusades, the new learning gave impetus to a Renaissance which now renewed contact with the parental Orient.

The Chinese Empire, however, remained aloof, suspecting the avarice and fearing the implements of seafaring Occidentals. Centuries of commerce with the West prior to the thirteenth century, and the recurring impact of barbaric tribes in the north and west, had accustomed the ministers of China to relations with those quarters; this fact in part explained the moderate successes of the Russians. Moreover, the Manchus, themselves aliens from the north, feared the undermining of their administration and a possible foreign alliance with native malcontents. In the later eighteenth century, the drain of Chinese silver also became alarming and was largely explained by ever increasing importation of opium.

48. The Age of Philip II

INTERNATIONAL RIVALRIES

POLITICAL STATES IN EUROPE acquired and lost extensive empires in the three centuries after the discovery of America. The period was one in which Spanish command of the seas was lost to Holland, France, and England. Hapsburg dominions were divided and changed hands. Traders from Holland and England broke down Spanish and Portuguese monopoly. The strong became weak, and occasionally the weak became strong.

Strength and ambition to become stronger were sufficient reasons for the appearance of a system of alliances against any dominant nation. The balance of power in Europe was frequently off-center, especially when allies shifted from one major antagonist to another. Spain, Austria, Prussia, and France were constantly maneuvering for an advantageous position in European politics. The bones of contention were generally portions of the Germanies, the Netherlands, Italy, or Poland. England, too, after George II came to the throne, was interested in Hanover.

Alliances made by Spain and France also concerned England because of the struggle for oversea empires in the Far East and the Americas. England eliminated the Dutch from the Hudson Valley, but found France a more tenacious opponent in North America and India. A series of wars that lasted for a century finally left Britain the supreme colonial power and undisputed mistress of the seas. England blundered so seriously in dealing with her American colonies that a princely realm was forever lost to the Empire. France and Spain, although on the verge of catastrophe, took satisfaction in promoting English disasters.

The degeneration of France finally brought on the Revolution and gave the Corsican adventurer his chance to pick up the Bourbon crown. Yet, Napoleon failed to effect a permanent restoration of French leadership.

His invasion of the Iberian peninsula precipitated the wars for independence in Spanish America. In less than ten years after Waterloo, the Spanish empire was reduced to a faint vestige of what it had been for three hundred years.

ABSOLUTISM AND INTOLERANCE

A popular international sport after the middle of the sixteenth century was to plague and ruffle the proud Philip II. Under the guidance of the great Catholic Monarchs, numerous territories were added to Spanish dominions, territories in Europe, the Americas, and Asia. Charles I, who was also Holy Roman Emperor as Charles V, thus ruled over one of the most extensive empires known to history. This heterogeneous collection of possessions was divided when Charles abdicated in 1556 to seek the solace of monastic seclusion.

Philip II, his son and heir, inherited Spain, the Netherlands, the Sicilies, part of Burgundy, Milan, and the vast American colonies. Over these territories Philip ruled until 1598, guided by two main principles: he would restore Catholicism to the commanding position in the religious world, and place Spain first among nations. While attempting to realize these two grandiose schemes, Philip dominated international affairs to such an extent that the period of his reign, from 1556 to 1598, is sometimes known as the Age of Philip II.

The Catholic Monarchs, Ferdinand and Isabella, achieved wonders in driving the Moors from Spain and in bringing political unity to the Iberian peninsula. They did not succeed in eliminating the spirit of individual-

"Surrender of Granada, 1492." This picture by the 19th century Spanish painter, Francisco Pradilla, shows Ferdinand and Isabella receiving the surrender of the last Moorish stronghold in Spain, Jan. 2, 1492

ism which still persists as a characteristic of the Spaniard, and it was to this task that Philip devoted much of his time. One of the main dissenting elements in the population was the group of half-hearted Christians known as Moriscos. These people were Moors who gave lip-service to Catholicism while persisting in their own customs. Their practices were so abhorrent to the Inquisition that Philip took measures to reduce the Moriscos to obedience. The result was armed rebellion which lasted from 1567 to 1571 and ended with the expulsion of the Moriscos from Spain. This act, combined with the persecution and expulsion of the Jews, deprived Spain of some of its most energetic groups of people and became an important factor in the economic decline of the kingdom.

Portugal, long independent of Spain, was added to Philip's dominions in 1580 by bribing the House of Braganza to relinquish its claims to the succession. During the sixty years of this captivity, Spain was in possession of the important Portuguese colony of Brazil as well as the eastern territories. Toward the end of Philip's reign, in 1591, the kingdom of Aragon rebelled against the odious absolutism which was being enforced. Again Philip was triumphant, but the Aragonese were by no means resigned to their fate. These measures against the Moriscos, the Aragonese, and the Portuguese, combined with a high-handed treatment of the Spanish parliament or *Cortes*, consolidated Philip's position in the peninsula. He was to meet with greater difficulties in the attempt to extend his policies abroad.

Only a portion of the gold and silver stream from the Americas found its way into the royal coffers. The many enterprises undertaken by Philip were so costly that oppressive taxation became necessary, a policy which was to have evil effects upon Spanish trade. The revolt of the Netherlands deprived Philip of large revenues which his father had received from those provinces, while foreign attacks upon Spanish shipping were especially annoying and expensive. The expulsion of the Jews and Moriscos deprived Spain of a large mercantile and industrial population, while the Spaniard's traditional contempt for productive labor added a fatal weakness to Spanish economic life.

Philip II was a devout Catholic, secure in the belief that God would not desert the faithful

Philip II of Spain, his three wives, and his son, bronze figures from his mausoleum in the Escorial, the royal monastery he founded

in the hour of need and that Spain was the nation chosen by Heaven to restore the true faith to its commanding position. The Inquisition, that remarkable institution for the suppression of heresy, was encouraged to extend its activities. Even in the Netherlands, where Protestant doctrines were sweeping away loyalty to the papacy, Philip attempted to enforce a return to Catholicism. This effort brought about a costly rebellion which finally resulted in the loss of the northern provinces of the Low Countries.

SPAIN'S INTELLECTUAL GOLDEN AGE

The Golden Age in the intellectual development of Spain, which came to full fruition in the seventeenth century, really began during the reign of Charles I and received added impetus in the age of Philip II. At least twenty universities were founded between 1516 and 1600. Valladolid, Salamanca, and Alcalá possessed universities of especial prominence, with thousands of students in attendance. These institutions were allowed a surprising amount of independence in the development of the curriculum. More than four thousand schools for the study of Latin and Castilian were in existence early in the seventeenth century, while numerous Jesuit colleges concentrated on the study of the ancient classical authors. In spite of certain restrictions, the publication of books increased rapidly under Philip II. Libraries were established, and Philip himself founded important archives whose priceless documents are still in the infancy of exploitation by historians.

The great philosopher Luis Vives (1492-1540) advocated "the observation of nature as the basis of knowledge" a century before Francis Bacon. Many of the ideas of Montaigne, Descartes, and other thinkers found an early expression by Spanish philosophers. Only the necessity of conforming to Catholic doctrine prevented the development of a great Spanish philosophical school.

Spain contributed writers on politics and jurisprudence who laid the foundations of international law before Grotius. In the field of economics Spaniards contributed many ideas which were later to find expression in Adam Smith, Tolstoy, and others. Luis Vives was also far ahead of his age in this field of thought. Vives, together with Páez de Castro, advocated the writing of history from the social point of view, to include an account of all social institutions rather than concentrating attention upon the political development of a nation. In the age of Philip II appeared great chroniclers, chief of whom were Zurita and Morales. Mariana, the Jesuit historian, deserves mention for his *Historia General de España*, first published between 1592 and 1595. Other writers, many unknown, contributed important works in cartography, geography, metallurgy, mathematics, and engineering. New World explorers advocated a Panama canal nearly four centuries before Theodore Roosevelt.

FINE ARTS AND LITERATURE

Cervantes (1547-1616). (Brown Bros.)

Spanish achievements in the fine arts kept pace with other developments under Philip II. The great actor and playwright, Lope de Rueda of Seville, restored the theater to prominence. Cervantes, author of the immortal *Don Quixote de la Mancha*, belonged to this period. Lope de Vega, one of the most prolific writers in the history of drama, achieved great renown before his death in 1635. Periodical literature, the novel, and poetry also received lasting contributions from Spanish authors. Juan de Herrera established a school of architecture that embodied the elements which he himself incorporated in the famous Escorial built for Philip II.

While depending primarily upon Italian

"Philip IV," by Velasquez. (Frick Coll.)

"The Virgin with Saint Inés and Saint Tecla," by El Greco. (Natl. Gallery, Wash.)

painters for inspiration, Spanish artists gradually developed an independent school in the age of Philip II—a school which was to produce such masters as El Greco, Ribera, Velasquez, Murillo, and Goya. In such composers as Morales and Victoria, Spanish music reached new heights. Although religious music was the most prevalent form of musical expression during the age of Philip II, the guitar had become the most popular instrument by the close of the sixteenth century.

Great as were these achievements in so many realms of activity, and although Spain was the mightiest European power in the sixteenth century, Spanish prosperity and leadership rested upon the insecure foundations of absolutism, religious intolerance, monopoly, and a deteriorating economic order. The international conflicts of Philip II and his successors resulted in a loss of world leadership, and the rise of France, England, and Holland as powerful nations threatened Spain with the loss of much of its American empire.

Bartolome Murillo (1617-82)

REBELLION IN THE NETHERLANDS

Of all the brilliant jewels in the crown of Philip II, few shone with greater brilliance than the Netherlands. But the monarch in his clumsy efforts to secure his hold more firmly, lost half of these gems forever.

Charles V was regarded as a native of the Netherlands, but Philip was a foreigner. Loyalty under Charles turned to hatred under the oppression and arrogance of Philip. The traders and shippers of the Netherlands occupied a strategic position to profit from the swing of trade routes to the Atlantic, but Philip was persuaded to continue a system of monopoly in favor of Spanish merchants. The wealth of the East and West Indies was guided toward Spain, while merchants from the Netherlands were largely excluded from participating in the profits. These restrictions on commerce were sharply resented by a people capable of erecting a far-flung commercial empire.

Attempts to collect high taxes in the Netherlands added fuel to the smouldering embers of rebellion. Philip could have won political support in the Netherlands by wisely permitting native participation in important political positions, but he neglected the opportunity and so alienated an influential class. The Spanish garrisons, looked upon as forerunners of the Inquisition, aroused more opposition, especially in the northern Protestant provinces. Even in the Catholic provinces, now comprising Belgium, opposition to Philip's policies was strong. Indeed, it was these very Catholic areas that provided the first leaders for the rebellion against Philip.

THE HATED DUKE OF ALVA

The revolt of the Netherlands against Spanish domination entered a military phase with the appearance of the hated Duke of Alva as governor in 1567. His orders were to suppress religious heresy and execute the leading rebels, measures calculated to prevent the recurrence of riots like those in 1566 which despoiled Catholic churches. Alva succeeded so well during his six years in the country that the prosperity of the Netherlands was almost destroyed. Many of the one hundred thousand refugees from the Low Countries found a welcome in England where they contributed much to the strength of Philip's great enemy, Elizabeth.

William of Orange, (called the Silent, for no good reason) became the leader of the revolt and around him centered the opposition to Spain until his assassination in 1584. Wil-

William the Silent
(Netherlands Info. Bu.)

liam commissioned privateers, collected armies, and kept alive the spirit of rebellion.

When an unpaid Spanish army perpetrated terrible acts of vandalism in 1576, the seventeen Catholic and Protestant provinces united in the Pacification of Ghent until such a time as the Inquisition should be abolished and their former privileges restored. This union lasted until 1579 when Philip's capable governor, the Duke of Parma, convinced the Catholic and industrial provinces that they had more to fear from the Protestant and commercial provinces than from Spain. The Catholic leaders signed the Treaty of Arras to effect a reconciliation with Philip. The northern provinces in the same year, 1579, united in the Union of Utrecht and continued the war. Henceforth the Catholic provinces, known as the Spanish and then the Austrian Netherlands, were separated from the Protestant north. Amsterdam soon developed as a great commercial center at the expense of Antwerp.

The Dutch traders and empire builders penetrated to the Spanish dominions, established a colony in South America, gained control over the Spice Islands, captured ports in India, began a colony in South Africa, and even challenged English and French supremacy in North America. During the greater portion of this period the war with Spain was continuing, although a truce was declared for a time in 1609. Not until the Peace of Westphalia in 1648 did Spain recognize Dutch independence as an established fact.

Philip made the great mistake of trying to keep too many pots boiling at the same time. Any one of the numerous projects in which he was engaged would have required the complete attention of a great power. He sought, while trying to suppress revolt in the Nether-lands, to interfere in the domestic politics of France and Spain. He succeeded in placing his nation on the toboggan for the dizzy plunge that may be said to have ended with the loss of the American colonies in the early nineteenth century.

STRUGGLES WITH ENGLAND AND FRANCE

There were numerous reasons for enmity between England and Spain. The island kingdom had become a strong national state under the guidance of the early Tudors. English commerce was developing, and men like Richard Hakluyt were calling attention to the rich rewards of a colonial empire. The Spanish effort to monopolize the world carrying trade could not go unchallenged by the future mistress of the seas. An important element in the rise of English nationalism was the break with the papacy under Henry VIII. This schism, so hateful to Philip II, challenged the crusading spirit of the Spanish monarch. He had been married to Queen Mary, and for a time wooed Elizabeth, but she scorned his advances and secretly gave countenance to the depredations of Hawkins, Drake, and similar heroic pirates. At the same time Elizabeth looked with more than passive favor on the revolt of the Netherlands. The final result of these circumstances was the building of a fleet which was known as the "Invincible Armada" until English seamen and a bad storm defeated it in 1588. The destruction of the great Armada did not blast Spanish power to pieces, but the Dutch, the English, and the French no longer shivered at the thoughts of Spanish galleons and Spanish infantry.

Philip should have learned a lesson from the disastrous result of his intrigues with Mary Queen of Scots; instead he became embroiled in the internal politics of France, a country already uneasy because it was hemmed in by Hapsburg possessions. Catherine de' Medici, who dominated French politics from 1559 to 1589, found her power threatened by Philip II, the Huguenots, and the nobility. Most of this period, extending until 1593, was made turbulent by a series of religious wars in which the Protestant Huguenots and the Bourbon family

The St. Bartholomew's Day Massacre, Aug. 24, 1572

opposed the Catholics and the Guise claimants to the throne. Catherine played first with one side and then with the other, always attempting to maintain her own supremacy. Until his murder during the horrible massacre of Saint Bartholomew's Day, August 24, 1572, the great Huguenot leader was Admiral de Coligny. Under his patronage and encouragement a French colony was begun near the present St. Augustine in Florida, and another at the site of Rio de Janeiro. Philip's agents succeeded in destroying these colonies, but the trespass was not forgiven.

When it became apparent that the strongest claimant to the French throne was the Protestant Henry of Bourbon, King of Navarre, Philip II allied himself with the Duke of Guise, an uncompromising Catholic. The war that resulted saw three Henrys fighting for the throne. Henry of Navarre led the Protestants; Henry of France, the reigning king and son of Catherine, led the moderate Catholics, or Politiques. Henry of Guise soon established his influence over Henry of France, while Queen Elizabeth of England gave aid to Henry of Navarre.

The succeeding events in this confused period of intrigues came swiftly. The king under-went a change of heart and caused Henry of Guise to be assassinated, and the next year, in 1589, he himself made his exit in the same fashion. But with one of his dying breaths, the king named Henry of Navarre as his successor. Henry of Navarre became a Catholic in 1593, made peace with Philip II a few years later, and was himself assassinated in 1610.

END OF THE TURKISH THREAT

This discouraging account of the failures of Philip II should be tempered by acknowledging his great service to Europe, and especially to Italy, as a result of the defeat of the Ottoman fleet at Lepanto in 1571. The Ottoman Turks not only had a secure hold on Hungary, but also committed annoying depredations on Mediterranean commerce. With the cooperation of Genoa, Venice, and the papacy, a great fleet was prepared which destroyed the Ottoman armada. Don Juan of Austria, an illegitimate half-brother of Philip II, commanded this Christian fleet in what has been aptly called the last Crusade. Henceforth the Mediterranean was to be free from Mohammedan piracy except for a brief period at the end of the eighteenth century, and western Europe no longer had cause to fear an Ottoman conquest.

49. France and England Struggle for World Dominance

HENRY OF NAVARRE AND RICHELIEU

Henry of navarre, whose conversion to Catholicism gave Philip II no little satisfaction, started France on the road to continental supremacy. Bourbon rulers of France in succeeding years contributed much to the further decline of Spain's international power. Henry devoted his attention to restoring France to economic and political health. In this difficult enterprise he had the co-operation of the Duke of Sully who, as chief minister of finance, revised the system of taxation and saved large sums for the treasury. Sully gave his attention to encouraging agriculture, which he believed to be the basic French industry. Henry balanced this activity by encouraging trade and commerce. Within a few years large French cities became industrial centers. French traders began to compete with the Dutch and the English for world trade. Factories (trading posts) were established in India, and the French Empire in North America began to take shape, guided by Champlain.

An assassin put an end to the life of Henry of Navarre in 1610, and for fourteen years confusion again prevailed in France. One of the most colorful figures in European history emerged from this chaos to become the virtual dictator of France in 1624. This remarkable man was Cardinal Richelieu. The cardinal was a great diplomat, unsurpassed in the art of intrigue. Until his death in 1642, Richelieu used every means to make royal power supreme in France, and to make France supreme in Europe. The first of these objects was accomplished by disregarding the French parliament, known as the Estates General, and by abolishing the power of the nobles. Royal officers, called intendants, were appointed to take charge of financial, judicial, and political affairs in different parts of the country. The policies of Richelieu were continued by Cardinal Mazarin, who governed France until 1661 while Louis XIV was growing up.

HAPSBURGS AND BOURBONS

Two great ruling houses were prominent in Europe during the seventeenth century, the Hapsburgs and the Bourbons. Spain and all of her possessions were ruled by one branch of the Hapsburgs. Austria, Hungary, Bohemia, and other territories were ruled by another branch. Against this great house the power of the French Bourbons seemed small indeed. The most terrible wars in history, before World War I, were the result of this struggle between Bourbons and Hapsburgs.

The first phase in the conflict was known as the Thirty Years' War, a series of bloody conflicts which lasted from 1618 to 1648. Cardinal Richelieu did everything possible to help the enemies of the Hapsburgs, and from 1635 to 1648 French armies played a leading role in the war. Richelieu declared war on Spain, and, although the efficient Spanish infantry gave a good account of itself, the French generals were superior. Even after the Peace of Westphalia in 1648, France and Spain continued the war for eleven years. The result was a French victory. French control was extended over Roussillon, Artois, and Lorraine. Metz, Toul, Verdun, and Alsace went to France in 1648, so French gains from the Thirty Years' War were of great importance. Louis XIV, in addition to having these territories added to his dominions, gained a Spanish princess, Maria Theresa, as his wife.

The Spanish cup of sorrows was overflowing, and in the midst of these disasters Portugal began a revolt in 1640. The war dragged on for twenty-eight years and ended with complete independence for the Portuguese. Brazil, which had been ruled by the Dutch from 1624 to 1654, was returned to Portugal; but that little country, which had done so much to increase geographical knowledge, lost many of her prized possessions in the Far East as a result of the Spanish dominance.

DECLINE OF THE DUTCH COMMERCIAL EMPIRE

Philip II might logically be considered as one of the Dutch heroes. During the wars precipitated by the policies of that Spanish monarch, the commercial power of the seven northern provinces of the Low Countries developed with astonishing swiftness. The defeat of Philip's great fleet in 1588 broke Spanish sea power, and within a decade Dutch traders were sending fleets into the stronghold of the enemy. Many of the colonial possessions of Portugal, which were captured by the Dutch in the war with Spain, remained in the hands of their new owners after the general settlement in 1648. Dutch prosperity was so marked and Dutch ships were so numerous that the little nation was a genuine threat to England. Dutch and English traders were in competition not only in the East Indies but also in the Hudson Valley area in North America.

This Anglo-Dutch rivalry produced a series of short commercial wars in the second half of the seventeenth century. For a time the issue was in doubt, but English supremacy was gradually established. New Amsterdam fell to the Duke of York in 1664, and later naval victories seriously crippled the Dutch carrying trade. The peace concluded three years later confirmed English possession of the former Dutch colonies in North America, as well as some of the Dutch West Indies.

FIRST ADVANCE OF LOUIS XIV

Louis XIV, the Grand Monarch of France, was fired with a consuming ambition to extend the frontiers of his country. Holland was by no means anxious to have the greedy French king as a neighbor; but, when Louis moved his armies toward the Spanish Netherlands in 1667, the Dutch were still at war with Eng-

land. The conclusion of this conflict was quickly followed by an alliance of Holland, England, and Sweden to prevent Louis from carrying out his design. France made peace, but the Dutch were blamed for the failure of Louis' grand scheme. Louis bribed the English and Swedish kings to withdraw from the alliance with Holland. This country of the dikes was in poor condition to resist the military might of France. Wars with Spain and England as well as internal conflicts, had made serious inroads on Dutch strength.

Louis XIV declared war on Holland in 1672; but the popular Dutch leader, William III, resorted to a measure which effectively dampened the ardor of the French army. He ordered the dikes to be cut and so flooded much of northern Holland. While the French were

William III

wishing for boots and boats, European rulers became alarmed and formed a new coalition which forced another peace. Holland emerged from the water and the war in a better condition than was to be expected. The English revolution of 1688 brought William III of Holland to the English throne; so the colonial empires of the two rivals were combined, at least for the time being.

After this union was dissolved early in the next century, the history of the Netherlands was relatively smooth until the first wave of successes won by armies of the French revolutionists. Then Holland was reduced to the status of a dependency. The unfortunate country became the Batavian Republic in 1795 and remained under French control until the fall of Napoleon. Since England was at war with France during most of this period of captivity for Holland, the Dutch colonial possessions became legitimate prizes for the English fleet. Capetown, which the Dutch East India Company had founded in 1652, fell to the British in 1806. Arrangements at the Congress of Vienna nine years later confirmed English posses-

The Child King, Louis XV of France being greeted by Peter the Great of Russia

and pestilence cast their horrible shadows over the land. Bankruptcies were common in a time when taxation was especially oppressive. More curses than tears followed the Grand Monarch to his tomb.

Not even Louis XIV could have healed the wounds he brought to France. His great-grandson and successor, Louis XV, had none of the qualities needed by the ruler of a great country. This unfortunate monarch was only five years of age when he became king. For nearly thirty years France was ruled by the Duke of Orleans and Cardinal Fleury. When Louis XV took active charge of the government about the middle of the century, French affairs continued to be mismanaged. But Louis didn't care. France would last as long as Louis —and then the deluge.

John Law

It was under the Duke of Orleans that the famous John Law formed a huge corporation to make money in colonial enterprises. Unwary investors bought shares in Law's enterprise which was very active between 1715 and 1720. Although the Mississippi Bubble, as this enterprise became known, popped quickly with an attendant shower of bankruptcies, John Law was responsible for adding strength to French possessions in the lower Mississippi valley.

sion of Dutch South Africa, and also deprived the Dutch of Guiana and Ceylon. In spite of these reverses over a span of more than two centuries, Holland retained an important commercial empire. The Dutch colonial possessions at present, including the Indonesian Union, amount to about 800,000 square miles of territory, much of which consists of the still important Spice Islands of the East Indies.

PRELUDE TO THE DELUGE

France and England were clearly the leading nations of Europe after the middle of the seventeenth century. England, victorious over Spain and Holland, entered a contest with France for world supremacy. Each of the antagonists possessed an expanding colonial empire which produced considerable friction in the West Indies, India, and North America. England was superior in sea power, but France had the finest army in Europe. The struggle was by no means an unequal affair, and the outcome was uncertain until the Seven Years' War was nearly over. The European wars invariably had colonial counterparts, and, although France retained her continental territories, the colonial empire was lost to England.

Louis XIV practically took France into the grave when he died in 1715. His incessant warfare had consumed the wealth of the country. Trade and commerce were stagnant; famine

The Mississippi Bubble was thus caricatured in a drawing which had wide circulation at the time

Cardinal Fleury, who succeeded Orleans in control of the government, had more ability than his predecessor; however, France continued to decline. One wonders at the courage and tenacity the French people displayed while faced with almost inevitable defeat. During the interval of peace between 1713 and 1739, French positions in North America and India were considerably strengthened.

WAR OF THE AUSTRIAN SUCCESSION

France might have recovered some of its former prosperity with the passing of time, in spite of Louis XV and his expensive court; but international affairs soon embroiled the nation in other wars. English merchants were responsible for much ill feeling between England and Spain in the early eighteenth century. Spain had granted England restricted trading privileges with her colonies in 1713, but the concessions merely whetted English appetites.

Spain was determined to keep foreign merchants out of her American colonies, and those foreigners were determined to get in.

One of the English traders, a Captain Robert Jenkins, appeared in England with a highly embellished story of how his vessel had been plundered by Spaniards. In the fray,

Robert Walpole

according to Jenkins, the Spaniards cut off one of his ears but obligingly left the severed member with its owner as a souvenir. Demand for war against Spain was so great that Robert Walpole gave way. This war, which began in 1739, soon developed into a general European conflict known as the War of the Austrian Succession.

Frederick II of Prussia inherited a marvel-ous army from his father, and developed in his own right a hunger for territory. Although Prussia agreed to respect Austrian territory before the death of Charles VI and the succession of the beautiful Maria Theresa, the promise was quickly forgotten. Frederick made arrangements with France and Bavaria to participate in depriving Maria Theresa of choice morsels in the Austrian empire. France hoped to acquire the Austrian Netherlands. Frederick marched his army into Silesia, control of which would add much to Prussian power and lessen Austrian influence in the decrepit Holy Roman Empire. Hungary and Bohemia rallied to support the beautiful queen of Austria. England, jealous of her trade with the Austrian Netherlands and opposed to any increase in French power, entered the contest for Austria. Holland also was anxious to keep France out of the Netherlands, and so joined the alliance of Austria and England. The alignment, then, was one in which Prussia, France, Bavaria, and Spain were opposed to Austria, England, Holland, and Sardinia.

Maria Theresa could not drive Frederick's armies from Silesia; so she ceded the territory to Prussia in 1745. Frederick withdrew from the war, and thereafter Austria and her allies were successful in repelling the Bavarians, French, and Spaniards, except in the Netherlands where the French penetrated even into Holland.

The war in America between France and England was known as King George's War, and, with the exception of the English capture of Louisburg, a strong French fortress, in

Capture of Louisburg in 1745 by British and Colonial troops

Columbus Lands in the New World, 1492. Columbus landed on an island in what is now the Bahamas, and named it San Salvador. Other explorers had touched the shores of the western hemisphere, but the record and memory of it was vague. Columbus' discovery led to further exploration and settlement of the new lands.

Armed Pilgrims Going to Church. When the Pilgrims landed at Plymouth in 1620 they faced a wilderness, disease, hunger, and Indian attacks. Their steadfast faith endured through all hardships. Expressing this faith was a daily part of their lives, even though it meant that they had to carry arms on their way to church.

Patrick Henry Speaking on the Stamp Act. He summed up public resentment in a speech before the Virginia House of Burgesses, "Caesar had his Brutus, Charles I his Cromwell, and George III . . ." "Treason!" cried the audience. Henry went on, "may profit by their example. If that be treason, make the most of it."

The Signal Given for the Boston Tea Party, 1773. Boycott of tea shipments had not been recognized, so colonists, disguised as Indians, tossed tea into the harbor.

Paul Revere's Ride, April, 1775. Revere and William Dawes warned the countryside of approaching British troops. The battles of Lexington and Concord followed.

Washington Takes Command of his Troops. The Second Continental Congress appointed him commander-in-chief of the Continental Army, June, 1775. He joined his army at Cambridge, near Boston, on July 3, 1775. After the battles of Lexington and Concord in April, Massachusetts became the center of military activity.

Burgoyne's Surrender at Saratoga. Burgoyne's army planned to join Howe's in New York City and cut communication between the colonies. Gates defeated him in upstate New York and British victory was improbable. The French heard of Gates' victory and sent military assistance. It was the turning point of the Revolutionary War.

Signing the Constitution, Sept. 17, 1787. The chaos which followed the end of the Revolution made a stronger federal government necessary. The present Constitution was drawn up at Philadelphia by a Constitutional Convention. Washington presided. The states ratified the document and the new government was installed in 1789.

George Washington in the Battle of Monongahela, or Braddock's Field

1745, the outcome was not decisive. In India the French leader Dupleix won some initial successes, but the British recovered the lost ground at the end of the war. The conflict ended with the treaties of Aix-la-Chapelle in 1748. Frederick II was allowed to keep Silesia, but all other conquests were restored.

THE SEVEN YEARS' WAR

Prussia and Austria had begun in the Germanies a rivalry for supremacy which was to continue until the time of Bismarck, more than a hundred years later. Anglo-French rivalry had as its primary issue the fate of colonial empires. During the few years of peace before the next conflagration, Maria Theresa and her great minister, Count Kaunitz, concentrated their efforts toward isolating Frederick on the Continent. Louis XV of France was persuaded by his mistress, Madame de Pompadour, to desert Prussia and ally himself with Austria. In the meantime Frederick came to an understanding with George II of England who also possessed the German territory of Hanover. This shifting of allies has been called the "Diplomatic Revolution." France shifted its support from Prussia to Austria, while England shifted from Austria to Prussia. It was in this manner that the European countries were aligned in 1756 when the Seven Years' War broke out.

THE WAR IN THE COLONIES

Just as the War of Jenkins' Ear between Spain and England in 1739 expanded into a European conflict, so also did the border warfare between French and English colonies in 1754 develop into an even greater international war. The American phase of this struggle, known as the French and Indian War, occurred as a result of French and English competition for the Ohio Valley. French activity in this region after 1713 greatly alarmed the British both at home and in the colonies. A number of forts were built at strategic points before the English in America were aroused to action. The Ohio Company, organized in 1749 in Virginia to colonize the old Northwest, built a small post at the junction of the Monongahela and Allegheny rivers in 1754. The post was captured by a French force from Canada and rebuilt as Fort Duquesne. George Washington was sent into the region to assert English claims, but he met with defeat and retired. General Braddock, who undertook an ambitious campaign against the French in 1755, was defeated disastrously in the Battle of Monongahela. It was during this same year that the Acadians were removed from Nova Scotia and distributed through various parts of North America.

The Death of General Wolfe after his victory over the French in the Battle of Quebec, in 1759. From a famous painting by Benjamin West. (National Gallery of Canada)

French successes in America continued until the elder William Pitt came into power in England. Pitt infused new life into British resistance, and with important cooperation from the colonies France was defeated in Canada. Quebec, valiantly defended by General Montcalm, fell before the strategy of General Wolfe in 1759. Montreal capitulated the following year and the French empire in America was doomed.

Dupleix, builder of the French empire in India, met a far greater man in his opponent, Robert Clive. This former clerk executed a series of daring strokes which culminated in the Battle of Plassey in 1757. Four years later Pondicherry fell to the British and France was defeated in India.

THE WAR ON THE CONTINENT

Frederick II had his hands more than full with his European enemies while England was defeating France abroad. Armies from Russia, Sweden, Austria, and France marched against Prussia from various directions. Frederick held his enemies at bay. The defeat of a French army at Rossbach in 1757 was followed by a crushing blow against the Austrians at Leuthen. A Russian army captured Berlin, but Frederick continued his desperate fight.

William Pitt was generous in his support, especially with money. England could afford heavy expenditures in order to prevent France from sending reinforcements abroad. It was in this fashion that Frederick the Great did much to conquer India and America for England by fighting France in Europe. In spite of the heroic resistance of the Prussian armies, Frederick would have been defeated disastrously had not Russia suddenly changed sides when the Czarina Elizabeth died in 1762.

Spain entered the war in support of France in 1761, but it was too late for the French Bourbons to save much from the wreckage. Before the conclusion of peace in 1763, France ceded to Spain the French territory of Louisiana west of the Mississippi. This cession more than compensated Spain for the loss of the Floridas to England. Practically all of the remainder of the French empire in North America and India was surrendered to England. Austria definitely renounced all claim to Silesia. The House of Hohenzollern was thereafter to be supreme in the Germanies, a supremacy that endured until the upheaval following World War I which sent William II as an exile to Holland.

British gains from the Seven Years' War were so great there is danger in not appreciating their full significance. British mastery of the oceans was secured, the merchant marine increased rapidly, and the British Isles became the commercial center of the world. Territorial acquisitions in North America and India gave Britain one of the greatest empires of all time. France took revenge by helping the colonies during the American Revolution, an act which further weakened the tottering Bourbon dynasty. France was humbled. Let the years bring what they might. Great Britain was supreme in 1763.

50. Grievances of American Colonies

ENGLISH COLONIAL POLICY BEFORE 1763

THE TREATY OF PARIS IN 1763 marked a distinct turning point in English colonial history. Former economic and administrative policies were found inadequate to meet the needs of an empire enlarged by the acquisition of the vast American possessions of France.

England, like other European countries, had early accepted the principles of mercantilism. As previously stated, this theory maintained that colonial possessions were valuable only in proportion to the amount of raw materials and markets they furnished. In other words, the mother-country must accumulate gold and silver bullion, particularly by keeping a favorable balance of trade—a favorable ratio of exports over imports.

British legislators sought to accomplish this end by a series of navigation and trade laws passed intermittently from 1651 to the end of the French and Indian conflict.

In general, these acts provided for the carrying of colonial exports in ships owned and manned by British subjects. Certain colonial products, such as tobacco, sugar, cotton, wool, indigo, and dyes were to be exported only to England or her possessions.

The growing dominance of the English landed gentry and merchant middle classes after 1688 explains the gradual tightening of economic restrictions on American commerce. An excellent example of such regulation was the Molasses Act of 1733. This forced the colonies to buy their sugar and molasses from the planters of the British West Indies. Naval stores and furs were added to the enumerated articles, while the manufacture of iron, hats, and woolen cloth was restricted.

The colonists regarded these trade regulations as oppressive and unjust, and in most cases entirely disregarded them. Smuggling became very common, and customs officials received slight cooperation from local merchants.

ROYAL CONTROL OVER THE COLONIES

English colonial officers were perplexed, not only by the difficulty of enforcing trade acts, but also by the threatening political discontent in America. Despite the growing supremacy of Parliament after the Glorious Revolution of 1688, the English Crown still controlled colonial administration. The royal governor acted as the direct representative of the king, having extensive veto powers over provincial legislation which might injure British commerce or interests. Colonial laws could not go into effect until approved by the Crown advisory body—the Privy Council. Royal influence increased steadily in each province. In fact, by the opening of the Revolutionary War, all but four of the original thirteen colonies were royal colonies (see the section on Colonial Government in the chapter, "Development of the English Colonies").

The colonists feared this growing domination and strove to maintain a position of independence. They quarreled continually with the governor over acts for raising and appropriating money. During the French and Indian struggle, necessary funds and troops were often withheld by stubborn legislators. Inefficiency, graft, and petty disputes between royal and local officers caused general resentment and misunderstandings. One bitter controversy followed another.

To remedy this universal dissatisfaction and lack of cooperation, American and British leaders suggested proposals for joint action. Such a scheme was discussed in an intercolonial conference called by the British ministry in Albany in 1754. Some practical plan of action was sought to meet the impending French menace. A proposal, known as the Albany Plan of Union, drafted by Benjamin Franklin, failed to pass. The British maintained that it gave America too much self-government, while the colonists argued the plan did not go far enough in that direction.

COLONIAL SELF-CONSCIOUSNESS DEVELOPS

By the middle of the eighteenth century the colonists had evolved some sense of national consciousness. They regarded America not merely as an English overseas domain but as an equal commonwealth, united with Great Britain only in the person of the king. They were willing to accede in theory to legislative regulation so long as it was laxly administered. By 1763, however, American manufactures and shipping had grown enormously. With almost 3,000,000 people, a strong, diversified economy, and political traditions reaching back 150 years, America had come to have political ideals divergent from those of the Englishmen carrying on the government in the mother country. There were three great differences: (1) a differing theory and practice of representation; (2) different ideas of the rights of the individual, or a disagreement as to the extent of proper governmental authority over individuals; (3) conflicting ideas as to the extent and character of local self-government, or a differing opinion on the problem of distributing governmental authority between the center and the outlying parts in an imperial system. These differences in political theories were reflected in controversies of a more practical nature over economic issues.

Another factor sometimes overlooked, but very important in this period, is the great westward trek. Thousands of Scotch-Irish, Germans, and English moved toward the frontiers of New York, Pennsylvania, and Virginia. Isolated as they were, amid physical danger and hardship, they developed a spirit of independence which resented all restriction. Also, the non-English groups had no traditional affection for the British Isles and added their influence to the general eastern reaction against the mother-country.

Despite the increased unrest in the colonies, they enjoyed more self-government and political freedom than was accorded to any other European possession. Provincial assemblies assumed more and more control over local legislation and royal enactments. Commerce and business flourished in spite of trade acts.

Yet, the whole system of English colonial administration was based on a false economic theory and stimulated by a narrow nationalism. Dangerous potential grievances lay concealed in the colonial economic and political structure. These were to burst into flame during the next quarter-century.

John Hancock. (Acme)

ENGLISH COLONIAL POLICY AFTER 1763

The victory over the French in 1763 multiplied England's colonial problems. She was faced with a tremendous war debt, a vast unorganized western domain, and a serious Indian revolt known as Pontiac's Conspiracy. The Ottawa chieftain, fearing further advances into his territory, decided to strike in 1763 before the English frontier defense was

Meeting of Pontiac and Major Rogers probably took place on Rogers' expedition to Detroit, 1760

Benjamin Franklin's Printing Shop near the new market, Philadelphia. (Continental Dist. Corp.)

organized. Fort Detroit withstood the attack, but before order was restored all but two of the English forts in the West were destroyed and the frontiers horribly ravaged.

In order to meet such Indian hostility, the British ministry issued the Proclamation of 1763. This provided for establishing the provinces of East and West Florida in the south, and Quebec along the St. Lawrence River. The large territory west of the mountains was designated as Indian Country. All grants of land to settlers were expressly forbidden for that time. This restriction was expected to quiet the natives and provide for an orderly, supervised partition of the trans-Allegheny region. Officials also hoped to safeguard the fur trade by closing this vast border to hordes of restless settlers.

Storms of protest at this new restraint came from traders, frontiersmen, and land speculators who were operating in this area. At the end of the French and Indian War many land schemes were under way. Among the more prominent promoters of such plans were Samuel Wharton, a wealthy Philadelphia merchant, and Benjamin Franklin. Their organization, known as the Vandalia Company, sought a grant of land, roughly coinciding with West Virginia and eastern Kentucky. Permission for this colony was withheld until just before the Revolution. This was due to the hostility of Virginia, which maintained that the territory lay within her charter claims. Also, many of her leading citizens, including George Washington and Henry Lee, wished to obtain exclusive grants in the same general area.

WESTWARD MOVEMENT

In 1768 the Treaty of Fort Stanwix was negotiated by the northern Indian agent, Sir William Johnson, with the tribes known as the Six Nations. It opened for settlement a large tract east and south of the Ohio River. A second purchase, by John Stuart, the southern agent, allowed settlers to move into the West Virginia and eastern Kentucky districts.

Frontiersmen began to pour into these regions where, before 1763, only a few squatters had built their tiny cabins along the lonely trails. By 1770, a number of fortified stations dotted the banks of the Watauga and Holston rivers on the boundaries of Virginia and North Carolina. Here in 1772 came the Scotch-Irishman, James Robertson, from the Carolina frontier, and John Sevier, the Virginia Huguenot. As early as 1772 these settlements drew up a written compact of government, the first one west of the mountains.

The natural highway to the "dark and bloody ground" of Kentucky was known as

"Daniel Boone Coming Through Cumberland Gap," a famous painting by George C. Bingham. (Washington University)

The Old Fort at Boonesborough

the Wilderness Trail. Over its narrow pathway, hunters and scouts, such as Daniel Boone, made their way to the rich blue-grass hunting grounds of the Indians. Trained as he was in the use of the gun and the knife and accustomed to the dangers of frontier life, Boone has come to symbolize for us the characteristics of the sturdy pioneer of the period.

Just a few weeks before the historic clash on Lexington Common, Judge Richard Henderson of North Carolina, head of the Transylvania Company, negotiated a treaty with the Cherokees. Through it he acquired title to much of the land included in the present states of Kentucky and Tennessee. Hunters and pioneers had already found their way into this area. The tiny settlements of Boonesborough and Harrodsburg had been made here a few years earlier. A written constitution was drawn up at Henderson's behest, with the hope that Transylvania might become the fourteenth colony. The scheme failed, for Virginia and North Carolina were not ready to surrender their western lands.

Continued Indian raids kept the frontiersmen in a state of perpetual alarm. Nearly every family that trudged over the famous trail, or pushed down the Ohio River, had lost some loved one at the hands of the hated "redskins."

To meet this situation, England determined to provide for frontier defense by establishing troops at strategic points. The erection of such an extensive military organization meant heavy financial burden. The attempt to pass on a portion of this expense to the colonies led directly to financial and political controversies. These in turn led to the break-up of the empire. The colonists insisted that this new program for western defense was but a pretext to get revenue for a depleted British treasury.

RESISTANCE TO NEW COMMERCIAL POLICIES

George Grenville, as Prime Minister, determined to bring some order into the chaotic American administrative system. Early in 1764, he proposed a number of acts designed to increase colonial revenue. The first of these measures was known as the Sugar Act. It had a dual purpose: to provide revenue and to tighten the enforcement of the earlier trade regulations. The act reduced the duty on molasses from the West Indies, but levied additional duties on sugar, wines, coffee, silks, and linens.

The prospect of such a duty, collected by a reorganized customs service, caused consternation among the New England merchants. For over a generation they had disregarded the Molasses Act of 1733, and had become wealthy from illicit trade with the connivance of dishonest revenue officials. The most unfortunate feature of the Sugar Act, however, was the implication stated in the preamble. This expressed the theory that Parliament had the right to tax for purposes of revenue. The colonists had early accepted the idea that the British legislature had the power to tax for the purpose of regulating imperial trade. They were not willing, however, to accept its right to tax for revenue only.

Merchants, assemblies, and town meetings protested against the law. Colonial lawyers like James Otis, Patrick Henry, and Samuel Adams, found in it the first suggestion for their dynamic phrase, "no taxation without representation." Other measures of the Grenville program, such as the Currency and Quartering acts, only added to the general

Patrick Henry speaking to the Virginia assembly against the Stamp Act, May 29, 1765

reaction against English rule. The former enactment forbade the issuance of colonial paper money, while the latter compelled the colonists to furnish lodging and supplies to British troops.

THE STAMP ACT

Organized opposition was crystallized when the Grenville government passed the Stamp Act on March 22, 1765. Every legal paper, bill of lading, newspaper, or book was taxed under the act. This tax, the British felt, was more equable, and fell on all groups of people.

The violent reception of this measure in America astonished British officials. Merchants, businessmen, lawyers, journalists, and clergymen of all sections were aroused. Respectable citizens organized the "Sons of Liberty." Mobs, harangued by Samuel Adams, paraded in Boston, ransacked the home of

Lieutenant-Governor Hutchinson, and destroyed his remarkable library.

American hostility took unified form in the Stamp Act Congress, held in New York City on October 1, 1765. This was the first intercolonial meeting called by the colonists themselves definitely to oppose English policy. The resolutions and petitions drawn up by this body are representative of colonial opinion of the time. The colonists willingly gave their allegiance to the Crown. In return, they insisted that they were entitled to all the rights and privileges of English subjects. Chief among these opinions was the theory that no taxation could be levied without their consent.

The constitutional issue centered about the question of representation. In America there had developed the tradition that the representative must live in the geographical district he was chosen to represent. It was impossible then, from the colonial viewpoint, for Americans to be represented in Parliament. The English held, on the other hand, that their system of stratified representation, by class and estate rather than by geographical unit, represented all interests and groups in the empire.

REPEAL OF THE STAMP ACT

To bring pressure to bear on Parliament, the Stamp Act Congress resolved to refrain from buying, using, or selling English goods until the obnoxious measure was removed. This boycott was so effective that soon English merchants, fearing bankruptcy, bombarded Parliament with petitions asking for the immediate repeal of the stamp duty.

Revenue Stamps ordered by the Stamp Act being burned in South Carolina, in 1765

The Sons of Liberty in New York City had their headquarters in this building

The Boston Massacre, March 5, 1770

paint, lead, paper, and tea. The customs service was reorganized, and new admiralty courts were established, writs of assistance or general search warrants were authorized, and offenders were to be tried by the new admiralty courts with no jury.

To the Americans, the most insulting feature of the whole program was the provision to use the revenue to make the royal governors and judges independent of the colonial legislatures. The colonists saw in this another threat to their liberties, for their assemblies had, by the control of colonial finances, kept the governor in check.

THE BOSTON MASSACRE

Massachusetts took the lead in opposing the new restrictions. Her legislature sent out a circular letter in 1768 to the other colonial assemblies. This called for united resistance, and stated that the people of each colony could be legally taxed only by its own provincial legislature. When Massachusetts refused to rescind her action, Parliament ordered the assembly dissolved and radical agitators brought to England for trial. The only result was heightened feeling against English policy. When customs officials attempted to collect duties from John Hancock's vessel Liberty, they were badly treated by a Boston mob.

Such action brought two regiments of British troops to the Massachusetts capital. The presence of "redcoats" led to irritating

Joseph Warren

Repeal was effected in March, 1766, but only after the passage of the Declaratory Act which reaffirmed parliamentary right to tax the colonies.

Few Americans stopped to worry about the implications of this last decree. They celebrated the repeal of the Stamp Act with extravagant demonstrations of loyalty and gratitude. Changes in the trade laws, which made them no longer regulatory but clearly revenue-raising schemes, were scarcely noticed. If England had been able to take immediate advantage of this favorable colonial reaction, the Revolution might possibly have been postponed or even avoided.

Unfortunately, American rejoicing was short-lived, for the matter of taxation was reopened. The brilliant and injudicious new Chancellor of the Exchequer, Charles Townshend, in temporary leadership of the government, soon brought about a second crisis in colonial affairs. He showed at once that he was in accord with the Grenville policies. Using admirable cleverness, he attempted to straddle the colonial distinction between duties for revenue and duties for trade regulation. Townshend proposed to reduce the cost of Indian control and to retrench in military appropriations. Colonial revenue was to be increased by import duties on

436

clashes, which culminated in the famous "Boston Massacre" in 1770. When the affair was over, four Bostonians lay dead. Such radicals as Samuel Adams and Joseph Warren shrewdly seized upon the incident further to inflame the populace against British "tyranny." Prominent among the liberal agitators in the other colonies were the young Virginians, Thomas Jefferson and Patrick Henry. They represented the democratic

The Boston Tea Party, December 16, 1773

philosophy of the frontier counties, and reflected, to a certain extent, that section's clash with some of the interests of the eastern planting aristocracy.

BOSTON TEA PARTY

Under the leadership of Adams and the southern radicals, Committees of Correspondence were organized throughout the colonies. These bodies acted as the propaganda machine of this insurgent group. They continued their activity even after the Townshend duties were repealed by Lord North. As a gesture of maintaining Parliamentary supremacy over colonial taxation, however, a tax of threepence was kept on tea. The powerful East India Company, facing bankruptcy at this time, appealed for a government subsidy. Instead, it was given a monopoly of all tea imported into the colonies. This unwise and ill-considered act threw the conservative colonial elements in with the more radical groups. Now the interests of

Samuel Adams.
(Brown Bros.)

the commercial classes and the provincial policy against taxation for revenue were both challenged.

American reaction took various forms. In Charleston, Philadelphia, and New York, East India agents were forced to resign. Several ships were compelled to sail back to England with their tea cargoes. In Boston, however, Governor Hutchinson refused to allow the ships to return without unloading. The radicals decided to take the next step, and on the night of December 16, 1773, a number of them disguised as Indians, boarded the vessels and dumped the whole cargo, worth $75,000, into the Boston harbor.

THE COERCIVE ACTS

The liberal Whig groups in England immediately withdrew their support from the colonial cause. Such disregard of property rights, as exhibited in the "Boston Tea Party," was abhorrent to them. English opinion almost universally demanded stern coercive measures. The erring colony must be forced to return to respectability and reason.

Early in 1774, five punitive acts came from an outraged Parliament. They were labeled at once by the colonists the "Intolerable Acts." The first proposal, known as the Boston Port Bill, closed the port to commerce until Bostonians repented of the infamous "Party" and agreed to compensate the East India Company for the cargo.

The next measure, the Massachusetts Government Act, disregarded what the provincials had come to hold as their most cherished political safeguard—their charter. They looked upon this document as a contract which could be abolished only when one party broke its provisions. Since it was granted by the king, the colonists insisted that only the Crown could abolish it. Naturally, then, a storm of angry protest arose when Parliament revoked the Massachusetts Charter of 1691, and substituted a royal government. The council and judges were no longer to be elected by the people, but appointed by the Crown. What struck at the foundation of the personal liberty of all classes, however, was the prohibition of town meetings. These strongholds of Samuel Adams and his cohorts were regarded in British eyes as centers of treasonable propaganda.

The third irritating act provided that persons charged with murder in connection with law enforcement should be transported to England for trial. A fourth measure compelled Massachusetts towns to provide quarters and food for British soldiers. The last parliamentary enactment, the Quebec Act, particularly inflamed the Puritan fathers. This plan extended the boundaries of the province of Quebec to the Ohio River, disregarding colonial claims to that area. Perhaps the most significant feature of the act, was the provision granting religious and civil toleration to Catholic French-Canadians.

Still smarting under the restrictions of the Proclamation Line of 1763, the colonists were incensed by this new prohibition. Extravagant speculation and magnificent land promotion schemes faced destruction. New Englanders felt especially offended by the extension into their western claims of the hated French Catholicism, laws, and customs.

In order to make this coercive program more effective, Parliament issued supplementary administrative acts, one of which resulted in the appointment of General Thomas Gage, head of the British army in America, as civil and military governor of Massachusetts.

Some of the more conservative groups in the disciplined colony were anxious to reinstate themselves in British favor by paying for the tea. The radicals, however, would not consent to this and seized the opportunity of capitalizing on the universal anger against Britain. The movement for resistance developed rapidly under their skillful guidance. City workingmen, frontiersmen, merchants, and planters—all clamored for action against their common oppressor. Samuel Adams, Patrick Henry, and James Madison, in legal and extra-legal assemblies, insisted that immediate steps must be taken to relieve the distressing plight of Massachusetts.

The day the Boston port was to be closed, June 1, 1774, was designated by the Virginia legislature as a day of fasting and prayer. When, on account of this, the governor dissolved its session, some members of the assembly gathered in the famous Raleigh Tavern, in Williamsburg. They resolved to invite the other colonies to meet in a continental congress. The acceptance of this invitation by every colony, except Georgia, proved conclusively that the crisis was no longer local but national in character.

The Raleigh Tavern, Williamsburg, Va., famous meeting place of Revolutionary patriots

Carpenters Hall, Philadelphia, where the First Continental Congress met, September 5, 1774

51. American War for Independence

REBELLION!

WHEN THE CONGRESS MET IN PHILADELPHIA, September, 1774, it dispatched a petition to the king asking a return to the political status of 1763, which the colonists felt to be the true constitutional division of imperial and provincial power. It also urged that the colonists abide by the rules of the proposed association, whose provisions forbade the importation of British goods. A Declaration of Rights and Grievances, an ultimatum stating the American position, was also drafted. Finally, after providing for another Congress the following year, the members adjourned.

Within the year, however, war had been precipitated. Pitt and Burke in Parliament had urged conciliation, but the majority in England realized that the revolutionary movement in America was led by radicals who were really asking for a return to nonenforcement of law; hence they supported the king, who urged General Gage to be firm.

When Gage tried to seize Samuel Adams and John Hancock as rebel ringleaders and to destroy colonial military stores, the quarrel broke into open conflict, and the "shots heard 'round the world" were fired on Lexington Green and Concord Bridge. Thereupon, militia from New England flocked to Boston, and, although driven from one height in the Battle of Bunker Hill, they harried the British and threatened their hold on Boston by fortifying the surrounding hills. The die was cast. About one-third of the colonists had forced the war. Another third hoped and continued throughout the war to hope for conciliation. The remaining third was indifferent to the controversy before the war, and stayed aloof during the actual fighting.

The Second Continental Congress met on May 10, 1775. It recognized that a state of war existed by appointing George Washington commander in chief of the colonial army, and by issuing a "Declaration of Causes for Taking up Arms."

The Battle of Lexington, April 19, 1775

The Battle of Bunker Hill, June 17, 1775. (Chicago Historical Society)

MOVEMENT TOWARD SEPARATION

Conservative groups in America were slow to support any movement toward separation. Such a step meant severing the sentimental ties to the mother-country, and economic interests dictated hesitation. Not only would commercial privileges within the empire be lost, but there was danger that the resulting revolution might bring on anarchy or military rule, more to be feared than parliamentary taxation. The Whigs in England tended to support the liberal demands of the colonies and to aid them in reducing the royal power. However, patriotism and the whole background of the mercantile system, which would keep the colonies subservient to England, influenced the majority of Parliament—perhaps as much as did royal patronage—to vote support for the war. Lagging enlistments forced the English government to adopt the common practice of purchasing the services of soldiers from other countries; the ruler of the German principality of Hesse supplied England with mercenaries.

In the colonies, resentment against this hiring of Hessians, as well as the reputed incitement of Indians on the frontier, added fuel to the revolutionary propaganda being poured out. Press and pulpit recited tales of

Thomas Paine

British spoliation of American territory. Thomas Paine's *Common Sense* and John Dickinson's *Letters of a Pennsylvania Farmer* were two of the more influential pamphlets published.

DECLARATION OF INDEPENDENCE

By July 1, 1776, representatives of nine states in Congress were ready to support a resolution of independence. Later the vote was unanimous, and on July 4 a formal declaration was adopted. Jefferson prepared the document which asserted the principle earlier developed by John Locke—that men have certain inalienable rights. This was fol-

The Final Drafting of the Declaration of Independence, in Philadelphia, June, 1776. (Continental Dist. Corp.)

lowed by a list of acts of the king in opposition to these rights. Finally appeared the statement that hence "these colonies are, and of right ought to be, free and independent states."

This Declaration marked a definite turning point in the war. Henceforth, "Loyalists" were not thought of as individuals who merely differed in opinion. Now they were branded as enemies of the new nation, and were punished accordingly. Imprisonment, banishment, detention camps, tarring and feathering, and confiscation of property made the life of the Loyalists wretched and dangerous. It must be remembered that this group, as was admitted even by John Adams, comprised a third of the population.

"The Declaration of Independence," a famous painting by John Trumbull

Secret aid in the form of money and supplies came from France, which was glad to assist in the disruption of the British Empire. France, as a government, had no love for, nor interest in, the colonies. Frenchmen and liberals from other nations, who were interested in the democratic philosophy of the Revolution, flocked to America. While some of these caused much embarrassment and gave little service, others, like Lafayette, De Kalb, Von Steuben, and Kosciuszko, were invaluable to Washington and his army.

WASHINGTON'S STRATEGY IN THE FIRST PERIOD OF THE WAR

The scene of the war shifted to New York after the colonial troops evacuated Boston. Washington was dislodged from Long Island, and escaped with his army only because Howe decided to wait until the next morning to bag the "sly fox."

The next four months after the New York campaign, from September through December, 1776, allowed Washington to exhibit his talents as a clever and efficient general who displayed unusual strategical ability. He realized that his task was to keep the small colonial army from dispersing, and to keep it out of reach of the superior English forces. He seized every opportunity to retreat after making sudden and unexpected attacks. These maneuvers made it difficult for his less able

opponent to take advantage of British numbers.

Such tactics were necessary. A decisive defeat or capture of the small American army, which was supported by only one-third of the colonial population, would put an end to the Revolution. At least some victories, no matter how small, were necessary as arguments if American ministers abroad were to secure the foreign aid which seemed to be essential for final victory.

Washington continued to prove his ability as a general by the manner in which he carried on his maneuvers. From New York he retired across New Jersey, keeping just ahead of the British forces. On Christmas night in 1776, knowing that attack would be unexpected, he crossed the icy, dangerous Delaware River, and won decisive victories over

The Battle of Princeton, January 3, 1777, from a painting by John Trumbull. (Three Lions)

The Liberty Bell being removed from Philadelphia for safekeeping on the approach of Howe's army

Burgoyne's Surrender at Saratoga, Oct. 17, 1777. The American victory here helped bring French aid

detachments at Trenton and Princeton. Before the startled Cornwallis could gather his wits, as well as his army, Washington went into fortified winter quarters at Morristown, New Jersey.

SARATOGA AND FRENCH AID

The next year the British planned to cut off New England from the rest of the colonies by capturing the strategically important Hudson River. Three armies were to cooperate. However, Howe took his army south instead and captured the seat of government, then at Philadelphia. A second army, commanded by St. Leger, was defeated by the Americans in the Mohawk Valley. The third army, under Burgoyne, advanced from Canada and was harassed on every side by New England and New York militia. Finally, Burgoyne's long line of communication was cut behind him. Frantic appeals to Howe for aid went unanswered by that Philadelphia-bound general. On October 17, 1777, Burgoyne surrendered his army of five thousand men to General Gates at Saratoga.

The Battle of Saratoga put an end to the military plan of the British to divide the colonies. Colonial aspirations, by then at low ebb, were revived. More important still, Saratoga proved to be the decisive victory upon which the hopes of Washington and other Americans rested— the victory destined to bring foreign aid.

Benjamin Franklin, the American agent in France, had reason to rejoice when he heard of the victory at Saratoga. Beaumarchais, the French playwright and amateur diplomat who had acted as the agent in bringing secret French aid to the colonies, was also encouraged. These men realized that Saratoga

Pierre Beaumarchais. (Brown Bros.)

was a convincing argument to promote an open alliance between France and the rebellious colonies. In fact, Beaumarchais was so excited that on his way to the court with the news he wrecked his carriage and broke his arm!

A treaty of alliance was soon signed. Although military aid in the form of land and naval forces did not arrive immediately, ammunition, clothing, shoes, and other necessities, as well as money, flowed steadily from France. Later Spain and Holland declared war on England and sent some financial assistance and supplies across the Atlantic.

FINANCING THE REVOLUTION

The importance of this foreign aid in the field of finance alone can be deduced from the fact that $8,000,000 was secured from Europe in the form of loans, while the states contributed a total of only $6,000,000. For additional money to carry on the war, Congress resorted to the printing presses. By 1780, $240,000,000 in paper money was

Benjamin Franklin being officially greeted at the court of France, in 1778

The Capture of Vincennes by George Rogers Clark. (Indiana Historical Bureau)

issued and depreciation naturally became an acute problem.

THE WAR IN THE WEST AND IN THE SOUTH

Just before the Revolution began, a continuous stream of colonists flowed into the valleys of the Virginia and Carolina frontiers. Led by Daniel Boone, James Robertson, and John Sevier, a large number of settlers entered Kentucky and Tennessee during the Revolution. These settlements, as well as the frontier communities of the colonies north of the Potomac River, suffered from British-inspired Indian raids. There was, in addition, the constant threat that the British would succeed in their attempts to form an Indian confederacy and attack the colonies from the West.

To forestall this eventuality and to end British control over the Indians, Virginia sent George Rogers Clark and a small de-

tachment into the West. Surprise attacks and the willingness of Clark's volunteers to march through waist-deep water, won the British posts in the Illinois country and established the American claim to the region.

Clark's victory was almost the only encouraging note for the Americans in the military campaigns from Saratoga to Yorktown. In 1778, the British transferred the war to the South, capturing Savannah as the first step of a new plan. They proposed to march north, taking and controlling one state after the other. This "rolling up of the South" was successful for the most part, although on the frontiers of these states, guerrilla warfare, led by Marion, Sumter, and Pickens rendered

Yorktown, 1781: General Washington receiving the first surrender proposals from General Cornwallis, commander of the British forces. (Three Lions)

British rule ineffective as rapidly as it was established. Along the coast the British plan was successful and was stopped only by the defeat of Cornwallis at Yorktown in 1781.

ENGLAND LOSES CONTROL OF THE SEA AND THE COLONIES

Throughout the world, England was facing the combined forces of France, Spain, and Holland. In 1781 a hostile Armed Neutrality League was formed by Russia, Denmark, and Sweden. In the same year, Cornwallis had reached Yorktown, Virginia, in his process of "rolling up the South." A rapid march from New York by Washington, and a cooperating expedition under Lafayette and the French general, Rochambeau, closed the neck of the Yorktown Peninsula. Admiral de Grasse, with a French fleet, cut off hope of escape or reinforcement by sea. The control of the sea was the deciding factor, and Cornwallis was forced to surrender his army.

Count de Rochambeau. (Chicago Historical Society)

That ended the Revolution as far as America was concerned. Her European allies spent the next two years trying further to weaken the British position on the Continent and in the Orient. However, England maintained her position at Gibraltar, in India, and defeated a French fleet in the West Indies. So important had become the world phase of the war that by 1782 England was willing to concede American independence.

THE TREATY OF PEACE

France, Spain, and Holland entered the war not because of any love for Americans or their philosophy of government; they sought only to weaken England and had no wish to see a great nation arise on the North American continent. In the last analysis, France was willing to sacrifice American interests rather than those of her close ally, Spain, which feared the influence of the Revolution on her colonies. Sensing the attitude of France, the American ministers, Jay, John Adams, and Franklin disregarded the treaty of alliance which bound them to keep the French informed of the progress of peace negotiations, and signed a preliminary treaty with England in 1782 without French knowledge. In the following year, a definite treaty was signed by all the warring nations.

Marquis de Lafayette. (Metropolitan Museum of Art)

By this treaty, the United States was given all the territory between the Atlantic and the Mississippi River, from Canada to Florida. The right to fish on the Newfoundland banks was granted. In return, the United States promised not to put any legal impediments in the way of collection of British debts and to recommend that the states return the confiscated property of the Loyalists. British generosity in this treatment of her former colonists was an attempt to woo the Americans from the side of the French.

AFTER THE WAR

Social and economic development usually quickens in any period of stress. America was no exception to the rule. During the Revolution, manufacturing was stimulated as a result of the increased demands of the war and the removal of British restrictions. Privateering and war profiteering created a new moneyed class. Changes in the laws of inheritance and confiscation of Loyalist property caused smaller estates and wider property holding.

The philosophy of the Revolution extended into religious and social life. Toleration had been developing slowly during the colonial period. Now the last steps were taken, and freedom of religion became almost universal. Even suffrage requirements were made more liberal in the older states, and in the new western commonwealths, manhood suffrage was written into the constitutions.

LIFE IN THE NEW NATION

Top left, voting in Vermont, the first state to give all adult males the right to vote. Top right, the waterfront at Arch Street, Philadelphia, from a print made about 1800. Above left, director of the first U. S. mint inspecting the first coins made there, 1792. Above right, a Colonial Philadelphia volunteer fire company responding to an alarm. Below left, building of the U. S. frigate "Philadelphia". Below right, public market at the foot of High Street, Philadelphia, about 1795. (National Life Ins. Co., Continental Dist. Corp.)

52. The Confederation and the Constitution

SOLVING OF THE PROBLEM OF FEDERATION

THE REVOLUTION was mainly a result of Britain's failure to solve the problem of federation—that is, there was a failure to distinguish between the rights, interests, and duties of the individual colonies on one hand, and the central government of the empire on the other. The outbreak of war turned this problem over to the Second Continental Congress, which came into session in May, 1775. A central government had to be set up to take the place of government from Britain. It was the problem of Congress to work out a division of powers, satisfactory to the individual colonies and yet granting enough power to the central government so that it would be effective. If Congress failed, the Old World would see across the Atlantic thirteen jealous states, easy prey to European intrigue.

A committee of thirteen was appointed by the second Congress to draft a satisfactory plan of government. They found the solution as difficult as had the British Cabinet. The Articles of Confederation, drawn up by this committee, proved to have grave weaknesses even before the last state, Maryland, ratified them in 1781, four years after they were drafted. As in the case of the British administration, the central government was given power over foreign diplomacy, Indian affairs, and disputes between states. Matters of taxation, control over courts, the right to regulate commerce, in fact those questions which had been in dispute between the colonies and Britain, were all left to the states.

The central government soon found itself ineffective. The states refused to vote money to support it, and there was no power to enforce its demands since an executive department had not been provided. Nor was there a judicial system to interpret the laws of Congress uniformly; instead, the courts in each state interpreted Federal law individually.

There was little possibility of remedying these defects because a unanimous vote was needed to amend the Articles. In fact, the passage of any law was difficult, for each state had one vote and all important laws needed the approval of nine of the thirteen states. Attempts to correct the most serious omissions of the Articles—the lack of a Federal executive and judiciary, of the power of the central government to enforce its laws, to regulate commerce, and to levy taxes—failed repeatedly.

Within two years after the war, the prestige of the Congress had fallen so low that state legislatures often neglected to choose delegates, members failed to attend Congress, and sessions could not be held because of the lack of a quorum. The first American solution to the problem of federalism had failed.

LAND CLAIMS

Maryland refused to ratify the Articles of Confederation until 1781, because of the immense territorial claims of Virginia, Massachusetts, and the Carolinas. She feared not only that these states would in time have an overwhelming voice in Federal councils, but also that they would profit by the migration of Maryland citizens to the West. Her ultimatum was that those states which claimed western territories should cede them to the central government. The older states without western lands, including New Hampshire, Rhode Island, New Jersey, Delaware, and Pennsylvania, naturally supported Maryland. They argued that the lands thus ceded could

The Northwest Territory

tion, and for full religious toleration. In addition, slavery was excluded.

EUROPE AND THE CONFEDERATION

Control over this region by the United States was insecure because the British refused to give up the posts they held at Niagara, Detroit, and other places along the Great Lakes. England justified this breach of the peace treaty because of the refusal of Americans to return Loyalist property and to pay pre-Revolutionary debts to British merchants.

Spain held the mouth of the Mississippi River and refused to grant American shipments free access to the sea. Kentuckians and Tennesseans, who would profit from the free navigation of the river threatened secession from the Confederation and talked of capturing New Orleans.

Attempts to reach some diplomatic solution of these difficulties failed because of the weakness of the Federal government in international and interstate relations, a weakness well understood in Europe. England, in fact, refused to send a minister to the United States saying that she did not know whether to send one or thirteen. Spain, too, realized the impotence of the new Federal government, and paid little attention to American demands for free navigation on the Mississippi River.

DEPRESSION

Congress was not allowed to levy taxes and was dependent upon contributions from the states, each of which jealously watched lest it pay more than its share. In time, money ceased entirely to flow from the states for the support of the government. Borrowing had to be resorted to, even to pay the interest on former debts. As a result, exorbitant interest rates were charged on government loans. Bonds and paper money continued to drop to new lows. One of the after-effects of the Revolutionary War was a depression, soon felt by the American people. In the 1780's, conditions were complicated by the lack of gold and silver, the lack of a uniform currency, and the uncertain value of paper money. American foreign commerce was destroyed since the right to trade with the British

be sold and the proceeds used to pay off the national war debts which, as Maryland pointed out, had been incurred in a common cause.

Another reason for the necessity of such cessions was the dispute between the states over the extent of their overlapping claims. New York, with a weak claim based entirely on Indian treaties, was the first to agree to Maryland's proposal. Virginia had extensive claims based on charter provisions and Clark's conquest. She agreed to cede her lands to Congress, and Maryland announced her willingness to ratify the Articles. The last cession was not made, however, until 1802. Common ownership and interest in this Federal domain acted as a strong bond in holding the new states together.

After providing in 1785 for the survey and sale of the lands northwest of the Ohio River, Congress passed the most important legislation of the entire period of the Confederation. This famous act, the Northwest Ordinance, provided for the government of the territory and its admittance to the Federal union. Used as a basis for all future territorial organization, it provided for a governor with ample power, assisted by a popular assembly. Provisions were included for the creation of three to five states when warranted by sufficient population, for the support of public educa-

colonies was lost when the states left the British Empire.

In addition, trade wars developed between the states. One after the other passed customs laws aimed at its neighbors. No control over foreign commerce was possible because as soon as one state passed a customs act, its neighbors reduced all corresponding duties in an attempt to win trade.

Trying to remedy a hopeless financial condition, Rhode Island inflated its currency. Massachusetts farmers advocated the same policy. When state officials attempted to foreclose farm property, the rural districts rose in Shay's Rebellion, demanding cheap money. Printing-press money was made legal tender for payment of debts, and it was so worthless that the creditor actually hid from those who owed him money. If he were found he might have to acknowledge payment of a hundred-dollar debt with paper money that would perhaps buy only a dozen eggs.

DEMAND FOR A NEW GOVERNMENT

These conditions caused certain economic groups to unite with those who saw in the state rivalries and the ineffective central government the destruction of the infant Federal union. Those who held government securities, manufacturers, financiers, and landowners, wanted a government able to control radical groups in the states, able to demand concessions from foreign nations, as well as one able to stabilize domestic economic conditions.

Delegates from Virginia and Maryland met at the home of George Washington in 1785 to discuss navigation of the Potomac River. They decided to invite all the states to meet in 1786 at Annapolis to confer on commercial problems of the Confederation. The representatives of the five states who attended this conference adopted Alexander Hamilton's resolution, which called for a meeting of all the states in May of the next year at Philadelphia to consider desirable and necessary changes in the Articles of Confederation. A second attempt to solve the problem of the relationship of state and central governments was to be made.

THE FEDERAL CONVENTION

Delegates from all of the states except Rhode Island arrived in Philadelphia in 1787. Not all of them came in May, the month designated, and not everyone remained during all the sessions of the convention. The average age of the group was about forty and it was the younger delegates who did most of the work, although the tempering influence of the few older men must be recognized. The membership, in general, was from the propertied and conservative classes. While these men were not demigods, their average of competence and ability was probably higher than in any other group which has ever met in a convention. Most of them had served their states or the nation as governors, congressmen, judges, or diplomats, and came to the convention convinced that the very existence of their nation depended upon their labors.

From Virginia came James Madison and George Mason, while James Wilson and Gouverneur Morris represented Pennsylvania. Others who were to be leaders in the convention were the Pinckneys of South Carolina, John Dickinson of Delaware, Luther Martin of Maryland, and Alexander Hamilton from New York.

George Washington, whose ambition and patriotism were above reproach, was made chairman. The venerable Benjamin Franklin was present among the Pennsylvania delegation, and his wise counsel often calmed the scene when excitement and conflicts of ideas threatened to disrupt the assembly.

THE GREAT COMPROMISE

One of the first of these conflicts occurred when the question of state representation in the Federal government arose. The large states, headed by Virginia, wished representation according to population. The smaller states, led by New Jersey, wished a continuation of the system of equal representation. Finally, Connecticut suggested two houses of Congress: a Senate in which the states were equally represented, and a House of Representatives based on population.

Return of Benjamin Franklin from Europe, Sept. 14, 1786. Franklin landed at the Market Street wharf in Philadelphia. (Continental Dist. Corp.)

Another compromise settled the question of the counting of slaves. The South wished them included in enumerating the population for apportioning representation, but not when taxes were levied. The North took an opposite stand. The final compromise provided that three-fifths of the slaves should be counted both for representation and taxation.

SUBORDINATION OF STATE GOVERNMENTS

Since the greatest defect of the Articles of Confederation was the inability to enforce the acts of Congress, several remedies were suggested in the convention. It was proposed that the army be available to coerce the states into line with Federal policy, and that Congress have the right to nullify a state action. The logical and purely peaceful solution of this problem is contained in two clauses. The first provides, "This Constitution, and the laws of the United States which shall be made in pursuance thereof . . . shall be the supreme law of the land; and the Judges in every state shall be bound thereby, anything in the Constitution or laws of any State to the contrary notwithstanding." This may be thought of as the core of the Constitution. The second coercive clause required that all state and Federal officers take an oath to uphold the Federal Constitution when they entered upon the duties of their offices.

In this way the national government was made supreme in those powers assigned to it by the Constitution, including control over conflicting state laws, and cases arising over this point could be transferred from state to Federal courts.

Since the Constitution was defined as a law, it operated directly on the individual rather than on the states. This principle was perhaps one of the most important departures from the Articles. Since state officers had to swear to uphold the Constitution, even when it conflicted with state law, hampering action by any state official could result in his trial in a Federal court for violation of the "supreme law of the land."

There was no attempt to make the government responsible to popular demand and opinion. The president was chosen by electors who, the convention thought, would use their own judgment in selecting the executive and not be bound by parties, which were not in existence then nor foreseen by the makers of the Constitution. Senators were to be chosen by state legislatures and judges appointed by the president with the approval of the Senate. Only the delegates to the House of Representatives were chosen directly by the people.

The Constitution followed the plan of a French philosopher, Montesquieu, to divide the functions of government among legislative, judicial, and executive departments. An attempt to make the three departments equal, balanced, and a check on each other, resulted in giving the president a veto over Congress, and the appointment power over the judiciary. Congress had the power to disapprove all appointments and could impeach both executive and judicial officers. The judiciary in like manner was made independent of the other two departments by providing for life appointment.

JUDICIAL INTERPRETATION AND REVIEW

Some agency was necessary to interpret the meaning of the Constitution. Obviously, this power could not be given to the states or thirteen different decisions might result. Congress and the president were frowned on as judicial interpreters, since they had such great powers in making laws. The logical place to put this power was in the courts, since they would have to pass on cases arising under the Constitution.

No specific clause was placed in the Constitution giving the courts the power to declare unconstitutional laws passed by Congress or the states. There are three reasons, however, which indicate that the framers expected this power to reside here. First, as has been noted, the interpretation of the Constitution and laws most logically falls here. If the courts were to consider the Constitution the *"supreme law* of the land" and a state or congressional law came into conflict with it, they had no choice but to exercise this power.

Moreover, precedents were by no means rare. State courts, and before them colonial courts, had set aside laws as unconstitutional. Finally, if the equality of the three departments was to be maintained, the judiciary had to be given the power to decide on the constitutionality of proposed laws, since the other two departments already had it. Congress could refuse to enact legislation of which it disapproved. The president had the power to make a like decision and veto a law passed. The fact that three agencies might restrain legislation, while only Congress can initiate it, is an indication of the cautious procedures embodied in conservatism of the Constitution.

RATIFICATION

The completed document was finally submitted to the states for ratification by conventions in each state, with the provision that as soon as nine states took favorable action it was to go into effect in those states. This provision was made in spite of the Articles of Confederation, which provided that any amendment must be unanimously adopted.

The campaign for the adoption of the Constitution showed, in general, rather definite cleavage between two groups which had existed in America from Colonial days. The conservative, tidewater, creditor, strong government advocates, who had been in control of the colonial governments, now sought a return to leadership. The back country, radical, debtor, local rights advocates, who had opposed the colonial governments and had seized the helm at the outbreak of the Revolution and maintained control up to this time, naturally threw all their strength against the adoption of the conservative Constitution.

In Delaware, Connecticut, New Jersey, Georgia, Maryland, and South Carolina, ratification was secured with little difficulty. In Massachusetts, Virginia, Pennsylvania, and New York, favorable action was secured by the Federalists only after bitter and close fights and the promise to Antifederalists that the main objections would be corrected by amendment. This promise resulted in the Bill of Rights, or the first ten amendments, which were adopted within two years. North Carolina and Rhode Island did not ratify until after the new government had been set up.

As soon as nine states had ratified the Constitution, Congress set dates for the election and inauguration of the new government. Federalists were busy in the resulting elections, for they realized that, if the new government were to succeed, its friends must be in office to see that it started in the right way. Fortunately, they could count on Washington's popularity and the popular realization of his ability to carry him into the presidential chair. In addition, they obtained a majority in Congress. With the inauguration of Washington, April 30, 1789, the new government began.

53. Early Years Under the Constitution

HAMILTON AND FEDERALIST POLICIES

THE NEWCOMER to the society of nations made its debut April 30, 1789, in New York City when George Washington was inaugurated President of the United States, thirteen years after the Declaration of Independence. Alexander Hamilton, the financial wizard of his day, was appointed Secretary of the Treasury. He favored a strong central government. "Let the Union," we can imagine him saying to himself, "take over the war debts of the states as well as the Confederation. Let the Union collect the revenue and pay the full amount to the creditors, who held the states' notes. The Federal government then will be looked to as a rightful taxing agency and as a savior in time of need—savior of the states which could not pay, savior of the creditors who had expected to get only thirty cents on each dollar owed them." He also felt that the government should pay the holders of continental notes one hundred cents on the dollar, even though speculators had purchased most of them at very low rates. This is the first instance of the desire on the part of Federal officials to take over responsibilities which people had expected the states to handle, and is evidence of the so-called tendency toward centralization.

A second of Hamilton's recommendations was a protective tariff to encourage American infant industries. Finally, the Secretary of the Treasury proposed establishing a Bank of the United States with $10,000,000 capital stock, one-fifth bought and held by the government, the rest sold to the public. The bank was to issue "sound" currency, that is, only as much was to be issued as could be backed by the government's gold and silver.

These three policies, assumption and full payment of debts, a protective tariff, and a sound currency, were supported by the Federalists, the group who wished to see a strong federal government. In general those making money from commerce, banking, foreign trade, or manufacturing, and the holders of the state and continental notes, followed Hamilton's leadership, carrying with them the commercial towns, and the tidewater plantations of the South.

JEFFERSONIAN AND REPUBLICAN DEMOCRATIC IDEAS

Hamilton's proposals were not without bitter opposition. Washington appointed Thomas Jefferson Secretary of State. He was the philosophical, democratic, country gentleman who wrote the Declaration of Independence. Although a friend of the Constitution and the Federal union, Jefferson had always held republican or democratic ideals. He spent the troubled period of the Confederacy in France and retained his ideals after most of the revolutionary leaders had decided that a strong government, dominated by educated and propertied people, was necessary. This Virginian felt that the ideal America would be a society of small free farmers, very small towns, with as little government as possible and what there was directly controlled by the people. Jefferson was supported by the farmers, craftsmen, laborers, and small shopkeepers, mostly in the rural areas of the North and the frontier parts of the South.

These beliefs were in direct opposition to Hamilton, who wished to aid commerce and industry, in which he felt the real vigor and safety of the new nation would lie. This meant the growth of cities and the rise of at least two classes, laborers and capitalists, and it also

On his Estate, Mount Vernon, Washington was actively interested in the practical farming operations

Washington's Marriage to Mrs. Martha Custis, a widow, took place in 1759

Valley Forge: Washington and Lafayette visiting the suffering soldiers in their winter quarters

The First President being greeted on his arrival in New York for the inauguration ceremony

"Palmy Days," Washington and Lafayette at Mount Vernon, a painting by Thomas Rossiter

Washington in Consultation with Jefferson and Hamilton, members of his cabinet. (Three Lions)

meant a restricted ruling class, the very thing that Jefferson feared.

FEDERALISTS AND DEMOCRATS UNDER WASHINGTON

Washington attempted to keep the peace between the followers of Hamilton, known as Federalists, and the followers of Jefferson, known as Republicans (later called Democrats), for two terms, though he was too worn out by the effort to run for office again. At first Hamilton had somewhat the better of the struggle. Jefferson allowed him to put his debt funding plan through Congress, in return for Hamilton's support of a southern location of the future national capital. Congress also passed a tariff law and authorized the bank suggested by Hamilton.

Temporarily, also, Jefferson's group lost power as a result of foreign affairs. He had sympathized with the French because of the republican principles proclaimed by their early revolutionists. The Federalists, in opposition, tended to favor the conservative, industrial English, upon whom American commercial life depended. A general European conflict broke out, in which most of the monarchical nations were aligned against revolutionary France. By the terms of the treaty of alliance with France, made during the American Revolution, the Jeffersonians felt the United States was obliged to help the French. However, the French emissary to America, Citizen Genet, behaved so rashly before his official reception that Jefferson with his French sympathies had to take to cover; the Federalists won their point when Washington issued a proclamation of neutrality in 1793.

THE JAY NEGOTIATIONS AND TREATY WITH ENGLAND

Eventually, however, the Jeffersonian party won public approval. The Federalists sent John Jay to London in 1793 to negotiate a treaty. His instructions were to secure the removal of the British fur posts in the United States Northwest Territory, in accordance with the treaty of 1783; to end Britain's policy of keeping the Indian tribes hostile to the Americans; to end the impressment of Ameri-

John Jay. (Chicago Historical Society)

can seamen into the British navy; to stop British seizure of American ships trading in the French West Indies; and to secure the opening of British West Indies ports to American trade.

Jay, however, had little to offer in return, and, in the treaty which he brought back, the English agreed only to surrender the fur posts in 1796, to open their East India ports to American shippers, to be somewhat more liberal with American ships in the West Indies, and to let commissions arbitrate certain other matters. The seizure of American ships and the impressment of sailors were not even mentioned. The treaty was ratified in the Senate, although popular feeling appeared to be opposed to it.

Despite the unpopular Jay Treaty, the Jeffersonians were not able to place their leader in the presidency. The Federalists still remained in control by electing the aristocratic New Englander, John Adams, with a majority

John Adams. (The Metropolitan Museum of Art)

of only three votes in the electoral college.

THE ADAMS ADMINISTRATION

One event in his administration was an undeclared war with France. News that the Americans had signed a treaty with England so angered the French that Adams decided to appoint a commission of three able men to confer with officials in Paris. There Talleyrand, the French foreign minister, sent three agents to negotiate with them, known to history as Messieurs X, Y, and Z. They intimated to the American envoys that for a bribe they might secure a favorable treaty. When Americans heard the news they were furious. Such an in-

Talleyrand

sult must be avenged! Fortifications and warships were built, French vessels were seized by privateers and by the navy, and Washington was recalled to command an enlarged army. "Millions for defense, but not one cent for tribute!" was the war cry. Luckily, war was not formally declared, as the officials in both France and America saw the folly of conflict. A new commission was sent to France in 1800. Napoleon who had just come to power, received them courteously and agreed to end the old military alliance and to sign a friendly commercial treaty.

Meanwhile there was growing indignation in the trans-Allegheny region. The western farmers disliked the tax on distilled liquors, and the Whisky Rebellion resulted. The unpopular Alien and Sedition laws, passed in 1798 as war measures, were also causing great annoyance in the West and in the South where Jeffersonianism had its greatest support. The most drastic clauses of these laws permitted the president to remove aliens from the country merely by declaring them dangerous, and proposed fines and prison terms for those opposing the execution of laws, or criticizing the president and government. Such laws, so obviously in contradiction to the spirit of the Bill of Rights, have been passed under war pressure, even by liberals like Lincoln and Wilson, and are frequently left on the statute books long after the crisis is over. It is evident that Adams and his party were unduly alarmed, for war was never declared.

The Republican newspapers, however, continued to attack him and raised a hue and cry over fundamental liberties and freedom of the press. Indignation was so great that Jefferson wrote a set of resolutions passed by the Kentucky legislature, condemning the Alien and Sedition Acts, and claiming that the states should prevent the Federal government from exercising too great powers. Madison pre-

pared a similar one for passage in the Virginia legislature. Using these resolutions as a platform, Jefferson successfully waged his campaign for the presidency in 1800.

JEFFERSONIANS IN POWER

This election marks the emergence of the West as a factor in national politics. The democratic tendencies of the adventurous pioneers were outraged by the aristocratic leanings of the Federalist party. They eagerly joined the mechanics, laborers, small farmers, and non-propertied classes in their struggle to gain suffrage and political recognition. All these groups heartily endorsed Jefferson's philosophy of government, and were elated at his election. America for them now gave promise of being a democratic republic, instead of an eastern aristocratic oligarchy.

Although the Federalist party had definitely lost its control except in New England, the Republicans accepted the groundwork laid by Washington and Hamilton. They adopted the financial and credit system, the tariff laws, and continued the foreign policy along lines proposed by the Federalists. Cities, commerce, industries, and foreign trade all continued to prosper.

Even Jefferson's dislike of the "loose construction" interpretation of the Constitution gave way under the pressure of his great interest in the Louisiana territory. The growth of centralized government, given its start by the Federalists, continued in the Republican regime as interstate and international relations became more complex and important.

One phase of Federalist policy, however, caused Jefferson grave annoyance. Adams had bequeathed to his administration courts filled with judges of Federalist leanings, including a large number of last minute political appointments. Jefferson greatly resented the presence of these men on the bench and he recommended that Congress repeal the Judiciary Act. Republican ire went so far that impeachment proceedings were started in Congress against certain judges and, as a result, John Pickering, an aged and incompetent Federal judge in New Hampshire, was removed. When Justice Chase of the United States Supreme Court was

John Marshall, "Father of the Supreme Court"

Monticello, Jefferson's home, was designed by him

Thomas Jefferson, third President, painted by Gilbert Stuart

brought to trial, however, he was not convicted; his acquittal discouraged prosecution of the man who finally did most to strengthen the court and oppose Jeffersonianism, Chief Justice John Marshall.

Albert Gallatin, (1761-1849). (Metropolitan Museum of Art)

Aside from judicial appointments, Jefferson was able to accomplish many of his aims, for he was an able politician as well as a philosopher. Much of the ceremony of an aristocratic government was abhorrent to him, and instead of riding in a coach he walked to his inauguration. However, his supposedly radical ideas did not create the revolutionary violence which the conservatives had feared. Instead, he "out-Federalized the Federalists."

Albert Gallatin, whose financial genius approached Hamilton's, was appointed Secretary of the Treasury. He pursued a policy of economy in order to reduce tariffs, eliminate internal excises, and balance the federal budget. James Madison, a close friend of Jefferson, was made Secretary of State.

Transfer of Louisiana to the United States: the formal ceremony in what is now Jackson Square, New Orleans. (Chicago Historical Society)

PURCHASE OF LOUISIANA

The most important domestic event of Jefferson's administration was the Louisiana Purchase. Since the Northwest Ordinance of 1787, settlers had been moving rapidly into the trans-Allegheny region north of the Ohio River. Land was cheap, wages were high, and in a few years a laborer could earn enough to purchase his own farm. The area south of the Ohio River was so well settled that by 1792 Kentucky was ready for admission to statehood, while Tennessee followed in 1796. Ohio also was sufficiently populated by 1803 to be admitted into the Federal union.

With an enlarged western population came a corresponding need for manufactured goods and markets for their agricultural products. Unfortunately, the mouth of the Mississippi River, their most logical and accessible water highway, was in the hands of the Spaniards. Repeated diplomatic protests and sporadic intrigues and armed outbreaks finally resulted in the Pinckney Treaty of 1795. This agreement

The Lewis and Clark Expedition meeting some Indians, a painting by Oscar Berninghaus

with Spain opened the river and gave the frontiersmen the right to deposit their produce at New Orleans. Naturally, then, Jefferson was alarmed when rumors came that Spain had retroceded Louisiana to Napoleon in 1800 in the Treaty of San Ildefonso.

Congress, duly aroused, appropriated $2,-000,000 for the purchase of New Orleans and named James Monroe and Robert Livingston as American agents to the French court. Napoleon's plans for rebuilding the French empire in North America had been defeated by native uprisings and disease in Haiti. Fearing the collapse of his European policy also, the French dictator astonished the American agents by offering to sell the entire Louisiana territory extending from the Mississippi River to the Rocky Mountains. Livingston and Monroe hastened to accept the offer before Napoleon might change his mind. The sum of $15,000,-000 was agreed upon, and thus for a relatively insignificant sum the young republic more than doubled its area. Jefferson put aside his constitutional scruples and urged Congress to ratify the purchase at once.

His interest in western expansion was further proved by his sponsoring of the Lewis and Clark Expedition (1804-1806) which ascended the Missouri River, crossed the mountains, and entered the Columbia River valley. These explorers laid the foundation of later American claims to the Oregon territory.

OPPOSITION TO JEFFERSONIANISM

Jefferson's second term was not as popular as was his first one. Not only did he break with a faction of his own party, headed by John Randolph of Virginia, but he also faced renewed opposition from New England and New York Federalists. A radical faction of this group, fearing complete loss of political influence, even suggested the formation of an eastern federation. To accomplish this, they backed Aaron Burr for governor of New York in 1804. Largely through Hamilton's efforts, this plan failed. The antagonisms aroused in the incident resulted in Hamilton's death in a duel with Burr. For Burr it meant the end of his active political career in the East, and the beginning of his colorful and unfathomable quest for power and dominion in the West and in Mexico—finally ending in his conspiracy trial in 1807.

JEFFERSONIAN NEUTRALITY

Perhaps the most serious foreign problem that Jefferson had to meet was in his struggle to safeguard American maritime neutral rights. With both England and France engaged in the Napoleonic struggle, American commerce was greatly hampered. English admiralty courts held, in the famous Essex case in 1805,

The Burr-Hamilton Duel

456

that neutrals could not carry on trade with France even if the enemy cargo were landed in a neutral port and then reloaded and reshipped. This struck a deathblow at the American West Indies trade. England further antagonized the United States' commercial interests by issuing Orders in Council which closed the northern European ports and forced all continental trade to go through the British Isles. The English practice which irritated the United States' pride most of all, however, was the halting and searching of American vessels for deserters from the British navy.

Napoleon struck back at Great Britain in the Milan and Berlin Decrees, which in effect prohibited commerce with England and provided for the seizure of neutral vessels that obeyed the English regulations.

Jefferson was in a dilemma, with both European countries so materially restricting neutral trade. He felt that the most effective way to force the belligerents to respect American neutrality was to issue a nonintercourse act. In 1807, Congress passed such a measure, in the Embargo Act, forbidding all foreign commerce with the United States. Unfortunately, it did not have the reaction Jefferson had hoped. In fact, English and French merchants paid little attention to the act, while New England merchants protested vigorously at their loss of markets and profits. This protest became so alarming that even Jefferson admitted the failure of his theory of economic sanctions, and in March, 1809, the act was repealed. American ports and commerce were opened to all nations except France and Great Britain.

This was the situation that Jefferson turned over to his successor, James Madison. The latter, hoping to end this perplexing commercial plight, listened to the unauthorized proposals of the British minister in Washington. According to them, England promised to revoke the hated Orders if the United States would reopen trade with her. Madison ordered trade relations resumed with Great Britain on these conditions, and forbade commerce with France. England, however, refused to ratify the agreement. Congress, still perplexed, decided to restore commercial relations with both Great Britain and France. It proposed

James Madison (1751-1836), fourth President of the United States, was in office 1809-17

that, in the event either country rescinded its edicts against the United States, it would forbid trade with the other.

Napoleon saw in this action an opportunity to stir up war between his British enemy and the United States. He announced that he intended to repeal the French decrees. Madison, not questioning Napoleon's sincerity, immediately announced the revival of nonintercourse measures against British goods. America unwittingly had joined Napoleon's continental system, aimed at stifling British trade. As a matter of fact, France had violated American neutrality repeatedly, seized and confiscated American ships, and frequently submitted their crews to indignities in French ports. The French dictator was clever enough to see that he could use American complaints against Britain to his own advantage.

England was not anxious to add the United States to her list of enemies. Her merchant classes protested against the continuance of the Orders in Council, and Parliament finally yielded on June 16, 1812—just four days after the American Congress had declared war against England.

THE "WAR-HAWKS" IN POWER

The commercial groups in the United States were not anxious for war because they were receiving handsome profits in evading the

The Chesapeake Affair. British Officers taking deserters from the U. S. frigate "Chesapeake" in 1807, an incident that caused American indignation

fluenced by British commercial restrictions, which cut the new West off from its markets abroad.

"War-hawk" enthusiasm for war reached a high pitch after Tecumseh's Indian rebellion was crushed by William Henry Harrison. It was universally believed that the savages fought with English guns and ammunition. War hysteria finally carried away even Congress, which embarked the United States in June, 1812, on a struggle for which she was totally unprepared.

THE WAR OF 1812

French and English trade regulations. Other Americans, however, smarted under England's insolent treatment of their trade and the imprisonment of American seamen. Perhaps the primary urge for the War of 1812 came from the frontiersmen and southern planters. The western "war-hawks," led by Henry Clay of Kentucky, and Felix Grundy of Tennessee, were anxious to acquire more free land and the control of the fur trade. They looked longingly on the Indian lands and on Canada. On the other hand, the southern "war-hawks," led by John Calhoun of South Carolina, hoped to gain Florida from Spain, which was then an ally of England. Both sections may have been in-

With a small, untrained, and poorly equipped army led by incompetent officers, the American land campaigns were far from successful during the first year. The attack on Canada in 1812 was a failure. Hull surrendered at Detroit; Smythe and Van Rensselaer at Niagara; while Dearborn's army mutinied before it got to the Canadian line, enroute to Montreal. The next year, however, Perry's victory on Lake Erie and Harrison's success at the Thames River re-established the original American military frontier in the Northwest. On the sea, for the first few months, American vessels had brilliant success; but Britain's superior naval forces finally completely blockaded the American coast. Privateers, however, captured over 300 British merchantmen as prizes.

England now determined to push the war to a

The Battle of Tippecanoe, Nov. 7, 1811. U. S. regulars and militia won a victory over Indians

Oliver Hazard Perry during the Battle of Lake Erie, an important American victory

close by invading the United States on four fronts: Niagara, Lake Champlain, New Orleans, and the Atlantic coast. At Niagara the Americans under General Jacob Brown forced the surrender of the fort, while the American fleet under Commander MacDonough in the Battle of Plattsburg won control of Lake Champlain. The British plan to strike at the Chesapeake Bay regions along the coast was also doomed to failure, although General Ross did burn Washington. Andrew Jackson, the Tennessee Indian fighter, who had been quelling the Creek Indian raiders near Mobile, hurried to New Orleans to meet the British forces. In a signal victory fought, ironically

enough, after the peace treaty had been signed, Jackson inflicted a disastrous defeat on the British and completely endeared himself to the West.

New England hostility continued during the duration of the war. Both financial and military aid were refused to the national government. Farmers and merchants living along the Canadian border smuggled goods to the British forces. Finally, in October, 1814, the Hartford Convention assembled to draw up some plan to limit the powers of Congress and the president, and to restate the principle of state sovereignty. Delegates were on their way to Washington with this report when news of the

General William Henry Harrison in the Battle of the Thames, an American victory in Canada

American troops in the Battle of New Orleans, fought after the signing of a peace treaty

Treaty of Ghent came. This dying gesture of the New England Federalists was lost in the general rejoicing over peace.

END OF A FUTILE WAR

The British at first made excessive demands regarding the Canadian boundary, the control of the Great Lakes and fisheries, and the creation of a northwestern Indian territory. As news of each successive American victory came, and upon the advice of Wellington, who practically refused to take over any command in America, however, the British diplomats gave way. The final treaty provided merely for a return to conditions before the war. Nothing was said about impressment, blockades, or rights of neutrals. Vital matters, such as boundaries and fisheries, were left to future commissions, setting a notable precedent for treating Anglo-American disputes.

Although the War of 1812 was not a decisive one from a military standpoint, it did have far-reaching effects. No longer was American policy to be dictated by European diplomacy—by a French emperor or a British Parliament. Divorced from Old World domination, the young republic could now turn its attention to internal development and expansion. Industries grew rapidly, American commerce expanded to the far corners of the globe, and the United States was ready for the first time to take an independent position among the nations of the world. For three quarters of a century America looked to the West, turning her back on Europe. Domestic concerns, rather than foreign affairs, were of prime importance.

The Burning of Washington by the British, 1814. General Ross burned the White House, the Capitol, and certain other public buildings in retaliation for the American burning of York, Canada. (Brown Bros.)

John Wesley Preaching in the Street. Wesley was an English clergyman who founded Methodism about 1744. He was one of the first evangelists to stress social reform and create a taste for good reading among the poorer classes in England. He had a genius for organization, and in 1768 a chapel was opened in New York City.

Milton Composing "Paradise Lost." The great English poet became blind at the height of his career, but continued composing in spite of his handicap. He dictated *Paradise Lost*, his greatest work, to his daughters. Milton was also a strong supporter of Cromwell and the Commonwealth, and wrote tracts in its favor.

Captain James Cook Landing in Australia. The Australian coast had only been thoroughly explored on its eastern portion. Cook charted the west coast and took possession of the land for the British crown in 1770. He discovered Botany Bay, New South Wales, Broken Bay, and Port Jackson, claiming all for England.

Jenner and the First Vaccination. Knowing that infection with cowpox produced immunity to smallpox, Edward Jenner, in 1796, used pus from a human case of cowpox to vaccinate a child, James Phipps. Subsequent efforts to inoculate the child with smallpox failed, and the principle of smallpox vaccination was established.

The Court of Louis XVI of France. Mismanagement, bankruptcy, and chaos during the reign of Louis XVI brought the end of the old regime in France. The peasants and the working classes joined in the French Revolution. Louis XVI was executed in 1793. "Liberty, equality, and fraternity" became the French national slogan.

Liberty Leading the People, a painting by Ferdinand Delacroix. It symbolizes the July Revolution of 1830 in France, a liberal uprising against Bourbon Charles X, who was replaced by Louis Philippe. Charles had attempted to abolish many of the freedoms gained by the people, but popular resentment made this impossible.

Marie Antoinette in Prison, 1793. Marie Antoinette, wife of Louis XVI, was also declared guilty of treason and died on the guillotine during the "Reign of Terror."

Anton Rubenstein Playing for the Czar. The famous Russian composer and pianist was one of the first modern Russian composers to gain an international reputation.

Napoleon I after Friedland, June 14, 1807. This was one of Napoleon's greatest victories. He was at the height of his power, and not only was the Peace of Tilsit signed, but Czar Alexander became an ally of France. From this time on, Napoleon was thought of as a tyrant by most Europeans, rather than as a liberator.

54. The Age of Enlightenment

RENAISSANCE INFLUENCES IN ART AND LITERATURE

WHILE THE NATIONS OF EUROPE were engaging in their titanic struggles for power during the eighteenth century, significant changes took place in European culture. Indeed, the foundations of modern science and thought had been laid by 1815. One field in which this progress did not occur to any considerable extent was that of the fine arts. Here the admiration for classical models and masterpieces, characteristic of the preceding years, continued and even increased during the eighteenth century. Regularity and finish were praised highly, and the art of the Middle Ages was scornfully termed "barbaric."

One notable new strain of culture was introduced from China and affected many of the arts. There was great interest in the paintings, furnishings, and architecture of China, and many porcelains, embroideries, and similar wares were imported. It was fashionable to include some Chinese atmosphere in building, and even Frederick the Great built an oriental pavilion at Sans Souci. The influence was felt in gardening, and it also appeared in literature as descriptions or imaginary tales of oriental life, or as impressions of Western life as it might appear to an oriental visitor.

In literature the devotion to classicism is especially clear. In the seventeenth century Italy and Germany produced little of importance. Spain, however, was more distinguished with Cervantes' great study of human nature in *Don Quixote*, the hundreds of plays by the great Lope de Vega depicting contemporary life, and later with the less significant poems and dramas of Calderón. In the eighteenth century, Italy's most important writer was Alfieri, who continued the classical manner.

Eighteenth century German writers, led by Lessing, demanded a "pure" classicism, rather than a slavish imitation of French models. His *Laocoön*, a treatise on Greek aesthetics, and his classical dramas illustrate this direct connection with ancient Greece. About the same time, there was an opposite reaction in the direction of imitating nature. This "romantic" movement began with imitating Shakespeare, Ossian, and medieval folk poetry, while ignoring classical rules. Klopstock, Herder, and, somewhat later, Schiller, were leaders in creating a great national literature. The dominant figure of the romantic and classical movement was the great statesman, poet, scientist, and dramatist, Johann Wolfgang von Goethe. An ardent romanticist during his early years, he became a thorough classicist for the rest of his long life. He wrote a number of polished plays in the classical tradition. His greatest work, *Faust*, is perhaps the highest expression of the innate longing for infinity.

CLASSICAL ENGLAND AND FRANCE

In England, Milton's great poetry followed the ancient classic models, with baroque elaboration and colorful detail. John Dryden, in elegant classical poetry, expounded the political and religious ideas of the time. Later, Alexander Pope not only expressed the philosophy of his time, but also wrote light, penetrating

461

Goethe

Milton

Johnson

Sterne

satire in his polished and witty poetry. The eighteenth century contributed some great prose, from the political and economic works to the literary criticism of Samuel Johnson, best known for his dictionary. The dramas of the time portrayed the elegant manners of contemporary society. This was also the period in which the novel first became popular, with the portrayal of contemporary life by such men as Fielding and Sterne. The eighteenth century also witnessed the beginnings of newspaper publication and popular essays.

In French literature the height of classical poetry and drama was reached during the time of Louis XIV, in the work of Corneille and Racine. Equally great was Molière, though his work was less classical and portrayed more of the actual life, particularly the follies, of the time. Another great figure was Boileau, whose classical poetry and criticism had wide influence. Even later in the eighteenth century, classicism was important, with all the orators modeling their speeches upon ancient masterpieces. As in England, this was a great period of prose, which was the medium of Voltaire and other great thinkers. One type of prose literature was the novel, the growing importance of which is illustrated by the popularity of such works as Prévost's *Manon Lescaut*.

ROMANTICISM

Toward the end of the century, discontent with the classical restrictions upon subject matter and manner of writing led to a freer, more natural treatment of every day subjects and scenes. This romantic movement in Germany has already been noted. In England, Thomas Gray praised simple, poor people in his poetry. Robert Burns wrote poems about the humble Scots in their own dialect. There was also a group of poems supposedly by an ancient Scot named Ossian, and, although they were proved to be a hoax by a young man of the day, their continued popularity shows the interest in this type of poetry.

The great pioneer in French Romanticism was Rousseau, who expressed in many works a love of nature and man, while praising the "noble savage"—the simple primitive man uncontaminated by what we consider civilization. Although classic ideals had governed most of the period, there had begun a romantic trend which was soon to achieve dominance.

Classical and baroque styles continued to be popular in eighteenth-century painting. English portrait painting reached its climax in the grand works of Reynolds, the more realistic ones of Raeburn, and the more delicate ones by Gainsborough. Watteau painted classically the gay, elegant aspects of French aristocratic life. In addition to this type of painting, there developed a group of artists who avoided this beautiful and elegant manner and sought rather to paint things as they actually appeared to be.

Haydn

Mozart

Gray

Burns

The English Hogarth went so far as nearly to caricature people, so unfavorable were his representations of them. The great Spanish painter Goya combined satire and realism in his portraits of nobility as they appeared to his peasant eye.

The baroque style was principally evident in architecture, represented by the palace of the French monarchs at Versailles, the added ornamentation of St. Peter's at Rome, the Jesuit churches in Spain, St. Paul's Cathedral in London, and the structure which Peter the Great erected in his new capital. The simpler forms of classical pillars and other details were found in American colonial architecture, notably on Washington's estate at Mount Vernon.

Music also reflected the admiration of classicism. A graceful, cultivated phase is represented by the dances of the French composer, Rameau. More impressive were the symphonies, string selections, and Masses of Haydn. Gluck used Greek subjects and style in opera in an effort to achieve the "pure Classicism" which Lessing advocated in literature. The tendencies of the period are personified by Mozart, who wrote all types of instrumental and vocal music, including opera, sometimes lofty, sometimes gay and graceful, with the charm, elegance, and good taste which characterized the period.

ACHIEVEMENTS IN THE SCIENCES

Seventeenth and eighteenth century scientists made great contributions upon which our modern sciences rest. Bacon and Descartes in the seventeenth century paved the way for future progress by insisting that man should learn not from books, but from observation of the facts around him. Descartes stressed the need of testing systematically all material things of the world. In addition to this theory, Descartes made practical contributions to mathematics and physics.

The greatest physicist and mathematician of this age was Sir Isaac Newton. He experimented in light and discovered that all color is found in white light which, when broken down, reveals the series of rainbow hues. His most important contribution was the theory of gravitation, which explained not only the falling of objects, but the reason that the earth, stars, and planets move and yet retain the course and relationship which they have.

Newton's work in turn inspired others to study natural phenomena. Halley observed the movements of heavenly bodies and discovered the comet which bears his name. Leibnitz worked out a system of calculus which proved valuable in engineering. During the two centuries other contributions were made to the knowledge of physics, such as the principle of the barometer, worked out by Torricelli; the invention of the air pump; and the improvement of the mercury thermometer by Fahrenheit.

Leibnitz   Halley   Boyle   Lavoisier

Important contributions were made to the knowledge of electricity by Franklin's work on conduction through "lightning rods," by Volta in his work with batteries, and by Galvani on reactions to electricity.

Modern chemistry also began in the period of the Enlightenment. Robert Boyle made a valuable contribution in the seventeenth century when he developed the theory of the relation between pressure and volume of gases. Boyle also wrote a book in which he distinguished between chemistry and alchemy. He developed the modern idea of chemical elements, and devised many practical laboratory processes. Chemical science was further advanced through the discovery of carbon dioxide by Black, of hydrogen by Cavendish, of oxygen by Priestley, and the composition of air and water by Cavendish. The Frenchman Lavoisier perfected and systematized many of these experiments.

Some advances were also made in the field of medicine. The Italian, Malpighi, an expert in the use of the microscope, contributed to the knowledge of blood circulation and anatomy. The work of von Haller, a Swiss, was so significant that he has been called the founder of modern physiology. Jenner developed a vaccine to prevent the dreaded smallpox, and an able Dutch maker of microscopes, van Leeuwenhoek, discovered protozoa and bacteria.

Linnaeus   Buffon

The first important work in geology was done by the Scot, James Hutton. After studying minerals and rocks, he propounded in 1785 the theory that in the earth's crust lies the history of all that has happened in the past and that the age of the earth is much greater than that suggested by the story in the Bible. The full import of the doctrine, however, was not realized until the nineteenth century, when further progress was made.

There were also gains in botany and zoology. In the former field, Carl von Linné, a Swede known by his Latinized name Linnaeus, made a new classification of plants which superseded the work done before his time. A new classification in zoology culminated in the works of Buffon, the French scientist.

Geographical knowledge was extended through the travels of Captain Cook to Australia and of de Bougainville in the South Seas.

SPREAD OF SCIENTIFIC INFORMATION

These scientific contributions are in themselves interesting, but they gained added significance because of their great popularity in this period. In the first place, scientific knowledge was exchanged and disseminated by scientific academies. Several of these academies were established in Italy during the early part of the seventeenth century. Two of the most famous scientific societies were founded later in the century—the English Royal Society, chartered in 1662, and the French Academy, organized in 1666. Both academies, and academic groups in other countries as well, published journals through which scientific information reached the educated upper and middle

Anton van Leeuwenhoek (1632-1723).
(Lambert Pharmacal Co.)

Swedenborg

Wesley

classes. Even royalty was interested in and encouraged science. Observatories and museums began to flourish; Paris and Greenwich observatories were founded in the sixties and seventies, and the Oxford Museum to house curiosities was established in 1683. These measures increased the popularity of science and made possible further progress.

PHILOSOPHY AND THE FAITH IN MAN

The progress of scientific thought also involved a development of philosophy. Philosophy had rested upon theology during most of the Christian Era. As natural science developed, however, it began to displace theology as the basis of thought. An important step was taken by Descartes, who distinguished between mind and the things it could perceive on the one hand, and matter which could actually be measured, on the other. Then such men as Hobbes, Leibnitz, Locke, Berkeley, Hume, and Kant successively took up the problem of man's mind and body, their relation to each other and to the universe. They often differed radically in their explanation of reality—thus Hobbes taught that reality was matter and motion, Berkeley believed that all reality is in the mind, and Hume contended that the mind was nothing but a sequence of perceptions. But they were consistent in ignoring theology or dissociating it from philosophy, though many of them were devout Christians and few were complete atheists. The philosophers all believed that they were "enlightened," in contrast to the superstition and misunderstanding which preceded them, and soon people in all classes stressed the

importance of being enlightened. The main points of this new philosophy, as typified by Kant, were these: (1) Natural law and science were substituted for the all-powerful God and theology as the guiding force of the world. (2) Man's reason was regarded as the highest thing in the world, and only the facts he could discover need rule his life. (3) If man is supreme, then by seeking to improve his lot he may progress and eventually become perfect. (4) If man is so important, then his care and protection are the main concern; in other words, a humanitarian attitude should prevail.

CHANGES IN RELIGIOUS THINKING IN THE EIGHTEENTH CENTURY

In religion too there were important changes. There was a spiritual revival, and different groups maintained that men should stop quibbling about dogma and try to find true piety through experience. One of these groups was the so-called German Pietists; another was composed of the followers of Swedenborg, a Swedish Pietist.

At the same time in England the Friends, or Quakers, led by George Fox, preached similar opposition to formal doctrine, emphasis upon personal inspiration, and opposition to war. An extremely important phase of this general trend was the Methodist movement, led by John Wesley. He too emphasized personal experience above formal observance, and while he did not originally intend to break from the English national church, it was inevitable that he should. Similar stress upon feeling rather than reason occurred in other denominations. Even the English church, which had for a long time neglected the lower classes in its contentment with cold formalism, was spurred to spiritual revival and a drive to inspire and convert more people.

In France, the emphasis upon the inner spiritual life was advocated by the Jansenists, who thereby gained the enmity of the Catholic Church and were subsequently banned. Even in Russia, stronghold of Orthodox Christianity, there were similar movements. Meanwhile the other Protestant sects, which had arisen during the Reformation, continued to grow without diminishing the strength of Catholi-

Bayle

Gibbon

Voltaire

Locke. (Brown Bros.)

cism in the primarily Catholic countries.

While the movement toward greater piety and religious feeling gathered strength, there was a strong movement in the opposite direction. Many intellectuals, and those who desired to be classed with them, were discarding mystical or "revealed" religion. Influenced by scientific thought and the exaltation of reason in philosophy, they felt that reason should rule in religion also. These skeptics doubted and criticized the doctrines set forth in the Bible. Some of them discarded traditional belief and acknowledged only that there is a God of Nature. Prominent among this group called Deists, were Hobbes and Pope; Pierre Bayle, who expressed his beliefs in his *Dictionary;* and Diderot and the Frenchmen who compiled the great *Encyclopedia.*

Voltaire was the outstanding Deist, philosopher, and advocate of the Enlightenment. A brilliant thinker, he poured out many volumes on different subjects, of which his essays and letters are most interesting. His keen mind investigated numerous phases of life, and his support of Deism contributed greatly to its importance. Deism was also strengthened by the rise throughout Europe of Freemasonry which had similar doctrines. Some thinkers went to the full extent of atheism—the belief that there is no God at all.

The result of this freedom of religious thought was an increasing tendency toward toleration. Signs of this broadened attitude were the decline of beliefs in witchcraft, the beginnings of greater freedom for the Jews, and the suppression of the Jesuits, who had been accused of fanaticism and temporal interests.

NEW HISTORICAL WRITING

The growth of the scientific spirit, which had revolutionized the natural sciences, also revealed itself in the writing of history and in the development of the social sciences. Historical narratives before the seventeenth century had been semitheological in character and were concerned chiefly with the fortunes of kings and battles. Historical occurrences were not described dispassionately as natural events, but rather as if guided by a divine will. For example, a victory in war was often ascribed to God's aid, and a defeat might be pictured as a punishment of His people. The new historical writers were more skeptical and rationalistic. They regarded history as a series of natural consequences. The method of the natural sciences was applied to history.

Thus Gibbon in his noted work, the *Decline and Fall of the Roman Empire*, attributed the destruction of Roman pagan civilization to the growth of what he scornfully called Christian barbarism. David Hume, in his *History of England*, placed less emphasis on politics and wars, showing the historical importance of the social life of the people. Herder, a German clergyman, in *Ideas on the Philosophy of History*, emphasized the humanitarian aspect of society and human nature and accomplishments as revealed in literature, science, and social affairs. The historical works of Voltaire and Raynal were even more popular at that time. Their works consisted of rationalistic and sarcastic attacks on contemporary royal despotism, comparing it with conditions in countries, real or imaginary, where actual liberty prevailed.

Montesquieu. (Brown Bros.)   Rousseau   Bentham

POLITICAL THOUGHT BECOMES LIBERAL

There were also important developments in political thought. Thus far political philosophers had spun themes designed to explain and defend either papal or monarchical authority and absolutism, often thereby ingratiating themselves with their rulers. Of royal abuses and extravagance, of the exploitation and ignorance of the people, little was said; and the common people were regarded as incapable of having a hand in their own government. Thus Hobbes believed that man, by nature bad, had entrusted his welfare to absolutist rulers, to whom he was forever subjected.

John Locke developed a different approach in his political writings. He was the first philosopher to make popular the idea that sovereignty does not ultimately reside in the monarch but in the people, and that the king's power is derived from a grant of power given to him by the people. When the king abuses this power the grant may then be revoked. This theory of social contract became of great significance in Locke's day and thereafter. It was the theoretical backbone of the English Revolution in 1688, and had great influence on the American and French Revolutions.

A different approach to the problem was made in France by the great lawyer Montesquieu who, after studying history, argued that government, instead of being built upon some general abstract theory like a social contract, must be fitted to the particular country and time. Oddly enough, his praise of English government caused many people to do just what

he argued against: to assume that the English system should be used in France and in the American colonies.

Rousseau, whose best known political work is *The Social Contract* (1762), held an opinion similar to Locke's, and greatly influenced his age and subsequent times. His praise of natural man, his interpretation of popular sovereignty, and his concept that government depends on the consent of the governed, were among the ideas which were regarded as so revolutionary he was forced to flee from France.

Also advocating reform, but from a different approach, was Jeremy Bentham. He stressed Utilitarianism, the idea that an act should be measured by the happiness of its doer, a selfish standard. Yet in the long run, in order to be happy a man will act in a way which also makes others happy. The aim of society, therefore, becomes the happiness of the largest possible number of people or in other words, "the greatest good of the greatest number" a phrase already used by the Italian reformer, Beccaria.

RADICAL CHANGES IN ECONOMIC THOUGHT

There were also attempts to develop economics into a science as mercantilism suffered a loss of popularity. The great exponent of the new economic theory was Adam Smith. In France the Physiocratic school of economic thought, led by Quesnay, already had expounded the theory that economic wealth is not the product of rigid government regulation; that such regulation instead, hampers economic production. Adam Smith, in his memorable work, *The Wealth of Nations* (1776), elaborated on this idea. He argued that labor was the basic source of all wealth and that it alone created capital. The entire productive process was governed by rigid natural laws, which automatically determined the importance of the various factors of production. That labor received little, and lived in misery on the verge of starvation, was deplorable but should not be remedied by government action. Nothing should interfere with this inexorable natural law which, as by an invisible hand, governed the economic process. Because it demanded a hands-off policy, this school of economic thought became known as laissez faire, which means "let alone."

Adam Smith thus revolutionized economic thinking. His ideas were also to have great practical consequences. The manufacturing and commercial interests soon advocated the complete elimination of tariffs and monopolies, which was carried out to the fullest extent in England. For the same reason, these classes also opposed any legislation aimed at alleviating the lot of the working class. Both of these factors were to be significant in future world history.

HUMANITARIAN AGITATION

The principle of Enlightenment, besides making for change in the fields already mentioned, gave rise to Humanitarianism. One phase of this movement was a growing demand for the abolition of Negro slavery, begun early in the eighteenth century by the Quakers, and favored by various individuals in both England and America. Likewise the Quakers, and such writers as Abbé Saint Pierre as well, raised their objections to the horrors of war. They offered various plans for courts or leagues of nations to achieve international peace.

Horrified by the deplorable treatment of criminals, such leaders as the Italian writer, Beccaria, and the English economist, Bentham, advocated the improvement of prison conditions, and a decrease in the use of torture and of capital punishment.

The other principal problem which faced humanitarians was that of education. Both Catholic and Protestant groups in European countries founded day schools and Sunday schools in which the poor received elementary instruction, both in secular and religious subjects, while in America the colonies provided for education which they regarded as basic for good citizenship.

ENLIGHTENED DESPOTS

The pervasiveness of these doctrines of Enlightenment is perhaps best illustrated by the fact that their influence extended even to the rulers of the day. These so-called enlightened despots aspired to exercise complete power in the best interests of their people.

An outstanding ruler in this respect was Frederick the Great, whose broad education fitted him for his position, and whose own active life was a model for his people. He had read widely, and as a ruler he enacted many reform measures which have already been discussed. Throughout his life, he continued to interest himself in scientific and artistic progress, enjoyed discussing it, and greatly encouraged German activities in these fields. Thus both theoretically and practically, he was the personification of enlightenment.

Maria Theresa in Austria was less brilliant and thorough, but in addition to centralizing government, decreasing the power of religious groups, and in other ways increasing her power, she improved the educational system and patronized the arts.

Her son, Joseph II, was well read in the works of the enlightened writers and aspired to apply their theories. Unfortunately, he lacked administrative skill. He failed to acquire desired territory. A true believer in reason, he tried to reduce the power of the Catholics and increase the rights of the Jews, two projects which rapidly aroused opposition. Furthermore, his attempts to decrease the powers of the nobles and improve the lot of the peasants were bungling and were opposed throughout the empire.

The attempts at enlightened despotism by Catherine the Great, on the other hand, were insincere since she was, in reality, a tyrant. In contrast to her were Charles III of Spain and Joseph I of Portugal. The former, by measures similar to Frederick's, increased the population and prosperity of Spain, while the latter appointed as minister Pombal, who likewise promoted education and measures for the welfare of the lower classes. Some of the rulers of minor states of Europe during the eighteenth century followed some of the same principles.

55. The French Revolution

UNFORTUNATELY, the enlightened theories of the eighteenth century were not translated into action. The theorists stressed the importance of liberty, yet Europe was governed by absolutist rulers who believed in the divine right of kings. There were all-powerful kings in France, Spain, Portugal, Prussia, Sweden, and Denmark; emperors in Austria and Turkey; and petty but equally absolutist rulers in the little German and Italian states. As we have noted, even the rulers who claimed to be enlightened were, nevertheless, despotic, and absolute. A rigid class system prevailed throughout Europe in spite of pleas for freedom and admiration of the "noble savage" who lived unfettered by society.

In a Europe professing liberal ideas, yet ruled by despots, bound by class distinctions, and hampered by economic regulations, England was the only relatively free country. However, the situation in France is especially interesting, since France was the cultural center of Europe and was to be the political center of European activities for the next twenty-five years. What will be said of France was also, at least partially, true of all Europe.

PRIVILEGED NOBILITY

Far above the mass of the people stood the clergy and the nobles, the members of the First and Second Estates, relatively small in number, but having enormous power. Conspicuous in the social scale were the nobles of the Second Estate. Most of them had great landholdings, from which they received large incomes enabling them to live in leisure and luxury. Some also held important church offices, from which they derived additional income.

A minority of these nobles in France were called the nobility of the gown (*noblesse de la robe*). They were wealthy middle-class men who either inherited titles or who acquired them by buying a position in a law court, which carried with it a title and a judge's robe, whence came their name. The majority, however, were nobles of the sword (*noblesse de l'epée*). They had inherited their titles from medieval ancestors and still owed feudal allegiance to the king.

It is true that not all the nobility were in the same position: some had relatively little property and were forced to live upon their estates in a none too prosperous condition. Frequently this group treated their tenants well and took a neighborly interest in their welfare. Others were wealthier and lived in the country by choice. Many held government positions, but they were also members of the highest social class. On the other hand, many nobles were immensely wealthy and lived a life of indolent pleasure and vice at the court. There, in addition to their own wealth, they received money from the king in the form of high-salaried positions for which no work was required. They were absentee landlords with efficient but uncharitable managers who ran their estates and extracted as much money as possible from the peasants.

There was some desire for reform, but as a group the nobility led a life devoid of useful activity. They collected feudal dues from the peasants; yet, despite the great wealth they possessed, they paid almost no taxes. This privilege was inherited from the Middle Ages, when the nobles were expected to contribute to the protection of their inferiors and, though they no longer did much for their people, they still enjoyed exemption from taxation.

PRIVILEGED CLERGY

Ranking even higher, since they constituted the First Estate, were the clergy. As in the case of the nobles, the clergy varied greatly in wealth and character. There were many priests who were truly concerned over the condition of the poor people, and who devoted their time and what little money they had to the relief of the unfortunate. On the other hand, the higher clergy were wealthy, powerful men, men with vast lands, who lived luxuriously and, because of the similarity of their interests, co-operated with the nobility. In fact many were also nobles. The clergy also enjoyed the privilege of exemption from taxation.

THIRD ESTATE

In contrast to approximately 280,000 nobles and clergy stood some 24,750,000 members of the Third Estate. Some of these were artisans, city workers in trades and industries, hard working, poorly paid people who were under great restrictions and had practically no political rights.

Far outnumbering them were the peasants, about 21,000,000 in all, for agriculture was still France's main activity. In France, it is true, there were only about 1,000,000 serfs—people, tied to the land, whose lives were completely at the mercy of their lords, and who owed the lords half their laboring time—in contrast to the almost complete serfdom in other European countries. Some peasants owned their own land, yet most of them were subject to old feudal regulations. They were forced to work upon the roads. They paid rent to their overlords, and in addition paid fees for the use of the mill, the bridge, and the oven. The kind of farming they might do was limited to the cultivation of strips of land under old medieval customs. There was no progressive farming with crop rotation, fertilization, and improved methods such as English gentlemen farmers used. If a peasant owned a few farm animals and managed to raise enough for bare existence and payment of fees and taxes, he was fortunate. If not, he might starve to death.

Not only did the peasant have to pay fees to his lord, but he also was forced to make a contribution of somewhat less than a tenth of his produce, for the support of the Church.

The royal government imposed an especially odious tax burden on the unfortunate peasants. Taxes were levied with complete disregard for justice or the ability to pay. There were land taxes, poll taxes, and income taxes. Theoretically at least, the land tax was supposed to be proportional to the value of the property; but the tax collector followed the practice of getting all he could from his victims. Even the necessities of life did not escape the insatiable government. Salt, pots and kettles, paper, cards, starch, and alcohol all paid tribute to the Old Regime.

Bad as were the principles of the tax system, even more intolerable abuses were prevalent in the manner of collection. A person or company could buy the privilege of collecting taxes by paying a fixed sum to the government. The difference between the cost of the privilege and the amount collected represented the profit of the collector.

LEADERSHIP OF THE BOURGEOISIE IN THE THIRD ESTATE

Members of the middle class, or bourgeoisie, were the leaders of the Third Estate. Capitalists and financiers, lawyers, doctors, writers, artists, tradesmen, and wealthy farmers belonged to this Estate. Their importance increased steadily throughout the eighteenth century as towns, industry, and commerce grew. This growth had occurred in spite of the fact that surviving guilds still restricted industry. Mercantilism regulated foreign commerce, and poor transportation and internal duties hampered domestic commerce.

The wealth of the bourgeoisie lessened the severity of the tax burdens they shared with the peasants, but these exactions were far from popular. Particularly annoying to the business men were the internal customs duties, tolls, and levies at the gates of the cities. Their business also suffered because of French wars and colonial losses. Naturally they resented the discrimination against them. Since they constituted the bulk of the reading public,

King Louis XVI, 1754-93. (Chicago Historical Soc.)

Marie Antoinette, 1755-93

they were familiar with the advanced scientific and philosophic ideas of the day, and sought to put some of these principles of enlightenment into practice. It is not surprising that the bourgeoisie led the opposition to the king.

The problem of public finance was aggravated by the fact that money once collected was squandered upon the royal family and the court, with no real benefit to the nation. Added to this deplorable situation was the confusion in political and legal organization. The government, because it had grown in a haphazard fashion, was badly organized as well as arbitrary, and plagued with overlapping powers. There existed side by side six different political divisions: judicial, ecclesiastic, educational, and three administrative divisions. Each had its own officials supported by taxes. Then, too, the towns elected their councils in different ways. Weights, measures, and coins differed through the country. There were even many different law codes. These conditions increased the hardships that were normal in carrying on business during this period.

ROYAL WEAKNESS

In spite of all these difficulties, France might have continued for years, if really able kings had been on the throne. Unfortunately, the successors of Louis XIV were not only inefficient, but, perhaps, the most wretched possible under the circumstances. Louis XV was too young to rule when he succeeded to the throne in 1715. There was no efficient body to take charge because Louis XIV had kept all government in his own hands in the latter part of his reign. The ministers of Louis XV ruled in their own interests exclusively. When Louis XV finally assumed control, he was so interested in a life of pleasure and so completely controlled by his mistresses, most of whom were hated by the people, that upon his death in 1774 there were cheers rather than sorrow.

Louis XVI proved to be well meaning but weak and rather unintelligent in state affairs. Unwilling to see any of his immediate family or friends discontented, he reversed national policies to please them. His marriage to Marie Antoinette was unfortunate because she was an Austrian and was considered an enemy by the French, who traditionally regarded Austria with suspicion.

FINANCIAL CONFUSION

The incompetence and increasing unpopularity of the royal family was aggravated by the growing disorder of the public finances. The king chose as minister of finance the admirable Turgot, an expert theorist who wished to put laissez faire principles into operation. Industry and commerce were to be allowed unrestricted activity, finances were to be reformed, and taxes lowered—a program necessary to the preservation of the French monarchy. Naturally, however, he was opposed by all persons who would have lost their privileges and even the peasants, who misunderstood his intentions, were aroused.

Necker, a practical middle-class man, then succeeded to the ministry of finance. He made a step in the right direction by publishing a report on the hitherto unknown condition of French finances. All business men welcomed this information, but Necker was ousted because he tried to force economy upon the court. Marie Antoinette refused to have her friends lose their pleasures and, to placate her, Louis replaced Necker with Calonne.

Jacques Turgot, 1727-81, French economist who was Louis XVI's finance minister for a time

Instead of trying to economize, Calonne borrowed even more money and at high interest. He spent large sums in an effort to make France appear solvent. Intervention in the American Revolution was a very unprofitable venture, for, although France had the satisfaction of humbling England, the expense was enormous. The treasury was bankrupt when Calonne resigned in 1787.

At this point Louis called a meeting of the Assembly of Notables, a group of about 150 of France's most important men, to consider the finances. The nobles would agree to surrender only a few privileges, and recommended that the Estates General handle the tax problem. A new finance minister began by making beautiful promises of reform, but soon resorted to making loans. The Parlement of Paris, the Supreme Court, refused to assent to new loans or taxes, and demanded the meeting of the Estates General, the national legislature, which had not met for 175 years. Annoyed at its impertinence, Louis XVI dissolved the Parlement of Paris, thereby causing much indignation in Paris.

Having asserted his authority by dismissing the Parlement, the king was, nevertheless, forced to call a meeting of the Estates General for May, 1789. Elections were held during the winter of 1788-1789. The Estates General was composed of the three Estates: there were 308 clergymen, 290 nobles, and 598 commoners. This meant that in number of representatives the Third Estate equaled the two upper groups. Since some of the upper classes sympathized with the Third Estate, the latter would have an excellent chance to control the Assembly if all three Estates met together and voted by individuals. On the other hand, if each Estate voted as a unit, the upper Estates would lead two to one, since the nobles and clergy usually voted on the same side.

Before the meeting, groups of each Estate presented their grievances and suggestions, formally drawn up in petitions known as Cahiers. Unfortunately, the ministers of the king, instead of studying the Cahiers and outlining a program for the Estates General, did nothing and had no leadership to offer.

THE CRISIS

When the Estates General convened, therefore, confusion reigned. At once there arose the question of how the Estates should vote. The king in his opening speech, which said very little, indicated that he favored a vote by order—that is, he wished each Estate to vote as a unit. The Third Estate objected because it would be outnumbered two to one. It preferred a vote by head because, they said, the nation would be truly represented that way. Practically, of course, as has already been pointed out, they would have at least an equal chance this way.

The Third Estate consisted largely of the bourgeoise, who desired greater power. They had the advantage of two excellent leaders. Mirabeau, a noble whose sympathies drew him to the Third Estate, was a brilliant orator and a wise and courageous man. The Abbé Sieyès, less outstanding, was nevertheless prominent, especially because he had written a pamphlet in favor of the Third Estate just before the assembly of the Estates General.

Under these leaders the Third Estate carried on fruitless debate for a month. During this time tension increased because the peasants and city proletariat were on the

The Estates General's Opening Session, May 5, 1789, its first meeting in 175 years

verge of starvation. Finally, since the clergy and nobles showed no signs of yielding, the Third Estate declared itself a National Assembly on June 17, 1789. The king tried to make them subservient to his wishes by barring them from the chamber in which they were to meet; so they assembled instead at a place where tennis matches were held. Here they took the "Tennis Court Oath," swearing that they would not separate until they had drawn up a national constitution. Thus they assumed the task of providing a constitutional government for France, and made the first move of the French Revolution.

The king had failed to enforce his will: the Third Estate, backed by some members of the other two Estates, continued to insist

Mirabeau, the early French Revolution's great exponent of a constitutional monarchy

Members of the Third Estate meeting in the tennis court where they took an oath to draw up a constitution

Storming of the Bastille, July 14, 1789. Artist's conception of the mob's attack on the Paris fortress used as a prison and regarded as a symbol of Bourbon tyranny. Actually, at the time the prison had only seven inmates, none of them political prisoners. The Bastille was destroyed after its capture

on their rights. After a week, in his usual timid fashion the king submitted and the Estates General met together on July 1, 1789 and voted by head.

VIOLENCE

When troops were brought into Paris from the frontier, it was feared that the royal government would use force against the Assembly if necessary. The Assembly's request for removal of the troops was refused; and the people of Paris, desperately hungry and seeing their only hope in the Assembly, began to riot. The rioting continued for three days until, on July 14, 1789, the mob destroyed the Bastille, an arsenal formerly used as a prison for political offenders and regarded as a symbol of Bourbon tyranny. Its destruction made the upper classes realize at last that revolution was under way. The middle class people of Paris established a local government of officials chosen by popular election. This Commune, with Lafayette in charge of the National Guard, for the most part controlled the city without royal approval.

But quiet and order did not last long. The peasants in the provinces had taken up the agitation, destroying property and organizing armed groups and local governments. While the Assembly met at Paris and began the program of reform, the dire distress and threatened starvation of the mob continued. The unrest was increased by news that new troops had been brought to the royal court in Versailles and at a lavish entertainment had expressed their enthusiasm for the king.

Finally on October 5, a mob of the women of Paris marched to Versailles and, nearly maddened by hunger, rioted for bread. After a night of terror, during which Lafayette barely succeeded in protecting the royal family, the king and queen consented to move to Paris, as a guarantee that food would be provided for the mob, and the middle class might exercise power. The people in many towns throughout France had refused to pay taxes and had assumed control of local affairs. Under these chaotic circumstances the royal government had collapsed, and the royal family's removal to Paris made them virtually prisoners. The mob was in command.

At last the people had an opportunity to put into effect the principles of liberty—freedom of property, of religion, of speech, of press; equality—the end of all class distinction; and fraternity—a nation of men working together for the good of France.

REVOLUTIONARY LAWS

During these months of chaos, the pressing problems of finances, which had originally caused the crisis, became increasingly complicated because no taxes had been paid. The Assembly therefore undertook taxation reform, and relieved the situation by the issue of paper currency or *assignats*. As security for this issue, the Assembly confiscated large blocks of church lands, in partial return for which the clergy were to be paid salaries.

Thus in an attempt to ease the financial strain, the power of the Church was reduced.

The subjection of the Church was furthered by confiscation of church property and the suppression of the monasteries. In 1790, by the Civil Constitution of the Clergy, the number of the higher clergy was reduced, and they were made a civil group, elected by the people and forced to take an oath of allegiance. Many of the clergy fled rather than take this inferior position. As a result a large number of devout Catholics, who had thus far favored the Revolution, now turned against it.

Meanwhile the National Constituent Assembly, as it was now called, continued to work on reform. During the August days, the nobles, frightened by the violence of the mob, and perhaps moved by generosity, surrendered their feudal rights. Serfdom was ended, servile fees ceased, and ecclesiastical privileges were discontinued. By these and other enactments the lower classes were relieved of many grievous burdens of taxation and service. However, the nobles were to be reimbursed, and it was not until 1793 that the feudal abolition was made without indemnity.

As a statement of their basic principles, the Assembly adopted the "Declaration of the Rights of Man," guaranteeing rights of liberty, property, and security of the individual. Important administrative reforms were also made, and the French Revolution was well under way.

FRANCE UNDER A NEW GOVERNMENT

Most of the immediate problems in connection with a new system of government were solved by the National Assembly in 1791. The results of its labor appeared in a written constitution for France. There was to be a separation of powers, with the executive function vested in the king and the legislative power vested in an elected assembly. The king's executive capacity was limited primarily to the exercise of a suspensive veto. The assembly was controlled by the middle classes because only property owners were allowed to vote.

Thus were made in two years sweeping changes which had not been achieved in centuries. However, as might be expected under such conditions, few people were satisfied with what had been done. The nobles, many of whom fled from France and were called emigrés, naturally wished to recover their property. Many devout Catholics resented the revolutionary attacks on religion and their discontent was expressed in a riot at La Vendée. The royal family could not be expected to enjoy its new fetters. Louis XVI and Marie Antoinette made an attempt to flee from their rebellious subjects, but they were recognized and compelled to return to Paris.

This attempted flight increased the wrath of radicals, a group which was growing rapidly in numbers. The middle classes, motivated by the desire for power and genuine sympathy with the proletariat, led the radicals. Their activities centered in Paris where political clubs had come into existence. Chief among these clubs were the Cordeliers who were radical from the beginning, and the moderate Jacobins who later became extremely radical. Three great leaders appeared among these extremists. Marat was a brilliant and vigorous advocate of direct popular rights. Danton was a deliberate agitator, calm, practical, and a good orator. Robespierre was a scholar who believed ardently in popular rights. All three of these men met violent deaths early in the Revolution.

Charlotte Corday in prison. She had killed Marat. She was executed on July 17, 1793

UNITED OPPOSITION OF EUROPEAN MONARCHS

France was seething with discontent, but the immediate cause for the downfall of the monarchy came from abroad. The first incidents of the Revolution were observed with sympathy in England where liberal Britons approved the limitation of monarchical power. But British alarm was aroused by unbridled radicalism in France, and by 1790 many influential Englishmen agreed with Edmund Burke in his opposition to the Revolution across the Channel.

On the Continent, however, the feeling was clearly against the French people from the beginning of the Revolution. The Bourbon family, ruling in Spain and the two Sicilies, were united by family compacts with the rulers of France, and their wrath was aroused. Worse still, the sympathy of Leopold II of Austria was alienated from the revolutionists. As a Hapsburg he was expected to protect his sister, Marie Antoinette. As a ruler of Austria, he feared that revolt in the Austrian Netherlands, recently suppressed with difficulty, might break out again. As Holy Roman Emperor he wished to keep ideas of revolution out of the German States.

Cooperation of Austria and Prussia, enemies for many years, would have been impossible had Frederick the Great been alive, but his weak successor, Frederick William II, was willing to act with Austria. The two rulers proclaimed their views in August, 1791, when they stated that the restoration of monarchy and order in France was the common interest of all European sovereigns.

The possibility of war was welcomed by many groups in France. The court group believed that should the allies win, its supremacy would be re-established, and even if the French won, the victory would so add to royal prestige that their positions would be improved. The middle classes saw in war a factor to unify all France, now so divided in sentiment. Even the radicals, with the exception of a few who feared that a military dictatorship would follow, regarded war as an opportunity to achieve a truly democratic government.

Therefore the question of war became the main interest of the Legislative Assembly. About half of the deputies, who represented many shades of opinion, at first voted independently; but as time passed they tended to side with one of the two groups which constituted the balance of the members. They

The Marseillaise, French national anthem, being sung for the first time by its composer, Claude Joseph Rouget de Lisle (1760-1836). From a painting by Isidore Alexandre Augustin Pils

were the Feuillants, who favored a monarchy restrained constitutionally, and the radical Girondists, whose leaders came from the department of Gironde, who desired a republic. Although these groups opposed each other in internal problems, they agreed on the foreign problem, and in April, 1792, Louis XVI was persuaded to declare war.

The people were united in enthusiasm for their cause, but they were wretchedly equipped and badly organized. Furthermore, members of the royal family, although supposedly loyal to France, were naturally fearful of the growth of Republicanism. They regarded the foreign armies as possible deliverers and were even suspected of revealing French plans to the enemy. It is not surprising that when the French suffered a series of defeats, they blamed their king and became increasingly bitter and violent.

THE END OF THE MONARCHY

At this point once again an incident abroad incited action at home. Late in July, 1792, the Duke of Brunswick, commander of the allies, issued a proclamation declaring his intention to restore order in France and threatening to destroy Paris completely if any of the royal family was harmed. This proclamation roused the proletariat and extreme members of the bourgeoisie to fury, and on August 10, 1792 they revolted. They displaced the Commune by a new revolutionary body headed by Danton; broke into the palace, killed the Swiss Guards, and forced the royal family to flee to the Assembly for protection. Under the influence of the Paris mobs the weakened Assembly suspended the king and called for an election of a new National Convention by universal suffrage.

When the Convention assembled on September 22, 1792, it declared that France was a republic. The Convention was supposedly elected by universal suffrage, though many of the lower classes had been kept away. However, many degrees of opinion were represented. On the right were the Girondists, who were theoretically democratic but actually feared the proletariat. On the left were a smaller number, the Jacobins, members of the middle class but thorough disciples of Rousseau and sympathizers with the proletariat. Their leaders included Robespierre, Danton, Carnot, and St. Just. Between them was "The Plain," the majority, who had no set policy; but as the course of events revealed the strength of the proletariat, they tended more and more toward the left.

Members of the National Convention leaving their meeting place after the arrest of 31 Girondist deputies, forced on the Convention by an uprising planned by the Paris Commune and the Jacobin group in power

The Convention was faced with the necessity of running the war, continuing the work of the Revolution, and improving organization at home. One of the first problems confronting them was the disposal of the king. Louis XVI was tried in January, 1793, for betraying his people. He was convicted and executed. Among those who voted for the execution was the king's cousin, the Duke of Orleans, who had turned Revolutionist, taking the name of Philippe Égalité.

THE REIGN OF TERROR

Meanwhile the tide of the war had turned. The news of a French victory had been received on the day the republic was proclaimed. Success continued as the French under Dumouriez not only drove the allies out of France but actually conquered Belgium. The proclamation of the French intention to spread the revolution to all countries aroused Great Britain, Holland, Spain, and Sardinia to join Austria and Prussia in a coalition against France. Even within France there was some reaction against revolutionary policies, and Dumouriez himself deserted to the Austrians.

Military success continued in spite of this desertion. Carnot, one of the Jacobin leaders, took command, drafted and drilled men, devised such new features as making the division a military unit, and perfected plans of strategy. Under his brilliant leadership the French broke up the coalition. By the treaties of 1795, Spain made peace; Prussia granted France a free hand on the left bank of the Rhine; William V was deposed and Holland was transformed into the Batavian Republic; and France held the Austrian Netherlands. France, in controlling the territory east to the Rhine, had accomplished what Louis XIV with his great organization had failed to do. Only Great Britain, Austria, and Sardinia continued the armed opposition.

Meanwhile violence increased at home. Danton had become virtual dictator, and in the September massacres of 1792 the royalists were ruthlessly executed. Still there was opposition from the middle classes and the people of the provinces. The military machine built up for the foreign war was used to stamp out this opposition. The Jacobins had become supreme, with Robespierre, St. Just, and Carnot directing the Committee of

On the Way to the Guillotine. Girondins being sent to their execution during the Reign of Terror

The Trial of Louis XVI. By a vote of 361 to 360 the king's sentence was fixed as death

Public Safety, the supreme executive organ of France.

The year of their rule, 1793, is frequently termed the "Reign of Terror," so bloody were its results. The Committee felt that terrorism was the only way in which to deal with their many enemies. The Revolutionary Tribunal was empowered to try and convict suspects, who were not allowed counsel, and were tried without jury. The bloody horror of the French Revolution's Reign of Terror is shown in the number of executions, which rose from 13 per month before November, 1793, to 65 a month through February, 1794, and 135 a month in March and April. Between April 20 and June 10, 636 persons were guillotined. The last days of the Terror were the bloodiest; from June 11 to July 27, 1794, there were 1,366 executions. These were only the deaths ordered in Paris. In the provinces, where there had been several royalist uprisings, thousands were killed by the Revolutionary tribunals. At Nantes alone, 15,000 persons were put to death in three months.

REVOLUTIONARY LEGISLATION

In addition to these violent activities, the Convention enacted much in legislation. It began the task of unifying the law code and adopted some radical social reforms: the abolition of imprisonment for debt, of Negro slavery in the French colonies, and the pro-

tection of women's property rights. Primogeniture was abolished so that property, instead of being willed to the eldest son alone, was divided among the nearest relatives. The metric system of weights and measures was adopted.

An interesting experiment which typified the desire to sweep away all manifestations of the old regime, was the calendar reform. The year was to be divided into twelve periods with new names, each in turn into three weeks of ten days each, with every tenth day set aside for rest, and the remaining few days at the end of the year to be holidays.

The Convention likewise turned its attention to religion. In 1792 it had decreed an entirely new religion of reason to be expounded in the churches. Later, under Robespierre, Deism, including belief in a Supreme Being, was substituted. Finally, at the end of the "Reign of Terror," the Convention decided that religion was a private matter in which the state should not interfere.

Extreme economic measures were enacted, whereby further confiscations of property occurred. Land was divided into small parcels

Marie Antoinette after she was declared guilty of treason. She was guillotined Oct. 16, 1793

Robespierre

Danton

and sold. Furthermore, laws were enacted fixing maximum prices.

The radical nature of this legislation, and particularly the bloodiness of the "Reign of Terror," inevitably led to reaction. Danton, wearying of violence, now favored moderation and consequently was guillotined. Finally Robespierre, after a short dictatorship, was executed, together with St. Just.

This decline of radicalism, known as the Thermidorian Reaction, because it occurred in the month called Thermidor, marked the end of terrorism. Bourgeois groups were once more in the ascendancy, but they continued their homage to republicanism. The Convention, called to draw up a constitution that had never gone into effect because of the Terror, now provided one in harmony with the prevailing bourgeois spirit. Effective in 1795 and known as the Constitution of the Year III, it provided for two legislative chambers elected indirectly: a lower house to propose the laws and an upper house to examine and enact them. Executive power was delegated to a Directory of five persons elected by the legislature. The Directory was to appoint ministers and supervise law enforcement.

THE DIRECTORY

The four years of the Directory were characterized by domestic dissension and dissatisfaction. With the exception of Carnot, who was expelled in 1797, the members of the Directory were of mediocre caliber. Interested mainly in the amount of profit they might acquire, they paid little attention to the welfare of the country. Political and social dissension continued. On the one hand there were many royalists and reactionaries in the legislature, who were restrained only by illegal force. At the other extreme were such men as Babeuf, a socialist radical leader, whose indignation at the still unimproved lot of the underdog caused him to lead an insurrection for which he was subsequently executed.

An increasingly serious problem was the financial situation. The issue of the *assignats*, or paper currency, which had been instituted as a temporary measure, was continued until by 1796 three hundred livres in *assignats* were required for one livre in cash. In 1797, a partial bankruptcy was declared and the *assignats* repudiated. The financial situation was worse than it had been in 1790.

56. The Napoleonic Wars

RISE OF AN UNKNOWN CORSICAN—NAPOLEON BONAPARTE

THE CHIEF THREAT TO THE POWER of the Directory was the increasing popularity of Napoleon Bonaparte. The man who molded the destiny of Europe by his own personal power, was born on the small Mediterranean island of Corsica in 1769. The Bonapartes were an old and honored family, prominent in Corsican politics. Charles-Marie Bonaparte had some political influence at the French court, and obtained an appointment for his son Napoleon to attend the military academy at Brienne. Four years of military training were followed by a year of specialized preparation as an artillery officer at the École Militaire. Then, like any other soldier in his class, the future master of Europe was commissioned a sub-lieutenant and detailed to a provincial post.

There was little that distinguished the young Bonaparte from other lieutenants of artillery except his short stature and his interest in the ideas of Rousseau. The outbreak of the Revolution and the subsequent reorganization of the army gave Bonaparte ample opportunities for advancement. As tactical adviser in the siege of Toulon, a town on the Mediterranean coast that rebelled against the Parisian authorities, he established a reputation as an artilleryman and strategist. His superior officers next honored him, so they thought, by giving him command of the infantry in western France. Bonaparte refused the dubious honor because of his pride in believing himself an authority in the use of artillery, especially as applied to the peculiar conditions of warfare in southern France and northern Italy.

Left without a command and disgraced because he had refused one, Bonaparte lived in poverty and disrepute until called upon to assist in suppressing a royalist uprising in Paris in 1795. The ambitious young Corsican saved the Convention with a "whiff of grape-shot" and at the same time caught the scent of power. Raised to the position of a hero, Bonaparte was eventually rewarded with the command of the army in Italy.

ITALY AND EGYPT

The French military strategy called for two major campaigns. One army was to move in a northeasterly direction, and the other was to advance into Italy against Sardinia and Austria. This latter campaign was entrusted to Bonaparte. In a series of brilliant maneuvers through the Alps into Italy, he swept away the armies of the Sardinians and the Austrians. By the Treaty of Campo Formio in 1797, France was given the Ionian Islands and the Austrian Netherlands. As partial compensation for the loss of the Netherlands, Austria was given the Venetian Republic, but only on promising to stay out of other parts of Italy. Both Austria and Sardinia were thus removed from the conflict and only Great Britain remained to oppose France.

Members of the Directory realized the danger to their position in having a military hero in Paris. Bonaparte himself favored an Egyptian campaign as a means of striking at England and his wishes were followed.

Bonaparte's soldiers won new laurels in the shadows of the pyramids and suffered terrible hardships on a futile Syrian campaign. But Lord Nelson defeated the French fleet and maintained the supremacy of English sea power in the Mediterranean. The most significant accomplishments of the Egyptian cam-

Napoleon at the Battle of Rivoli, Jan. 14, 1797, during his victorious Italian campaign

paign were scientific rather than military. Bonaparte encouraged the study of Egyptian antiquities by the archaeologists who accompanied the expedition and returned to France with many Egyptian treasures.

Bonaparte was well aware that his Egyptian adventure was a military failure; but the French people were willing to believe that their remarkable young commander had won new honors for the republic. When he received the news of French reverses in Europe, Bonaparte decided to desert his army in Egypt and return to France. He managed to escape capture by a British fleet and landed to receive a tumultuous welcome which was by no means wholly deserved. But the French people were looking into the future as well as toward the past, and Bonaparte was expected to save France from an uncomfortable position.

COUP D'ÉTAT OF 1799

The Directory had decided that the best protection for France would be a ring of dependent republics around the country. Holland became the dependent Batavian Republic in 1795. The Swiss Confederation be-

came the Helvetic Republic. The Duchy of Milan, the city of Genoa, the Papal States, and the Kingdom of the Two Sicilies had all become republics. But the enemies of France formed a new coalition. Great Britain, Austria, and Russia made an alliance in which the British statesman, William Pitt, was an important leader. Armies of the coalition won victories over French troops, and in France itself there was domestic chaos. No wonder then that Bonaparte's return was regarded with so much favor!

For a few weeks after his return from Egypt, Bonaparte lived in conspicuous retirement in Paris. During that time he was plotting with the Abbé Sieyès for the downfall of the Directory and the establishment of a military dictatorship under three consuls, two of whom would be Sieyès and Bonaparte. A coup d'état was scheduled for November 9, 1799, and was to be accomplished in one of the sessions of the legislature. When the time came, the *coup* all but miscarried. One branch of the legislature, the Council of the Ancients, agreed to the proposed changes on November 9. But the Assembly, strongly Jacobin in membership, violently opposed modifications in the government. The conqueror of Italy fainted at a critical time in the proceedings on November 10, and the whole plot would have failed had not Lucien Bonaparte saved the day by dispersing the Assembly with a force of grenadiers.

FIRST CONSUL

Bonaparte himself became the First Consul in the reorganized government. There were two others, but they became mere phantoms when the powerful personality of Bonaparte began to make itself felt. His popularity and the prospect of a capable government overcame the momentary distaste for the dictatorship. Although France under the Consulate was nominally a republic, it was not long until First Consul Bonaparte adopted the pomp of royalty. Before long, too, occurred the psychological transformation of Citizen Bonaparte into Napoleon, Emperor of the French.

Early in 1800 Bonaparte saw his enemies of the second coalition seriously weakened by the withdrawal of the Russians from their ranks. Only England and Austria remained in arms to threaten France. He sent one army into German territory and personally undertook an expedition to humble Austria and drive her armies out of northern Italy. The campaign was a distinct success. Italy was bound securely to France, and Austria was again defeated. In the Peace of Lunéville (1801) which confirmed the conquest, Bonaparte assured the security of France by establishing a series of friendly Italian republics, the Rhine River as a "natural" boundary, and a respite in the war with Austria. England, the only power remaining at war with France, ceased her hostility in the same year. The speed, with which Bonaparte was able to bring peace, clearly proved him a genius in handling international affairs.

BONAPARTE'S ADMINISTRATIVE GENIUS

When he grappled with the internal problems of France, the First Consul showed an equal genius for administration. In short order he solved monetary problems, thereby restoring confidence in his central government and a measure of prosperity to the people of France. Almost overnight he wiped out the republican government of the provinces and substituted *prefects*, appointive officials who were responsible to him alone. He knew how little the uneducated people of the provinces cared to exercise their voting power. The system of prefectures, so efficiently administered, brought provincial France into the closest union that had ever existed. Thus Bonaparte was always in contact with the minds of his people.

The status of the church was the next problem to be solved. Catholicism, although in official disfavor, had remained a powerful force throughout the Revolution. Restoration of order under the Consulate required that the relations of church and state be established on a permanent basis. Negotiations with the papacy finally resulted in the mutually satisfactory concordat of 1801.

The legal problems of France were simplified by the preparation of a concise code which was published in 1804 and took as its popular name the *Code Napoléon*. Paris was beautified and France was given a system of good roads. The Louvre was enlarged to house the precious booty of Napoleon's Egyptian and Italian campaigns. Everywhere France blossomed anew under the stimulating personality of the First Consul.

EMPIRE—1804

Subject states, such as the Italian republics, were also included in the general reorganization which Bonaparte brought to France. One after another they were brought under his personal power. In a similar manner he built up a colonial empire. Spain ceded to France the vast trans-Mississippi region known as Louisiana, and a French army took the island of Haiti in the Caribbean Sea.

Building an empire, Bonaparte waived republican principles aside. In 1802 he had himself elected consul for life. Late in 1804, he dropped all pretense of republicanism and assumed the title of Emperor. Amid all the pageantry that was characteristic of his public appearances and those of Pope Pius VII, who came from Rome to grace the occasion, Napoleon placed the crown on his own head.

Pius VII, Pope from 1800 to 1823

Napoleon meeting Francis II of Austria after the smashing French victory at Austerlitz

France's foreign enemies were alarmed by the growing power of Napoleon. The imperial designs of the little despot became a matter of international concern. England induced Austria and Russia to join a new coalition of powers to curb the increasing might of France. Napoleon was not unmindful of his responsibilities to his people and to his own ambition. In 1803 he had sold Louisiana, his greatest American possession, to the United States to raise money for the impending war. Although Napoleon began to build a navy, he became convinced of the impossibility of carrying the war to the British Isles, so he attacked England's continental allies.

His genius did not fail him. In less than six months his citizen army and Bavarian allies captured the Austrian capital and dealt the combined Austrian and Russian armies a crushing defeat at Austerlitz. He next turned on Prussia, another of the allies, and drove its army from the field at Jena and Auerstadt on October 14, 1806. Of the continental members of the coalition, only Russia remained to be humbled.

The march from the Prussian battlefields toward Russia was impeded only at Friedland, where the French army signally defeated a Russian army augmented by a remnant of Prussians. Czar Alexander of Russia did not risk further defeat but agreed to meet Napoleon on a raft in the river to sign the Treaty of Tilsit. More than a peace was concluded, since Alexander soon appeared as an ally of France and an empire builder in his own right. Sweden, in spite of feeble aid from England, lost Finland to the Czar in 1809. In only two years Napoleon had asserted his mastery over continental Europe.

THE "CONTINENTAL SYSTEM"— A BOOMERANG

Unable to cope with England directly, the master of Europe devised an indirect war on Britain. The French navy, which had been reconditioned and augmented, lost its effectiveness in the Battle of Trafalgar in October, 1805, and so in a single stroke, Napoleon's chief weapon against England was taken from him. His plan of indirect war on Britain was to strike at her trade with continental Europe. As master of the continent, he closed all of its ports to British goods, hoping thereby to starve Britain of her life's blood—trade and commerce. Further decrees, after 1806, even allowed confiscation of English goods found on the continent. England, unable to attack Napoleon on the continent, issued counter-decrees prohibiting the world's trade with France, and ordering the seizure of vessels that complied with French decrees.

Napoleon's plan, which has come to be known as the "continental system"—economic war of the continent against England—was intended to injure Britain. Instead, his decrees worked hardships on his continental subjects and on the neutral powers whom Napoleon expected to supply Europe. Among the latter was the United States. American merchants were subjected to both French decrees and English counter-decrees. The difficulties of legal traffic with the combatants were a major cause of the American war with England which began in 1812. It was the despotism of Napoleon, typified in the Continental System, that contributed to his ultimate failure. Its application from 1806 onward turned Europe's thoughts from Napoleon the liberator to Napoleon the tyrant.

NAPOLEON'S EUROPE

The French invasion of Europe was at first viewed by the European peoples as a liberation from the tyranny of their own monarchs. Everywhere the Napoleonic army was welcomed as the herald of a new day.

When Napoleon entered a European state, he intended to stay there. The newly enlarged France was administered by his prefects; the lesser states of Europe were given over into the hands of persons who could be relied on to give Napoleon support when needed. Close relatives of Napoleon and trusted generals were raised, in many instances, to the positions of highest authority in some of the European states. Holland, the principalities of the east bank of the Rhine River, and Italy were among the states that were placed in the hands of his relatives and favorites.

Napoleon's policy was to keep his subject states so weakened that none could rise against him. Groups of smaller states, such as the Confederation of the Rhine, were banded together to balance the power of Austria and Prussia. The reorganization of Europe was accomplished at the expense of the old Holy Roman Empire, an organization which had been superfluous for more than a century. Napoleon merely laid its ghost and thereby compelled the Emperor, who was also Emperor of Austria, to restrict his power to his Austrian possessions.

Russia was the only continental power that did not feel the force of the Napoleonic program for Europe. The fickle Czar escaped its rigors because he had, by chance, become the ally of the master. For a short time Portugal, too, held out against the new order. But, although supported by England, the country fell before Napoleon in 1807. When Portugal and Spain fell, all continental Europe was in the hands of Napoleon or his friends.

Spain, ruled by a Bourbon who had bowed to the inevitable and become friendly to France, suffered without fault on her part. In order to secure the Portuguese conquest, Napoleon took the crown from the Spanish

The Battle of Trafalgar: a French officer's drawing of the "Redoutable" engaging British ships

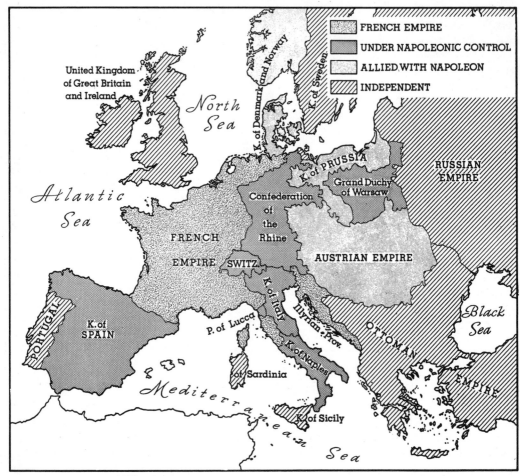

Europe in 1812, showing the extent of Napoleon's domination of the Continent

king and gave it to his brother, Joseph. It was an insult to Spain, and the Spanish people took it as such. A revolt broke out and England hastily sent a force to aid the fighting Spaniards. The stubborn resistance of the Spanish forces could not be overcome. Other European peoples, seething under the heel of the oppression, took heart and made ready for the day when they could also rise. Napoleon had lighted the fuse to the keg of powder on which he sat.

DISCONTENT IN LATIN AMERICA

Napoleon's difficulties in Spain were important in bringing about his final downfall in Europe. Moreover, he was badly mistaken if

he expected to secure control over Spain's American colonies by placing his brother Joseph on the Spanish throne. The colonies were far from being contented under Spanish rule, and they welcomed the opportunity to escape from oppression.

There were many causes for rebellion in Spanish America. Before the reforms of Charles III toward the close of the eighteenth century, the monopolistic trade practices were especially burdensome. However, corrupt officials and greedy merchants developed an extensive system of smuggling to modify the restrictions. Foreign goods found their way into the colonies in spite of efforts to exclude them. Taxation within the colonies was also oppressive, and Spain failed to encourage industrial development overseas. There is danger of overemphasizing these economic reasons for discontent in the colonies, but there is little doubt that they were factors in the loss of the Spanish-American empire.

There were religious causes for discontent, centering around objectionable practices of the Inquisition and on the part of a minority of the clergy. Scandalous conduct by unworthy clerics provided ammunition for detractors of the Church which had done so much to civilize two continents. The Inquisition attempted to stamp out heresy and to prevent the introduction of certain publications. These efforts could not fail to arouse the hatred of the people involved, especially among the small educated groups.

Colonial government was largely centered in the hands of native Spaniards, to the practical exclusion of Creoles, as American-born Europeans were called. This Creole group was vociferous in all of the Spanish colonies, and should have found support among the mestizos, the numerous offspring of unions between Spanish men and Indian women. Below this mestizo caste was the large mass of Indians whose every attempt at self-assertion was severely suppressed. Broadly speaking, the interests of Spaniard and Creole were similar, while the mestizo and Indian should have been sympathetic toward one another. The mestizos held the Indians in contempt; the Creoles scorned the mestizos; and even the most insignificant European Spaniard considered himself far superior to the Creole. These mutual animosities helped prevent the cooperation necessary to carry the subsequent revolutionary movements to early and successful conclusion. Another factor that prevented a vigorous independence movement was the lack in the Spanish colonies of the traditions of self-government in the English colonies.

PRELIMINARIES OF REVOLUTION

Many of the viceroys and captains-general were very capable rulers. Their efforts were largely responsible for maintaining Spanish authority and extending Spanish rule in spite of decadence in the mother country. But all of

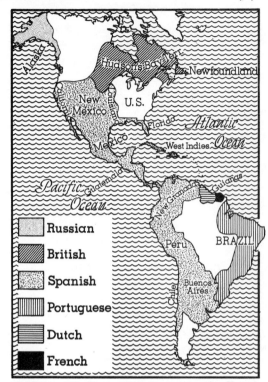

The New World in 1789. Except for the United States, unshaded areas show unexplored regions

their efforts, sincere as they were, could not build an impregnable Chinese wall against the revolutionary ideas then current in the European world. Spain gave her colonists dangerous ideas by joining France in fighting England during the American Revolution. Then came the French Revolution and the Rights of Man, with propagandists like Antonio Nariño to spread the new gospel in northern South America. But still Spanish power remained unshaken in her part of the Americas.

Godfather to Spanish-American independence was a colorful adventurer, Francisco de Miranda. This knight errant was intimate with American and British statesmen, a general in the French Revolution, and a favorite of Catherine the Great. After a series of disappointing experiences with English promises, Miranda found aid in the United States for an expedition to carry the torch of liberty to his native land. He sailed from New York in 1806 on the *Leander*, but the people of

Venezuela refused to be liberated. Miranda sailed away with those of his companions who had not been captured, and returned a few years later when the outbreaks of 1810 occurred.

The people of Buenos Aires gained valuable experience and self-confidence in 1806 and 1807 when they repulsed British efforts to conquer their city. Sir Home Popham and General Beresford turned from Capetown, which they captured from Holland, to an unauthorized attack on the cities at the mouth of Río de la Plata. Buenos Aires fell in 1806, but was retaken by the colonists under the newly elected viceroy, Liniers. Beresford surrendered his army. General Whitelocke captured Montevideo in 1807, but he met with a crushing defeat in Buenos Aires. Although British arms were sadly tarnished, British goods were introduced in sufficient quantities to increase discontent with Spanish trade restrictions.

THE INFLUENCE OF NAPOLEON

Napoleon Bonaparte more or less unwittingly cut the ties between Spain and her American colonies. The Corsican moved an army into Portugal in 1807, but the British admiral succeeded in pursuading the Portuguese court to take refuge in Brazil. French troops then occupied important positions in Spain. Charles IV abdicated in favor of his son, who became Ferdinand VII. Father and son were induced to confer with Napoleon at Bayonne. Ferdinand, too, abdicated, and Napoleon placed his brother Joseph on the Spanish throne.

Local governing bodies in Spain united to oppose the French invaders, and through their guerrilla warfare and English aid, they developed a "Spanish ulcer" which proved fatal to Napoleon. One of the proposals of the Central Junta of Spain was to give Spanish Americans equal voice in colonial government with the European Spaniards. The proposal satisfied few of the influential colonial leaders. Eventually the Spanish colonies were allowed to send thirty delegates to the Spanish parliament, or *Cortes*. Again colonial leaders were disappointed and began to think in terms of independence from Spain.

REBELLION IN THE NAME OF FERDINAND VII

The struggle in Spain and the hateful rule of Joseph Bonaparte gave the Spanish-American colonies a valid political basis for establishing their independence. Sporadic outbreaks in Chuquisaca, La Paz, and Quito were suppressed by royal troops in 1809. These movements were just a year too soon, for in 1810 a number of separate wars for independence broke out in the Spanish dominions. These armed revolts occurred in so many places that one is justified in stating that rebellion was an endemic political disease in Spanish America. Revolutionary *juntas* or committees were created in various colonies to rule in the name of Ferdinand VII. The most important of these committees were those in Buenos Aires, Chile, and Venezuela. Royal power was concentrated in Peru, from which region armies were sent out to subdue the rebellious *juntas*, since the Spaniards and many of the Creoles knew perfectly well that loyalty to Ferdinand VII was merely a screen behind which the leaders were fighting for independence.

This first period of the wars for independence terminated in 1814 when Ferdinand VII was restored to the throne. By that time royal power had been fairly well secured in most of the colonies with the exception of the modern Argentina. In the very year of Ferdinand's restoration, the great José de San Martín was given command of an Argentine army. This remarkable soldier, who must be given a high place in military annals, was destined to become the liberator of Chile and Peru.

Simón Bolívar, the Liberator, also played a prominent part in the first period of the wars for independence. He was especially

José de San Martín

Simón Bolívar, the "Liberator"

active in northern South America between 1810 and 1815, although in the latter year he was forced to flee to Jamaica. Bolívar gained valuable experience as a revolutionary general, and in the second phase of the wars he accomplished more than enough to entitle him to be called one of the greatest sons of America.

An inspired parish priest, Miguel Hidalgo y Costilla, led the rebellion in Mexico. He raised the standard of revolt in September, 1810, and rallied Indians and mestizos around his banner. "Long live the Virgin of Guadalupe! Death to the *Gachupines!*" became the battle cry which threw all Mexico into civil war. Hidalgo and some of his companions were captured and executed in 1811, but José María Morelos continued the fight. A constitution was drawn and independence was declared in 1813. Two years later Morelos, a priest like Hidalgo, was captured and executed. Until the final stroke by Iturbide in 1821, the war in Mexico was little more than a series of guerrilla raids by petty leaders.

SOURCES OF DISCONTENT IN EUROPE

Having seen the results of the combined forces of international politics and economic and social dissatisfaction in Latin America, we now return to the empire of Napoleon, where these factors, working under widely different conditions, had a similar result.

Although the conquests of Europe were first understood by European peoples as an extension of Liberty, Equality, and Fraternity—the three ideals of the French Revolution—it was not long before they felt the tyranny of Napoleon's rule. In the workings of the "continental system," which has already been described, they found themselves subjected to poverty because Napoleon wanted

to humble England. His numerous demands for soldiers to fill the ranks of many armies depleted the population and filled almost every continental family with the sorrow of parting or death.

A ray of hope that the day of Napoleon need not go on forever came from Spain. Napoleon's inability to quell that revolt gave the Austrians an opportunity to stimulate the revolutionary spirit in the German states in the hope of a general European clearing of the Napoleonic influence. But the efforts were premature—the states of the Rhine were too closely allied to their master's interest, and the French army was in possession of all strongholds of anti-French influence. In midsummer, 1809, Napoleon easily disposed of the abortive uprising. Austria was again crushed under the heel of despotism.

DISASTER IN RUSSIA

Yet the spirit of the people of Europe was not broken. French armies marched up and down the bypaths of Europe, but the spirit of revolt against Napoleon's despotism could not be suppressed. His Russian ally, the czar, also began to slip out of his position as a friend of France. Russia was no longer cooperating with Napoleon by 1810; she had opened her ports to British goods. Italian states were likewise beginning to circumvent the rigors of the Continental System.

Napoleon realized that he needed to mend the situation. He quickly chastised the Italian states and laid the plans for a Russian campaign. First, he secured a nominal Austrian alliance by marrying an Austrian princess. Next, he collected the largest army Europe had ever seen and marched it toward Russia.

One-half million men were in the Grand Army that entered Russia to find burned villages and a denuded countryside. The Russians had evacuated their towns, set them afire, and sought the safety of the hinterland. Napoleon found even Moscow a mass of ruins. There the victorious army camped amid desolation and the swirling snows of a Moscow winter awaiting the surrender of a foe who would not chance open battle. Napoleon might have been able to defeat the

Napoleon Retreating from Moscow in 1812. (Bettmann Archive)

Russians had they fought; but, as it was, his only enemies were cold, hunger, disease, and the maddening raids of elusive Cossack warriors. In the late days of the year 1812 Napoleon began a fateful retreat. Few of the half-million soldiers ever saw their homes again. Napoleon's power dribbled away on the long road home. It was the beginning of the road to Elba and to Waterloo.

THE FALLING HOUSE OF CARDS

The European countries did not remain idle when they saw their hated master so seriously weakened. Prussia, particularly, was ready to lead the way in a general European revolt. The earlier victories of Napoleon's armies, composed of citizens fired with nationalistic ideals, taught Prussia that the disinterested professional armies were outmoded. Prussian military leaders trained a national army in spite of the various restrictions. As in the case of the army, other national institutions were brought up to date and to the peak of efficiency. Under the stimulus of a rising nationalistic feeling that penetrated to the humblest citizen, Prussia joined Russia in a war on Napoleon in March, 1813. Other European states were making ready to join the two leading powers.

Napoleon struck at Prussia immediately, but, while winning battles, was unable to demoralize his enemies. At this juncture Austria, wavering for a time to see which side would win, chose to risk her lot with that of the allied powers. For the first time in the years of war against Napoleon, the enemies were united in both spirit and purpose. Together they struck at Napoleon's tired army and administered a crushing defeat at Leipzig. Methodically, relentlessly, they followed him into the very heart of France.

In lower France, also closing in on Paris, were the forces of the Spaniards and English led by Sir Arthur Wellesley, later to become the Duke of Wellington. The Allied forces had not been content with driving the French out of Spain, but resolutely continued to hammer away at the retreating army. With an enemy before him and an enemy behind him, each stronger in men and fired by a nobler cause than his, Napoleon saw his end was near.

On April 6, 1814, Napoleon abdicated and was given an asylum on the Mediterranean island of Elba. In a few short years the master of Europe had fallen from the greatest heights any man had ever reached in modern times. His own methods, which had carried him into

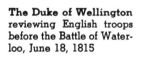

Louis XVIII, king of France, 1795-1824

The victorious powers faced many problems. The overthrow of Napoleon had left many lands without constituted authorities. In many instances the puppets of Napoleon had managed to retain their thrones, but, if the rule of Napoleon were to be set aside, his puppets must be removed from their positions. Problems of territorial division, always thorny, arose when the will of the master was no longer felt.

The problem of providing governments for the regions which Napoleon had ruled was the most immediate problem faced. Having been subjected to the will of a tyrant for a decade, the European states turned to the standard of legal rights. On this basis a Bourbon, Louis XVIII, a brother of the late king, was given the throne of France. The Spanish throne was given back to its former possessors, another branch of the Bourbon family. Having determined the location of national authority, the concerted powers assembled in Vienna a few months later to re-establish Europe on a basis that would afford peace and security to every country. It was a war-tired Europe that was represented at Vienna in the fall of 1814.

THE HUNDRED DAYS

every corner of continental Europe, were taken over by his enemies and were used to drive him from his pinnacle. The enthusiasm for nationalism and liberalism, which he had given Europe, turned on him and drove him whence he had come—to a Mediterranean isle. With an honorary guard of 800 old veterans, Napoleon was interned at Elba.

While the leaders of Europe discussed the fate of the world in Viennese drawing rooms, the world was electrified by the sudden appearance of Napoleon in lower France. While all Europe shuddered at the news, Frenchmen

The Duke of Wellington reviewing English troops before the Battle of Waterloo, June 18, 1815

again placed their country at the disposal of the exiled hero when he entered France in 1815, less than a year after his abdication.

Louis XVIII, the Bourbon king placed on the throne of France by the powers, sent an army to take Napoleon prisoner, but the army, too, joined Napoleon. Louis fled across the border for safety as Napoleon triumphantly marched to Paris.

The Congress at Vienna acted quickly. Napoleon was outlawed and the generals of the concerted powers, the English Wellington and the German Blücher, were ordered to unite their forces and defeat the army Napoleon was gathering. Napoleon acted even more swiftly. He first attacked Blücher and defeated him. Dispatching a part of his army under Grouchy to chase Blücher, he turned on Wellington near Waterloo.

Wellington was ready for him. All the afternoon of the single day of battle, June 18, 1815, Napoleon attempted to dislodge Wellington from his positions but utterly without avail. Late in the afternoon Napoleon was surprised to see Prussian forces coming up on his right. Instead of retreating, Blücher had moved to join Wellington; Grouchy failed to intercept the Prussians, partly because of Napoleon's faulty orders. Napoleon detached the VI Corps and the Young Guard to meet the Prussian vanguard, then massed the remaining Imperial Guard for a final attack on Wellington's center. The assault was repulsed, Blücher's forces began to arrive about 7:30, and the French began a retreat that soon became a rout. Napoleon fled to Paris, where he abdicated a second time.

Now deserted by all his friends, he planned to escape to America. But England had been careful to blockade the entire French coast. He found he could do nothing but surrender to the British. They held him in custody until it was decided to place him on the bleak, mid-Atlantic island of St. Helena. There, after six lonely and bitter years, he died.

He could not stem the tides he had loosed upon Europe. His magnetic personality had drawn men to live and die for him. His despotism and overweening ambition drenched Europe in blood and despair. Yet, in that same Europe made bloody and despairing, he spread the ideals of the French Revolution that still thrive in Europe. He found Europe a poorly organized continent and re-cast its three hundred odd states into thirty-three, each driven by new urges—nationalism and liberalism.

In a few short years Napoleon passed from obscurity to power, and from power to an island prison. Soon after his death, the "Napoleonic legend" began to take form. The bloodshed and tyranny of his grip on Europe were ignored; and Napoleon became the great French symbol of military and national glory.

Napoleon during the Battle of Waterloo, from a painting by Karl Wilhelm von Steuben (by permission, Macmillan Co.)

57. Conservative Reaction in Europe

THE EVENTS THAT TRANSPIRED in the early days of the French Revolution stimulated liberal leaders in every land to believe that the principles of liberty, equality, and fraternity need not be confined to drawing room discussions. This fact was particularly true in England where philosophers and scientists had sought for more than a century to solve social problems.

GREAT BRITAIN AND THE FRENCH REVOLUTION

Great developments were taking place in England during the years immediately preceding the crisis in France. The series of inventions that heralded the Industrial Revolution were being put into use, while small landholdings were being consolidated into large, scientifically operated farms. These industrial and agrarian problems concentrated much attention on domestic economic issues. The close relation of the government and the people made possible the amicable settlement of many major problems; the political parties, highly developed in England, closed the gap between rulers and ruled. England, when compared to Europe, was advanced in putting liberal ideas into practice.

The formation of certain organizations in most of the large cities indicated that there was sympathy for the French ideals. One of these groups was the London Corresponding Society, whose members met together to eat and drink at a local tavern, and to read revolutionary pamphlets and draw up revolutionary programs. The most frequent proposal of these clubs was that England adopt a real, written constitution like those of France and the United States.

English Whigs—the party of the merchants and middle class—were generally in sympathy with the upheaval in France. The Tories—the party of the landed class—looked upon it as the rising of the rabble against authority. However, as the radicalism of the Parisian mob mounted, even the Whigs became alarmed at its disrespect of property and changed their sympathies. Soon "law and order" societies were formed among the conservatives to combat the activities of the liberals. Generally, however, there was in England little revolutionary activity beyond loose talk. Restrictive laws were soon passed.

When England went to war with revolutionary France it became the patriotic duty of every Englishman to hate France. Led by Prime Minister William Pitt, they fell to it with a will, and few men were able to resist the patriotic call. The few who retained their revolutionary principles soon found themselves faced with governmental action. None the less, they were leniently treated.

This intensified patriotism, called nationalism, increased throughout the war. When the Irish, stimulated by the French movement, rebelled in 1798 under the leadership of Wolfe Tone, English opinion was so united that the revolt was easily suppressed. Two years later the English completely subordinated Ireland in the Act of Union, by which Ireland lost its autonomy.

William Pitt the Younger (1759-1806)

Conservatives representing traditional England, grew in power as public sympathy with France waned. Whig leaders lost their following and the Tories, led by Lord Castlereagh, gradually assumed the responsibility of leading England against France and Napoleon, who, after 1800, became Britain's "must-be-destroyed" enemy.

As the war became more critical, British feeling crystallized despite domestic economic disagreements. Losses on the continent were, in a measure, offset by gains elsewhere. Britain remained mistress of the sea, and she incorporated into her domain foreign islands once held by France.

THE GERMAN STATES

Before the French Revolution the Germanic states—over three hundred of them—were loosely bound together in the decrepit Holy Roman Empire. Liberal theory was not unknown, but the practice of liberal principles was generally lacking until the French army entered these lands.

When the Frenchmen first arrived, freeing the land-bound serfs and abolishing the innumerable feudal taxes, the people received them with open arms. French domination was not irksome until the iron hand of Napoleon was felt. Then they were forced to submit to the despotism he instituted: they served in his Grand Army and furnished the grain with which he fed his great military machine.

Prussia and Austria were the greatest of the Germanic states. Pre-revolutionary reforms had been initiated by their enlightened despots and liberal leaders. These reforms lapsed when popular clamor subsided or successors mounted the thrones. When the impact of revolutionary France was felt, liberalism took a new turn. Secret clubs were formed among the professional classes. Some of their members were thrown in prison.

It was not until Napoleon pressed at the gates of Prussia and Austria that the full power of the French Revolution was felt. The new principles of warfare as well as the new ideals were overwhelming. For a time these nations resisted but in the end, shorn of their extensive possessions, they learned the lessons of defeat and met Napoleon with his own methods. Prussia and Austria adopted the principles of nationalism and strengthened their relative positions in Europe. To accomplish this end they had to circumvent the will of Napoleon. For instance, he had limited the size of the Prussian and Austrian armies, but by a process of rapid turnover in training, these states raised armies many times more numerous than the number of men under arms at one time would indicate.

Liberal leadership gained most ground in Prussia. In that state the poet Herder carried the message of nationalism to the Prussian people. Liberally inclined Baron von Stein introduced financial reforms. Wilhelm von Humboldt pressed his cause for popular education. Prussia increased her strength under the tutelage of such leaders.

The most obvious change effected by the French Revolution and by Napoleon was the dissolution of the Holy Roman Empire. First

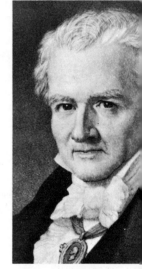

Von Humboldt.
(Chicago Historical Society.)

attacked by the invading army of republican France, the fading decrepit Empire was finally erased, even to its name, by Napoleon. Since the Empire was no longer of great political significance, there was little concern over its demise. The Emperor, who was also Emperor of Austria, contented himself with his Austrian possessions. No effort was made to revive the Empire when Napoleon fell and Europe was remolded in 1815.

SOUTHERN EUROPE

In southern Europe, especially in Italy, peasants were exploited economically and had little freedom before the eighteenth century. Tuscany was well governed, but the rest of Italy languished under an antiquated social system. When the revolutionary ideas came to the kingdoms of Italy, it was the professional classes which arose, not the oppressed masses who were in utter ignorance of idealism such as that of France. As elsewhere, they formed clubs and, as elsewhere, suffered for doing so.

The French armies conquered Italy on repeated occasions but, although they established nominal republics, really left little more than the all-pervading principle of patriotism. Italian leaders took up the tune, and the song of patriotism rang throughout Italy. Napoleon came, despoiled their cities of their richest art treasures, and left his sister, brother, and his favorite general to rule over portions of it. Reactions varied, it is true; Alfieri, the dramatist, condemned the French, maintaining that Italy should free herself of them, while the poet Foscolo praised Napoleon for freeing Italy. However, both agreed in their hopes for a new Italian nation, as did the secret society of the Carbonari, which developed in southern Italy after 1808. Thus, instead of winning Italy to his cause, Napoleon really strengthened Italian nationalism.

THE PENINSULAR WAR

Spain was not a fruitful ground for revolutionary principles, especially since much of the economic life of the country was in French control, greatly to the dislike of the impoverished Spaniards. The Bourbon king of Spain, in an attempt to save his cousin Louis XVI from death, took his country into war. He wisely gave up the idea before he suffered a serious defeat, and so saved his peninsula from what would have been certain ruin.

When Napoleon came to hold the reins of France, the king postponed disaster by becoming friendly to the ambitious dictator. His friendliness did not spare him, for when Napoleon wanted Portugal, the Spanish king was forced to allow the French army to pass through his lands. Then Napoleon used his ally in niggardly fashion. He deposed him and his heirs to give Spain to his brother, so that Portugal could be held in check.

Spain had suffered much, but this act was an unnecessary insult. The Spanish people arose in arms almost immediately and began to fight for their homes and the homeland. England, ever ready to strike a blow at Napoleon, sent soldiers and equipment to fight the French. Under the leadership of the "Iron Duke" Wellington, British forces drove the French army out of Spain and followed it into France.

NATIONALISM IN THE TURKISH DOMAIN

To the southeast in Europe lay the lands of an oriental empire. The Balkan Peninsula was bound to the Ottoman Empire under the sultan and his pashas or viceroys. The government was a typical oriental despotism administered by favorites; the subjects of this empire were Europeans and Christians.

For almost a century the borders of the empire were steadily pushed back by the growing European states, particularly Russia. There were also signs of disintegration within the structure of the empire.

Of all the Christian subjects of the Mohammedan sultan, the Greeks were allowed a

Wellington Crossing the Pyrenees in his pursuit of the French during the Peninsular War

certain amount of freedom in their church affairs and commerce. The other Christian portions of the Ottoman empire were less favored.

The memory of past independence and glory stirred in the hearts of the Greek upper classes. Under the leadership of such men as Korais and Rhigas, who had studied and traveled in western Europe and were inspired by the French Revolution, Greek nationalism was stimulated by revolutionary ballads and propaganda. Societies were formed with the same purposes as those in other countries. They were repressed, indeed, but the movement gained strength.

North of Greece in the Balkans similar national feeling was aroused among the people whom we know as the Yugoslavs. The Serbs were influenced less by the French example than by local conditions. Russia, which wished to weaken the Ottoman Empire, had for many years encouraged them to oppose the Turks, and even subsidized one section known as Montenegro. Then in 1804 a Turkish massacre of Serbs in Belgrade roused their countrymen to fury. Under Karageorge, a brilliant leader, though a peasant, they set up their own legislature and planned their own government. Aiding Russia in its war against the Turks, they were for the most part freed of Turkish control. Unfortunately for them, the Russian troops were withdrawn for use against Napoleon, and the Sultan re-established his authority. The Serbs were in subjection, but their national feeling was not destroyed and gave promise of surging up again in the future.

Near by were the Slovenes and Croats who lived along the east shore of the Adriatic. They had been organized into an "Illyrian" state by Napoleon, who introduced his usual progressive measures in law and public works, and in order to secure their cooperation encouraged them to use their language and recall their past glory.

THE RUSSIAN SPHERE OF INFLUENCE

In northeastern Europe, also, the revolutionary national spirit was felt. The example of France had inspired the futile Polish attempt at reform under the valiant Kosciuszko in the 1790's just before the final partitions removed Poland from the map.

Polish national feeling continued, however, and Napoleon renewed their hopes when he set up part of the country as the Grand Duchy of Warsaw. In return, the Poles under the able Prince Jozef Poniatowski, nephew of the last king, supported the French against Russia. Another great Polish patriot and disciple of enlightenment, Prince Adam Czartoriski was friendly with Russia and obtained a promise of Polish autonomy when the war was over. Thus whether France or Russia won, the prospects for a new Poland were bright. Russia was finally victorious, and Czar Alexander renewed his promises.

Alexander likewise improved the condition of his people in the Baltic provinces. By abolishing serfdom there he began a social reformation which promised future liberty for the Esths and the Letts, who had thus far been subject peoples.

Strangely enough, although Alexander was encouraging social reform and national feelings among his subject peoples, conditions in Russia proper remained much the same. Some of the upper class, who had absorbed the same ideas of enlightenment as their Czar, favored reform. The mass of the people, however, had been so completely subjected by their autocratic rulers that they were impervious to the liberal thought and activities of the age.

SCANDINAVIA

Northern Europe, too, was affected by the liberal and national movements. Finland, while it was a grand duchy under the enlightened Gustavus III of Sweden, had been granted a measure of autonomy. In 1809, it was conquered by Alexander of Russia and, like the Baltic provinces, benefited by his generosity to national groups. He united it with the Finnish territory that had belonged to Russia since the time of Peter the Great. Under the title of Grand Duke of the Finns, he ruled over this state as a unit distinct from Russia. He was assisted by a national legislature in which the nobles, clergy, middle class, and peasants were represented. As might be expected, this

Gustavus III, king of Sweden, 1771-92. (Swedish Traffic Assoc.)

support to Napoleon, Denmark was forced to cede Norway to Sweden, the Norwegians took advantage of the occasion to declare their independence, and set up a constitutional government under a Danish prince. However, General Bernadotte intervened and persuaded them to accept him as king, agreeing to rule in accordance with their new constitution. Thus Bernadotte ruled as king of both countries, and although Norwegian nationalism was unsatisfied, greater power had been granted to the people of both countries.

Thus did the influence of the French Revolution and of Napoleon extend throughout Europe in varying degrees. What the future would bring seemed largely in the hands of the Congress of Vienna, which had been summoned to meet in September, 1814, to arrange the formal peace terms.

THE CONGRESS OF VIENNA

The Congress of Vienna was one of the most brilliant assemblages in history. Its members included, first of all, six sovereigns: Czar Alexander I, whose liberal ideas have already been mentioned; Frederick William III, rather weak, but an admirer of the Czar; Francis I of Austria, and the Kings of Denmark, Bavaria, and Württemberg. There were also three of the outstanding nonroyal diplomats of the day: the shrewd representative of Great Britain, Lord Castlereagh; the wily and unprincipled Talleyrand, anxious to protect the interests of France; and above all, Count Metternich, the experienced, conserva-

greater freedom instead of satisfying the people only increased their national enthusiasm and promised future agitation for complete liberty.

In Sweden, the unfortunate war with Russia in 1808 discredited King Gustavus IV. The legislature assumed control, deposed the king, chose Charles XIII as his successor, and adopted a constitution. Later, they named General Bernadotte, of Napoleon's army, as successor to Charles, who had no children.

Norway, long under the sway of Denmark, also absorbed the French principles of liberty and nationalism. When as punishment for its

"The First Norwegian Constitutional Assembly, at Eidsvold," a painting by Oscar Wergeland of the group which drew up the Norwegian constitution in 1814. (Consulate General of Norway)

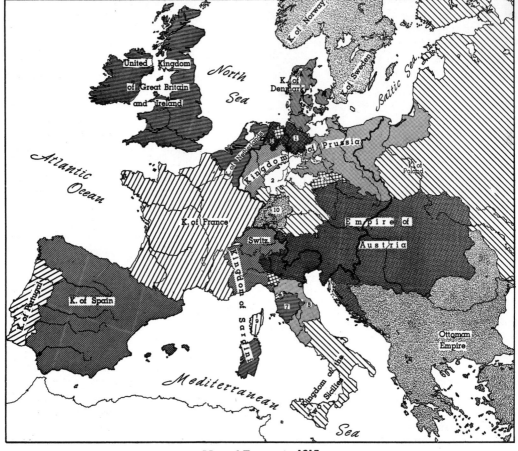

Map of Europe in 1815

SHEPHERDS & BREASTED

1. Hanover	4. Bavaria	8. Montenegro
2. Hesse	5. Papal States	9. Corsica (to France)
3. Saxony	6. Lucca	10. Baden and Wurttemberg
	7. Tuscany	

tive Austrian minister. In addition, all the minor states of Europe were represented.

Not only were the delegates outstanding, but the pomp and gaiety were memorable. The entertainments were in keeping with the wealth and rank of the guests. The assembly has often been called "The Dancing Congress," so numerous were the balls which were held. Here for one of the first times in high society, the waltz was danced, to the horror of some conservative people, who considered it ungraceful and indecent.

These festivities, however, served merely as a camouflage for the negotiations which were being quietly carried on. For instead of general sessions of all the delegates, which the name "congress" would suggest, most of the discussions were held secretly by small groups.

Metternich had hoped to confine the major decisions to the victorious countries—Austria, England, Russia, and Prussia. Talleyrand, however, was determined that France, although conquered in battle, should have some voice in the negotiations. It was not necessary for him openly to oppose them because before long, the "Big Four" were themselves divided on a major issue, and he was able to insinuate himself into their councils.

This issue was the fate of Poland. It will be remembered that Alexander had promised the Poles that he would reinstate them as a united nation under his sovereignty. Accordingly he made this request at the Congress, suggesting that in compensation for her Polish losses Prussia be given Saxony, whose king was to be punished for supporting Napoleon. Frederick William III favored this idea.

Metternich, however, feared that by these means Russia would become too powerful in Europe; and, supported by England, he refused to assent. Only by the skillful compromise of Castlereagh and Talleyrand was the problem solved. The Czar received most of Poland, which he promised to govern by a constitution; the rest remained under the control of Prussia and Austria. Prussia received only part of Saxony. In this way Poland was redivided and the king of Saxony was punished.

With various groups of countries thus conferring, the negotiations continued throughout the entire winter of 1814-15. The resulting provisions, together with some temporary agreements which had been made before the Congress assembled, were embodied in the peace settlement of June, 1815.

LEGITIMACY AND COMPENSATIONS

One of the ruling principles of the settlement was "legitimacy," that is the restoration of territory to the rightful monarchs who reigned before the war. By this principle, the Bourbons recovered the control of Spain and the Two Sicilies; the house of Savoy was reinstated in Sardinia and Piedmont; the Orange family in Holland; the pope in his temporal possessions; and the German princes in their states. The principle of legitimacy was also invoked to restore the Swiss confederation with its neutrality guaranteed, and to enable Austria to recover the Tyrol and the Illyrian provinces. This was also the reason for the repartition of Poland.

On the same principle of legitimacy, the French monarchy was restored and the boundaries of 1790 guaranteed. France was required, however, to return the art treasures which Napoleon had looted from other countries, and to pay an indemnity of seven hundred million francs. Furthermore, the principal French fortresses were to be occupied by foreign troops for five years.

Another principle, however, also determined the territorial distribution. "Compensations" were necessary as rewards to victors or in return for the cession of other lands. Thus Great Britain was allowed to retain the colonies which she had captured from Spain, Holland, and France. Then to compensate for its loss of colonies, Holland was given the Austrian Netherlands, despite their differences in religion and sympathy; and the Orange ruler of the two countries assumed the title of king. To offset this loss, Austria was given Venice and Milan, while members of the Hapsburg family ruled Tuscany, Modena, and Parma; thus Austria became an important force in Italy. The awards of Norway to Sweden and of part of Saxony to Prussia were also made upon this principle.

THE SUCCESSOR TO THE HOLY ROMAN EMPIRE

Another important work of the Congress was the formation of the North German Confederation. There had been some talk of establishing a single German state; but the weak King of Prussia, the logical person to rule such a state, was hardly suitable. Furthermore, the southern German states had been promised their freedom. So a federation of thirty-eight states was formed, with an assembly of princes presided over by Austria.

Thus the Congress of Vienna arranged the map of Europe. So far as possible, the conditions before the French Revolution had been restored. The provisions frequently disregarded nationalistic ambitions, and the entire arrangement ignored the liberal tendencies which had been developing in the preceding years.

Yet despite its reactionary aspects, the Congress of Vienna marked the end of an era. Weak though the republican spirit was in 1815, it had left its mark upon all countries. Europe would never return to the absolutism of the days before the French Revolution, and whatever events might follow, they would constitute a new phase in world history.

58. The Age of Metternich

EUROPE was weary of war in 1815. Napoleon's armies had crossed and recrossed the countryside making demands on peasants and bourgeoisie for men and food, for money and munitions. There were crippled and blind men in every town, for these wars had been fought by larger armies than any which had previously taken the field. Ruling classes knew that the people were aroused by revolutionary ideas which marching armies had carried with them. But Europe was on the verge of exhaustion, and peace was desired by all classes.

From all this confusion and unrest one man emerged as the central commanding figure—Count Metternich. Just as Napoleon dominated the European scene with his armies from 1795 to 1815, so Metternich with his diplomacy was the central figure from 1815 to 1829. He was attending the University of Strasbourg when rioting broke out among the populace in 1799 as a result of the revolutionary trend. We can imagine the feelings of this aristocratic youth upon seeing an undisciplined mob daring to question the right of his class to rule!

By reason of his pleasing appearance, his wit, his clever maneuvering, and his supremely keen mind, Metternich rose rapidly in the politics of the German states, and served as emissary to the great courts of Europe. He married into an important family and became chief adviser to Francis I in 1809. Finally, in 1814, partly in recognition of his political genius, Vienna was chosen as the city to which the nations would come to repair the damage caused by Napoleon and the new ideas.

"What the European peoples want is not liberty but peace," he said. He set up a system like Clemenceau's early plan for a league of nations to bind the victors together in order to hold in subjection the nation and the ideas over which their armies had just triumphed.

By the Treaty of Paris in 1815, Russia, Prussia, and Britain agreed to preserve the status quo in Europe, and to meet in the future in international congresses. France was soon admitted to the system.

THE "HOLY ALLIANCE"

To smooth over the rivalry and conflict of the various states, Metternich and the British minister, Castlereagh, worked to keep the powers acting in harmony—"the Concert of Europe." The famous but really unimportant Holy Alliance was sponsored by the visionary Czar Alexander I. The rulers of Russia, Prussia, and Austria pledged themselves to act in a true Christian manner, behaving as good fathers to their people. Like many other plans for peace, the Holy Alliance was ineffective. Only its sponsor ever intended to abide by it; in fact, he alone really knew its meaning, and he soon changed his mind.

METTERNICH'S POLICIES

Metternich and his fellow negotiators had to do more than merely draw up a peace treaty. Not only the boundaries of Europe had been upset, but the very fundamentals of society had been questioned. For centuries the ruling classes had been growing wealthier and farther removed from the peasantry.

Metternich saw that this upper class—the world he knew—depended for its very existence on the obedience of the lower classes. To question this order of affairs was revolutionary. Law and order, art and literature, work and production, peace and religion—all the things

Count Metternich (1773-1859). (Brown Bros.)

which made the life he knew worth while—would vanish if the people did not obey their rightful rulers. Metternich had seen the deluge follow the breakup of the Bourbon regime in France. Once liberal ideas were started, it would prove very difficult to stay the ultimate sinking of divine-right monarchs in a rushing flood of mob violence. Metternich was determined that such ideas should never again threaten Europe.

At home he showed the world how it was to be done. He imprisoned those leaders of the subject nationalities in the Hapsburg Empire, Czechs, Germans, Croats, Hungarians, and Italians, who questioned Austrian rule. He stationed imperial troops wherever there was discontent. He muzzled the press and strictly censored all printed matter from abroad. He discouraged all education not controlled by the conservative Roman Church, making "pietism a force for quietism." He strengthened the police, using them to spy on the actions of intellectuals.

EXTENT OF METTERNICH'S INFLUENCE

Metternich induced the German Confederation to pass the Carlsbad decrees. These provided for strict censorship and supervision of the press and universities, forbade any granting of constitutions contrary to the "monarchial principles," and created a permanent committee to investigate "the origin and ramifications of liberal ideas," which were fairly common among the university students.

Russia, too, experienced Metternich's reactionary policy. Alexander and his successor, Nicholas I, were perturbed by several flares of revolutionary spirit and were persuaded that there was no middle course between the overthrow of their rule by violence and the complete, ruthless suppression of the new ideas. Needless to say, these rulers chose suppression and Russia remained a chained and retarded country for another century.

In the Italian states, which had experienced a surge of nationalism, Metternich's influence was felt even where the Hapsburg emperor did not directly exercise authority. Even Victor Emmanuel I, king of Sardinia, followed the reactionary policy of Metternich, and in none of these states were nationalist or liberal reform policies adopted by the government.

Finally, if his Austrian example and the policy of the various states were not sufficient to maintain the old order, Metternich, by the protocol of Troppau, had the armies of Russia, Prussia and Austria pledged to march against the first popular uprising that should appear. This conservative success was more superficial than real, however. Metternich recognized liberalism as an enemy, but he did not realize how difficult it is to overcome the force of ideas. People seem unable to live without emotional dreams, a factor which Metternich failed to take into consideration.

ATTEMPT TO STIFLE NATIONALISM

More fatal than the suppression of liberalism, was Metternich's error in handling the second emotional dream of revolutionary Europe. Just as the French and American revolutions spread ideas of honest government, designed by the people and for the people's good—or at least by and for the middle, merchant class—so Napoleon's campaigns taught the lesson of nationalism to the subject states of Europe. By opposing the rule of the great dynasties over people who had no ties of race or language, by temporarily setting up peoples with their own national states, even by oppressing them, Napoleon aroused in all Europe patriot leaders burning to free themselves from foreign rule. Even his enemies, Britain and Prussia, were roused to nationalist fervor by their defeats and victories.

The Congress of Vienna, composed as it was of rulers, ignored this new force altogether. Most of Poland was given back to the czar, with parts of it going to Prussia and Austria. The Balkan states were dominated by the Turks with an altogether different religion and set of customs. Belgium was put under Dutch domination. Everywhere the new spirit of nationalism was sacrificed to legitimacy, the right of ruling families to hold their hereditary domains. Metternich's insistence upon this point was his greatest error.

President James Monroe. (The Metropolitan Museum of Art)

THE MONROE DOCTRINE

The most glaring violation of Metternich's system was in the Americas. During the Napoleonic wars and after, there was continued foreign meddling with the governments of Spain and Portugal. Colonial authorities in the New World received orders from several contenders for the thrones and assistance from none. One by one the colonies asserted their independence. The protocol of Troppau bound Austria, Prussia, and Russia to restore the Bourbon lands to the "legitimate rulers." But none of these powers had a navy strong enough to attack the rebellious colonies. Moreover,

England was hostile to any such intervention in South America. Although conservative in domestic politics, England had good reasons to pursue a different policy in foreign affairs. English trade with the Spanish colonies had increased rapidly during the period of revolution.

England had no desire to restore Spanish rule; rather, she asked French support in opposing Metternich's policy of intervention in rebellious countries. Failing to secure French cooperation, England sought support from the United States, a nation already suspicious of the Quadruple Alliance. Various negotiations were carried on between England and the

The Congress of Vienna, from an old engraving. The delegates began their work in September, 1814, and the Final Acts of the Congress were signed on June 9, 1815. (Bettmann Archive)

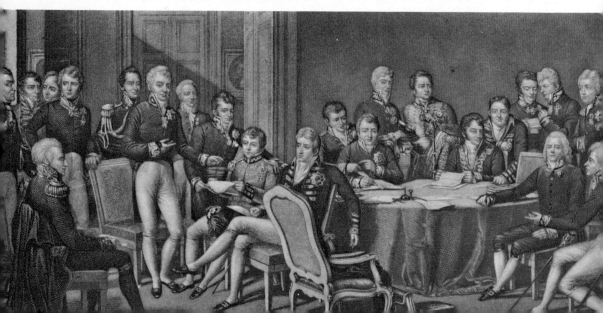

United States, but President Monroe finally decided to make a declaration of policy which was avowedly not dependent upon British support. A message to Congress in December, 1823, announced to the whole world that the United States would oppose any attempt to subjugate Spain's former colonies. Metternich did not become greatly alarmed at this declaration by such a weak power as the United States, but in the next year he renounced all hope of restoring the colonies to Spain.

INTERVENTION IN EUROPE

Even where Metternich intervened in Europe, national aspirations were merely driven underground and not eliminated. Secret societies spread the gospel of nationalism in Germany. The famous Carbonari spread revolutionary propaganda in Italy, where numerous rebellions called for the intervention of Austria to keep the legitimate sovereign on the throne. A notable outbreak against the hated Ferdinand I occurred in Naples. It was a year before the Austrian army obtained repeal of the constitution which the people had forced Ferdinand to grant them.

Victor Emmanuel was forced to abdicate his throne in Piedmont soon after. His successor, Charles Albert, granted a constitution, but Metternich sent in troops and threatened to punish him. Only by complete submission to the conservative philosophy was he saved.

Metternich's policy found difficulties in political-minded France. The liberals and the bourgeoisie wanted more democracy while the ultra-royalists—the returned émigrés and the clergy—wanted less. Louis XVIII was in a quandary. Maintaining the appearance of a divine-right monarch, he did not destroy Napoleon's national bank and educational system, religious freedom, equality before the law, or representative government. Nor did he attempt to restore serfdom and feudalism or punish sternly Napoleonic sympathizers.

Following a reactionary reign of terror, which made the liberals afraid to vote, the royalists got control of the government. When Louis saw the impossible nature of their demands and called a new election, the moderates won. Thus, as early as 1816 it was clear that

France, like England, would not cooperate with Metternich's reactionary policies. France, however, did cooperate in regard to peace, and the Quadruple Alliance was enlarged to a Quintuple Alliance to admit her.

In 1820 the reactionaries again came into power. They followed repressive policies both at home and abroad, sending armies to crush liberalism in Spain. Louis's successor, Charles X, was himself reactionary. Metternich was reasonably certain of French support for his system until 1827. In that year a new election showed that the French people would no longer stand for reaction.

NATIONALISM IN THE BALKANS

It was to be expected, perhaps, that the French and British governments would not follow Metternich's lead altogether. But the rising nationalism in the Balkan states, directed against the Turkish rule, was used by the ultra-conservative new czar of Russia, Nicholas I, for the profit of his country even though he disobeyed the Austrian's "legitimist" wish.

Following the failure of the earlier Serbian leader, Karageorge, Milosh Obrenovich led a successful revolt in 1815. Greece, too, was in revolt for some time. The ferocity of the Turkish suppression aroused the sympathy of all the world save Metternich. At London, in 1827, France, Britain, and Russia agreed to intervene if necessary in behalf of Greece. They finally went to war and defeated Turkey decisively. The Treaty of Adrianople, besides giving Russia concessions, recognized Serbia, Greece, and the two Rumanian provinces, Moldavia and Wallachia, as practically independent. Thus three great powers openly went to war to defeat the principles of legitimacy.

The forces of nationalism began to weaken Metternich's control over Europe several years before the revolutionary outbreaks of 1830. The spirit of liberalism, so odious to the reactionaries, could not be suppressed in a Europe which had thrilled to the ideas of liberty, equality, and fraternity. The Congress of Vienna made a valiant effort to organize central and eastern Europe on a permanent basis; but nationalism and liberalism rendered its effort futile.

59. Liberalism—The Creed of the Middle Class

LIBERALISM

THE SPECTER FROM WHICH Metternich was attempting to protect Europe was liberalism. Though its growth was impeded, he was unable to stifle this expanding, progressive movement, the roots of which are to be found in the various cultural, political, and economic changes of the previous centuries.

Liberalism had several foundations. In part, it was a child of the intellectual transformation which Europe had experienced in the eighteenth century. Colored by the skepticism of Voltaire and Gibbon, it inherited the scientific approach which that century had been seeking. "Natural rights" had been one of the slogans of the age. Liberalism took up this slogan, changing it but slightly.

The French Revolution, nourished in part by the Intellectual Revolution, proved a source of inspiration for liberalism. Although the rising of the French people had brought dismay to many, it remained a shining example to succeeding generations. It had left an indelible impression on Europe. Some viewed the possibility of the recurrence of 1789 with horror; the liberals wanted the principles of '89 without its excesses.

The Industrial Revolution provided another stone in the edifice of liberalism and a very important one. Many of the theories of liberalism and much of the support won by that movement were the results of the Industrial Revolution. New conditions and new classes were created, and there were new desires to be satisfied.

Liberalism changed its features often in the course of its history, but running through it constantly have been the main threads of social progress and rationalism. Faith in social progress is only a comparatively recent idea. Its basis was a belief that man could change his environment for the better and achieve the "good life" through his own efforts. One of the means of achieving social progress was, in the minds of the liberals, the use of reason.

ECONOMIC PHILOSOPHY

The economic philosophy of liberalism was born, appropriately enough, in England. In some measure it owes a debt to the physiocrats of France, who so vigorously attacked mercantilism. This new philosophy was to prove a boon to developing industrialism.

The economists who championed these new doctrines have been called the Classical school. Adam Smith's *The Wealth of Nations*, with its doctrine of economic liberty, has been the Bible of this movement. Jeremy Bentham, David Ricardo, James Mill, and others took up the new doctrines, developing them and giving them life. Nassau Senior, an Oxford professor, summarized and co-ordinated the work of his predecessors of the Classical school.

The basic tenet of the economic liberalists was laissez faire, essentially economic liberty. It was felt that if each individual were to pursue his own interests intelligently, prosperity for all would result. The natural wealth and possibilities of a country could be best exploited by individuals acting without restraint.

The Classical school believed that men would prosper if only the economic laws of nature were not violated. Nature, they maintained, provided the law of supply and demand for the perfect regulation of economic life. The function of government was to allow the free operation of natural laws and to prevent any hindrance of free competition. In practice, the capitalistic class was aided by this aspect of laissez faire. Labor was not allowed to combine within labor unions, in order to maintain the free operation of economic laws. Monopolies were likewise outlawed. Government was not to interfere in business again, so the economic laws would function freely. The industrialists were not to be subject to regulation. They could save on wages, buy cheaply, and sell dearly.

On a larger scale, laissez faire meant free trade. In theory, the removal of bars to international trade would further both prosperity and peace. By creating free competition on an international basis, each nation would be forced to produce only those commodities which it could turn out most efficiently. Thus, both wasteful production and one of the causes of war would be eliminated.

Free trade was favored by England, the most industrialized country in the world, because it desired free markets for its goods. Also, lack of English tariffs would enable foreign nations to sell raw products and foods to her and thus be able to buy manufactured products. By 1849, with the repeal of the navigation acts and the corn laws, England had achieved free trade. Continental Europe did not seize the idea so avidly. Even here, however, free trade made a few advances in Germany and France.

In France, J. B. Say began to import the new beliefs in the 1820's. Frédéric Bastiat was another crusader for the new cause. John Prince-Smith spread the gospel through Germany. As the industrial classes grew on the continent, economic liberalism likewise grew.

POLITICAL PHILOSOPHY

The political theories of liberalism were, in large part, shaped by the stirring examples of the French and American Revolutions. The eloquent words of the Declaration of Independence and the Declaration of the Rights of Man echoed throughout Europe and provided a battle cry and a creed for the liberals.

Government was to be bound by laws and to be responsible to the representatives of the people. To guarantee a government of laws, a constitution was necessary. The United States had been the first to draw up and abide by a written constitution, which was regarded by the liberals of the early nineteenth century as a magical guaranty of liberty and progress. They believed that the mere embodiment of rights in a written document would safeguard those rights from impairment. By expressly allowing opposition, the constitution would provide for peaceful change. The liberal emphasized the doctrine of liberty. He would allow any citizen to do whatever he pleased so long as his actions did not harm other citizens.

Under the old political regime, the unit of society was the caste. Laws were made in terms of class. Liberalism thought in terms of individuals. All individuals were equal in the eyes of the law, and government was based on the idea of individuals, banded together for a common purpose.

The crowning feature of political liberalism was its championship of civil rights—natural rights in new dress. The liberal asserted that each individual had certain *inalienable* rights which society could not abrogate. These were life, liberty, property, and resistance to oppression. No life could be taken without fair trial. No man was to be imprisoned without a warrant and a trial. In addition, liberty implied religious tolerance, freedom of speech and assembly, and the freedom of the press. Liberalism also recognized the right to revolt when government ceased to guarantee natural rights.

Civil rights, as applied in the sphere of peoples, were the basis of nationalism. Every people, said the liberal, must be given the right to achieve statehood and independence. In this way liberalism was linked to nationalism.

SUPPORTERS AND OPPONENTS OF LIBERALISM

Liberalism was a middle-class philosophy and as such found its support among that class. As citizens they would gain a greater voice in government and political liberties; a participation which had previously been denied them. As business men they saw in liberalism freedom from governmental interference and protection of property. Hence in the ranks of the liberals there were found industrialists, capitalists, merchants, members of the professions, shopkeepers—in short, the middle class.

Liberalism had more than an economic and political appeal. Its gospel of liberty exercised a somewhat romantic appeal. Students, professors, an occasional army officer, a few government officials, and intellectuals were attracted by the new philosophy. Liberalism exercised a profound influence on the European mind from 1830 to 1871.

Of the opponents of liberalism little need be said. Their number was legion. Those who stood to lose—nobles, kings, officials, generals—united in energetic opposition against those who threatened their dominance and the perpetuation of the traditions they considered essential to the fabric of European civilization.

THE LIBERAL REVOLTS OF 1830

The rising spirit of liberalism found expression in a series of revolts in 1830. In France, the rule of the Bourbon Charles X had elicited almost universal disapproval among the middle class. In an attempt to silence the criticisms which were growing in volume, Charles issued a series of reactionary ordinances which were answered by a revolution in July, 1830. In the place of the deposed Charles X, the liberal Louis Philippe, duke of Orleans, was seated. The bourgeoisie was now in control with a pliant noble as king.

The July Revolution seemed to be a call to arms to the liberals of all Europe. Southern (Belgian) Netherlands, which had chafed at domination by the Dutch, expelled the masters and set up an independent liberal kingdom in October, 1830. There were reverberations in central and southern Europe, but Metternich was still firmly entrenched. The faint rumblings in Italy and Germany soon died down. The Polish revolt of 1831 was drowned in blood by the ruthless Czar Nicholas I, while Metternich looked on with approval. The liberal movements throughout southern

Nicholas I, Czar of Russia 1825-55. (Chicago Historical Society)

and central Europe had not amassed sufficient strength to achieve success.

England was not unaffected by the events on the Continent, but the changes that occurred in the 1830's were peaceful. The factory owners and tradesmen were practically unrepresented in Parliament. Their desire for parliamentary reform was seconded by minorities, such as the Catholics, who resented the restrictions imposed on them.

The July events in Paris stimulated the demands for reform. The political leaders began to respond to this ever increasing pressure, and finally capitulated, passing the Reform Act of 1832. The number who thereby held the franchise was but a small part of the population, but by the reapportionment of seats in the House of Commons, the bourgeoisie gained a voice in the government of the country.

The masses had been disregarded. The working men found that the Reform Act had ignored them. The demand arose among them for a "People's Charter," to assure every man a vote. The resulting Chartist movement spread rapidly, so that by 1842 alarm was felt by government circles lest a revolt break out. Although the movement died down soon afterward, eventually many of the demands of the Chartists became law.

REVOLTS OF 1848—THE END OF METTERNICH

The bourgeois monarchy of Louis Philippe had left much undone. Democrats, republicans, and socialists were dissatisfied with the complexion of the new regime. They found its liberalism was not satisfactory, and its democracy was nonexistent. On the other hand, supporters of the Bourbons and Catholics found the rule of Louis Philippe equally unsatisfactory, for opposite reasons.

In the years 1847-1848, the opposition gathered momentum. As a means of propagandizing the reform doctrines, banquets of a disquietingly radical character were held. One planned for February 22, 1848, was forbidden by the frightened government.

The Parisian populace was aroused. Rioters filled the streets. In two days Louis Philippe prudently quit the country. A republic was set up. After the suppression of an abortive revolt of workers, the foundations of the republic were laid. It was to be a democratic one, but its complexion was moderate, not radical.

Southern and central Europe had failed to respond to the liberal revolutionary movement of 1830 and had remained under the sway of conservatism. But a new factor, industrialization, was changing the social makeup of large sections of Austria, Bohemia, Galicia, Italy, and Germany. Simultaneously, the liberal movements assumed larger proportions. Here, as well as in other parts of the Austrian domains, symptoms of a coming eruption were evident. Local revolts, growing revolutionary movements, and petitions showed that all was not well. At last, revolts broke out in Vienna which sent the arch-enemy of liberalism, Metternich, into exile.

REACTION AGAINST LIBERALISM

Central Europe was rocked to its foundations. Every capital and city was the scene of riot and bloodshed. The granting of a liberal constitution to Austria prompted uprisings in other parts of the Austrian Empire. Under the leadership of Louis Kossuth, Hungary demanded and received a liberal constitution which provided that Hungary should be ruled separately from Austria. Bohemia likewise obtained a relatively liberal constitution.

Many Italian cities soon were in rebellion. Austrian troops were expelled from most of northern Italy. Charles Albert dispatched his troops to help in the war for independence. Even autocratic Prussia experienced a revolution which was successful for a time. Frederick William IV promised reforms, and the smaller German states followed suit.

With revolution throughout the lands of the German Confederation, it was natural that reform of that body should be desired. An assembly was called at Frankfurt during May, 1848, to consider the revision of its constitution. The assembly, liberal in composition, passed innumerable liberal resolutions but liberalism had almost run its course. The monarchs of the Germanies were regaining their courage; they resisted the demands of the Frankfurt Assembly, and it ended in futility.

For a time constitutions, parliaments, and liberal guaranties were the order of the day but, as we have intimated, the tide was turning. Austrian troops succeeded in subduing the Bohemians and reinstating autocracy. The "War of Liberation" of Charles Albert likewise ended in failure. The rest of Italy witnessed the triumph of counter-revolution in 1849. Austrian generals converged on Vienna and soon brought it under control. Austrian and Russian armies restored the power of the emperor in Hungary. The liberal Prussian constitution of 1848 was abolished by the king in 1850.

Although the revolutions had been crushed in central Europe, they left more than one trace. A few liberal reforms were retained in Austria. Scandinavian states and Switzerland kept their highly liberal constitutions. Prussia, Denmark, and Holland made concessions to liberalism in their constitutions. It was in England and France, however, that liberalism achieved its greatest triumphs.

The expectations and hopes of the liberals in 1848 were not fully realized. Conservatism, it appeared, had again triumphed over the new forces. But liberalism was not dead. It was to raise its head again and flourish.

60. Romanticism and Realism

THE ROMANTIC MOVEMENT, which began late in the eighteenth century, became the dominant cultural development in the first half of the following century. It gained considerable force from current political and military events which could not fail to exercise a profound influence upon intellectual movements.

The eighteenth-century thinkers had exalted man as a rational being within whom lay the power of ruling his destiny; but the irrational occurrences of the revolutionary period and the Napoleonic episode convinced many people that man's reason was far from reliable. As a result they placed an increasing emphasis upon man's feelings and his relations and responsibilities within society. This romantic tendency is clear in the idealistic German philosophy which was begun by Kant who had emphasized man's spirit and duties. Fichte and Hegel continued this trend in the nineteenth century.

In religion the Christian revival of the preceding period was fervently and emotionally continued. The Catholic Church was conspicuous in this movement, and Pope Pius VII was a notable world figure. His dignified conduct during mistreatment at the hands of Napoleon excited admiration. Under his guidance Catholicism recovered much of the ground it had lost during the French Revolution.

Nationalism of the Napoleonic era was another element contributed by the political background. The deeds of patriotic leaders inspired Romanticists and permanently influenced the arts. This emotionalism and nationalism became increasingly important when combined with the interests of Romanticism which appeared in the eighteenth century. Those interests were rejection of classical restrictions, description of natural scenes, interest in man's daily life, portrayal of the past, and study of man's thoughts and aspirations.

All these elements are perhaps best seen in literature, in which two general trends can be found in all nations. An earlier phase of Romanticism, from approximately 1800 to 1830, was dominated by one group of writers, while a new group appeared from about 1830 to 1880, in the period which has become known as the Victorian Age.

VARIETIES OF EUROPEAN ROMANTICISM

In England, beautiful poetry was written by five great authors on a vast number of subjects. Wordsworth glorified nature and the simple man, while Coleridge told of mysterious, supernatural happenings. Byron narrated exciting adventures of sinister, romantic young men who defied social conventions, while Shelley's passionate cry for freedom verged on hysteria. Keats reveled in beautiful sights and sounds and romantic love.

Immanuel Kant   **William Wordsworth**

In prose, Scott's novels told stirring tales of history and Scottish life. The essayists of the day described everything from roast pig and prize fights to the pleasures of opium.

In the Victorian period, Tennyson wrote poems of past chivalry and modern

Samuel Coleridge

Lord Byron

Percy Bysshe Shelley

achievements, and Browning in his highly complicated and obscure style portrayed nobles, artists, musicians, and lovers, respectable and otherwise, in all periods of history. Later, the so-called pre-Raphaelite writers sought to paint portraits in their poems; and in his rebellion against the restrictions of society, Swinburne used such free language that he scandalized his generation.

The innumerable novelists treated various realistic subjects: the struggles and misfortunes of lower middle-class people, the follies of the day, and incidents of the past; but a romantic glow was clearly apparent. In more serious prose, Carlyle, Newman, and Ruskin were romantic in their stress upon man's spiritual uplift as well as his material welfare, while Macaulay glorified his country in a nationalistic interpretation of history.

The earlier German romantic movement was enthusiastically continued by Schlegel, while Goethe and Schiller gained greater fame by their romantic dramas. Romantic

poetry was made memorable by the great Heine's exquisite songs. The later period, however, produced no outstanding writers.

In France, Italy, and Spain literature was so traditionally bound to Classicism that few notable romantic contributions appeared in the earlier phase. In the later period, however, France assumed a leading position with poets such as De Musset, but even more through the writings of its novelists. Victor Hugo gained fame by his great novels of the French people of the Middle Ages, the Revolution, and his own day, while Dumas wrote exciting novels of adventure and George Sand produced many highly romantic stories. Balzac memorably portrayed the characters and lives of all sorts of middle-class persons. In Italy, the romantic and nationalistic movement produced many notable writers, among whom perhaps the greatest was the poet and novelist, Manzoni. The romantic drama flourished especially in France, where its brief but brilliant course began with Hugo's flamboyant *Hernani* (1830) and ended with his play, *Les Burgraves*.

John Keats

Sir Walter Scott

Goethe

Victor Hugo

The Romantic Era in Painting. English landscape painting in the early 19th century reached its culmination in the work of Constable and Turner. Constable's "Hay Wain," above left, shows the artist's chief inspiration, his native countryside. (National Gallery, London). Turner's scenes, such as "Dutch Fishing Boats," above, were full of his preoccupation with subjective light, air, and water. (Art Institute of Chicago). Left, Corot's "Gypsy Girl." (Philadelphia Museum of Art)

ROMANTIC APPROACH IN PAINTING

In painting, the transition to Romanticism is suggested by Goya, whose later paintings of the cruelties of the French war, if not romantic in themselves, aroused romantic indignation in the beholders. In France, however, Classicism long persisted. It characterized revolutionary painting and architecture because the revolutionists believed the simplicity of pure Classicism most suitable to their virile republic, in contrast to the luxurious baroque of the preceding monarchy.

The trend continued under Napoleon, since he fancied himself a successor to the ancient emperors. Besides encouraging Classicism, he introduced an Egyptian strain into the arts, and in furniture the resulting combination of the two is known as "Empire style." Classicism in portrait painting and architecture likewise continued in Italy and England, while in America its influence was evident in the new capital city of Washington, particularly in the Capitol and the White House.

True Romanticism, however, is illustrated by Delacroix, whose strong brilliantly colored paintings of military scenes revealed the pain of battle; by the more serene landscapes of the English painter, Constable; and the vivid water scenes of Turner.

THE SPREAD OF ROMANTICISM IN LITERATURE

Even in Russia Romanticism became prominent, with Pushkin glorifying Russian heroes and history in a romantic manner in the earlier period. He was succeeded in the next generations by Turgenev and Dostoyevsky, who vividly and impressively depicted the miserable lot of the mass of the Russian people. At the same time, Polish national glory was recalled by the patriotic Mickiewicz.

The later period was marked by the leadership of France. The charming landscapes of Corot were widely influential, and in France their effect is seen in the work of Millet, famous for his depiction of poor but inspiring peasants. In England the only painting of any significance was done by the pre-Raphaelites, so called because they went back to the Middle Ages for their inspiration in chivalric and religious subjects. At the same time, there was also a more realistic trend, exemplified by the brilliant caricatures of the English Cruikshank and the French Daumier, who also painted religious themes.

STYLES IN ARCHITECTURE

In architecture the particular manifestation of Romanticism was the revival of Gothic, or medieval style, which during the classical period had been banned as barbaric. An important force in this movement was the writing of John Ruskin, who pointed out the beauties and advocated the use of medieval forms. The movement, which spread throughout Europe, is illustrated by the restoration of Notre Dame Cathedral in Paris and by other religious and business structures in this mode.

This movement, however, could not supersede the classic style which had dominated architecture for so long. Classicism in public buildings continued in all countries, with modifications to suit each nationality, as in the Palace of Justice in Belgium.

ROMANTICISM IN MUSIC

The great early exponent of Romanticism in music was Beethoven, whose symphonies and other instrumental and choral works are outstanding for their depth of feeling. At the same time, in obscurity, Schubert was writing his beautiful melodies, while Mendelssohn was popular because of such romantic works as incidental music for *Midsummer Night's Dream*. The later period was distinguished by the exquisitely delicate piano music of Chopin and the brilliant piano and orchestral music of Liszt.

In opera, during the early years, Weber introduced fairy lore and other romantic subjects. Italian operas also replaced ponderous classical subjects with the charming gaiety of Rossini's *Barber of Seville* and similar treatments of romantic subjects with warm melody. A particularly romantic aspect appears in the beginnings of light opera, exemplified by *Fra Diavolo*.

The later period was marked by a succession of notable composers, who because of their national characteristics are thought of in connection with their native countries. In France the leaders were Gounod, best remembered for his adaptation of Goethe's *Faust*, and Bizet, whose *Carmen* has become immensely popular. Verdi was the outstanding Italian composer, remembered for the florid Romanticism of *Aida*, *Rigoletto*, and others. In the union of music and drama perhaps the height was reached by Wagner. His operas, dealing with German mythology, chivalry, romance, and mysticism mark a high point in genius, technical skill, and embodiment of a national culture.

Richard Wagner (1813-83), German operatic composer. (Paul's Photos)

Thus Romanticism influenced all of the arts. The nationalistic aspects of the Romantic movement were reflected in economics, history, and political science, all of which stressed the importance of adapting theories to individual countries. The nationalistic spirit was reflected in the interest in folk cultures, and above all in the emphasis given to political incidents. In fact, all life of the period had its romantic aspects. Such a tendency may seem surprising at a time when business, science, and practical affairs were in the ascendant, but things romantic served as an outlet and escape from the humdrum of daily affairs.

THE RISE OF REALISM

Near the end of the century, however, the influence of science and practical business was so great that the insistence upon gathering and interpreting facts permeated all phases of culture. The practitioners of the arts sought realism, and in so doing tended to go to the extreme and see only the unpleasant side of things.

Romanticism did not disappear at once, of course. In English literature sentiment was represented by Sir James Barrie, while the nationalistic and imperialistic feeling was enthusiastically expressed by Rudyard Kipling. The realistic approach, however, was made in Meredith's psychological studies of characters, Hardy's portrayal of the hard-

Anatole France

ships of peasant life, and James's complicated representation of upper class society. Particularly outspoken novelists were Samuel Butler, whose denunciations spared neither heaven nor earth, and George Moore, who expounded pagan ideas. In the drama, Shaw presented the problems and ridiculed the foibles of the day. Wells began by writing novels of daily life, but soon was picturing imaginary worlds.

These English writers clearly owed some of their inspiration to the French writers who were among the earliest Realists. Flaubert, who had pioneered in portrayal of the seamy side of life while most writers were still writing romantically, had been condemned as immoral. With the growing popularity of Realism after his death, however, his work was

Henrik Ibsen

highly praised. In the short story, realism was skillfully handled by Maupassant, while in his novels Zola turned his searching eye upon contemporary problems. Most notable of this group of writers was Anatole France, who produced numerous brilliant and ironical novels, short stories, and critical works.

A similar examination of man and society was occurring throughout all Europe, especially in drama and fiction, by such writers as Ibsen in Norway, Hauptmann in Germany, Pirandello in Italy, and Chekhov in Russia. The novelist and dramatist Gorky, in his protests against Russian conditions, became increasingly revolutionary and eventually found himself a hero of the Soviet republics.

Sometimes writers combined realistic material with nonrealistic qualities. Thus Daudet, the Frenchman, used a romantic approach at times. Tolstoi infused spiritual and mystic qualities into his work, and the colorful D'Annunzio was distinguished by his intense national enthusiasm.

A somewhat different offshoot of Realism was Impressionism, which advocated the mere suggestion of an idea or emotion, which the senses can then interpret and appreciate. This method, putting the maximum value upon words themselves and the resulting sensations, is seen in the work of such individuals as Pater and, more particularly, Oscar Wilde in England. It was condemned by many who saw in it only decadence. With less sensuousness and more mystical quality, the movement was taken up by the Irish poets and playwrights and the Belgian Maeterlinck.

PAINTING IN MANY STYLES

Similarly in painting, both classical and romantic creations continued. But here also were new developments wherein France clearly took the lead. As in literature, Impressionism became important. Its treatment ranged through the Spanish subjects of Manet, the ballet girls and other characters of Degas, the landscapes and nudes of Renoir, and the ocean and city scenes of Monet. Its influence spread even to America in the paintings of Whistler and the more distinguished portraits of Sargent.

"Man in a Blue Cap," by Paul Cezanne.
(The Museum of Modern Art)

"The Old Musician," by Edouard Manet.
(National Gallery of Art)

"Argenteuil (on the Seine)" by Claude Monet.
(Art Institute of Chicago)

"Starry Night," by Vincent van Gogh.
(The Museum of Modern Art)

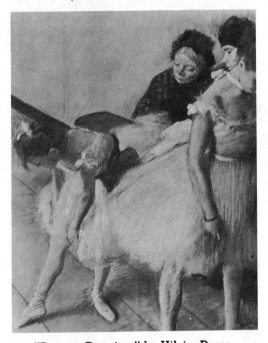

"Dancers Dressing," by Hilaire Degas.
(The Denver Art Museum)

"Oyster Gatherers," by John Singer Sargent.
(Corcoran Gallery of Art)

Johannes Brahms (1833-97). (Paul's Photos)

Cézanne's rejection of impressionistic vagueness in favor of simpler, more vivid painting, places him as a forerunner of Post-Impressionism. Also notable were the crudely vigorous and intensely colorful primitive works of Gaugin and the sunlit landscapes and bright flowers of Van Gogh.

Cartoon and caricature art was extremely popular in the new age of realism. The French artist, Daumier, an American, Thomas Nast, and Tenniel, the English illustrator, were among the leaders in the field of humorous and satirical art.

Edvard Grieg

In sculpture, the same tendencies were present. Among the more famous sculptors of the time is the American Saint-Gaudens, while in France the genius of Rodin expressed itself in startlingly forceful creations.

CONFLICTING TRENDS IN OTHER ARTS

Classicism remained dominant in architecture, with the majority of public buildings designed in this manner. A new trend, however, was also present, for Byzantine architecture was occasionally used in Catholic church construction. Of even greater significance was a more modern tendency. As steel increased in industrial importance, it became a building material. The resulting structures were in their utilitarian simplicity unlike anything in earlier periods.

In this age of realism, however, music remained romantic. In instrumental music, the genius of Brahms was conspicuous, both for his lofty symphonies and his dance forms which drew upon Hungarian folk tunes for themes. Particularly nationalistic were the composers of some of the smaller nations, such as Dvorák who glorified Bohemian music and Grieg who conveyed the scene and traditions of Norway. The operas of Puccini, Massenet, and Strauss continued the trends of their respective nationalities. In Russia, old history and legends were embodied in opera by Moussorgsky, Tschaikowsky, and Rimsky-Korsakov. The vogue for light operas increased, with Gilbert and Sullivan humorously satirizing their times in popular melody.

Peter Tschaikowsky

REALISM IN PHILOSOPHY AND RELIGION

A schism between science and religion had been developing steadily since the seventeenth century, when such revolutionary thinkers as Galileo and Newton rejected the idea of "final causes" as useless for the purposes of science. In the nineteenth century this schism reached a critical climax with a series of epochal scientific discoveries—all of which seemed to controvert traditional ideas on philosophy and religion. The geology studies of Charles Lyell (1830-33) and the discovery of primitive man by Boucher de Perthes (1846) called for a new interpretation of Biblical chronology; Charles Darwin's theory of evolution (1859), at least implicitly, challenged general belief in a "special creation";

Charles Darwin

Wilhelm Wundt

works on anthropology by James Prichard (1843), Theodor Waitz (1859-64), Edward Tylor (1871), and James Frazer (1890) questioned the supernatural origin of religion; and Wilhelm Wundt's *Foundations of Physiological Psychology* (1872) introduced the study of thought and behavior on a physical basis.

The skepticism generated by these discoveries was strongly implemented by the prevailing materialism in philosophy, politics, and economics. Ruthless practicality had become a commonplace in politics, a pre-eminent virtue in business. Writers and intellectuals propounded many varieties of agnosticism: either Haeckel's atheistic optimism, the optimistic positivism of Auguste Comte, Schopenhauer's pessimistic idealism, or Herbert Spencer's philosophy of "struggle."

Herbert Spencer

In the face of all this, believers were set busy reversing and testing their attitudes. In trying to reconcile science and theology, they obtained varying results; some had their faith strengthened, others, such as the theologian Friedrich Strauss and his "school of Tübingen," retained a belief in God but rejected the details of Biblical theology, while still others became atheists. The reaction to materialistic doctrines was strongest among the various Protestant sects, but Catholicism, too, in spite of its unity and discipline, was suffering from the inroads of the new agnosticism. Pius IX in the *Syllabus of Errors* accompanying his encyclical *Quanta Cura* (1864) specifically condemned various materialistic philosophies, and Pius X published a

Pius IX

syllabus of the errors of "Modernism" (1907). The "Modernist" movement, making considerable headway in Protestantism, brought about a leveling of belief among the various sects, and induced a strong spirit of cooperation. Among the Jews, the liberal trend in religion manifested itself in the development of Reformed sects, which retained most of the doctrines of Judaism while rejecting traditional beliefs and customs which were considered incompatible with modern life and thinking.

The skeptical attitude in science, philosophy, and religion became even stronger during the first decades of the twentieth century. The aftermath of World War I brought disillusionment not only in politics, but also in other aspects of life. Schisms in political and religious thought were reflected in the art and literature of the period, which were characterized by violent distortion of form and a purposeful neglect of meaning. Modern composers, in an attempt to convey more accurately the ideas and emotions of the modern tempo, employed eccentric rhythms and strident tonalities. New "isms" were invented to solve new social problems. Furniture and architecture became increasingly functional and severe.

In the nineteenth century and throughout the first half of the twentieth, art and philosophy, closely connected with other movements in history, became increasingly practical and realistic. Following World War II a revival of religious activity in various European countries, coupled with a mystical trend in literature and art and an increasing interest in indeterminism in science, were interpreted by some as a significant reaction against the predominant materialism. Only time could reveal whether these phenomena were tokens of a renewal of spirituality or the last gasp of the age of idealism.

61. A Century of Latin-American Development

SECOND PHASE OF REVOLUTION IN THE SPANISH COLONIES

WHILE THE UNITED STATES was passing through eras of nationalism, civil conflict and industrialization, the younger nations of the Americas made little progress toward national stability. Even the appearance of nations among the Spanish colonies had to wait for the completion of the wars of independence against Spain. Although the first phase of these wars ended in 1815 when Spanish armies restored royal control in the colonies, the desire for independence was by no means overcome.

The military aspects of the revolt consisted of two movements, one beginning in the north and the other in the south, both converging in Peru. Miranda gave over his active leadership in the north to Bolívar, who before 1815 attempted to set up a republic in Venezuela. With the help of British volunteers, he proceeded in the next few years to incorporate Ecuador and New Granada with Venezuela under the name of the Republic of Colombia.

REVOLT IN SOUTH

In the south, the struggle was handicapped by factional strife. By 1816, however, Argentina had established a republic and proceeded to direct revolutionary efforts in the La Plata Valley. The Argentinian, Belgrano, marched northward, but was defeated by royal forces in Bolivia. In Paraguay, however, Dr. Francia crushed the royalists and became dictator. Artigas, the picturesque cowboy of the South American plains, expelled the Argentinians and royalists from his native Banda Oriental. Brazil took advantage of the situation and recovered the region, but finally relinquished it in 1828 and it became the Republic of Uruguay.

Early revolts in Chile were crushed, but with the rise of San Martín to leadership a new era was at hand. He gathered an army at Mendoza, and, after a courageous march to the west coast, won command of the Chilean government. He then turned his attention northward. With more troops and aid from the British Admiral Cochrane's fleet, San Martín defeated the royalist forces at Lima and prepared to establish the Republic of Peru. In the meantime, Bolívar's army had arrived. San Martín, after meeting temporary reverses, gave over the leadership to the northern revolutionist, Bolívar.

In the meantime, Sucre led his troops over the Andes. At Ayacucho he crushed his foes. The royalists were soon defeated at Charcas and the Republic of Bolivia was a fact. The wars for independence in South America were over.

BRAZIL'S REVOLT AGAINST PORTUGAL

Brazil, alone, achieved her independence by peaceful means. The impulse was provided by Napoleon. The prince regent of Portugal, John, fled to Brazil when the French emperor threatened the ruling house of his country. John infused new life into the country by his liberal rule. Brazil was soon elevated to the

José Artigas

516

status of a kingdom. When John returned to Portugal in 1821, he named his son, Pedro, regent. In the following year, Pedro declared Brazil independent with himself as emperor. Despite an auspicious beginning and the granting of a liberal constitution in 1824, Pedro antagonized the country. He abdicated in 1831, placing his five-year-old son on the throne. The minority of Dom Pedro II was a period of internal dissension and division. By 1840 wiser counsels prevailed and the country united around the king, who had been declared of age.

The long reign of Pedro over a period of fifty years was one of wise and democratic rule. The civil rights of the people were maintained. Free political discussion was encouraged, and a spirit of moderation prevailed. Dom Pedro visited the United States and Europe in order to broaden his outlook. He encouraged the building of railroads and industries. Surprisingly, slavery was still strong in this "enlightened" country. With some urging from England, Pedro came out for the abolition of slavery. Finally in 1871, a law for the gradual abolition of the institution was passed and by 1888 emancipation was a fact. In 1889, the monarchy was overthrown and a republic proclaimed.

Latin America after the Revolutions

MEXICAN INDEPENDENCE

The death of Morelos in 1815 gave the insurgent movement in Mexico a temporary setback. Guerrilla warfare, however, continued in the south. Meanwhile the revolt had spread to the north of the country, where Mina, with a small force largely recruited in the United States, met defeat and execution. The revolutionary movement was now nearly extinct except on the fringes of Mexico, although Guerrero was still carrying on active guerrilla warfare in the south. General Iturbide, a royalist officer, was sent in 1820 to check the activities of Guerrero. Instead, Iturbide joined forces in that year with the guerrilla chief and, by the Plan of Iguala, united the contending factions. Iturbide assumed the title of emperor, but a revolt in 1823 resulted in his overthrow. In the same year, a republic was established and Central America, which had been annexed by Iturbide, declared itself independent.

SOUTH AMERICAN REACTION TO THE MONROE DOCTRINE

Although sympathetic toward the efforts of Latin-American revolutionaries, the United States felt obliged to maintain a pretense of official neutrality. In fact, the efforts of American filibusters, adventurers who aided the revolutionaries, were tacitly encouraged. The new republics of Latin America clamored for recognition. The question, which aroused considerable debate, was complicated by boundary difficulties with Spain. Finally, in 1822, recognition was granted.

The European countries followed the example of the United States after the formulation of the Monroe Doctrine. England was the first of the European nations to extend recognition to the new republics.

The issuance of the Monroe Doctrine elicited very little notice from Latin Americans who were much more closely allied economically and culturally with Europe than with the United States. England had early captured the most lucrative Hispanic-American commerce at the expense of the American merchants. French revolutionary philosophy was more popular and influential in directing the course of the uprisings in Spanish America than was the example of the American Revolution.

Bolívar, however, never gave up his hope for an American League, which would guarantee the independence of the new republics. Such a plan was discussed in a congress held in Panama in 1826. It failed, however, for the new republics got to quarreling among themselves and the United States refused to assume leadership because the slavery interests feared that Latin America would attempt to free Cuba and Puerto Rico. Bolívar had hoped that the United States would now join in the freeing of Cuba, but the intervention of the slavery interests of the United States prevented the country from assuming the leadership of the movement.

RISE OF DICTATORS IN SPANISH AMERICA

The post-revolutionary period in Spanish America was one of turbulence and change. Whether the republics should be large or small proved to be a thorny question. At first the plan of a large confederation was attempted. In the end, Spanish America was broken up into nineteen republics.

The turbulence of the period was caused by many factors. The new republics were sadly lacking in political experience and unity. Racial and social antipathies complicated the struggle even more. Political issues were also at stake. Federalism, liberalism, militarism, and clericalism found their advocates and opponents and kept the Latin Americans in a constant state of unrest. In the ensuing disorders, elections were decided by the force of arms, resulting in the establishment of dictators who were to become so characteristic of the Latin-American political scene.

INDEPENDENCE AND CHAOS IN MEXICO

Santa Anna

The history of Mexico after 1824 was typical of that of the other Hispanic-American republics. War, revolutions, and counter-revolutions were the order of the day. Within the space of thirty years, fifty men ruled the unfortunate country. Santa Anna assumed the dictatorship, to be displaced when Texas and California were detached from Mexico by the United States in the Mexican War. Under his Indian successor, Juárez, the republican constitution was restored.

Benito Juarez

The machinations of Napoleon III soon changed the scene. In his effort to erect a colonial empire, he sent French troops into Mexico who set up an empire under the puppet emperor Archduke Maximilian of Austria. Juárez resisted, but could do little. After the conclusion of the Civil War, the United States turned her attention to the situation. Partly as a result of her protest based on the Monroe Doctrine, the French troops were withdrawn. Deprived of their support, Maximilian was captured and killed by the Mexican rebels.

Porfirio Díaz, a follower of Juárez, was elected to the presidency on a platform promising no re-election. He then proceeded to assume dictatorial powers which he

Maximilian

held with little interruption from 1877 to 1911. During his long regime, Mexico experienced a period of great material growth.

Díaz encouraged the entry of foreign capital into Mexico. Her mines and oil wells were opened to exploitation, railroads were built, and the owners of the great landed estates prospered. But this apparent material abundance was dissipated by the time it seeped through to the lower classes. The peasants, or peons, were in a condition of serfdom, and in their land hunger lay a fertile field for revolution. In this instance, as in other revolutions occurring in the name of liberalism, the seeds were sown by the middle class.

Porfirio Díaz

At first the rising discontent showed itself in a demand for the popular election of a new president and for the dissolution of the great estates. But, when peaceful agitation proved futile, violent revolution was resorted to and Díaz was forced into exile. Years of turmoil and bloodshed followed the fall of Díaz in 1911, but by 1914 the reformers under Carranza had definitely gained the ascendancy.

THE RISE OF THE ABC POWERS

The republics of Argentina, Brazil, and Chile during the last half-century have come to be known as the ABC powers. Their remarkable development was made possible by political stability and economic progress.

The first one to achieve successful consolidation was Brazil, a nation of some thirty million inhabitants and extensive natural resources. Argentina, although broken by exhaustive wars with Paraguay and internal provinces during the first half of the century, after 1852 established a stable constitutional government. Chile, in the War of the Pacific (1879-1881), gained valuable nitrate deposits at the expense of her neighbors, Peru and Bolivia. The erection of the famous statue, the Christ of the Andes, in 1904, commem-

orated the settlement of a boundary dispute with Argentina. These two countries were further drawn together with the completion of the trans-Andean railway in 1910.

Great numbers of Germans, Italians, and Spaniards emigrated to these countries before World War I. Foreign capital, especially German and English, was largely responsible for the development of their natural resources. The beautiful, progressive cities of Santiago, Buenos Aires, and Rio de Janiero, resemble, in some respects, North American metropolitan communities.

Cultural achievement followed political stability. Universities of these countries have modernized their curricula in law, science, engineering, music, art, and architecture, while distinguished Argentinian and Chilean writers have given the world many notable literary and intellectual contributions. In fact, by 1914, these prominent ABC powers of South America, through their active participation in the Pan-American congresses, and The Hague Tribunal, had shown Europe and the United States that they could play an active, if minor, role in world politics.

Christ of the Andes commemorates 1903 treaty ending Argentine-Chilean boundary dispute. (Ewing Galloway)

62. England and the British Commonwealth of Nations

FOREIGN AND DOMESTIC POLICIES

Eᴺɢʟᴀɴᴅ shared Europe's lean years of depression following the Napoleonic crash. As conditions became progressively more disturbing, the electorate tended to turn on the party in power. The Tory cabinet had seen the country through twenty critical years of war, but was inexperienced in handling problems of peace and reconstruction. That aristocratic party, still representing the landowners, continued passing legislation that favored their own prosperity. Industrial overproduction, the mass of unemployed created by demobilization, and labor riots led some to argue a need for remedial legislation.

Castlereagh would not extend British cooperation to the reactionary Quadruple Alliance, but neither would he break with it. Public opinion, increasingly sympathetic to the outbursts of repressed peoples, was to use this further grievance against the Tories. When Canning replaced Castlereagh, he openly championed popular national movements, and in 1823 successfully defied the intervention of the Alliance in the Spanish revolt and the wars for independence in Hispanic America. British interest in the Hispanic trade prompted that stand. The determination to defend it with British naval power made the American Monroe Doctrine effective.

In internal affairs, the new spirit bore fruit in the modification of the criminal and corn laws, repeal of the combination acts against labor organizations, and of the civil disabilities of Dissenters and Catholics. The reform of the House of Commons emerged as the chief party issue in the general election of 1830. After the decline of the violent reform element, the moderates, under Lord John Russell, exerted a growing influence. Their groundwork from 1820 to 1830 had given the Whig party a principle on which to unite and successfully contest the election.

POLITICAL AND SOCIAL REFORMS

Earl Grey and his colleagues in the new ministry favored liberal reforms. Debate, dissolution, re-election, and a threat to swamp the Lords with new Whig peers, were necessary to put Lord John Russell's broad parliamentary Reform Bill on the statute books. This act removed the worst features of the electoral system by extension of the franchise,

Lord John Russell, prime minister, 1846-52, 1865-66. (Brown Bros.)

John Stuart Mill, political economist and philosopher

Sir Robert Peel, prime minister, 1834-35, 1841-46

Victoria, queen of Great Britain, 1837-1901, in the robes worn at her coronation in 1838

tion, formerly known as the Tories, and this combination from now on was known as the Conservatives. Meanwhile, the progressive Whigs and unaffiliated radicals were aligning themselves as Liberals.

After the accession of Victoria in 1837, it was four years before a clear majority put the Conservatives under Peel in office. A new popular demand for reform was sweeping the country. Chartism voiced the demand of the working classes that parliamentary reform be extended. The Anti-Corn Law League, led by Richard Cobden and John Bright, wielded an influence that the government could not ignore. The Oxford Movement carried the reform agitation into the church where it sought moral and cultural refinement in a return to ritualism.

FREE TRADE

The Whig achievement of the Reform Bill was given a Tory equivalent in the repeal of the Corn Laws in 1846, by which Peel embarked England upon her historic policy of free trade. With the final repeal of the Navigation Acts in 1849, the conversion was complete. But the break with tradition split the party which sponsored it. The breach widened because of the differences between John Russell and Lord Palmerston on foreign policy. Weak coalitions alternated in office, bungling the Crimean War. The period from 1859 to

improvement in the conduct of elections, and some reapportionment of representatives.

The mid-nineteenth century marked a high point in the reform movement. Legislation was regarded as the instrument through which Bentham's utilitarianism could become effective. The old doctrine of laissez faire was losing its hold before John Stuart Mill's argument that the fair distribution of wealth rather than its accumulation should be the end of economic policy. Of wider immediate influence, because more simple to comprehend, was the current wave of humanitarianism.

In the Factory Act of 1833, abolition of slavery in the colonies, reform of the poor laws and municipal administration, the government moved with crusading fervor against outstanding social injustices. Its record of success was halted when it became impaled upon the difficult Irish problem. The compulsory tithe in support of a Protestant established church, and the predominance of Protestants in civil offices, were opposed with systematic agitation which in many sections became open anarchy. The abolition of tithes and extension of the recent reforms to Ireland temporarily quieted that country.

A party transition gradually took place during an interim of relative inactivity. Some of the conservative Whigs joined the opposi-

The Charge of the Light Brigade, an incident of the Crimean War, celebrated in a poem by Tennyson

1865 marked Palmerston's complete ascendancy, characterized by great changes in India and by blustering diplomatic gestures toward Europe and America—gestures regretted by all but the Palmerstonians.

GLADSTONE AND DISRAELI

Gladstone now succeeded to the leadership of the Liberal party. During the thirty years of his early parliamentary career, he had moved from high Toryism to the front Liberal rank where his unmatched oratorical powers won him great popularity. The brilliant Disraeli was the intellect and guiding hand of the Conservative party. He matched wit, imagination, and daring against Gladstone's sober reasoning and high moral tone. Both parties

Gladstone

acknowledged that developments seemed to require the extension of parliamentary reform. However, the public remained apathetic, and the Liberals advocated several measures without success. In 1866 a reactionary wing of that party blocked the bill and forced the Liberal ministry to resign. Lord Derby and Disraeli formed a Conservative cabinet and, on the wave of aroused popular enthusiasm, won Liberal support by passing a new reform measure. The Act of 1867 practically established universal suffrage in the boroughs, thus enfranchising a large part of the working class.

Ireland was aflame once more, the blaze having been set by the Fenian movement. Gladstone rallied the Liberals for a legislative settlement and succeeded Disraeli as prime minister in 1868. During the next two years he brought about the disestablishment of

Disraeli
(Brown Bros.)

the Anglican church in Ireland, and obtained a land law intended to prevent eviction of tenants without compensation for property improvements.

An act of 1870 provided for local and national aid to local governments throughout England in establishing tax-supported schools where the private school systems were insufficient. A series of governmental reforms included the placing of the civil service on a competitive basis, and the introduction of the secret ballot. In its foreign policy, the cabinet was deemed weak, because aggression in the Near East went unchecked and Gladstone accepted the Geneva award of 1872 regarding the American *Alabama* claims which originated from the destruction of United States' shipping during the Civil War.

Disraeli returned to office in 1874. Although his social and economic measures seemed moderate after the sweeping reforms achieved, he loosed his energies upon a brilliant imperial

The House of Commons during the time of Gladstone, from a painting by T. Walter Wilson

policy, beginning by purchasing control of the Suez Canal in 1875. He increased British prestige in Africa and in the Near East, and won a diplomatic victory over Russia at the Congress of Berlin in 1878. When the Disraeli ministry swung once more to reaction, Gladstone triumphed in 1880.

One more great step toward parliamentary reform was taken by the Liberals. The acts of 1884-1885 extended the franchise qualifications of 1867 to rural laborers, while the principle of representation according to population was applied in the distribution of seats. The Irish question came to the fore again when the calculating Charles Parnell became leader of the Irish Nationalists. A new land law could not halt the outrages committed by Parnell's followers. Gladstone compromised with Parnell, achieving a breathing spell.

Salisbury replaced Gladstone in 1885 and headed the new Conservative cabinet. The Ashbourne Act solved the Irish land question by providing government loans enabling tenants to purchase their holdings. Gladstone and his Liberal government introduced a home rule bill for Ireland in 1886. The Conservatives opposed it, while Joseph Chamberlain led the Liberal Unionist wing out of the Liberal party to defeat the measure. The Conservatives held office from 1886 to 1906, with the exception of Gladstone's brief fourth cabinet from 1892 to 1894. The Boer War, discussed later in this chapter, was fought from 1899-1902.

Parnell

EARLY TWENTIETH CENTURY CHANGES

The Liberals won the election of 1906 on a program of social changes. They proceeded to regulate hours and minimum wages, establish workmen's compensation and insurance, old-age pensions and the labor exchange system, and provide salaries for members of the House of Commons.

Lloyd George

Lords and Commons finally reached a deadlock in the battle over Lloyd George's 1909 budget for social reform. The persistent upper chamber veto was met by the re-election of the government. Asquith received the royal promise to create enough new peers to pass a bill for the reform of the House of Lords.

Asquith

The act of 1911 established the constitutional principle that the Lords may delay, but cannot forever block, legislation demanded by the Commons.

Foreign relations involving principally imperial and naval rivalries, tended to crowd out domestic bills in the period immediately before World War I. The third Irish Home Rule Bill was introduced and passed the Commons in 1912. After the new two-year lapse, it became law without the Lords' approval, although its operation was postponed for the duration of the war.

CANADA DURING THE NINETEENTH CENTURY

For Canada, the hundred years from 1815 to 1915 were years of nation building. The United Empire Loyalists, refugees from the American Revolution, were the nucleus of the new Canadian nation. Trained in English institutions of self-government, their agitation had led to the constitutional act of 1791 which separated Upper and Lower Canada, providing separate governments for the British and French units. Although the measure was intended to reduce friction, and did grant a few representative institutions, it perpetuated the alien characteristics of the French population and postponed their ultimate absorption.

Mackenzie, Canadian insurgent leader

RELATIONS WITH THE UNITED STATES

All was not quiet on the American front for some years. The westward expansion of the two peoples brought trade rivalries, tariff duels, problems of Indian control, and other questions which Jay's treaty did not definitely settle. When war broke out in 1812, the Americans sought to conquer Canada and incorporate it with their expanding state. The sturdy defense against the invaders forged a bond of unity when Canadians of English and French extraction fought side by side.

Diplomatic negotiations in 1817 and 1818 resulted in solving major diplomatic problems. The boundary between the United States and Canada was to be unfortified, and the fisheries dispute was settled temporarily. A territorial dispute in the Lake of the Woods region was arranged through mutual concessions. Two other disputed boundaries, on the northeast and the northwest of the United States, were drawn satisfactorily in 1842 and 1846, respectively.

DEMAND FOR POLITICAL REFORM

Grave abuses in the governmental system in Canada came to light between 1815 and 1837, and a spirit of rebellion was growing. In Lower Canada, the antagonistic assembly demanded control over all expenditures and poured its wrath upon the "château clique" of local British officialdom. Great Britain transferred the permanent crown revenues of the province to the assembly in 1831. Instead of granting in return the desired civil list, irate members led by Papineau prepared the ninety-two resolutions of 1834, a document of extreme demands.

The conflict between elective assembly and appointed legislative council was repeated in Upper Canada. The "family compact" of official oligarchy was no more popular there than cial oligarchy was no more popular there than

in Quebec. Many of the residents were Dissenters, and the extensive lands held as Anglican clergy's reserves created a fundamental grievance. By 1828, the reform party under William Lyon Mackenzie obtained a majority in the assembly. When the governors charged the radicals with disloyalty, many moderate reformers were reluctant to be associated with them. The rebels were armed and made plans to cooperate in the two provinces. The revolt was not against British tyranny from overseas, but against incompetent officials in the province. It was, at best, the disorganized attempt of a minority. After the skirmishes of the autumn of 1837, Papineau, Mackenzie, and others fled across the border.

DURHAM REPORT

The British government sent Lord Durham to Canada to investigate and make recommendations. The famous Report, submitted in February, 1839, recommended without reservation complete internal, responsible self-government and the union of the provinces. Without enthusiasm either in England or Canada Lord John Russell carried the Union Act in 1840. The provinces were united under one governor, an appointed legislative council of twenty, and an elective assembly of forty-two members from each province.

Through succeeding ministries the new government lumbered along attempting to fit the constitution into the parliamentary system, and meeting the indifference or opposition of governors who believed colonial self-government incompatible with imperial control. In 1847 Lord Elgin, Durham's son-in-law, became governor. Undaunted by opposition in Parliament, Elgin risked personal violence and stood by the principle that the executive must approve all legislation passed by the two Houses. Also, in accord with constitutional practice, Governor Elgin set a precedent by absenting himself from cabinet meetings.

CANADIAN ECONOMIC EXPANSION

In the meantime, social and economic progress was being made. The waves of immigration, improvements in farming, industrial beginnings and the linking of communities by

Queen Victoria's First Privy Council. The Privy Council met on the morning after the death of Victoria's uncle, King William IV. The proper oaths were administered at once, and Victoria was proclaimed queen on June 20, 1837. Her reign, until her death in 1901, was conservative, but it marked a period of great prosperity.

The Charge of the Light Brigade. This incident occurred at the battle of Balaklava, October 25, 1854, during the Crimean War. The Earl of Cardigan, under mistaken orders, led the English light cavalry in a foolish dash against Russian positions. Their defeat was immortalized in a poem by Alfred Lord Tennyson.

Captain Cook on Vancouver Island, 1778. On his third voyage of exploration, Captain James Cook covered most of the Pacific coast of North America from what is now Oregon to Bering Strait. He was the first to make a thorough survey. British claims to what is now British Columbia were based on Cook's explorations.

The Founding of Toronto, 1788. The city was at one time a French fort. The British destroyed the fort when they occupied the site in 1759. The land was purchased from the Indians in 1788. The Loyalists, fleeing from the American Revolution, settled there in 1793. Toronto became Canada's second largest city.

First Parliament of Upper Canada, 1792. A certain measure of self government had been established by the Constitutional Act of 1791. The British Parliament allowed Canada a local parliament for each of its two provinces. Canada gradually developed dominion status from a desire for unity within its own boundaries.

Captain Vancouver at Burrard Inlet. George Vancouver explored the northwest coast in 1792. The city of Vancouver, founded near the inlet, was named for him.

Canada's First Railway. The pioneer Champlain and St. Lawrence Railroad was opened in 1837. Major railroad development took place later in the century, however.

Victoria, Vancouver Island, Founded, 1843. The Hudson Bay Company formed a trading post here in 1843, but the city was not laid out until 1851-52.

Fathers of Canadian Confederation in London. Lower and Upper Canada had been joined by the Act of Union of 1840. It was proposed that the maritime provinces join them in a confederation. Thus, Parliament, acting on resolutions drawn up and ratified by provincial parliaments, enacted the North America Act, 1867.

Winnipeg About 1872. The first settlement took place about 1738, but growth was slow until about 1881 when transcontinental railroads were built. The city of Winnipeg, the fourth largest in Canada, was incorporated in 1872. It is a railroad and commercial center for the great wheat-growing prairie area of central Canada.

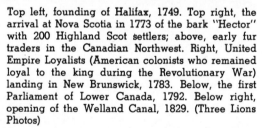

Top left, founding of Halifax, 1749. Top right, the arrival at Nova Scotia in 1773 of the bark "Hector" with 200 Highland Scot settlers; above, early fur traders in the Canadian Northwest. Right, United Empire Loyalists (American colonists who remained loyal to the king during the Revolutionary War) landing in New Brunswick, 1783. Below, the first Parliament of Lower Canada, 1792. Below right, opening of the Welland Canal, 1829. (Three Lions Photos)

Fathers of Confederation, a representation based on the painting by Robert Harris of the Quebec Conference of 1864, which paved the way for the confederation of Canada in 1867. (National Film Board)

roads, canals, and railways—developments which had taken place below the border—were repeated in Canada. Economic necessity dictated that Canadians must trade with the United States. A minority of over-anxious business men signed the Annexation Manifesto in 1849. But regular channels of negotiation produced the Elgin-Marcy Reciprocity Treaty of 1854, which proved beneficial to both countries. It was terminated, however, by the United States in 1866.

DOMINION ACHIEVED

The ten years from 1854 to 1864 saw the collapse of party government. Sectional, racial, and religious antagonisms brought frequent deadlocks. There was an obvious need for a general legislature in which all sections would be equally represented. Statesmen began to think beyond the limits of "province" and to visualize another Anglo-Saxon nation stretching from coast to coast.

Just across the border a war was being waged in vindication of the vital necessity of unity. Much of the North's hostility for Britain during the Civil War was being deflected toward Canada. Possible consequences of this feeling could not be ignored. Delegates of the maritime districts were assembled at Charlestown, Prince Edward Island, when representatives arrived from the other provinces urging participation in a general conference at Quebec to consider Canadian confederation. Here the

proponents of confederation headed by Macdonald, Galt, Brown, Tilley, Cartier, and Tupper drew up the Quebec resolutions which became the British North America Act of 1867. This measure provided for a bicameral, or two-chamber Parliament, an elective House and an appointive Senate. The cabinet, of course, was the real executive; but the governor-general, the right of appeal to the British Privy Council, and certain imperial checks remained. Delegated powers were accorded the provinces, the residue resting with the Dominion.

WESTWARD ADVANCE

John A. Macdonald took up the manifold duties of premier. He was in office from 1867 to 1891, except for one interim. The old fur-trading companies in the west and north retained some land reserves, but surrendered all

Sir John Alexander Macdonald (1815-91)

rights of jurisdiction to Canada. The westward advance of civilization brought contact with half-savage frontiersmen, scarcely different from the *coureurs-de-bois* of two centuries before. The rebellion of Louis Riel and his malcontents of the Red River district led to the passage of the Manitoba Act in 1870, creating a new province. British Columbia entered the Dominion the next year. A series of treaties established Indian land reserves, and the government agreed to provide implements and means for farming, in return for the land titles and a pledge of peace by the tribes.

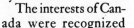
Louis Riel (1844-85), insurgent leader

The interests of Canada were recognized when Sir John Macdonald was named one of the British commissioners to negotiate the Treaty of Washington with the United States in 1871. Two years later the Macdonald government became involved in a scandal about bids for the transcontinental railroad which had been promised to British Columbia. Alexander Mackenzie headed a Liberal government for five years, but an economic depression and the lack of a program caused his downfall in 1878. Macdonald's new "National Policy" swept the country. A high protective tariff went hand in hand with a period of good harvest and a western boom. It was more than an economic policy; it was an appeal to nationalism and unity. This feeling was heightened in 1885, when the Dominion was spanned by the Canadian Pacific Railway. Riel attempted another rebellion in the northwest that year, but it was suppressed and its leader executed.

Macdonald, who had steadfastly advocated an imperial policy, was re-elected in 1891, defeating the Liberals, who were accused of favoring a policy of economic union with the United States. Sir John survived the election only a few months. Wilfrid Laurier, a French Canadian Liberal, won a clear majority in 1896 and became Dominion prime minister. In his term of office, the provinces of Alberta

Sir Wilfrid Laurier (1841-1919). (N.F.B.)

and Saskatchewan were admitted into the Dominion. The new government carried on an extensive program of social and labor reforms and also settled the questions of religious education in Manitoba schools.

TARIFF AND ANNEXATION PROBLEMS

Though not an imperialist, Laurier in 1897 extended to Great Britain an imperial preferential tariff. The problem of imperial responsibility and defense occupied much attention during this period. In fact, Robert Borden rebuilt the Conservative party by advocating Canadian financial contributions to the British imperial fleet.

After years of vainly seeking renewed tariff reciprocity, Canada was surprised to find Washington making that offer in 1911. Laurier was favorable, but the Conservatives and many others could not avoid suspecting some new annexation or union movement. The bold statements of certain American statesmen gave them some cause for hesitation. Once again the old loyalty issue triumphed over the ghost of annexation, and Borden and the Conservatives came into office on a veritable landslide vote.

An indication of the great changes which had come about in the relation of Canada to Great Britain, was given just before the outbreak of World War I. The Canadians, strongly nationalistic, nevertheless extended a promise of aid if Great Britain entered the war. Developments after World War I further revealed the place of dominions within the British Empire.

OTHER BRITISH DOMINIONS— NEWFOUNDLAND

In general, it may be said that the other Dominions passed through stages of development similar to those which occurred in Canada. The other old North American colony, Newfoundland, did not become a part of Canada. Concerned only with its fishing industry and having nothing in common with the continental problems of Canada, Newfoundland achieved responsible government as a separate Dominion in 1855.

AUSTRALIA AND NEW ZEALAND

Australia remained an insignificant part of the British Empire until the adoption of systematic colonization in the early nineteenth century. During the 1850's all but one of the states had achieved self-government as separate colonies. The gold rush of that period had a tremendous influence on Australia, increasing and diversifying the population.

New Zealand was colonized through the efforts of land companies and missionary organizations. An imperial Act of 1852 established a united New Zealand, consisting of six provinces. Maori, or native, wars continued till 1870. The provincial system of government was replaced by a single government in 1876. Dominion status was proclaimed in 1907, and New Zealand for some time was the scene of experiments in social legislation.

Meanwhile, exploration, industrial progress, and democratic experiments had been proceeding in continental Australia. The first conference of delegates was held in 1880 and plans for a federation were begun. The Constitution Bill of 1900 established a new dominion of six states, called the Commonwealth of Australia.

BRITISH DOMINION IN SOUTH AFRICA

In South Africa, the Boers had tired of living under British rule in Cape Colony. When slavery was abolished, they decided to move in order to keep their slaves, and from 1834 to 1840 made the great trek northward across the Orange River. When British jurisdiction was extended here, some of the Dutch migrated farther north into the Transvaal. In a convention of 1852, Britain voluntarily retired, recognizing the independent Orange Free State and South African Republic. Cape Colony became self-governing under the constitution of 1872.

Racial and economic friction between the Boers and the British continued. With the discovery of diamonds, the British frontier was advanced until Disraeli annexed the Transvaal in 1877. Under Gladstone, Conventions of 1881 and 1884 recognized the South African Republic once more. The gold rush in the Transvaal in 1884-1885 created a new situation. To preserve their wealth and ascendancy, the Boers refused practically all civil rights to foreigners. A raid led by Dr. Jameson and sponsored by Cecil Rhodes, premier of Cape Colony, brought on a fresh crisis.

Relations became steadily worse, and in 1899 the two Boer republics sent Britain an ultimatum which meant war. The British were unprepared and slow to get under way, but the outcome was inevitable. The generous peace of 1902 and the granting of complete responsible government to the conquered colonies, within five years were wise and brilliant measures. The South African colonies became the Union of South Africa in 1909.

BRITISH DOMINION IN INDIA

Although it neither attained dominion status nor remained completely a crown colony in this period, India made important progress. The governors of the early nineteenth century did valuable work in abolishing many of the old barbaric customs. The monopoly of the East India Company was being continually reduced to make way for greater imperial and native control of the government. There were also delicate situations on the northern frontiers which required preparedness. The Sepoy Mutiny of 1857 brought a rigorous revision in the supervision of India. The old company was dissolved and India came directly under the protection of the Crown. A secretary of state for India in the British cabinet was assisted by a council, as was the viceroy. A legislative council also served in India, an institution which was partly native and was the branch in which native responsibility was to increase.

The latter half of the century was largely taken up with the guarding of the frontiers against jealous powers, Asiatic or European. After 1905, the demand for reform was continuous, as the Indian National Congress grew in strength. An Indian Act of 1909 provided an electorate of some 30,000 which chose new members for the legislative council. These gradual degrees of participation in government gave the Indians some practical experience in home rule, but British control was still predominant. Further steps toward Indian self-rule were taken after World War I.

63. Nationalism in Continental Europe

UNIFICATION OF ITALY

IN 1815 ITALY was a "geographic expression." Napoleon had done much for the awakening of Italy, although he had not unified the peninsula. Austria, at the Congress of Vienna, regained her control over Italy, and enforced upon the various states her reactionary policy. In opposition to this repression arose a secret society, called the Carbonari, which by acts of terrorism and violence attempted to throw off Austria's rule. In 1821 rebellions in the north and south were quelled by Austria, with the aid of foreign troops.

Violence failing, Italian revolutionary movement broke out in a different field—that of letters. Joseph Mazzini, a writer with visions of a united nation, organized a society called "Young Italy," to further Italian nationalism and the expulsion of Austria from Italy. Gioberti, a priest with much the same ideas as Mazzini, though he was for an aristocracy instead of a republic, also wrote urging Italian independence. To this literary-revolutionary movement is given the name "Risorgimento," or resurrection.

Giuseppe Mazzini, who helped free Italy

In 1848, continent-wide revolutions embarrassed Austria. This was the signal for Italy to arise. Austria triumphed once more, however, and dealt severely with the liberals who had instigated the uprising. But the spirit of freedom was not to be denied. Piedmont, though defeated, achieved a constitution under Victor Emmanuel and now formed the center of the movement. The minister of Victor Emmanuel, Count Cavour, was the guiding force, and under his direction Italian unification was completed.

Cavour involved Piedmont in the Crimean War in 1855 with the hope of gaining the aid of France and England against Austria. In the congress following the war, Cavour partially succeeded in his hope and two years later, with the aid of France, the Austrians were defeated though they still retained the province of Venice because France deserted the Italians. The kingdom of Naples, and the Papal States were the scenes of the next step in unification. Giuseppe Garibaldi had little trouble in organizing and carrying through a successful revolution in 1860, which united Naples and part of the Papal States to Sardinia.

An Italian kingdom was formed, headed by Emmanuel, whose power was limited by a constitution. As a result of siding with Prussia in the war with France, when the French troops protecting Rome for the pope were withdrawn in 1870, that city was occupied and made

Giuseppe Garibaldi, Italian patriot

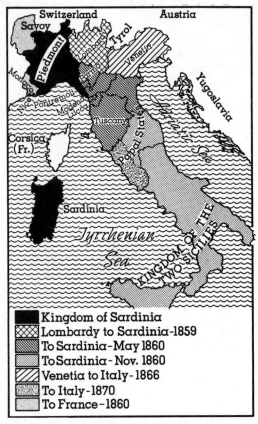

The Unification of Italy

Napoleon had attempted to merge many of the small political units, and his work was made permanent in 1815 by the German Confederation of thirty-eight states, instead of the three hundred of the sixteenth century. The middle classes, as well as other people who desired unification, resented Austrian domination of the Confederation, unequal representation, and tariff barriers between the separate states of the Confederation. In 1818 and 1833, led by Prussia, they formed a customs union, or Zollverein, which provided for federal tariff barriers against foreign goods, and free trade within the boundaries of the Confederation.

The middle classes, chafing under the still repressive control of their rulers, joined the general European outbreaks in 1848. Although they were unsuccessful, their spirit and desire for freedom remained. Prussia, under the pressure of liberal elements, achieved a constitution in 1847, but it was done away with in the same year. The Frankfurt Convention, representing the sentiment of the German people, offered an imperial crown to Frederick William, king of Prussia, who rejected it due to Austrian influence.

Frederick William died in 1861 and the crown of Prussia went to his brother, William I. The new king chose as his minister Otto von Bismarck, and as his army heads, von Moltke and von Roon. Under these three men, Prussia became the most powerful state in Germany. To attain to this position they had to fight the

the capital. Although the state sought to reach an agreement with the Church, the popes remained in the Vatican as "prisoners" until after World War I.

Internal improvements, including financial, educational, and electoral reforms, were instituted during the period preceding the war. Italy, laboring heavily under the then current delusion of grandeur, although her tax rate was the highest in Europe, attempted unsuccessful "imperialistic" conquests. Her attempts to retain a position as a "Power" caused expenditures which her relatively poor agricultural economy found it difficult to meet.

UNIFICATION OF GERMANY

The year 1815 found Germany, too, a "geographical expression" and under Austrian influence. Yet there was a strong feeling among the German middle class for a unified nation.

Bismarck Meeting Napoleon III in September, 1870, after the French surrender at Sedan

Bismarck in Versailles arguing with Louis Thiers and Jules Favre over the terms of the treaty ending the Franco-Prussian War. From a painting by Carl Wagner. (Ewing Galloway)

opposition of the Liberals, who objected to the heavy military expenditures. Bismarck, becoming Chancellor, practically suspended the constitution, announcing that not speeches but "blood and iron" would be the policy of the government, and cooperated in establishing a strong army.

War was the means by which Bismarck secured German unification. After defeating Denmark in a territorial dispute in 1864, he quarreled with his late ally Austria over the spoils of the war and defeated her in 1866. Prussia thus became the most powerful German state and brought most of the northern states under her influence in the North German Confederation. It was not until the Franco-Prussian War, however, that all of Germany achieved unification. Mutual confidence and patriotic strivings arose between the two sections at the outcome of the war, and served as the chief aid to union in 1871. Standing in the Hall of Mirrors at Versailles, in the defeated enemy's territory, Bismarck proclaimed the new German Empire.

Germany waxed strong under the guidance of Bismarck. To him the ever present fear of a French war of revenge provided a powerful motive for placating all classes of people. To the workers he gave important concessions, including insurance and old age compensation,

steps which put Germany years ahead of the rest of Europe. To the business classes he gave a tariff, and after 1884 pursued an imperialistic policy. Bismarck's adroit diplomacy placed Germany among the leading powers, and it soon became one of the most powerful. But Bismarck was displaced, in 1890, soon after the accession of the new emperor, William II, who directed German policy thereafter.

TURKEY

The Turkish empire, though diminished from its former size, was still great in extent and important in the affairs of Europe. A gradual disintegration, caused by the nationalistic spirit of the people within its boundaries, took place in the period from 1815 to 1914. Russia threatened her from the outside, and revolutions menaced completely to remove the empire from the map.

Serbia had revolted in 1804 and had achieved a measure of independence, and in 1821 the Greeks revolted. The revolt was not immediately quelled, and foreign powers intervened to aid the Greeks. The Treaty of Adrianople in 1829 considerably reduced the power of the sultan in Europe, and gave Greece her complete independence. Russia then supported Serbia which gained autonomy in 1829. Turkey gave up further powers in 1830.

531

Russia also gained control over the Rumanian provinces north of the Danube. England and France, disturbed by the growing power of Russia, combined against her in the Crimean War. The people of Moldavia and Wallachia began to think of themselves as a definite nation and, finally, in 1862, the state of Rumania was created. Beginning in 1875 revolts again broke out in the Balkans. Herzegovina rose in 1875, and soon Bulgaria, Montenegro, and Serbia took the field against the sultan.

War between Russia and Turkey broke out in 1877. By the following year Russia and the Balkan states had won. The Treaty of San Stefano forced Turkey to recognize the sovereignty of Serbia, Montenegro, and Rumania, and created an autonomous Bulgaria under the administration of the sultan. The Balkan peoples were disappointed in the provisions of the treaty, none of them having become as strong as they wished. But Russia had gained all she desired, to the dismay of the other nations. These nations, at the instigation of Disraeli, demanded a congress at Berlin which was held in the same year, with the crafty Bismarck presiding as an "honest broker."

This treaty weakened the Balkan states by dividing them. Bulgaria was divided into three parts. Austria was given administration over Bosnia-Herzegovina, though the inhabitants were predominantly Slav. In 1885 the Bulgarians revolted against this arrangement and announced themselves united. Immediately they seized East Rumelia and added it to their possession.

A movement to reform Turkish institutions came to a head in 1908. Corruption and an absolute prohibition of any new ideas or improvements had reduced the old empire to almost the status of a primitive society. The young Turks, headed by Enver Bey and Mustafa Kemal, had progress as their watchword. Gaining control, they enforced the long suspended constitution of 1876 and sought to wipe out corruption. In 1909 they deposed Abdul Hamid II and set up a national assembly. In two more years they established a virtually military dictatorship. While Turkey was becoming nationalistic-minded herself, her possessions were again on the verge of war.

In 1908, while Turkey was occupied with her revolution, Austria annexed Bosnia-Herzegovina which was under her protection. Serbia, infuriated by this annexation, almost declared war, but was restrained by Russia, which feared a general war. This intrusion by Austria set the stage for the overt act which later caused World War I.

While Turkey, dominated by the Young Turks, was involved in a war with Italy, the Balkan nations seized the opportunity to form a Balkan League, presenting a united front to Turkey. War resulted in 1912, the League emerging victorious. But dissatisfaction over the division of the spoils soon led to quarrels among the Balkan nations. In 1913 Serbia,

Signing the Treaty of San Stefano, March 3, 1878. In this contemporary drawing from Harper's Weekly, Russian and Turkish representatives are shown concluding the agreement which ended the Russo-Turkish War

aided by Montenegro, Rumania and Greece, declared war on Bulgaria, and defeated her. Turkey joined the war against Bulgaria and recovered a small part of her lost territory.

Thus by 1913 Turkey had completely disintegrated. But her internal reforms gave promise of making her once more powerful, and the friendliness of Germany, which sent officers to help the army, and otherwise showed willingness to aid, promised the New Turkey a place in the sun once more—certainly a place in the heart of European politics.

AUSTRIA-HUNGARY
(1815-1914)

Austria was the most powerful nation on the continent at the time of the Congress of Vienna; but by 1848 her power had been undermined by the rising tide of nationalism. The unification of Germany and Italy in the next generation dealt blows to her prestige and strength from which she never recovered. Austria was unable to join in the nationalistic movement and become a modern state, for the Hapsburg empire was not one nation, but several. The only means by which the empire could be maintained was by playing the several peoples one against another. Moreover, the state existed and expanded by the will of her aristocracy, not of her people, for accurately speaking Austria had no people. Austria-Hungary was not a nation, and no amount of propaganda could make her nationalistic.

The war with Germany in 1866 clearly illustrated this point. Germany was an intensely nationalistic and patriotic nation, and for that reason, as much as for any other, easily defeated the Hapsburgs. After the rout, Austria had to make concession to the rising nationalistic movements and in 1867 provided a new constitution. The empire was divided into two states under a single crown and certain other mutual agencies, such as army, diplomacy, and tariff. The constitution was a compromise, a living agreement between the two nations.

Internal troubles continued to plague the Dual Monarchy. Bohemia was desirous of getting the same place in the empire that Hungary had achieved, and her demands became so vociferous that Austria at various times seemed about to grant them. But the other nationalities of the empire, seeing the rise of Bohemia, protested bitterly, demanding like concessions. The minority races living in Bohemia also objected and the concession was never given. Other nationalities within the empire grew restless as they saw their hopes fade with the denial of Bohemia. Hungary, too, was plagued by internal groups which desired independence or autonomy within that half of the Dual Monarchy.

Yet Austria-Hungary still had interests in the Balkans, and here she came into direct conflict with Russia which was expanding into the peninsula from the opposite direction. In order to offset the power of Russia, Austria-Hun-

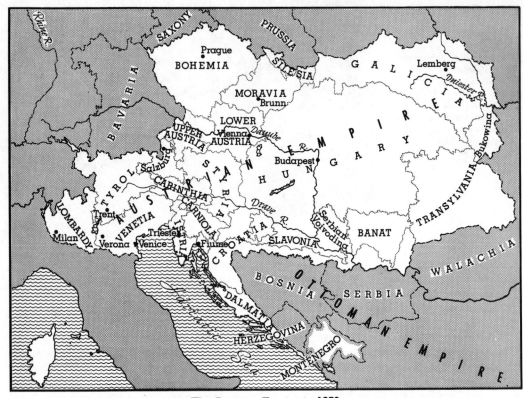

The Austrian Empire in 1850

gary formed an alliance with Germany in 1879.

At first retarded by the Russian alliance which formed part of Bismarck's policy, she had to wait until William II came to the throne. Then she became bolder in her opposition to Russia in the Balkans, and in 1908, by seizing Bosnia, created the first Bosnian crisis. Russia at this time was not ready for war, but the continued alliance and the continued foolhardiness of Austria indicated to the careful observer what the result must be.

SPAIN

Ferdinand VII was restored to the throne of Spain by the Congress of Vienna. A Bourbon, he was perhaps the most reactionary king of his time. In 1820 the Liberals rose against him, were put down, rose again three years later, and were defeated a second time. The succession to Ferdinand's throne was the next question to plague the country and cause the aristocracy to fight among themselves.

Ferdinand's daughter Isabella was the logical contender for the throne, but her uncle, Carlos, opposed her. Both had supporters, those of Carlos being called Carlists, and a series of wars resulted. From 1833, when Isabella began her reign under her mother's regency, until 1843, when the regent was forced to abdicate, violence reigned. Isabella continued to offend her courtiers and members of the aristocracy who finally forced her to flee in 1868. Civil wars resulted, with a republic occasionally varying the dictatorships.

Isabella II (1830-1904), queen of Spain from 1833 to 1870

After the crown had been offered to a Hohenzollern in 1870, a gesture which served as an excuse for the Franco-Prussian War, Amadeus of Savoy, younger son of Victor Emmanuel II of Italy, was called to the throne. His troubled reign lasted until 1873, when a republic was again proclaimed. A military

Amadeus of Savoy

dictatorship soon took power, and recalled Alfonso XII, son of Isabella.

A parliament had been established in 1834, but it had little or no influence. Universal suffrage was established in 1890, but the people, illiterate and unschooled, had little real voice in the government. Alfonso XII died in 1885 and was succeeded in 1886 by his posthumous son, Alfonso XIII. The queen mother, Maria Christina was regent until 1902. During this period Spain lost the Philippines and the last of her American possessions in the Spanish-American War. Alfonso XIII was declared of age in 1902. Elementary education was established in 1907, natural resources were exploited, and commerce began to prosper. But the country was still backward compared to the larger nations. Religious freedom was proclaimed in 1907. This was the situation in Spain at the outbreak of World War I, during which the country remained neutral.

PORTUGAL

The history of Portugal in this period is much like that of Spain. Civil wars and intrigues made the reign of Maria Christina II (1835-1853) a troubled one. The conflicting parties were the Regenerators and the Progressives, one the Conservative group and the other the Liberal group. A constitutional reform in 1852 enabled deputies to the parliament to be elected directly by the people.

Civil strife continued until 1910 when the monarchy was overthrown and a republic proclaimed. The incumbent king was Manoel II. The constitution that was set up provided for a popular body, which elected ministers who directed the country and were responsible to the Cortes, or parliament. Opposition aroused by the anticlerical attitude of the republicans made the country once more the scene of strife until 1914. Entering World War I on the side of the Allies, Portugal played a comparatively minor role.

BELGIUM

Belgium became independent from the Netherlands in 1830, and set up a constitutional monarchy. Leopold I reigned during 1831-1865, a period of peaceful internal development. Commerce flourished, schools and railroads were built, and freedom of press and religion was established on a firm basis.

Albert I, king of the Belgians, 1909-34

In 1865 Leopold II ascended the throne. Though there was little demand for reform, the constitution was revised to permit greater suffrage. Perhaps the most serious internal trouble was the sectionalism in the country. In the north were the Flemish (Dutch) who were more industrial and included more Protestants than the Walloons (French) of the south. A second issue was caused by the rise of the Socialist party and its demands, centering about education and opposing the aims of the Catholic Church. These issues were always peacefully settled. At no time did civil war break out—a tribute to Belgium in this period. Leopold's interest in the Congo region of Africa is discussed elsewhere.

Albert I ascended the throne in 1909, and was king during the period of the war. Since Belgium lay between France and Germany, her neutral position was important. At the time of her separation from the Netherlands, this neutrality had been recognized and confirmed by the four Powers: England, Germany, France, and Russia. The invasion of Belgium, in violation of this neutrality, was one of the first acts of World War I.

THE NETHERLANDS

Holland remained during the nineteenth century one spot in the world where freedom and peace were paramount. Her schools, her citizenry, her accomplishments in the arts and sciences, were those of a free country.

In 1848 Holland revised the constitution which had been set up in 1815 by William I. The revision diminished the power of the king and elevated parliament. The country prospered under this reform, and no other major change was made until 1887 and 1896 when the suffrage was extended, and 1917 when it was made universal.

The chief problem of the Dutch government was the administration of its great colonial empire, one of the most valuable in the world. Holland governed her colonies with an iron hand, and no troubles arose in these territories to harass the government at home. Continuing her policy of peace, Holland remained neutral during World War I.

SWITZERLAND

In 1815 Switzerland was composed of a group of states with independent governments. The Swiss Confederation, as this group was called, was held together by the Pact of 1815. In this federation the separate states, or cantons, were dominant, making their own trade treaties. But by 1830, and during the next two decades, there began a series of revisions which unified the states. Opposition to the policy of union by the *Sonderbund*, a group of Catholic cantons, resulted in civil war in 1847–1848. The outcome was the Constitution of 1848.

Under this constitution the Swiss nation became the most democratic in the world. The twin policies of the initiative and the referendum are the most striking examples of this fact. By the referendum, the Swiss legislature is compelled to submit all bills to the people for ratification. Under the initiative the people are allowed to submit their own bills to the legislature, which in turn must resubmit them to the people for ratification.

The neutrality of Switzerland, guaranteed by international agreement, has never been violated—at least, not by armed invasion.

SCANDINAVIA

Norway belonged to Denmark at the opening of the Napoleonic wars. The Congress of Vienna, to punish Denmark for her aid to France, and to compensate Sweden for the loss of Finland, forced Norway to exchange rulers.

Denmark developed quietly after the Congress, her people attempting to regain some of the ground they had lost during the wars. The population remained more interested in economic than in political affairs until 1830, when a strong liberal movement compelled the king to resort to repressive measures. The liberal movement played a large part in the internal affairs of Denmark from that time until 1849, when Frederick VII granted a constitution. The next break in the peaceful growth of the country occurred over the Schleswig-Holstein question.

In 1864 Denmark was forced into a war against Austria and Prussia over the two duchies. To prosecute the war, King Christian IX had practically suspended the constitution and this aroused the opposition of the liberals and the radicals. These parties, gradually becoming more powerful, succeeded in passing many socialistic measures, climaxed, in 1891, by an old age pension act.

The constitution had been revised so that a two-house parliament was established, but the various kings, disdaining democratic methods, usually relied on the upper house. This system of constitutional abuse lasted until World War I.

Norway, the pawn passed from Denmark to Sweden, had asserted itself at that time, and at Eidsvold formed a constitution. The Norwegians asserted that the Danish king surrendered his authority by ceding Norway to Sweden. Therefore, when the king of Sweden sent his son into Norway to take possession, a war resulted. Though Norway was victorious, the intervention of foreign powers compelled her to accept union with Sweden, although each was allowed to retain its sovereignty.

Bernadotte, a general in Napoleon's army, had become king of Sweden in 1818. Under him important internal reforms, such as the reform of the educational system, were instituted. The accession of Oscar II in 1872 opened a new era in the domestic development of Sweden. He accomplished sweeping reforms, establishing a two-chambered parliament, on the modern scheme, and widening the suffrage. Friction over the problem of Norwegian independence again arose to plague the Swedish ministers. Finally, the Norwegian leaders called the Prince of Denmark to be their king, and, after their action had been ratified in a popular referendum, they secured Sweden's grudging acceptance of separation in 1905.

RUSSIA IN THE NINETEENTH CENTURY

The Russian empire during most of the nineteenth century remained largely feudal in character. In this respect it was far behind the rest of Europe. Its industrial development did not take place till the latter part of the century, and despite large natural resources, never became very extensive. The country was ruled autocratically, the mass of people were illiterate, while a small landed aristocracy wielded much power and was checked only by the superior position of the czar. This general backwardness was largely due to Russia's relative isolation. Geographically it was far removed from the cultural centers of Europe and not till late in its expansion did Russia acquire warm water seaports which would give easy communication with the rest of the world.

The role of Czar Alexander I at the Congress of Vienna in 1815 has been related. Though Alexander was liberal in his youth, Metternich's influence led him to become more harsh and autocratic in later life. His successor, Nicholas I, who ruled from 1825 to 1855, was even more oppressive. He established what was called the "Nicholas System." All printed materials were subjected to a severe censorship to prevent the spread of liberal ideas. A thoroughgoing spy system made unguarded utterances or acts dangerous. Catholics, Jews, and other minority groups were persecuted, since the czar was the head of the Greek Orthodox Church and religious conformity was considered as important as national unity. A revolt of the Polish people in 1830 to regain national independence was ruthlessly suppressed and thereafter Russian administrators were installed in the Polish country. The defeat of Nicholas in the Crimean War at the hands of Turkey, France, and England, did much to weaken the prestige of czarist autocracy, and demands for civil and military reform arose on all sides.

Hence Alexander II (1855-1881) was forced to make concessions. He liberated the serfs, but their economic condition was not greatly improved. He also made other liberal advances. The cities in Russia were given councils, which, however, were only partially elected and had only limited powers. Representative bodies or *zemstvos* were established in rural communities. These had power to deal with

The Assassination of Alexander II—the Wounded Czar Being Conveyed to the Winter Palace

such matters as roads, schools, and other local improvements. They had no influence on national policy, and the demand for a national representative body was denied. Yet, the *zemstvos* provided a valuable forum where liberal and radical leaders could give speeches to arouse the people from their lethargy. All these liberal reforms occurred early in Alexander II's reign. Later, the growth of unrest in Poland and in Russia proper caused him to retrace his steps. He was killed by a bomb hurled at him while he was driving in his carriage.

EARLY REVOLUTIONARY MOVEMENTS

During the middle of the century radical ideas gradually filtered into Russia from abroad. The opposition to autocracy centered mainly around the intellectuals and students, while the mass of people remained illiterate and ignorant. Most of the former were liberals who desired peaceful reforms under a constitutional and limited monarchy. Some were extremists who demanded revolutionary action. Bakunin was a famous anarchist who advocated terrorism. The *V Narod*, or "Go to the People," movement was planned to arouse and liberate the people. Its adherents were mostly students, who employed any and all methods to gain their ends. The movement was smothered in blood and hundreds were exiled to Siberia.

During the nineteenth century a group of Russian literary geniuses astonished the world by their masterful portrayal of Russian life and social conditions. The names and works of Turgenev, Dostoyevsky, and Tolstoi are typical of this group.

Alexander III (1881-1894) expressly denied all demands for reform. He introduced methods to secure the complete extermination of the revolutionists. Thousands were executed or sent to Siberia. The motto of this czar was: "One Russia, one Creed, one Czar." The "Russification" of all national minorities was undertaken. Jews were impoverished, maimed, and killed in pogroms. The hand of a corrupt and ruthless bureaucracy weighed heavily upon the entire people. The secret police became an effective tool in the seeking out of all kinds of opposition. Such was the internal condition of Russia which led to its defeat at the hands of Japan in 1904, and to the revolution of 1905, which was also called the dress rehearsal for the October Revolution of 1917.

The Battle of Tsushima Strait, 1905, in which a Russian fleet was destroyed by the Japanese. (Acme)

64. Agricultural and Commercial Changes

WITH THE CONQUEST OF NAPOLEON and the repartition of his appropriated territories there arose among the victorious nations of Europe a system of thought and policy which was doomed from its inception in view of the prevailing trends. Inaugurated and largely enforced by the efforts of the Austrian noble, Prince Metternich, it was the product of the aristocratic classes, an incarnation of their hopes, wishes, and memories. It was, in effect, an attempt to turn back the clock to the period before the Revolution.

The teachings of Voltaire were to be eliminated from the minds of men: liberty, equality, and fraternity were to become less than words or even memories. No longer were corpulent and well dressed burghers to dictate the policies of nations or empires, or stir their bloodthirsty associates to fury. In Europe, the church was to assume its place again in the hearts of men—Protestant and Catholic alike.

Change was to be ordered carefully. The *ancien régime* was to be restored and the nobles were to take command. Arrayed on their side were the armies of continental Europe. Their opponents were the manufacturers and traders with their allies, the common people. An old order was struggling, in the only way it knew, against its destiny. Its use of force was to prove inadequate against the onslaught of propaganda, science, and free thought—the weapons of the new liberalism.

The Revolution in France had been important for its intellectual, political and institutional results. Over the same period of time there had been occurring in England a less obvious and spectacular series of events which even more profoundly changed the course of human progress. Changes in agricultural and industrial methods, taking place over a period of years, and producing in their wake radical social and economic innovations, started the development of the modern state. These changes, initially unnoticeable and seemingly inconsequential, became prominent in England. It is convenient, therefore, to take England as the pattern of the modern state, and by outlining the steps through which she became industrialized, sketch also the ways in which industrial progress came to other countries.

THE OLD AGRICULTURE

At Crécy and Poitiers in the Hundred Years' War, the English yeomanry had fought bravely and well. As a reward for their loyal service these men had been given grants of land. Other serfs, less fortunate or more crafty, had, by working for years for small wages, managed to purchase their land from the lord of the manor and sometimes were given the legal title to the property. Still others had simply worked the same land for generations and had attached themselves and their families to the soil.

They had no expectation of ever leaving their homes, simple huts though they were. The yeomanry were, in a fashion, happy and contented. They usually had enough to eat, were clothed sufficiently well, and amused themselves with games and holidays and their own particular celebrations and festivals.

As a leftover from the old manorial system, the typical farm of a great noble was divided into many small fields. The great bulk of the land was owned by the lord, while the strips were the property of his peasant neighbors. The great fields were cultivated *en masse*, with certain sections being allowed to lie fallow. Thus an area under cultivation presented a somewhat spotty appearance, with crops growing in certain places and bare fields in other sections. The process was wasteful of land and of effort as well; but for many decades the sight of strip farming, as it was called, did not overly distress the great lord. Gradually, however, a series of changes in agricultural theory revealed to the lord just how he might increase his income by eliminating strip farming.

IMPROVEMENTS IN AGRICULTURE

The wars in which England engaged during the period 1660–1815 took enough of her population from productive activities to help create a food shortage. England imported as much food as possible but it was not enough, and moreover the English people highly resented paying for food that they felt they could have raised. There arose a sentiment for increasing farm production, and in answer to the demand innovations in planting and reaping, in breeding, and in methods of fertilization shortly evolved.

Lord Townshend, who as minister under George III aided in accelerating the American Revolution, spent a great deal of time at scientific farming, devising the system known as crop rotation, by which method each field was made to yield each year, instead of lying fallow once every three years. Lord Townshend was so vigorous in pushing the cultivation of turnips that he was called, by his irreverent friends, "Turnip" Townshend.

Robert Bakewell, observing that animals were raised primarily for such products as wool, hides, and milk and not for meat, began a series of experiments which shortly produced sheep, cattle and horses of superior quality. His breed of cattle called the "New Leicestershire" is still remembered, and so famous was his breed of sheep that he was given twelve hundred guineas for the services of a ram for

one year. It is said that Jethro Tull made two blades of grass grow where one had grown before, through his invention of the drill. This was a planting device which, unlike the wasteful method of hand sowing, spaced seed evenly and in rows. Another of his useful inventions was a hoe by which the ground could be well turned. In a different sphere, Arthur Young, a propagandist for improved agricultural methods, succeeded in 1793 in his agitation for the establishment of an official Board of Agriculture, whose task was to encourage and assist progressive agriculture.

ENCLOSURES

Under these circumstances farming rapidly became a business wherever it was possible to practice these new methods. Profits had been impossible under the old strip system of farming, with each man doing his own work and consuming all he produced; but, if some method could be found to consolidate the small fields under one owner and thus open the way to large scale production, much money could be made. A speeding-up of the enclosure system was the logical solution of this problem.

Parliamentary acts providing for the enclosure of an area were granted on petition of the lord of the manor, or a large landholder, and required the consent of four fifths (later two thirds) of the holders of the land involved. The large landholders' political influence usually obtained enclosure acts' passage. When an act became law commissioners examined the villagers' claims to their land, and, if they found these demands good, placed a valuation upon the property. Then, when the total area had been enclosed, the villager was assigned a solid block of land in that section. The process was filled with discrepancies, because for various reasons the bulk of the yeomanry were unable to produce titles to their land. Over a period of centuries the title may have been lost or perhaps there had been only an unwritten agreement or mutual understanding. In the majority of cases dispossession was swift. The farmer-owners were simply turned adrift in the world, their one occupation and trade taken from them, their habits, customs, and lives disrupted.

THE DESERTED VILLAGE

Penniless, with no means of support except manual labor, the dispossessed yeoman left the village where he had spent his life, and where he had expected that his family would spend theirs, and wandered over England, seeking employment. Those few who managed to establish a title and achieve the position of competitor to the lord, found it impossible to meet the challenge of the new agricultural methods, and were easily bought out at the lord's price. Although agricultural productivity increased, large numbers of the English yeomanry were brought face to face with unemployment and starvation. The landowners grew rich. Crop production increased, and, although there was plenty, disease and starvation took an increasing toll among the landless poor. The contemporary poet, Oliver Goldsmith, wrote of the situation in enduring lines:

**Oliver Goldsmith
(1728-74)**

"Ill fares the land, to hastening ills a prey,
Where wealth accumulates, and men decay.
Princes and lords may flourish, or may fade;
A breath can make them, as a breath has made.
But a sturdy peasantry, their country's pride,
When once destroyed, can never be supplied."

The south of England, where there is the best land, at one time completely cultivated by the strip method, and dotted with small villages and clusters of homes, gradually became deserted. The enclosure movement was only one among numerous great changes occurring in England; the depopulation of half the land of the kingdom cannot be entirely attributed to it alone. Yet unquestionably the enclosure movement, producing as it did many social and cultural problems, and obviously marking the breakdown of feudal civilization, is a most important factor in the concentration of people in cities.

It must be remembered that the so-called Agricultural Revolution is a term used to describe, not a sudden upheaval, but imperceptible changes which took place in England and other countries over a period of many years. And England did not entirely lose its rural appearance because of the enclosure movement, nor was the small farmer everywhere crowded out. Despite the increase in the number of enclosure acts between 1750 and 1810, and the growth of the cities, even today much of England has a rural aspect.

AGRICULTURE IN THE GERMAN STATES AND FRANCE

The tendency toward the concentration of population in cities in the eighteenth century was distinctly an English phenomenon. The nobles controlling France and Germany during the period were intent upon confining the peasantry to the soil. In the tangle of independent states which made up eighteenth century Germany, a group of petty feudal princes and nobles held in check the peasants and commercial classes. Each state, in an attempt to gain as much as possible and also to discourage industry, built trade barriers. The few passable roads were well policed, and the merchant who attempted to carry goods along these routes was compelled to pay duties so many times that, if he added the accumulated taxes to the cost of his goods, he would find no market. If, on the other hand, he attempted to pay the taxes out of his own pocket, he found himself ruined. The same situation occurred along the rivers, and so, while there was commerce, it was only in the most necessary articles.

The great French nobles who still retained power under Louis XIV used force to keep their peasants bound to their land. The nobles managed their estates and raised their crops in the same unscientific fashion as they had for centuries. Under Colbert, minister for Louis XIV, French trade and industry made great strides, and the beginning of a merchant class arose. This class was so small proportionally, however, that its influence was unfelt. Since France was still essentially a feudal state with the peasants unable to move about, the mobile supply of surplus labor necessary for industrial

The Custom-House at Liverpool, a symbol of the era when busy British commerce dominated the trade routes of the world. The cornerstone of the Custom-House was laid in 1828

progress was lacking. The revolutionary movements in 1789 had swung the pendulum the other way, economically speaking, for the great estates of the nobles were confiscated and broken down into a great many small farms, upon which scientific methods of agriculture were impossible.

FACTORS FAVORING ENGLISH INDUSTRIAL DEVELOPMENT

England, having undergone her Glorious Revolution in 1688, and having established class rule, was politically adapted to the arising order. The enclosure measures, for example, brought about by ruling-class pressure, could not have attained their sweeping results under the feudal system. Thus new economic developments influenced political progress.

By the end of the eighteenth century, England was the leading colonial and trading nation. From all over the world, cargoes came to England, there to be turned into manufactured articles or to be resold directly. The merchant class in England had been powerful for many years when Charles was restored to the throne in 1660, and that class has continued to grow in power until the present.

Mercantilism as an economic system was still in vogue at the opening of the eighteenth century. Sir Robert Walpole, Prime Minister of England from 1721-1742, was a confirmed mercantilist. Under him England prospered. Though his efforts were directed largely toward the improvement of internal trade, he did not neglect to sponsor foreign and colonial commerce. England was at that time undergoing an era of speculating in stocks. Companies formed to colonize various parts of the world were numerous, and the desire to possess their stocks and to trade in them seized a large share of the population. The most famous companies were the East India Company and the Muscovy Trading Company, organized in the age of Elizabeth. Later on, the Hudson's Bay Company and the South Sea Company were founded. These were only a few of the many organizations, some of which were in operation from the Elizabethan era until comparatively recent times. The Hudson's Bay Company is still in existence. From the methods used to organize the stock companies and from the profits they produced as well, came another impetus which put England well along the road to industrial organization.

In countries other than England, capital was static. English banking houses developed early, offering a storehouse for surplus capital and a ready supply of funds for new ventures. With the growth of enterprise, insurance companies were organized, originally to protect shipping and later to underwrite almost anything capable of furnishing a premium.

Under these circumstances it is not surprising that invention flourished. Capital was waiting to be put to work. With a sufficiency of labor to do the work at "reasonable" wages and with world markets for the goods produced, a new economic era was at hand.

65. Industrial England

EARLY INVENTIONS

BASICALLY, the Industrial Revolution consisted in the application of power to existing tools, and the consequent improvement and replacement of those instruments. Such a movement had been under way some time before the eighteenth century. In Flanders and parts of Holland, wind power had been used for pumping water and for turning mills. Inventions tending to hasten production, or make it more efficient, were beginning to be adopted. The roots of the factory system, which is an integral part of the Industrial Revolution, were present. England received the benefit of these tendencies through the immigration of religious classes, such as the French Huguenots, and the Dutch Protestants, who left their own countries to escape persecution.

The series of inventions which produced modern industry were different from the previous great human discoveries. They were deliberate and planned, and were created to fill certain specific needs. The printing press had been invented by accident in the fifteenth century. Gunpowder was known for many years before it made essential changes in warfare. But in the modern age inventions are made to order. There occurs a lag in the industrial process, which, if removed, would profit someone. As the process is speeded up in one section, there comes a demand for an invention in some other field. The whole process of production, transportation, and distribution fits into an economic pattern. Changes made in one part effect changes in another part, and produce resulting innovations in society.

Perhaps of all the inventions in England during the early part of the Industrial Revolution, the steam engine was the most important. It furnished power for factories, trains, and vessels. In the process of its development, it awakened the industries of metallurgy and mining. These new industries demanded that new techniques be found for cheaper and more efficient operation.

Long ago Hero, a Greek scientist in Egypt, demonstrated the power of steam. But, other factors being lacking, it brought no change in production and disappeared for a while from history. A Frenchman, Denis Papin, modified the steam engine so that, by means of a long and complicated process, it would furnish power. An Englishman, Thomas Newcomen, produced a further modification of the machine which, with the addition of a boiler, was used widely.

Another Englishman, James Watt, however, really perfected the steam engine. With

James Watt (1736-1819)

James Watt demonstrating his first steam engine, at Glasgow, about 1765. From an original drawing made for the "American Peoples Encyclopedia"

some scientific training and a native ability, he noticed the defects of the atmospheric pump, and rectified them. Where the old engines had required the cylinder to be heated and cooled with each revolution, Watt, by using the power of steam to force the cylinder back and forth, reduced the waste and inefficiency and adapted for the first time, in reality, the power of steam. In 1769, Watt took out a patent for his new engine.

NEW METHODS IN IRON PRODUCTION

It was not until a great deal of further invention and progress had taken place that the steam engine was practical. Methods had to be perfected whereby the machine could be constructed. With the old method of making and working steel, it was impossible to do any fine cutting or grinding such as is done today in lathework. It was impossible also to make castings of a sufficient size and hardness in any quantity. Ultrafine work, as well as large castings, are indispensable to modern industry. Therefore, with the practicability of the steam engine demonstrated, new methods in metallurgy arose.

For centuries, iron had been smelted with charcoal. About 1620 a blacksmith named Dudley attempted to use coal, but since his methods were crude and his neighbors grew fearful that new processes would put them out of work, he was compelled to give up his efforts. But by the middle of the eighteenth century, coal and coke were being used. The

effect of the heat was further increased by the invention of a new machine bellows. Later, wrought iron was invented by Peter Onions and Henry Cort. This process, which resulted in strong iron, free of impurities, included the stirring or "puddling" of the molten iron, and the separation of the iron and the fuel. The puddling burned out most of the impurities by allowing air to come in contact with the metal.

Henry Cort, who had been purchasing agent for the British Navy, invented a method for making steel plates. With the aid of Purnell, he arranged a series of rolls through which the almost molten metal could pass, and thus be made as thin or as thick as desired. Earlier plates had been hammered out by a process so expensive and tedious that it would have greatly hampered the progress of the Industrial Revolution.

The acceleration given to the coal industry by the increased use of coal in steam and smelting, caused new methods to be developed in mining. The steam engine was used to pump water out of the mines and to hoist coal to the surface. In 1815, Sir Humphry Davy invented the invaluable miner's lamp which greatly lessened the danger of explosion below ground.

GROWTH OF THE TEXTILE INDUSTRY

Slightly prior to the advances made in the iron and mining industries were the developments in the textile industry. In this field arose many of the distinctive factors of what is known today as modern industry, and it is desirable, therefore, to discuss these changes in some detail.

About the end of the eighteenth century in England there was a great demand for the gaily colored cloth known as calico. It had been imported from India, but so popular was it that the woolen manufacturers protested. Laws were passed prohibiting the wearing of calico, but laws could not eliminate the demand. From 1721, the date on which the Calico Act was passed, the cotton industry became one of the most important in England. By 1735, the industry had become so strong that it secured from Parliament the repeal of the law against the wearing of calico, provided that a certain amount of linen or wool be combined with the cotton.

In America a young man named Eli Whitney, visiting at the plantation of a friend, was told of the planters' predicaments. They could sell more cotton if it could be prepared more quickly for market. The big drawback was the amount of seeds which had to be pulled from the bolls by hand. Whitney, with this difficulty in mind, perfected the cotton gin which solved the problem, thus giving new life to the institution of slave labor on cotton plantations. It might be said that Whitney, by making possible the production of cotton on such a large scale, laid the groundwork for the Civil War in the United States. At any rate, English mills eagerly snatched at this new source of raw material, and began to flood the world with cotton goods.

Eli Whitney (1765-1825)

THE FACTORY SYSTEM

The modern factory system also developed from the textile industry. From the middle of the fifteenth century, the old system of handicraft and guilds had been breaking down because of the rising demand which they were unable to meet. There had arisen in their place a system of manufacture which was called the putting-out system.

Briefly, the putting-out system was merely the distribution of raw materials to people who worked at home in the intervals between working in the fields. The middleman fur-

The First Cotton Gin, from a wood engraving in Harper's Weekly, 1869. The gin helped make possible the production of cotton on a large scale in the southern states

nished the raw materials and the workers furnished the tools. At certain times, the middleman would come around and collect the finished product and pay the workers. It was a simple system, and easy on the laborer, for it allowed him to choose his own hours and work as much or as little as he pleased. It kept him with his family, he could cultivate his crops, and his personal freedom was unrestricted.

When the demand for cotton goods and other textiles made itself felt, capitalism invaded the textile industry in full force. In its train came a host of inventions which shortly concentrated the workers in factories, took them from their families, and placed a premium not on any mental qualification but only on physical fitness.

Their sons were as well-fitted as they for factory work; and their wives soon found themselves with a certain number of cotton spindles to watch.

Sir Richard Arkwright (1732-92). (Brown Bros.)

CHANGES IN THE TEXTILE INDUSTRY

A weaver named Hargreaves was responsible in a great measure for the new methods in textile manufacture. He saw that a fortune awaited the man who could increase the amount of cotton yarn produced, and he proceeded to find a way. His invention, called the spinning jenny, consisting of a number of spindles run by one wheel, vastly increased the amount of yarn produced. It furnished more raw material to the weavers and makers of cotton goods. He had arrived at the idea, it is said, by watching his wife's spinning wheel, which had fallen upon its side while the wheel continued to spin around. The spinning jenny considerably increased the production of yarn. It soon became evident that the isolated weavers made but insufficient progress and that some more efficient method would have to be found to eliminate the lag in production. This realization was hastened by the invention of Arkwright's "water frame" in 1769, a water powered machine which spun even faster than did Hargreaves'.

Arkwright was a new type in the economic world, the forerunner of the modern captain of industry. He became wealthy through the use of the water frame, which he had taken over from its real inventor, financed, and made practical. His invention was too bulky and expensive to be used by any single merchant; so Arkwright, forming a company, set up his machine and started a factory. He is probably better known for his methods of business organization than for his invention. To him is given the credit for establishing the first disciplinary code governing factory workers.

Emphasis was now shifting from the primitive home manufacturing system to the complex factory organization. It was called forth, as we have seen, by improvements in machinery and methods of distribution. Some sort of factories had existed even before the Industrial Revolution. The yeomen, driven from their land and slowly gathering in the towns, were forced to seek some means of employment. Enterprising men quickly assembled them in groups. Using the tools and implements of the owner, they worked by hand to produce such materials as they could, and for which there was a sufficient demand. With the use of machinery came the necessity for the location of factories near water power and where raw materials were available. Thus the factory town grew up in England. These communities, built for economic reasons solely, were for the most part ugly and poorly planned.

SPREAD OF THE INDUSTRIAL REVOLUTION

Invention and improvement went on at a startling pace in all industrial fields, given the impetus by the early changes made in the basic industries. It is impossible to do more than summarize briefly the most important improvements and their broad effects upon society.

We have seen how changes were made in the methods of spinning, which speeded up the manufacture of textiles. The weaving process was next speeded up; then improvements took place in the dyeing industry. The rise of steam to the supreme place in the power field necessitated improved methods and growth in the steel industry in order to provide its engines and tools. Steel was improved by the introduction of air blasts into the metal, and the use of coal as a fuel greatly facilitated the methods of working in metal. The mining industry, in order to share the profits accruing from mechanization and large scale organization, improved itself, causing resulting changes in handicraft in other industries. To distribute the finished materials, roads had to be built and improved, for although England had depended in the past largely on water transportation for her internal trade, she now had such a volume of produce, needing to be moved quickly, that faster methods were imperative. The railroad and the steamship were invented and perfected to fill this need.

Every invention useful to industry brought forth a succeeding one. Each caused a dislocation and rearrangement of society. Since life and industry are inseparable, a change in one affects the other. As the wheels of the factories turned, meshing into the gears and wheels of the whole industrial fabric, life in England, both economically and socially, was accelerated.

EFFECTS OF THE INDUSTRIAL REVOLUTION

Working conditions in the early factories were generally poor. Sanitary and lighting conditions were inadequate, and the workers, even women and children, sometimes worked as many as 12 to 14 hours a day, or more.

Crowded together in the newly-erected cities in the north of England, thousands of the working people were killed by disease. Tuberculosis, a malady from which they had been free as farmers, afflicted the working population. Malnutrition left them in a wretched physical condition, an easy prey to every type of disease. Social diseases became rampant, and drunkenness and its accompanying evils increased.

Considering these facts, we can understand why the old institutions broke down. A father could offer little in the way of advice, example, or financial aid to his children, for they worked as long as he did and earned their own wages, and consequently were scornful of his authority. The influence of motherhood could not be felt, for mother and child were separated during the most important formative years. There was no place for religion in the crowded life of the working man, and the Church and its ministers lost what influence they possessed. There was no time to devote to learning or cultural pursuits. Physically and mentally the working man became corrupted and his family became disorganized.

These were the temporary, harmful effects of the Industrial Revolution on some of the new concentrations of workers in England. From the viewpoint of production, the large scale manufacturing and distribution techniques of the Industrial Revolution resulted in a wider diffusion of goods than there ever had been in the history of the world. All classes of people soon benefited from the cheaper clothing, tools, and household goods produced by the factories. Capital and labor, united by invention, and called into union by a great demand, utterly transformed the society of the Western world. That society, transformed, proceeded to carry its civilization throughout the world.

66. England in the Nineteenth Century

B Y THE END OF THE Napoleonic period, the middle class was strong in England. The wars had brought profits which could be used to purchase position and power. The slowly dying aristocracy was still in control of government and inclined to direct state affairs so as to perpetuate its supremacy. Industrialists challenged its position successfully in the nineteenth century. The growth of industry in other countries, together with the gradual decline of agriculture, set in motion the same type of social and political movements that evolved in England. The struggles of the decaying aristocracy to maintain its political power against the middle classes are an important factor in nineteenth-century European economic history. The most important development, of course, was the application of steam power to manufacturing.

MERCANTILISM CHALLENGED

The rise to power of the middle classes is a fascinating story. They became so powerful economically that their influence in social and political matters was inevitable. After gaining power over industry and labor, the next logical course was control of Parliament. The first step in the process was the substitution of the theory of free enterprise for the old mercantile theory of economic self-sufficiency and government subsidy, to which the landlords of England still clung tenaciously.

Under the eighteenth century interpretation of this system, internal and foreign trade were regulated for the good of the nation as a whole. In order to keep out a commodity which it was thought desirable to produce within its borders, a nation resorted to the use of tariffs on imported goods which raised their price so high that no one could afford to buy them. Within the country, bounties were offered to people who would produce the excluded commodity. We have seen how this worked in the case of calico. The most

serious defect in the practice of mercantilism was that it cut off a supply of some of the necessary raw materials. Forced to great lengths by this situation, the affected classes—which meant the middle classes—set up an agitation for the abolition of this doctrine.

ADAM SMITH AND LAISSEZ FAIRE

They advanced an opposing theory of their own, which was far reaching in its effects and implications. This theory was called "free trade," or to use the French name by which it is equally well known, laissez faire, which means "let alone." Its chief exponent, Adam Smith, later known as the father of political economy, expounded this theory in the classic *An Inquiry into the Nature and Causes of the Wealth of Nations.*

Adam Smith was born in Scotland in 1723, and devoted his life to literature and study. After some years of training and postgraduate work, he became professor of logic at Edinburgh. He wrote several volumes on philosophy, and was noted for his brilliant prose style as well as for the independent

Adam Smith (1723-90), Scottish economist

Edmund Burke

thought contained in his books. It was not until 1776 that Smith published his famous *Wealth of Nations*, after having spent years in its preparation. Dealing exhaustively with social and political problems, it propounded a new theory of economic and national policy.

Fundamentally the book extends the doctrines of the mercantilists, which declared that the preparation of the state for war was one of the most important functions of a government. But where they had declared that gold, which represented purchasing power, was the chief means to economic domination, Smith declared that consumable goods, or manufactured articles, were most important, for they could be exchanged at any time for gold which in turn could be exchanged for goods. Thus the acquisition of gold became a secondary interest, and the emphasis was shifted to the production of consumable goods as the chief aim of national economy. Trade, industry, and agriculture, Smith argued, interlocked to form an organic whole. If left alone, these various forms of production would seek channels automatically, "as though an Invisible Hand were guiding them," and each man by an appropriate display of industry could secure his just share of worldly goods. Therefore, the government was to keep out of business. By natural law, each man was allowed the rights of "life, liberty, and the pursuit of happiness," and interference with them was akin to interference with the Almighty. Thus the doctrines of free competition, self-interest, and natural law are the chief points in his theory; with the emphasis placed on capital as the basis of wealth. It is important to note here that Smith referred to the capitalist as the chief organizer of capital. He was the man with the means of production, who saw opportunities and was able to take advantage of them. The laborer was simply a part of the manufacturing process, a part of the raw materials, whose purchase price, or wage, was included in the cost of the finished material.

These revolutionary doctrines were eagerly adopted by the rising industrial class. These were the very theories industrialists had been seeking. They could now oppose to the impassioned, liberal, humanitarian orations of Edmund Burke, the choice phrases of Smith, or answer a question in debate with a detailed quotation concerning the making of a pin by piecework. The average middle class industrialist was glad to have at his command such a phraseology, and the logic of the theory appealed to his mind.

Enlightened self-interest became the order of the day. It was preached in the schools and in homes, as the rising tide of industrialism moved upon the weakened bulwark of English aristocracy. A new nation was arising in America, governed by a constitution which was gradually interpreted to follow the theories developed by Smith. After the defeat of Napoleon, France and Germany also produced industrial middle classes.

Attempts to restrain these forces and to turn back the course of history, or to crush the wealthy and powerful new middle class, inevitably failed. Events had moved too swiftly and too steadily to remain under Metternich's control. His system of thought was inundated by the flood tide of changing conditions, and all the soldiers of Europe could not impress it upon the rising class. Time would not stand still, nor progress cease.

MIDDLE CLASS IN POWER

The history of Europe after the fall of Napoleon is the rise to power of the middle class in different countries and the lengths to which they were forced in order to maintain their power. The wars and revolutions of this period arose directly from the struggle of the middle classes for recognition. They soon won the support of the most influential groups, the clergy and the intellectual classes, and through them gained the adherence of many people not of the middle class economically. Propaganda played a large part in the middle class revolutions of the period.

Throughout the nineteenth century England maintained its lead in the race for industrialization. English goods were purchased by the whole world, and the profits from this trade were invested abroad by English capitalists. America, for example, was largely financed by British money in its industrial development. American railroads, steel mills, canals, ships, and factories were made possible by English capital; and much the same procedure took place during the industrial development of France and Germany. The whole world became a profitable field for English investment.

MIDDLE CLASS REVOLTS

The English middle class became powerful enough to command a political majority in 1832, an important date in history. In order to understand this triumph, it is necessary to go back in time to the close of the Napoleonic wars in 1815.

The surrender of Napoleon seriously affected British industry, for it had become accustomed to produce great quantities of military and other supplies. England, to a large extent, had supplied the other belligerent countries with materials, and the loss of these markets was a serious commercial blow. The return of 400,000 soldiers to the ranks of civil life added to the numbers of unemployed. A depression resulted. Starvation and business failures mounted tremendously, although English warehouses were filled with goods ready to be sold, and other European countries had great quantities of grain.

Parliament was controlled by Tory landholders. In an effort to profit from the situation, they increased the tariffs upon imported grain, attempting to monopolize the home market for themselves. Since this legislation directly affected the laboring classes, and was in violent opposition to the doctrines of Adam Smith, the masses and the middle class were infuriated. Parliament did not attempt any legislation which might have benefited the manufacturing class. This group had been drawing money from all of Europe for a long period of time, and the other nations were exhausted. If these countries could have found a market for their farm produce in England, they might have accumulated enough capital to allow them to buy English manufactured goods; but the Tory Parliament refused to cooperate with this international conception of commodity exchange.

Therefore, they aroused the bitter opposition of the middle classes, who saw themselves becoming bankrupt because of the greed of an old entrenched group. As it became apparent that Parliament intended to do nothing for them, the middle class commenced an agitation which they hoped would achieve their end, in spite of parliamentary indifference.

Led by a little group of intellectuals who ceaselessly wrote and argued for political and economic reform, the movement quickly sprang into prominence. Leaders in the group were James Mill, the father of the economist and philosopher; the journalist William Cobbett, and the philosopher Jeremy Bentham. Their chief point of attack was the parliamentary system. A reasonable Parliament, they argued, operating on sound businesslike principles, could quickly pass legislation of a nature that would free trade from its artificial barriers, and end forever the economic miseries of the nation.

They told the populace that a reasonable Parliament would not refuse to admit cheap grain, which would mean an end to starvation. By this means, they managed to gain the support of the working classes, who might provide excellent shock troops in case of a rebellion. They also insinuated that many of the evils of the factory system could be eliminated by law; and intimated that reform, which would give the factory owners control of Parliament, would immediately better the working conditions of labor. This point of view was quickly adopted by several men who were sympathetic with the intolerable condition of the working man, and they became an important additional force to the agitation for reform. Their support allowed the factory owners, for example, to accuse the Tories of cruel and inhuman conduct and motives; to cry to Heaven at their greed; and, in general, to raise against them the finger of righteous scorn and indignation. In fact universal popular opinion soon became aroused against the conservative Tory program.

A riot broke out in London in 1816 when a crowd, inflamed by speakers, committed acts of violence. Immediately the Tories seized upon this as cause for action. They suspended the Habeas Corpus Act, which provided that persons arrested should be charged and brought to trial immediately. The Sedition Act was revised to include all meetings, even those of a literary and scientific nature.

Opposition only stirred the middle classes to increased fury. Juries refused to convict under the Sedition Act, and meetings were held despite the law against them. Many of the larger manufacturers were fearful of this "radical" movement, though they approved the ends toward which it was directed, and they refused to support it. They imagined that such action would lead to anarchy, or at least a "reign of terror," in which they would be the chief, though unfortunate, participants. Despite their attitude, the movement continued to gain power, and became very threatening. The military proved useless against it. It was, however, repressed for a time by the passage of the Six Acts in 1819. These limited the freedom of the press, forbade civilian military training, and made the libel laws and penalties more stringent. Under the measures, the more vehement leaders were imprisoned, and the movement lost much of its violent nature. The reformers were forced to find new channels in which to continue their agitation.

Failure of the grain crop in 1826 forced the Tory Parliament to allow the importation of foodstuffs. This allowed the laborers to buy food more cheaply, and proved to them that the cost of food was too high. The Tories were forced to revise their Corn Laws on a more liberal plan.

PARLIAMENTARY REFORM

By 1830 the majority of the English people had been convinced that parliamentary reform was necessary. They would have refused to support the Tories in a popular election, but

William IV, king of Great Britain, 1830-37. From a painting by Sir David Wilkie. (Toledo Mu. of Art)

by means of the "rotten borough" system they were not given the chance. The "rotten boroughs" were deserted districts, whose right to elect a member of Parliament had never been revoked, for obvious reasons, for the landlords controlled them, and through them, the whole country.

In 1832 popular agitation had reached such lengths that the Reform Bill, which included many other provisions than the redistribution of representation, was forced through the Parliament. It was held up in the House of Lords in a last despairing gesture on the part of the old regime. When William IV, recognizing the favorable popular demand, threatened to force passage of the bill by the creation of new peers, the Tories saw that further resistance was useless. The Great Reform Bill of 1832 passed, and the middle classes came into partnership with the aristocracy in political power.

The act modified the political system in three ways. The "rotten boroughs" were eliminated, and their votes given to the large cities. The conduct of elections was improved and made less expensive by the limiting of the voting period and the adoption of a new system of registration. People whose rent amounted to ten pounds a year or more, or who lived in tenements worth fifty pounds, were allowed to vote. Nevertheless, universal popular suffrage was far in the future.

LABOR REFORM

The wave of reform sentiment awakened in England was not to die with the mere passage of the Reform Bill. The factory owners were compelled to pass in 1833 a bill which did away with the worst features of child labor. This measure was largely the work of Robert Owen, a "utopian" socialist.

Owen had started as a laborer and had risen to the ownership of a factory by hard work and the display of considerable intelligence. Unlike the majority of his associates, he was interested in reforms because he knew from experience the conditions in factories. There was a strong economic motive in his reforms, for he had demonstrated in his own factory that children accomplished as much work, if not more, when they were allowed to rest and have shorter hours, without being driven by harsh overseers. The law applied to textile plants alone, and, while it indicated a tendency, child labor was not eliminated.

Robert Owen (1771-1858) factory reformer

Parliament continued to be besieged by people bent on industrial reform. In 1834 the Poor Law was altered, to bring it up to date from the time of Elizabeth. Many employers, taking advantage of the antiquated system, made their wages so small that laborers were compelled to seek the shelter of the Poor Law. Such a policy reduced payrolls, but it increased taxes correspondingly. The taxpayers protested, as did also the Tories and the smaller manufacturers who could not compete with cheap labor.

CHARTISM

The reforms of the period were largely beneficial to the middle class. The proletariat was little benefited by any of the measures, and, despite the glowing promises of orators and middle class propagandists, they began to feel that their lot was being overlooked. Hence arose the Chartist agitation, which was decidedly a proletarian and lower middle-class movement. It took its name from the "People's Charter," which, so its supporters said, followed in the line of political development begun with the Magna Charta, whose bill of rights had benefited the landlords. The political rights of the industrial class were safeguarded in the Reform Bill of 1832. It was but natural that British workingmen should demand their rights, among which were universal suffrage, annual election of Parliament, and the removal of property qualifications for members of that body.

The Chartist movement was well under way by 1838, and though opposed by all the higher classes, caused a great disturbance in the English life of the period. Its representatives visited all the large towns, where they held demonstrations calculated to arouse the working classes and make them active participants in the Chartist cause. The middle classes feared that the occasional acts of violence would develop into something more dangerous, and so the power of the army was invoked. However the Chartist movement, because of internal dissension, soon suppressed itself. Thereafter, the working classes, lulled by more or less improved economic conditions, made few outbursts.

REPEAL OF CORN LAWS

One other economic goal, the repeal of the Corn Laws, remained for the middle classes to achieve. This last vestige of the old mercantile system was still the chief plank in the platform of the Tories. The measures were recalled in 1846, through the efforts of Richard Cobden and John Bright, two middle class merchants, with an aptitude for expression and politics. The repeal of the Corn Laws, they told the laboring classes, would

Richard Cobden, the "Apostle of Free Trade"

give them cheaper food. They told the industrialists that their business would increase if the United States and other agricultural countries were allowed to sell grain to England, for then those countries in return could buy English goods. The Irish famines, which could have been greatly minimized by the importation of grain, were also a powerful factor.

LATER SOCIAL AND ECONOMIC CHANGES

By the 1880's labor reform demands became more and more insistent as the entire industrial process was speeded up. Liberals forced through Parliament in 1887 an act which forbade mines to employ children under twelve years of age. Four years later a compulsory education act, abolishing tuition fees in elementary schools, provided free training for the children of the laboring classes.

Nevertheless it was not until 1905 that a beginning was made in workingmen's insurance legislation, providing for certain trades.

A campaign against the free trade policy, led by Joseph Chamberlain, exerted considerable influence, although it did not result in a change in the tariff rates. Chamberlain proposed that Britain place duties on foreign foodstuffs and manufactures, but place colonial imports on a preferential list. He felt that such a program would encourage a better imperial feeling, and would benefit local industry and agriculture as well.

Trade-unionism had grown steadily in power and influence since the 1850's. Its agitation had been largely responsible for the granting of suffrage to the laboring classes in 1867, and a few years later for the legalization of the organization of unions and the use of picketing.

The Socialist movement in England took an intellectual turn in the 1880's under the leadership of the Fabian Society. Its membership included such literary figures as Sidney Webb and George Bernard Shaw, who agitated for a program of national socialization of agriculture, industry, and government.

The labor movement had become powerful enough in 1906 to elect twenty-nine workingmen to the House of Commons. With their added influence, considerable labor legislation was passed in the next decade. A new Workmen's Compensation Act increased the employers' liability in industrial accidents and illness. Free employment bureaus were established in 1909, while an attempt was made to set minimum wages in certain industries. Educational facilities were further extended to the lower classes, and old age pensions were established.

Housing legislation provided for adequate planning and building programs for industrial centers. Slums were torn down and parks and modern homes were built in their places.

Perhaps the most far-reaching social legislation came in the National Insurance Act of 1912, providing for an unemployment fund, contributed to by the employee, the employer, and the state.

Another important change, gratefully received by the laboring groups, was the Parliament Bill of 1910-1911, providing for control of finances and public legislation by the Commons and the general election of the members of the House every fifth year.

The reforming element, led by David Lloyd George and other Liberals, had just started a vigorous campaign against "landlordism" when hostilities broke out in 1914. Liberals, Conservatives, and Laborites hastened to fall into line with a policy of imperial defense and unified governmental control. Sentiment for continued changes in the existing social and political order gave way to a patriotic effort to win the war.

George Bernard Shaw, British playwright, one of the early advocates of peaceful socialization. (Copyright by Karsh)

67. Industrialism Comes to France and Germany

CONSERVATIVE REACTION IN FRANCE

THE Bourbon monarchy was restored by the Congress of Vienna. The new king, Louis XVIII, realizing that the France of 1815 would never accept a return to the old feudalism of the earlier period, wisely did not attempt to restore that system.

He gave his people, instead, a charter guaranteeing civil liberties, freedom of the press and religion, and freedom from arbitrary arrest. Despite his liberality, however, he was not popular with the emerging industrial middle class.

When Louis XVIII died in 1824, his brother ascended the throne as Charles X. The latter attempted to restore the old system of things, as well as to bring back the supremacy of the Catholic Church. Moreover, he endeavored to reduce interest on the bonds supporting the public debt, a measure that made him unpopular with the middle classes, whose income was affected. This procedure was adopted in order to give an annuity to the *émigrés*, whose lands had been appropriated during the Revolution. These and other restrictive measures convinced the people that Charles was merely trying to restore the old power of the Bourbons. Hence in July, 1830, when he issued a series of ordinances that repealed Louis XVIII's charter, the people, urged on by the liberal groups, rose against him. The ill-prepared government troops were defeated.

RISE OF THE INDUSTRIAL CLASS

The victorious middle class liberals had led the people to believe that they would set up a democratic state with a constitution and representatives, but, instead, they installed Louis Philippe, a Bourbon who was favorable to their plans. He at once accepted a constitution that guaranteed the same rights that the earlier charter had, and did all in his power to curry favor with the influential middle class.

The latter group was safely intrenched in control of the government, but the working classes and the small farmers were still unrepresented and received little consideration although they had supplied the sinews of war for two revolutions. They proceeded to form a party of their own, under the leadership of the socialist journalist, Louis Blanc. He advocated, as an ideal form of government for France, an industrial republic based on a system of "social workshops," operated by the workers. Competition would be replaced by the principle, "to each according to his needs, from each according to his abilities."

During the reign of Louis Philippe, the Industrial Revolution came to France. English capitalists were eager to invest in a country whose king had the support of the middle classes and who in turn upheld them. There was little coal or iron in France, and that of a poor grade; so the country never reached the stage of industrial development that England did, though water power and charcoal somewhat tended to offset that lack. Moreover, there was a large system of canals and roads which retarded the development of the railroads.

The Jacquard loom, which wove complicated patterns in silk, had been invented in 1804, and from that time on France gradually took the lead in the manufacture of luxury goods. There was a large market for French silks, wines, and brandies, which, together with surplus agricultural products, made France economically the second most important nation in Europe.

REPUBLIC AND EMPIRE UNDER LOUIS NAPOLEON

In 1848 a revolution occurred which swept Louis Philippe out of power; the middle class and the proletariat had again combined against governmental restrictions. Although Blanc, the proletariat leader, attempted to set up his system of national workshops, his plan was and were inclined to support him as long as he kept the revolutionary sentiment of the lower classes quiet. Under the Second Empire, as his regime is called, the middle classes prospered immensely, for Napoleon aided the growing Industrial Revolution to the fullest extent. Capitalism, the faithful ally of industrialism, flourished under his reign. Paris rivaled London as a financial center. The rail-

Louis Philippe, the "Citizen King," ruled France, 1830-48

Marie Amelie de Bourbon, wife of Louis Philippe

Napoleon III, founder and ruler of the Second French Empire

so poorly carried out that it was ineffective, and the schemes of the proletariat soon gave way to the less socially minded plans of the bourgeoisie. Defiantly, the proletariat attempted another uprising, but it was put down by the army. France was proclaimed a republic, and Louis Napoleon, a nephew of Napoleon Bonaparte, was elected president. Soon after he took office, he launched a plan destined eventually to re-establish the power enjoyed by the first Napoleon.

Louis Napoleon suppressed revolutionary movements, but was careful not to alienate the proletariat too much. He sought favor with the industrialists and placated the royalists. Napoleon thus consolidated the most influential elements of France about him, and, in 1851, by a coup d'état, announced himself emperor.

He put down the immediate uprising of the proletariat, although he continued to parley with the propertied groups. They, on the other hand, did not consider his *coup* seriously

roads were improved, roads built, and new factories erected. To improve marketing conditions, Napoleon abandoned the French high tariff policy and allowed the entrance of English iron and steel goods, with the understanding that French wines and brandies be given the same consideration in England.

DEFEAT BY GERMANY

The Emperor had imperial dreams which eventually led to his downfall. In Germany the crafty Bismarck, noting the trend of affairs, and realizing that a strong France meant a weak Germany, decided to end the matter as soon as an excuse presented itself. By interfering with the internal affairs of Spain, which had offered its empty throne to a Hohenzollern, Napoleon gave Bismarck an opportunity to force a war in 1870. This proved to be a succession of German victories, and in two months Louis Napoleon himself was surrounded and forced to surrender.

The provisional government at home attempted to re-equip an army which could cope with Von Moltke, the German commander, but France was forced to admit defeat. The failure of the armies and government produced a new revolutionary outbreak.

The Paris Commune, organized by radical groups, took advantage of the situation and revolted against the control of the National Assembly. They seized Paris with the aid of the mob and attempted to arouse the country. But the bulk of the people refused to join the radicals, and the revolt was suppressed. France was compelled to suffer the loss of Alsace-Lorraine, its chief source of raw materials, and to pay a huge indemnity. The Republic, set up after the fall of Louis Napoleon, struggled valiantly and successfully to provide for the treaty payments and to reorganize the country after the effects of a costly war.

DEVELOPMENT OF THE THIRD REPUBLIC

After a period of confusion and bloodshed, the Republicans assumed leadership under

Louis Thiers, French Republican leader

Thiers. By 1875, the Third French Republic was organized under a liberal constitution. Freedom of the press and of assembly were again guaranteed, while an act of 1884 enabled workingmen to organize into trade unions. Elementary public schools established at this time gave the lower classes welcome educational opportunities.

One faction of the radical and socialist element organized a program of cooperative societies and trade unions which sought to gain desired reforms through liberal legislation. By 1910, the Socialists had obtained over one hundred seats in the Chamber of Deputies. Another faction of the working element, disliking ordinary political methods, used the strike, boycott, and sabotage in an effort to achieve its aims.

Until World War I, France remained predominantly an agricultural nation. The smallness of the farms and the abundance of labor called for little agricultural machinery. As time went on, however, railroads and highways were opened, and market gardening and dairying overshadowed wheat and potato raising. In the eighties, French farmers turned to protective tariffs, cooperative associations, and rural education to offset foreign agricultural competition.

France lost to Germany valuable iron and steel plants, cotton factories, and iron deposits in the cession of Alsace-Lorraine. Industry suffered a staggering blow from this loss for almost twenty years. In 1890 the adoption of a protective tariff policy gave French manufacturers control of domestic and colonial markets. The cotton, coal, and iron industries received a new impetus, and by the time of World War I, France ranked third in Europe in the manufacture of steel.

GERMAN CONFEDERATION

The Congress of Vienna, in 1815, had formed the German states into a loose organization known as the German Confederation. The groundwork for this arrangement had been laid by Napoleon in 1806, when he abolished the Holy Roman Empire and united many of the German states in the Confederation of the Rhine. In order to facilitate the conduct of trade, some of these tiny provinces formed an economic alliance in 1833, called the *Zollverein*, or customs union. This league, brought about through the influence of Prussia, erected barriers against foreign goods but allowed German goods to pass between the members free of duty, established a system of weights and measures, and reformed the currency.

The benefits of this trade association were so apparent that a cry rose for closer union in other matters. The middle class, aided in their affairs by the *Zollverein*, clamored for a national government—not necessarily a republic, but a constitutional monarchy; and their views were elucidated by the remarkable intellectual movement known as German Romanticism. Heine, Goethe, and Schiller, as well as the famous German historians Von Treitschke, Von Sybel, and Ludwig Häusser, played a great part in this development. The philosopher Fichte also enunciated a doctrine of nationalism which had much vogue. This nationalistic spirit, combined with genuine liberalism of the period, resulted in the revolt of 1848 in Prussia. It was put down by the army, but the spirit remained and soon manifested itself in a different form.

Emperor William I of Germany

PRUSSIA SUPREME IN GERMANY

Austria was the dominant factor in German politics, although the state of Prussia was her most dangerous rival. The Frankfurt Assembly, a group of liberals, proposed that Frederick William IV of Prussia assume the leadership of the German people and form a federal empire. Since the proposition came from a revolutionary group rather than from a divine or royal council, Frederick William refused to accept the invitation. It was felt by the middle class that only a war against the power of Austria could unite the nation.

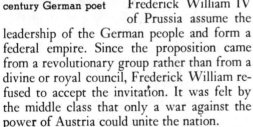

Heinrich Heine, 19th century German poet

Prussia was the logical leader of such a war, since she was the strongest of the German States. Under the leadership of William I and his prime minister, Otto von Bismarck, Prussia made careful military and diplomatic preparations for such a conflict.

The middle class liberals had forced William to accept a constitution, but he believed that he could rule as well as reign under it. In order to defeat Austria, it was necessary for him to build an excellent army, but his plans were fought by the Diet, which feared that a strong military organization would end its power. Bismarck handled the Diet as he pleased, paying as much attention to the Constitution as he chose, and no more. His famous defense of his actions, if so it can be called, explained his views: "Germany looks to Prussia's power, not her liberalism. The great questions of the day are decided not by speeches and majority resolutions . . . but by blood and iron!"

An excuse for war was soon found. In the Danish War in 1864, Austria and Prussia had combined to wrest from Denmark the two duchies of Schleswig and Holstein, to which Prussia laid claim, and which contained, among other prizes, the excellent harbor of Kiel. Isolating Austria from her allies, Bismarck forced a war by seizing both the duchies. In the resulting war (1866) Austria was easily defeated. Placating her, Bismarck turned his attention to France, for he knew that she would be unfriendly to a powerful nation on her border. This hostile reaction finally did result in the Franco-Prussian War in 1870, in which France was completely out-generaled and defeated.

The wars which Prussia fought during this period, the Danish War, the Austrian War, and the Franco-Prussian War, were all

Prussian Leaders in the Franco-Prussian War. King William I of Prussia, right, meeting with his military chiefs. Bending over the map is Von Moltke, and to the king's right is Von Roon. (The Bettmann Archive)

easily won. This gave the German people great confidence in their leaders and led to increased nationalism. Occasionally, to help keep the nation behind him, Bismarck would fling to the working classes some concession which satisfied them for a while and kept them in line with his nationalistic policy.

Germany was governed in effect by Prussia, and Prussia in turn by a king, chancellor, and parliament. The power of the latter body lay in the fact that it could delay or throw out legislation, though only in extreme cases. The Junkers, or Prussian nobles, had great influence, and they enforced many of their policies on the rest of the nation. But Bismarck was able and intelligent and realized that a unified state would have to take ad-

vantage of the industrial movement in order to gain strength, and must, at the same time, keep the working classes happy and contented.

SOCIALISM

Modern socialism, or "scientific socialism," originated with the writings of Karl Marx. A German of the bourgeois class, he was forced to leave Germany because of his agitation for a free press. In Paris, he met his future collaborator, Friedrich Engels. Forced to flee from France, Marx and Engels went to Brussels, where they published the *Communist Manifesto* in 1848. This work contains the essential points of Marx's doctrine, though his thought was later clarified and enlarged in the "Bible" of socialism, *Das Kapital*.

Prussian troops storming the Danish fortifications at Dueppel in 1864. (The Bettman Archive)

The Prussian bombardment of Strasbourg in 1870. (The Bettman Archive)

Briefly, the four essential points of "scientific socialism" are: the economic interpretation of history, the class struggle, the inevitability of a trend toward a socialistic program, and the labor theory of value. Marx, following the method of the German philosopher Hegel, taught that each system produces within itself the seeds of its own destruction; that for every tendency, thesis, in the social world there is a counter-tendency, antithesis, which will overwhelm it. Elements of the two are then combined to form a new, third tendency, synthesis,—which in turn is liable to the dialectic thesis, antithesis, and synthesis.

Capitalism, having overthrown the old feudal system, was itself to be overthrown by the contradictions contained within itself, or by labor. For, argued Marx, the capitalist adds to the value of an article—value being the amount of labor which went into its manufacture—a certain sum, in order to make a profit. The profit is invested in other capitalistic enterprises, which further speed up production, and the effect of which, when carried on for a time, leads to depressions. This in turn causes the common people to lose their buying and consuming power.

These depressions, with other factors, Marx argued, would lead the workers to realize that they were being exploited, and, starved and outraged, they would eventually

rise in wrath against the capitalistic system. For in the past, Marx said, the class struggle had usually resulted in an overthrow of the dominant but outmoded system. This he attempted to prove by his economic interpretation of history; for, he maintained, history is the study of the political forms and civilizations that have arisen in certain types of economic orders— the state and its culture being determined by the economy of the ruling class of people at that time. He predicted that the process which had operated so inevitably and so ceaselessly in the past would not fail to do so in the future. Therefore, said Marx, capital will be concentrated in the hands of a few; and the masses will be in poverty; and then will come the Revolution— the final Revolution, for, understanding the economic and historical process, the people will set up a state which will avoid all political and economic inconsistencies. Under a dictatorship of the proletariat, the people will learn to work and produce for themselves, and will finally be able to do without any state at all. His plea is expressed: "Working men of all the world, Unite! You have the world to gain and nothing to lose but your chains!" This clarion call brought results.

Friedrich Hegel (1770-1831), German philosopher

All over the world various groups arose to carry out the Marxian ideas. In most cases the principles became somewhat changed, as various men, agreeing on Marx's fundamental theses, differed as to the best way of putting them into practice. The First International Workingmen's Association was formed in 1864 by Marx himself; when it broke up it was followed by the Second International.

In Germany particularly the Socialist movement was strong. Therefore Bismarck, though he fought it bitterly, finally was compelled to grant it a certain amount of recognition; but to offset that concession Bismarck went directly to the workers with three radical measures for their benefit. In 1883 laws were passed which provided insurance against sickness; in 1884 against factory accidents; while in 1887 a law was passed providing for industrial regulation, including the limitation of working hours for women and children. In 1889 he established compulsory social insurance for working men. Labor gratefully accepted the three concessions and the threat of revolution dissipated.

To please the industrialists, he provided for a high tariff in 1879, which protected the empire against English and American trade encroachments. This move put the industrial and agricultural classes strongly behind him.

GERMAN INDUSTRIAL DEVELOPMENT BEFORE 1914

Large chemical and electrical works grew up—a tribute to the broad German scientific knowledge. Immense deposits of minerals, from which sulfur, sodium chloride, and potassium salts were extracted, proved invaluable to industrial development. Deposits of coal ·provided the source of the great German dye industry, while, from 1871 to 1914, the output of the mines increased nearly eight hundred per cent.

Industrial progress stimulated German commerce and shipping, and caused a demand for colonial markets in the expanding business field. Large industrial units adopted mass-production, employed scientific advisers, studied foreign markets, and organized cartels or national business trusts, that apportioned the trade among their members. German branch banking institutions appeared all over the world to aid her industrialists and to finance public improvements in near-by countries.

This great economic development affected the social and political life of Germany. Tariff restrictions came as a direct result, and a large urban working class population arose, with the accompanying problems of unemployment, old age, sickness, and accident disability.

Kaiser William II of Germany

Bismarck's program of social amelioration continued even after his dismissal in 1890. The action of the young William II, however, with his haughty, uncompromising attitude toward liberalism, only reinforced socialist reform sentiment. Military preparation went on with startling rapidity. Societies were founded to support the navy, the anti-Semitic feeling, and the spread of German culture. This new crusading spirit permeated all German society, tending to accentuate the European tension and undoubtedly contributing greatly to the war hysteria before 1914.

68. Young America

MONROE, ADAMS, AND JACKSON

JAMES MADISON WAS FOLLOWED in 1817 by his secretary of state, James Monroe. During Monroe's administration—the Era of Good Feeling—the Federalist party disappeared. In the confused election of 1824 no candidate received an electoral

James Monroe

John Quincy Adams

Andrew Jackson

majority, whereupon the House of Representatives chose John Quincy Adams, although Andrew Jackson had received a plurality of electoral votes. Political factions then sprang up, and developed into two new parties—the Whigs and the Democratic Party—the latter representing the so-called Jacksonian democracy. By the 1830's limitations on the franchise had given way almost everywhere to white manhood suffrage, while the principle of free public schools was making progress.

THE SUPREME COURT

Under John Marshall the Supreme Court played an important role in the building of a strong national union. As chief justice from 1801 until 1835, the Federalist Marshall was often a thorn in the flesh to the dominant Republicans. In Marbury v. Madison the Court held that a law of Congress was void if it was contrary to a provision of the Constitution. Later, state laws were similarly in-

Seminole Indian Chiefs being led to their execution, ordered by General Andrew Jackson in 1816

Erie Canal at Lockport, an early view of the locks, from a drawing by W. H. Bartlett. Note the freight boat in the lock, left

Steamboats on the Mississippi, with a flatboat in the foreground. From a Currier & Ives print

validated as being in conflict with the Federal Constitution. In other famous decisions, Marshall and the Court defended the sanctity of contracts and Federal control of interstate commerce, and insisted, in the doctrine of implied powers, that Congress had the power to enact laws broadly conceived in the general interest of the nation.

NATIONAL GROWTH AFTER 1815

With its course as an independent nation firmly established as a result of the War of 1812, the United States entered upon a period of territorial growth and westward movement. Florida was purchased from Spain in 1819 for $5,000,000, after Andrew Jackson had created an international incident by invading the Spanish territory in pursuit of marauding Seminoles. The settlement of the frontier was facilitated by such internal improvements as the National Road, the Erie Canal, and the Chesapeake and Ohio Canal, and by the development of steam navigation on the Ohio, Mississippi, and the Great Lakes. To the original 13 states had been added 11 others by 1830, while in four decades the population had increased from 3,929,214 to 12,866,020. Washington, D. C., a mere village when first occupied by the government in 1800 (the Federal government had first met briefly in New York and then 10 years in Philadelphia), had a population of 18,826 in 1830. Most of the population growth was natural increase; the immigration during the decade 1821–30 was 151,824, nearly all of which had come from the British Isles.

The Beginnings of Washington, D. C. The first White House under construction in 1798

SOCIAL AND ECONOMIC DEVELOPMENT

Among the significant events in the industrial growth of the country were: the spinning mill built in Rhode Island by Samuel Slater (1791); the invention of the Cotton Gin by Eli Whitney (1793); the introduction of a solid cast-iron moldboard for plows (1797); and the first successful trip of Robert Fulton's steamboat, the *Clermont* (1807). Aided by these inventions and many thousands of others, the Industrial Revolution was transforming American life, using water power chiefly at first but shifting to steam power about 1810. A new class of industrial workers appeared, and by 1830 they had begun to organize labor unions, although on a small, uninfluential scale. The first daily newspaper was published in Philadelphia in 1784; by 1809 there were 27 dailies in the country; in 1828 the number of all dailies, weeklies, and periodicals was 2,800.

With the coming of independence the American branch of the Church of England became the Protestant Episcopal Church. Other denominations likewise quickly reorganized as national churches. There was a serious decline both in religious activity and church membership during and after the Revolution; then came the "Second Awakening" (1797–1805), which swept the nation. Prominent in this revival, especially in frontier regions, were the new denominations, the Methodists, Baptists, and Disciples of Christ. The Methodists grew

The Clermont, built by Robert Fulton, was the first successful steamboat in the United States

from less than 15,000 in 1784 to 200,000 in 1816. Frontier "circuit riders," who rode from one small congregation to another, played an important part in this development. During this period the remaining state churches were deprived of public support; Connecticut took this step in 1818, New Hampshire in 1819, and Massachusetts in 1833.

CULTURAL DEVELOPMENT

From the early national period until at least the third quarter of the 19th century, American cultural life was dominated by romanticism and remained closely dependent on European traditions. In literature especially, however, native themes early found exponents of genius. Washington Irving (1783–1859) introduced American versions of European legends in his famous *Sketch-Book* (1819–20) and showed an urbane interest in the life of the western frontier (*A Tour on the Prairies*, 1835; *Astoria*, 1836); James Fenimore Cooper (1789–1851) achieved a fictional panorama of the frontier in his "Leather-Stocking Tales" (1823–41); Henry Wadsworth Longfellow (1807–82) turned native traditions into distinguished verse (*Evangeline*, 1847; *Hiawatha*, 1855); Nathaniel Hawthorne (1806–64) portrayed the Puritan soul in powerful, brooding novels (*The Scarlet Letter*, 1850; *The House of Seven Gables*, 1851); and the self-chanting poet, Walt Whitman (1819–92), sought to express the quintessential spirit of America in his facile, loping, exultant strophes (*Leaves of Grass*, 1855). Exceptionally, Edgar Allan Poe

Slater's Mill, in Pawtucket, R. I., built in 1793, was the second cotton mill in America

American Authors of the Nineteenth Century. Left to right: Washington Irving, James Fenimore Cooper, Henry Wadsworth Longfellow, Nathaniel Hawthorne, and Walt Whitman

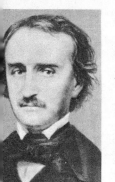

More Nineteenth-Century American Authors. Left to right: Edgar Allen Poe, Ralph Waldo Emerson, Julia Ward Howe, John Greenleaf Whittier, and William Cullen Bryant

(1809–49), who made a magnificent art form of the short story, generally ignored the American scene in his macabre verse and stories.

Much of the literature of the "American Renaissance" (1830–1860) reflects the influence of Transcendentalism, an eclectic romantic movement in philosophy and art which developed in New England among the followers of Ralph Waldo Emerson (1803–82). Preaching doctrines of optimism, self-reliance, individualism, and absolute personal liberty, this Yankee offshoot of Neo-Platonism and European romanticism was ultimately religious, being based on the notion of the immanence of God in the world and in the individual soul. These ideas tended to shape the ideas not only of Emerson and his friends (Margaret Fuller, Bronson Alcott, James Freeman Clarke, Orestes Brownson), but of many other contemporary writers. The inward-minded Hawthorne was drawn to the nebulous Transcendentalist creed, as was Julia Ward Howe, author of the stirring "Battle Hymn of the Republic." Similarly, various Transcendentalist notions found expression in the works of Longfellow and Whitman, in the rustic lyrics of John Greenleaf Whittier (1807–92), in the memorable verse of William Cullen Bryant (1794–1878), and in the various poems and essays of James Russell Lowell (1819–91). In a modified form, this curious mysticism also appears in the novel *Moby-Dick*, the greatest work of Herman Melville (1819–91).

American art and architecture closely reflected European trends. The most notable developments up to the Civil War were the establishment of the native Hudson River School of landscape painting (1803) and the Greek Revival in architecture, which began about 1815 and extended up to the Civil War.

69. Expansion, Sectionalism, and Slavery

TEXAS

With "MANIFEST DESTINY" dominating American foreign policy, the national boundaries reached their present continental limits before the Civil War. In the Southwest American settlers began entering Texas in the 1820's shortly after Mexico became independent from Spain. Conflicts over government, land, and slavery soon broke out between the Mexicans and the Americans. In 1836 the Texas colonists revolted and after bitter fights, among them the famous "last man" stand at the Alamo, and Sam Houston's smashing victory over the Mexicans at San Jacinto, set up an independent republic; they next asked for annexation to the United States. American politics delayed action, the principal objection being opposition in the North to the admission of another slave state. In 1844 the Democrats won the election with their candidate James K. Polk and a platform demanding "the re-annexation of Texas and the reoccupation of Oregon"; Texas was thereupon annexed and admitted to the Union in 1845.

MEXICAN WAR

The next year the Mexican War broke out when American troops were sent into a terri-

Last stand of the Texans, in the Battle of the Alamo. (Brown Bros.)

The Battle of Chapultepec, an American victory in the Mexican War. (Three Lions)

Gold Mining in California during the early days of the Golden State. A Currier & Ives print

tory claimed by both Texas and Mexico. Gen. Zachary Taylor led an expedition into northern Mexico and won the battles of Palo Alto, Resaca de la Palma, Monterey, and Buena Vista. Gen. Winfield Scott led a second expedition from the sea, which captured Veracruz, and then proceeded to Mexico City, winning battles at Cerro Gordo, Contreras, San Antonio, Churubusco, Molino del Rey, and Chapultepec; the capture of the capital practically ended the war. A minor but important expedition was led by Col. Stephen W. Kearny from Fort Leavenworth over the Santa Fe Trail; after capturing New Mexico part of the little force went on to California to help establish American control there. By

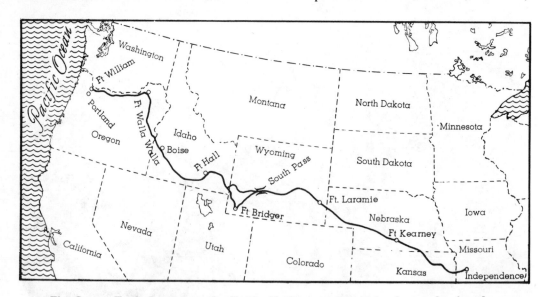

The Oregon Trail, the route to the Pacific Northwest followed by thousands of settlers

Martin Van Buren

William H. Harrison

John Tyler

James K. Polk

the Treaty of Guadalupe Hidalgo, Mexico in exchange for $15,000,000 gave up what is now the southwestern portion of the United States. By the Gadsden Purchase (1854) the United States acquired a small additional tract in what is now southern Arizona and New Mexico.

OREGON AND CALIFORNIA

Meanwhile in 1846 the dispute over Oregon had been compromised, the parallel of 49° being extended to the Pacific. Settlers had already been journeying the long way to Oregon, and now their numbers increased. Over the Oregon Trail, thousands, with their families, household goods, and supplies, drove their wagons into the Pacific Northwest, and others took the California cutoff. The discovery of gold in California started a rush to the new territory. The "Forty-niners" arrived in such numbers that, in 1850, after a bitter fight over its prohibition of slavery, California was admitted as a state. Oregon, settled more slowly, entered the union in 1859.

DEMOCRATS, WHIGS, AND REPUBLICANS

In the election of 1828 John Quincy Adams, running for re-election, was defeated by Andrew Jackson; party lines were confused, the factions being called Clay-Adams men and Jackson men, later National Republicans and Democratic Republicans respectively. By 1834, after the re-election of Jackson, the National Republicans had become the Whigs and their opponents the Democrats. Important events of Jackson's administration were: the establishment of the Spoils System in the Civil Service; Jackson's veto of a bill rechartering the Second Bank of the United States (established in 1816); and Jackson's firm stand in the Nullification controversy with South Carolina. The Democrats won again in 1836 with Martin Van Buren, but in 1840, weakened by the Panic of 1837, they lost to the Whigs, who conducted a spectacular campaign with a military hero, William Henry Harrison. The new president died a month after taking office; the

Zachary Taylor

Millard Fillmore

Franklin Pierce

James Buchanan

The Webster-Hayne Debate: Daniel Webster speaking during the Nullification controversy of 1830

ically profitable, the northern states abolished it between 1774 and 1804. In the South, however, the invention of the cotton gin revived slavery, and soon it was regarded as good for both whites and Negroes. The matter first became a political issue in 1819 when Missouri applied for admission as a slave state; the controversy was settled by the Missouri Compromise, which balanced Missouri with the admission of the free state of Maine, and provided that thereafter slavery should be prohibited in the Louisiana Purchase territory

John C. Calhoun (1782–1850)

presidency passed to John Tyler, who spent most of his term opposing the policies of the Whig leaders. In 1845 the Democrats returned to power with James K. Polk, but four years later they lost when the Whigs presented another military hero, Zachary Taylor. Taylor died in 1850, and his office passed to Millard Fillmore. The Democrats won in 1852 with Franklin Pierce and in 1856 with James Buchanan, both of whom were northern men satisfactory to the South. Minor parties during the period were the Anti-Masonic Party, the Free Soil Party, the Know-Nothing Party, and the Liberty Party. In 1854 a major political regrouping began with the appearance of the Republican party, which developed during the bitter slavery controversy which occurred after introduction of the Kansas-Nebraska Bill. In 1856 the Republicans nominated John C. Fremont, but lost in a fairly close election.

PRELUDE TO THE IRREPRESSIBLE CONFLICT

Before the Revolution Slavery was generally regarded with disapproval by most of the leading persons, even though it was legal in all the colonies. Finding slave labor not econom-

north of 36° 30′. The growing sectionalism was deepened by the tariff controversy, the industrial North favoring tariff protection, the agricultural South opposing it. Under the so-called American System tariff rates were raised in 1824 and 1828; this policy brought on South Carolina's threat of Nullification, which was settled by President Jackson's firmness and a compromise law reducing tariff rates. Meanwhile the Abolitionists were gaining strength, led by William Lloyd Garrison, James Birney, Elijah Lovejoy, Wendell Phillips, Theodore Parker, Gerrit Smith, and Lucretia Mott. In the controversy John C. Calhoun was the spokesman of the South, Henry Clay was "the great compromiser,"

The Compromise of 1850. Henry Clay speaking in the U.S. Senate in behalf of the compromise measures he introduced to settle the controversy over the admission of California as a free state

while Daniel Webster took a strong stand for the preservation of the Union.

The abolitionists were unsuccessful in opposing the annexation of Texas, but during the Mexican War through the Wilmot Proviso they proposed that slavery be forbidden in the territory about to be acquired. This issue was deepened when California asked to be admitted as a free state; its admission would upset the balance which had hitherto been preserved. Under the Compromise of 1850, sponsored by the aging Clay, California was admitted, territorial governments were set up in Utah and New Mexico without mention of slavery, and an amendment to the Fugitive Slave Law was adopted. In 1854 the South won what appeared to be a great victory in the passage of

the Kansas-Nebraska Bill, which was sponsored by Stephen A. Douglas of Illinois; this act repealed the Missouri Compromise, and permitted the people of each new territory to determine the matter of slavery—called Popular Sovereignty by advocates, squatter sovereignty by opponents. Out of this controversy came the new Republican party, which was founded to oppose the extension of slavery. The decision of the Supreme Court in the Dred Scott Case, which threatened the main tenet of the Republicans, only intensified their determination. Other events and forces which pointed to a clash were: the struggle over slavery in Kansas territory, the Underground Railway aiding fugitive slaves, and John Brown's raid on Harper's Ferry.

The Capture of John Brown. U. S. Marines, under the command of Col. Robert E. Lee, storming John Brown's "fort" at Harper's Ferry, October 16, 1859

70. Civil War and Reconstruction

SECESSION OF THE SOUTHERN STATES

IN 1860 THE REPUBLICANS nominated for the presidency Abraham Lincoln of Illinois, who in the senatorial election of 1858 had gained national prominence in the Lincoln-Douglas debates. The Democrats split, the northern group nominating Stephen A. Douglas of Illinois and Herschel Johnson of Georgia, the southern group choosing John C. Breckenridge of Kentucky and Joseph Lane of Oregon. The Constitutional Union Party—composed largely of remnants of the defunct Whig party—nominated John Bell of Tennessee and Edward Everett of Massachusetts. Lincoln received 180 electoral votes to 123 for his three opponents, but in popular votes his total of 1,857,610 was 930,124 less than the combined opposition. The southern secession movement began with South Carolina; it was followed by Mississippi, Florida, Alabama, Georgia, Louisiana, and Texas; after the beginning of hostilities Virginia, Tennessee, North Carolina, and Arkansas joined the secessionists. The southerners promptly organized the Confederate States of America with the capital at Montgomery, Ala. (later

Debates with Stephen A. Douglas in 1858 made Abraham Lincoln a national figure. (Brown Bros.)

Richmond, Va.); Jefferson Davis was chosen president with Alexander H. Stephens as vice-president.

PRELIMINARY MOVES AND OPENING BATTLES

Following President Lincoln's decision to send supplies to Major Robert Anderson at Fort Sumter in Charleston harbor, the Confederate forces of Gen. P. G. T. Beauregard began firing on the post (April 12, 1861), which surrendered the next day. Lincoln then issued a call for 75,000 troops, and soon afterward he ordered a rigid naval blockade of the Confederacy. The only important battle of 1861 was fought at Bull Run, which resulted in a serious Union defeat. Both sides spent most of the year recruiting and drilling troops. In the Trent Affair of late 1861, a U.S. naval officer forcibly removed two Confederate envoys from a British vessel. Lincoln was forced to yield to British demands that the two men be released, with an apology.

Abraham Lincoln, from a photograph made eleven days before he delivered his "Gettysburg Address"

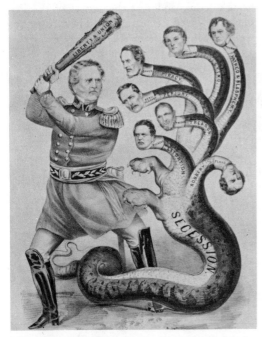

"The Hercules of the Union," a cartoon showing Winfield Scott, senior officer of the U. S. Army in 1861, attacking secession leaders. Too old for active wartime service, Scott retired in late 1861

BATTLES AND LEADERS

In 1862 Gen. George B. McClellan launched the Peninsular Campaign against Richmond, but in the Seven Days' Battle the Confederates, led by Joseph E. Johnston and Robert E. Lee, forced him to retire. Then after defeating Gen. John Pope at the Second Battle of Bull Run, Lee invaded Maryland but was checked by McClellan at Antietam. In December, 1862, Gen. Ambrose E. Burnside attacked Lee at Fredericksburg, but was repulsed with heavy losses. In May, 1863, "Fighting Joe" Hooker, the new commander of the Army of the Potomac, advanced against Lee's Army of Northern Virginia, at Chancellorsville. Although his troops numbered 60,000 as against Hooker's 130,000, Lee, with "Stonewall" Jackson, who was mortally wounded in the battle, soundly defeated the Northern army and forced it back across the Rappahannock. Meanwhile, in the West, Union forces led by U. S. Grant and Don C. Buell, captured Forts Henry and Donelson, and won victories at Shiloh and Perryville.

The First Reading of the Emancipation Proclamation, July 22, 1862

TURNING OF THE TIDE

On Jan. 1, 1863, President Lincoln issued his Emancipation Proclamation declaring free all slaves in the areas then "in rebellion against the United States." By this time both sides were fully mobilized to the extent that their inefficient conscription systems permitted. In the spring of 1863 Lee and his victorious army invaded Pennsylvania. Gen. George G. Meade, the new commander of the Army of the Potomac, followed Lee carefully. The two armies

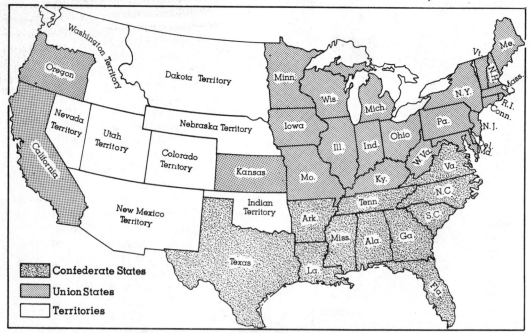

Union and Confederate States During the Civil War

Top left, photograph of a young Union soldier in full uniform. Top right, a Confederate camp in 1861. Center left, commissary department in a camp of the 6th Mass. Volunteers, 1861. Center right, "The Camp Barber," an 1863 drawing. Bottom left, Union prisoners in a camp at Salisbury, N. C. Bottom right, ambulance drill by one of the first army field medical units

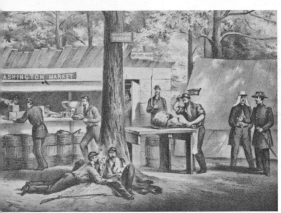

Lincoln and Officers of the Army of the Potomac after the Battle of Antietam. Facing the President is Maj. Gen. George B. McClellan, and on Lincoln's immediate right is Capt. (later Maj. Gen.) George A. Custer

met at the little town of Gettysburg, Pa., and in a great three-day battle (July 1–3) Lee was defeated. Meanwhile, Gen. Grant, after a skillful campaign had enabled him to approach Vicksburg, Confederate bastion on the Mississippi, was besieging the city. On July 4 he captured it, thus establishing complete Federal control of the Mississippi. (Commodores David Farragut and David Porter had captured New Orleans in April, 1862.) At Chickamauga the Federal army under William Rosecrans and George Thomas was seriously defeated by Braxton Bragg, but later in the Chattanooga Campaign Grant won a spectacular victory. By this time the fate of the Confederacy was sealed: the naval blockade had seriously crippled the Confederate economy; the hope of recognition by Great Britain and France had disappeared; Great Britain had tightened her neutrality regulations. Northern superiority in numbers, industry, and wealth was beginning to show its effect.

Gen. Robert E. Lee with his son, Maj. Gen. G. W. C. Lee, and his aide, Col. Walter Taylor. (Meserve)

Lt. Gen. U. S. Grant, commander-in-chief of the Union armies in the last year of the Civil War

LAST YEAR OF THE WAR

With Grant in supreme command the Army of the Potomac began a long series of hammering operations against Lee in Virginia; bloody battles were fought in the Wilderness, at Spottsylvania Court House, Cold Harbor, in the Shenandoah Valley, and in the siege of Petersburg. In the west Gen. William T. Sherman won a series of battles against Joseph E. Johnston and John Hood in his advance on Atlanta, which he captured in September, 1864.

"Monitor" and "Merrimack" in the first battle between ironclad warships

The Battle of Atlanta: a scene from the Cyclorama made by German and American artists

Sherman then began his March to the Sea. He cut a 60-mile swath across Georgia, tearing up railroads and burning cotton and grain. Sherman reached Savannah in December, 1864.

After a nine-month siege Petersburg fell on April 2, 1865, and Richmond was evacuated at the same time. The end came with Lee's surrender at Appomattox. Meanwhile Sherman had marched from Savannah through the Carolinas; on April 26 he accepted the surrender of Johnston near Durham, N. C. Jefferson Davis, his regime in complete collapse, was captured on May 10.

The Battle of Gettysburg, which marked the turning of the tide in the Confederacy's struggle

The Battle of Vicksburg: a Union assault on the Confederate lines guarding the city

General Lee signing the surrender terms at Appomattox Court House, Virginia, April 9, 1865

RESULTS OF THE WAR

The war sealed American unity; it was the victory of Nationalism over Sectionalism; it established a sound basis for the Federal Union, and it settled for all time the dispute as to the location of Sovereignty; it laid to rest the disruptive doctrines of Nullification and Secession. Slavery was ended: the house was no longer divided against itself. But the debit side likewise was heavily weighted: the War Between the States—an irrepressible conflict partly because of hot heads and weak statesmen on both sides—had cost the victorious forces 359,528 death casualties, while the Confederates had lost approximately 258,000, not counting the wounded and the permanently disabled; the financial cost is calculated at about $3,250,000,000 to the Union and $1,-500,000,000 to the Confederacy; with pensions and interest on war debt added the grand total would exceed $10,000,000,000. Large sections of the once prosperous South were devastated; the southern economy was wrecked, and its social order was undermined; and long after the healing of the physical destruction there lingered memories both fond and bitter—memories of a lost cause, celebrated in legend, song, and story, and memories of war's cruelties.

Interior of a Union military hospital, Carver Hospital, Washington, D. C., September, 1864

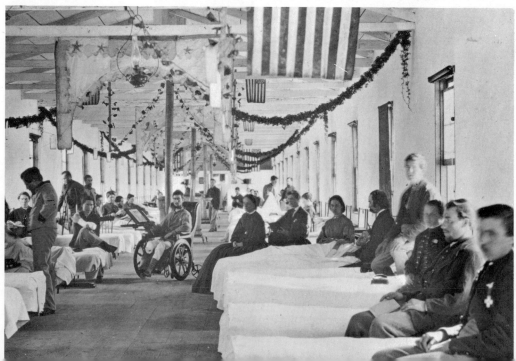

WARTIME LIFE AND POLITICS

In the North business prospered during the war. With southern opposition eliminated by withdrawal, Congress raised tariff rates to please the industrial community and enacted the Homestead Law for the benefit of farmers. In politics Lincoln's conduct of the war was complicated by a large Copperhead element opposing the war, by abolitionists demanding immediate emancipation of the slaves, by congressional committees appointed to investigate the conduct of the war, and by the "Radical Republicans" who advocated stern punishment for the southern "rebels." In 1864 the Republicans reluctantly renominated Lincoln and then named Andrew Johnson of Tennessee, a Union Democrat, as his running mate, while the Democrats nominated Gen. George B. McClellan and George H. Pendleton. Lincoln won with a large electoral vote but by a small popular majority. In the field of foreign relations a controversy developed with Great Britain over the *Alabama* and other Confederate commerce raiders built in British shipyards. When the American minister accused the British government of a breach of neutrality the practice was stopped. After the war the United States secured through arbitration arranged under the Treaty of Washington, in 1871, an indemnity of $15,500,000.

A BROKEN UNION RECONSTRUCTED

President Lincoln, holding that the states could not legally secede and believing that leniency was the best policy, adopted a liberal and easy program to restore the 11 states to the Union. After Lincoln's assassination (April 14, 1865) President Johnson adopted the policy of his predecessor. Congress, however, refused to accept the presidential reconstruction; this led to the historic feud between Congress and President in which the latter was impeached but escaped conviction by one vote. The southern states (except Tennessee) were subjected to military government and to domination by the freed Negroes, the "Scalawags," and "Carpetbaggers" before they were eventually restored to the Union. By 1870 the last of the states had been restored. Finally in 1877 President Hayes removed the Federal troops, thus permitting the South to wipe out every vestige of the reconstruction program. During this period three constitutional amendments were adopted—the Thirteenth abolished slavery, the Fourteenth was designed to confer civil rights on the freedmen, the Fifteenth was intended to guarantee them the franchise.

Death of Lincoln, April 15, 1865. From a painting

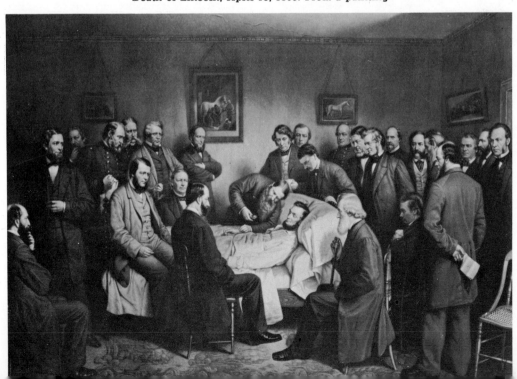

71. Industrialization
and Social Change

HALF A CENTURY OF GROWTH

From 1870 to 1920 the population of the United States increased from 38,558,371 to 105,710,575, while the number of states rose from 37 to 48. During the Civil War West Virginia was admitted in 1863 (following a Unionist revolt against Confederate Virginia) and Nevada in 1864; they were followed by Nebraska in 1867. Colorado was admitted in 1876; Montana, North Dakota, South Dakota, and Washington became states in 1889, and were followed by Idaho and Wyoming the next year; and by Utah in 1896; the last three were Oklahoma in 1907, New Mexico, and Arizona, both in 1912. During this half century 26,277,565 official immigrants entered the United States. Prior to 1890, most of the immigrants had come from northern and western Europe. After this date, the majority came from southern and eastern Europe.

MARCH OF THE IRON HORSE

The railroad age in the United States began in 1830, when steam engines were first installed on the Baltimore and Ohio and the Charleston and Hamburg Railroad (South Carolina). Many railroads were projected and started during the years following but progress was stalled by the Panic of 1837; by 1845 railroad construction was again under way, and was greatly accelerated during the 1850's. Canals were now almost forgotten. Soon the original small units were combined into great companies for efficiency of operation, an example of which was the New York Central, formed in 1853. The Galena and Chicago, later absorbed by the North Western Railway, gave Chicago its first rail service in 1848; four years later the Michigan Central reached Chicago to give the city rail connections with the East. Another notable event was the completion of the Illinois Central in 1856. The railroads played an important role during the Civil War. Transcontinental railway service first became a reality in 1869 when the Union Pacific united with the Central Pacific at Promontory Point, Utah. The period after the

Completion of the first transcontinental railroad at Promontory Point, Utah, May 10, 1869

General Custer's Last Stand, in the Battle of the Little Big Horn, June 25, 1876. An artist's conception, for there were no survivors in Custer's immediate command

Civil War was a time of great railroad construction, as shown by the following figures on rail mileage: 1840, 2,709; 1850, 8,683; 1860, 30,283; 1870, 53,878; 1880, 94,671; 1890, 163,597; 1900, 193,346; 1910, 240,439; 1920, 252,845.

LOST FRONTIERS

For nearly 300 years the moving Frontier was one of the strongest forces transforming Europeans into Americans. According to the theory of Frederick Jackson Turner the frontier was a state of society in which old processes and ideas underwent continuous adaptation to the requirements of the new communities. By 1890 the frontier had come to an end. According to the Turner theory the country had lost its "safety valve"; no longer did it have free cultivable lands beckoning to the discontented of the settled sections. The United States thereupon, according to this theory, began a new phase of its history. Some other historians disagree.

After the Civil War the tribes of the Great Plains and western regions, especially the Sioux, fought numerous wars to prevent the occupation of their homeland. The Indians won some victories, the most notable being the Little Big Horn battle, in which they killed General Custer and a large part of his command. But by 1880 most of the tribes had been removed to reservations, and after that time only sporadic Indian outbreaks occurred, and these were easily dealt with.

"A Dash for Timber," a painting by Frederic Remington. (City Art Museum, St. Louis)

WESTWARD, THE STAR OF EMPIRE

Scenes portraying the westward sweep of the American people in the nineteenth century. Top left, "Astoria, 1812," artist's conception of the fur trading post built in the Oregon country by an expedition sent out by John J. Astor. Top right, view in 1881 of Fargo, Dakota Territory, the head of steamboat navigation on the Red River. Center left, Overland Mail stagecoach used on route which ran from Tipton, Mo., farthest point west reached by Pacific Railway, and San Francisco. Center right, painting by John S. Curry of the Oklahoma land rush of 1889. Below, "Independence Rock," painting by William H. Jackson of an emigrant camp at a well-known point along the Oregon Trail. (C. S. Jackson)

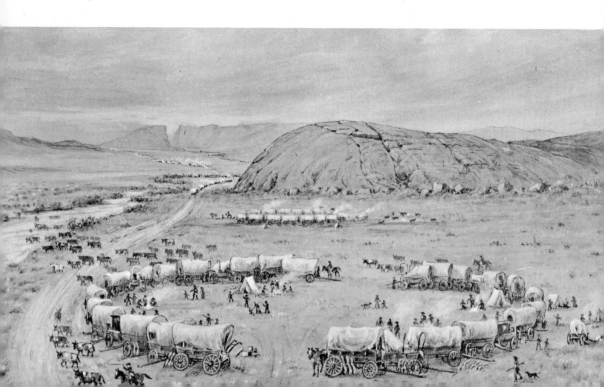

CAPTAINS OF INDUSTRY AND CAPITALISTS

Under the ruling doctrines of Individualism, Laissez Faire, and Liberalism, the Free Enterprise system reached its highest development in the United States in the decades after the Civil War. By 1900 Capitalism had transformed the country from an agricultural land to an industrial society. This American Industrial Revolution was characterized by the introduction of numerous new inventions (such as the telephone, telegraph, numerous electrical inventions, and later the automobile)

Andrew Carnegie
(Carnegie Inst.)

and by the exploitation of hitherto little used resources (such as petroleum, steel, and aluminum). Great industrial leaders appeared in many fields, an outstanding example being John D. Rockefeller of the Standard Oil Company. Other notable captains of industry were Andrew Carnegie and H. C.

J. P. Morgan
(Brown Bros.)

Frick in steel, Cornelius Vanderbilt and James J. Hill in railroading, George Westinghouse in electricity, Philip D. Armour and Gustavus F. Swift in meat packing. There was a corresponding growth in the banking field. Among the most prominent financiers were Jay Cooke and John Pierpont Morgan. Such men wielded much influence because of the part they played in financing new industries.

Agriculture was still dominant in large areas in 1914. But the rise of industry and its new production techniques were transforming America and giving it a standard of living higher than any the world had seen.

MERGERS AND MONOPOLIES

The trend toward Monopolies began in 1879 with the formation of the first Standard Oil Trust. According to the census of 1900 there were 185 industrial combinations, 73 of them capitalized at $10,000,000 or more, turning out 14 per cent of the nation's industrial production. In 1901 came the organization of the United States Steel Corporation. Among the forms of combinations and mergers were pools, Gentlemen's Agreements, Holding Companies, and interlocking directorates. By such methods the captains of industry managed to curb—and sometimes almost to eliminate—competition, which in practice was often wasteful. Another motive behind such combinations was the desire for greater economy of production.

ORGANIZATION OF LABOR

Although labor organization began in the United States before 1800 it made little progress during the first half of the century. By 1860 it was estimated that the total membership of all unions was under 250,000. In 1869 the Knights of Labor was organized; it grew slowly at first, but after 1880 it boomed in membership, reaching a membership of 600,-000 or 700,000 by 1886, after which time it declined rapidly. The Knights of Labor was organized as a single disciplined army for political action and social reform. The American Federation of Labor, which was organized in 1886, quickly replaced the older organization; under the able direction of Samuel Gompers the A. F. of L. dominated the American labor movement for nearly 50 years. Even so the great majority of American workers remained unorganized; in 1920, after a great wartime gain in membership, the A. F. of L. had about 4,100,000 members. A short-lived revolutionary organization of the World War I

Samuel Gompers

Haymarket Riot, 1886, in which eight Chicago policemen were killed by an anarchist's bomb

period was the Industrial Workers of the World. Notable strikes were the following: the railroad strikes of 1877, in which state militia and Federal troops were used to suppress violence; the widespread strikes in 1886 for the eight-hour day, resulting in the Haymarket Riot; the Homestead Strike of 1892; the Pullman Strike of 1893; and the coal strike of 1902.

UP AND DOWN WITH THE BUSINESS CYCLE

The period after the Civil War was generally prosperous for eight years; then came the Panic of 1873, which was one of the most severe in American history. The upturn came in 1879 and continued until the minor depression of 1883–85. Ten years later came the severe Panic of 1893, which lasted until 1897.

After 1900 the country experienced the moderate financial depression of 1903–04, the short but severe Panic of 1907, and the moderate depression of 1913. Thereafter war demands brought about a period of great prosperity, but after World War I came the depression of 1920–22.

POLITICS AND TWO PARTIES

From 1860 to 1912 the Republicans won every presidential election except two. General Grant was president from 1869 to 1877, a period during which scandal and corruption

Assassination of McKinley, in 1901. (Brown Bros.)

were connected with some members of the government. The outcome of the election of 1876 was disputed for a time, but finally an Electoral Commission, by a strict party vote of 8 to 7 gave all the contested states to the Republican candidate, Rutherford B. Hayes. His successor, also a Republican, James A. Garfield, was assassinated in 1881 and was

Andrew Johnson

Ulysses S. Grant

Rutherford B. Hayes

James A. Garfield

The McCormick Reaper being given its first public test, near Steele's Tavern, Va., July, 1831

Vulcanization of Rubber was discovered by Charles Goodyear in 1840. It made rubber much more useful

Early Rotary Press, from drawing in Leslie's Weekly, 1856. Richard Hoe invented rotary in 1847

Atlantic Cable was successfully completed in 1866. Men are checking cable message reception

The Telephone being demonstrated by Alexander Graham Bell to an audience in Salem, Mass., 1877

First Successful Incandescent Lamp. Artist's conception of final stage of Edison's experiments

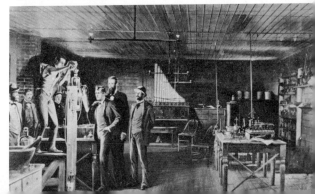

Chester A. Arthur

Grover Cleveland

B. Harrison. (Meserve)

William McKinley

succeeded by the vice-president, Chester A. Arthur. During his administration Congress, by the Pendleton Act, set up a Civil Service Commission to administer competitive examinations for government appointments.

In 1884 Grover Cleveland, a Democrat, was elected over James G. Blaine. During this administration the Interstate Commerce Commission was established. With the tariff as the principal issue, Cleveland failed re-election in 1888, although he won a small popular majority. The new president was Benjamin Harrison, grandson of William Henry Harrison, the victor of Tippecanoe and ninth president of the United States. During Harrison's administration Congress passed the Sherman Anti-Trust Law, the Sherman Silver Purchase Act, and the high-duty McKinley Tariff. Harrison was defeated for re-election in 1892 by Grover Cleveland, the only president who ever served nonconsecutive terms of office.

Cleveland's administration was marked by the Panic of 1893 and a conflict over currency. Various of the discontented groups in the country, such as the Populist party, joined to demand the free coinage of silver. To this Cleveland, other Conservative Democrats, and the Republicans were opposed. The discontented groups—farm, labor, and currency—captured the Democratic party in 1896,

William J. Bryan

with the fiery William Jennings Bryan as their candidate. However, he was decisively defeated by the Republican, William McKinley. War with Spain soon threatened over the Cuban question, and although he opposed it, McKinley bowed to the popular clamor and acquiesced in the declaration of war on Spain in 1898. Soon after the war was over McKinley was re-elected, again defeating Bryan, who ran on a platform of anti-imperialism and free silver.

McKinley was assassinated in 1901 and was succeeded by the vice-president, Theodore Roosevelt. His dominating personality and interest in reform led to the prosecution of several trusts and monopolies. The Interstate Commerce Act was strengthened and a Pure Food and Drug Act was passed. An ardent nationalist and imperialist, Roosevelt pushed the acquisition of the Panama Canal route and dominated the Caribbean. Roosevelt was re-elected in 1904, and in 1908 his good friend, William Howard Taft, was elected president.

ERA OF THE PROGRESSIVES

During the Roosevelt administration there was a faction in the Republican party which favored political and social measures considered by it as reforms. Feeling that the Taft administration was not carrying out the Roosevelt policies, these insurgents repudiated the President; in 1912 they attempted to supplant Taft with Roosevelt, but failed. The insurgents thereupon formed a new Progressive Party and nominated Roosevelt and Hiram Johnson. With the Republicans thus split the Democrats won an easy electoral victory with

Theodore Roosevelt

William Howard Taft

Woodrow Wilson
(Harris & Ewing)

Woodrow Wilson and Thomas R. Marshall. In 1916 Wilson was re-elected in a close election over Charles Evans Hughes and Charles W. Fairbanks. The Progressives, weakened by the legislation of the Wilson administration, disbanded in 1916 after Roosevelt had declined their nomination.

REFORMERS AND RADICALS

Although national politics were channeled through the two parties there were numerous insurgent groups and Third Parties. During Grant's first administration the Liberal Republicans led by Carl Schurz, Charles Francis Adams, and others, denounced the prevailing political corruption and demanded Civil Service reform; in 1872 they joined the Democrats in opposing Grant but were badly defeated. Republican factionalism continued, however, and was strengthened by the disclosures concerning the Credit Mobilier, the Star Route frauds, and the Whisky Ring. Yet the liberals, derisively called Half Breeds (opposed to the "Stalwarts"), and later termed Mugwumps, won a victory in the passage of the Pendleton Act (1883), and they helped defeat Blaine in 1884. On the currency issue the Greenback Party showed some strength in elections from 1876 to 1884. Farm discontent was expressed through the Grange, the Farmers' Alliance, and the Populist Party; in the election of 1892 the Populists gained considerable support. Labor discontent was expressed through the Antimonopoly Party, the Union Labor Party, the United Labor Party, the Socialist Labor Party, the Social Democratic Party, and the Socialist Party. Although the last showed con-

siderable strength in some American cities after 1890, it was never an important factor in national politics. The other third parties managed to elect some senators and representatives, and state and local officials, but were also unimportant nationally. Toward the end of the nineteenth century Anarchism made some headway among extreme groups. In the nomination of Bryan in 1896 the various discontented groups—farm, labor, and currency—gained complete control of the Democratic party against the conservative leadership of President Cleveland.

FROM LAISSEZ FAIRE TO SOCIAL CONTROL

The trend toward the public regulation of business enterprise began in the 1870's with the Granger Movement among the farmers of the Midwest, who demanded, and obtained, state regulation of railroads and warehouses. In 1887 the Interstate Commerce Commission was established to regulate railroad rates and services throughout the nation. In striking at monopoly, Congress passed the Sherman Antitrust Act (1890) and the Clayton Antitrust Act (1914). After 1900 the movement for the

President Taft signing the proclamation officially making Arizona the 48th state, Feb. 14, 1912. (Brown Bros.)

Top left, railway station at Chicago in 1870's. Top right, horsedrawn boat on the Delaware and Hudson Canal, opened in 1828. Center left, relay station of the Pony Express, which traveled between St. Joseph, Mo., and California before the completion of the transcontinental telegraph in 1861 (Western Union). Center right, clipper ship "Red Jacket" in the ice off Cape Horn, 1854. Bottom left, Brooklyn ferryboat about 1835. Bottom right, State Street, Chicago, 1889

President Wilson signing the Federal Reserve Bill, Dec. 23, 1913. (Brown Bros.)

government control of industry and commerce accelerated greatly. Under President Roosevelt the Conservation Movement for the exercise of foresight in the utilization of natural resources made considerable headway. During this trend toward the public control of business the Supreme Court acted as a moderating factor on political-minded legislators attempting to give expression to popular demands; the high tribunal in numerous decisions invalidated both Federal and state laws as in conflict with the "Due Process of Law" clause of the Fourteenth Amendment.

EXTENSIONS OF POLITICAL DEMOCRACY

The Australian Ballot, first used in the United States in 1888, was quickly adopted by most of the states to insure secret voting and to reduce election frauds. In order to permit direct legislation by the people a number of states, especially in the West and Midwest, adopted the initiative and referendum. Another innovation was the recall to permit voters to remove public officials from office. Shortly after 1900 the direct primary was introduced and widely adopted to permit the people to nominate candidates for public office. Also dating from the same period are the Corrupt Practices Acts, both state and Federal, to pro-

tect the honesty of elections. In 1913 the Seventeenth Amendment to the Constitution was adopted to provide for the popular election of U. S. senators, and in the same year the Sixteenth Amendment was ratified to permit a Federal Income Tax. The Nineteenth Amendment, ratified in 1920, provided for woman suffrage; this action was the culmination of a long movement which had been accepted by many states, beginning in 1889 with the admission of Wyoming to the Union.

THE PROHIBITION CRUSADE

As the Temperance Movement gained headway in the United States before and after 1900 there was much experimentation in liquor laws, but with the main trend toward Prohibition. The first prohibition wave appeared about 1840 and the second about 1880, but after a few years each subsided with most of the states repealing their prohibitory laws. The Prohibition Party was organized in 1869, but it never gained much support. The third prohibition wave, driven forward by the Woman's Christian Temperance Union and the Antisaloon League, developed great mo-

A Woman Suffrage Parade, part of the campaign which resulted in the Nineteenth Amendment

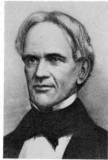

Horace Mann, Massachusetts educator

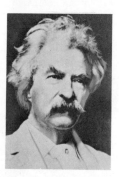

Joseph Pulitzer, big city journalist

Samuel Clemens (Mark Twain), writer

mentum among the states of the West and the South; by 1917, 26 states had prohibitory laws. In December, 1917, the Eighteenth Amendment was submitted for ratification; by Jan. 16, 1919, the requisite number of states had ratified it, and it became effective a year later.

EDUCATION FREE AND FOR ALL

Education during the Colonial period, although both common and general, was haphazard in system with varying combinations of private and public features. The Ordinance of 1787 in setting aside a section in each township for education gave a tremendous stimulus to public education. The growing nationalism and democracy were other factors of extreme importance. The public school movement made a great advance during the 1840's and 1850's under the leadership of such men as Horace Mann. Gradually state after state provided for free public schools supported by taxation instead of by rates; compulsory attendance developed after the Civil War. Systems of public education were introduced into the southern states by the Reconstruction regimes. The first public high school was established at Boston in 1821, but not until after 1890 did secondary public education make a great advance. The free public Library, which first appeared about 1830, was stimulated after 1881 by the generosity of Andrew Carnegie, who gave over $60,000,000 for this purpose. In the newspaper field the introduction of numerous improvements, including the introduction of wood pulp paper (1870) and the Linotype (1886), spurred the development of cheap daily papers; leaders in journalism were Charles A. Dana, Joseph Pulitzer, and William Randolph Hearst.

DEVELOPMENTS IN LITERATURE AND ART

The years following the Civil War saw the development of a native realism which had already appeared, at least germinally, in the frontier sketches and tall tales of such Old Southwest writers as Augustus B. Longstreet and Johnson Jones Hooper. Its first notable exponent was Samuel L. Clemens ("Mark Twain"), who recaptured the spirit and atmosphere of America's frontier age in such works as *Roughing It* (1872), *Life on the Mississippi* (1883), and *The Adventures of Huckleberry Finn* (1884). Similarly, Bret Harte caught the glamour of the California of Gold Rush days in a series of brilliant short stories (*The Luck of Roaring Camp and Other Sketches*, 1870). Two of the most significant postbellum writers were the sensitive recluse poet, Emily Dickinson (1830–86), and Henry James (1843–1916), who withdrew to England to write his subtle analytical novels; both revealed clearly a distrust of American ideals. The accepted leader of American novelists in the period was the sober realist, William Dean Howells

Henry James (Meserve Collection)

Wm. Dean Howells, realistic author

Isaac Singer Perfects his Sewing Machine, 1850. Elias Howe had patented a sewing machine in 1846, but Singer's was the first one to be manufactured.

The First Successful Steamboat, Robert Fulton's Clermont sailed from New York City on the Hudson River to Albany, N.Y. in 32 hours, August 17, 1807.

An Early Typewriter, 1829. William Burt's typographer was not practical. The first use of typewriters dates from Sholes's and Remington's machines, after 1867.

An Early Railroad in Connecticut, about the middle of the 19th century. Railroad building in the eastern U.S. flourished after 1826. A marked change in transportation had taken place in the Northeast before the Civil War. Transcontinental railroad lines were not constructed until after the Civil War, however.

The Battle between the "Monitor" and "Merri-mac." The first battle between ironclad warships took place on March 9, 1862 off Hampton Roads, Virginia. The *Merrimac* was a Confederate warship renamed the *Virginia*, built from a captured Federal hulk. The battle was indecisive. The *Monitor* was later wrecked.

Indians Attack the Overland Stage. Stage transportation began to serve the western U.S. in 1849. The California Gold Rush had made overland transportation necessary. The possibility of attack and robbery by Indians made travel by stagecoach dangerous. Stage lines were finally replaced by railroad and bus lines.

"The Peacemakers," March, 1865, a painting by George P.A. Healy, shows President Lincoln in conference with his high commanders. General Grant is in the center and General Sherman is on the left. Reconstruction of the South was being discussed, for the Confederate armies were virtually exhausted.

Landing the Atlantic Cable, July 27, 1867. This was the first successful cable. Two previous attempts had failed because of weather and cable construction. Cyrus W. Field was the guiding genius whose organization of the project and whose persisting faith in its possibility made it a success in spite of great adversity.

"The Last Spike," by Thomas Hill. The first transcontinental railroad line was completed May 10, 1869, at Promontory, Utah. A golden spike was driven into the last rail linking the Union Pacific and the Central Pacific Railroads. Construction had proceeded eastward from California and westward from Missouri.

Edison's Motion Picture Machine, 1889, produced in his laboratory at West Orange, N.J. The motion picture industry did not develop until the 20th century.

The First Successful Airplane Flight. Orville Wright flew the first heavier-than-air craft, 120 feet at Kitty Hawk, N.C., Dec. 17, 1903. Advances soon followed.

The Mergenthaler Linotype, 1884. This machine made mechanized typesetting possible. It revolutionized printing. Mass circulation of newspapers resulted.

Cotton Plantation on the Mississippi about 1880. A Currier and Ives print

"The County Election," painting by George Bingham of an early nineteenth century scene

"The Homestead," painting by John S. Curry. Homesteads dotted the prairies after the Civil War

"The Arkansas Traveler," a figure in nineteenth century American folklore

Broadway, New York City, from a lithograph made in 1885. Note the maze of telephone wires

The Peddler's Wagon, a common scene in nineteenth century rural America. (Culver Service)

The Brooklyn Bridge, opened in 1883, was the longest suspension bridge at that time

(1837–1920), whose masterpiece was *The Rise of Silas Lapham* (1885). Stephen Crane (1871–1900) was one of the first American novelists to adopt the techniques of the French naturalists. He was followed by Frank Norris (1870–1902), the stolid but conscientious Theodore Dreiser (1871–1945), and Jack London (1876–1916). A number of writers served their literary apprenticeship in the muckraking move-

followed the development of the American skyscraper and the appearance of the modernistic Chicago School, led by Louis Sullivan. American art continued to be dependent on European movements. The Hudson River School fell away under the impact of French Impressionism, and only a few individualists such as Winslow Homer, Thomas Eakins, and George Bellows remained impervious to

Theodore Dreiser
(Brown Bros.)

Jack London
(The Macmillan Co.)

Carl Sandburg
(Life Magazine)

Robert Frost
(Henry Holt & Co.)

ment, which began in 1902. Among these were the prolific Upton Sinclair, Lincoln Steffens, and David Graham Phillips. Among a host of writers who catered to the public's needs for romance and adventure fiction should be mentioned George Barr McCutcheon, Harold Bell Wright, Gene Stratton-Porter, John Fox, Jr., and Richard Harding Davis. William Sydney Porter ("O. Henry") was notable in the field of the short story with his skillfully plotted tales of city life (*The Four Million*, 1906). In poetry, a trend toward precise imagery and free, patternless rhythms was represented in the work of Carl Sandburg (*Chicago Poems*, 1916), Edgar Lee Masters (*Spoon River Anthology*, 1915), and Amy Lowell (*Men, Women and Ghosts*, 1916); while Robert Frost and Edwin Arlington Robinson produced distinguished work in traditional forms. The dramatists of this period were facile, amusing, rarely profound; typical were George M. Cohan and Clyde Fitch.

In architecture, a Gothic revival prevailed from the Civil War until the Philadelphia Centennial Exposition (1876), which marked the beginning of a period of eclecticism; there

foreign influences. On the eve of World War I, the New York Armory Show of 1913 introduced a new vogue of Continental modernism which was to dominate American art for generations.

NEIGHBORS IN THE WESTERN HEMISPHERE

The relations between the United States and Latin America were expressed mainly through the Monroe Doctrine and the Pan-American Movement. The Monroe Doctrine was proclaimed by President Monroe in 1823 at a time when the Holy Alliance was planning to help Spain recover her American colonies; at the end of the Civil War the doctrine was employed to force France to withdraw her troops which were supporting Maximilian in Mexico; in 1895 President Cleveland asserted it vigorously against Great Britain in the Venezuela boundary controversy; under President Roosevelt it was expanded to justify American policing of the turbulent Caribbean area. The Pan-American movement, first suggested by Henry Clay in 1820, and then discussed for

"The Fog Warning," by Winslow Homer

decades, came to fruition in 1890, when the first conference was held. After 1900 with the increasing Latin-American nationalism there was considerable suspicion of "the colossus of the North," especially on the part of the A.B.C. Powers. Relations with Mexico were generally friendly, but became strained during the revolutionary disturbances which began in 1910; Veracruz was occupied briefly in 1914 by American troops; in 1916 Gen. John J. Pershing led an expedition into northern Mexico in pursuit of Francisco Villa. Canadian-American relations were uneventful.

"Eleanor, Jean, and Anna," by Geo. W. Bellows, won 1922 International Exhibition. (Carnegie Institute)

Louis H. Sullivan, architect of the sky-scraper

Brig. Gen. John J. Pershing and members of his staff in the Mexican Punitive Expedition, 1916. (Acme)

FROM ISOLATIONISM TO IMPERIALISM

Before 1900 the United States was mainly occupied in developing her own vast natural resources. The prevailing sentiment was strongly isolationist and anti-imperialist. When Secretary of State Seward negotiated the purchase of Alaska from Russia in 1867 he had difficulty obtaining the approval of Congress. President Grant proposed the annexation of Santo Domingo but the Senate rejected his project. The Spanish-American War was brought about by a mixture of imperialism and humanitarianism. The defeat of Spain led to American annexation of Puerto Rico, Guam, and the Philippine Islands, but the continuing anti-imperialistic sentiment forced early American evacuation of Cuba and prompted a promise of independence to the Philippines. The Hawaiian Islands were annexed in 1898 by a joint resolution of Congress; the next year the Samoan island of Tutuila was acquired by agreement with Great Britain and Germany; in 1917 the Virgin Islands were purchased from Denmark. Under President Roosevelt, an advocate of American expansion, the negotiations for the construction of the Panama Canal were pushed to completion and the Caribbean area became practically an American Protectorate. President Wilson opposed such a policy in theory but supported it in practice.

Scene in Charlotte Amalie, capital of the Virgin Islands, bought by the U. S. in 1917

72. European Partition of Africa

BACKGROUND

THE STORY OF EUROPEAN DISCOVERY and exploration of the vast unknown areas of the world has already been told. Despite the fact, however, that large colonial empires existed on the American continents and in the East Indies, there were still lands of great potentialities awaiting exploitation.

England was, without question, the greatest colonial power in 1763. From that time until the advent of modern imperialism a century later, European nations were too occupied with internal problems and continental affairs to devote much thought or effort to expansion.

The earlier economic theory of mercantilism had emphasized the importance of colonies as a source of raw materials, a protected market, and the accumulation of gold. The newer policy of colonial expansion, known as imperialism, a product of the Industrial Revolution, demanded larger amounts of raw materials, and wider and freer markets and investment fields for surplus manufactured goods and capital.

The Adam Smith doctrine of laissez faire was eagerly adopted by the rising industrialists, who were irked by excessive governmental regulation. More extensive world or colonial markets were needed to absorb the increasing surplus of goods and capital; before long those same capitalists insisted on high tariff walls to protect their interests from foreign competitors.

From these various and conflicting economic motives, came the theory of modern imperialism, with all its implications of inflated national prestige, active trade rivalries, enlarged military organizations, and various methods of acquisition and exploitation.

As the industrialization process went on during the last quarter of the nineteenth century, this desire for economic expansion was closely allied with the emerging nationalism of the period. Such nations as Germany and Italy, which had recently achieved national unity, began to turn their attention to securing their share of unexploited areas in Africa, in the Near East, and the Orient.

France, still suffering from the staggering loss of Alsace-Lorraine, sought to regain her European prestige by acquiring territory and spheres of influence in Africa and the East. Russia, in a burst of national expansive zeal, penetrated into Siberia and southern Asia. England continued to consolidate her superior position in the colonial world in the extension of her imperial control, the maintenance of her navy and her great capitalistic organization. Even the United States was not immune to this nationalistic surge and found herself, at the turn of the century, an imperial world power, in spite of her earlier reaction against European imperialism.

An attempt was made to rationalize and justify the extension of European civilization to so-called "backward areas." Many imperialists were probably sincere in emphasizing the religious and moral responsibility of sharing the advantages of a superior culture with less fortunate people. In fact, those honest and earnest missionaries, who followed the explorer and trader, were often unconsciously preparing the way for new empires. Such was the case of the famous missionary-explorer, David Livingstone, whose initial efforts to elevate the black man of central Africa led to the inauguration of the British and Belgian imperialistic policy there. Although the medical missionary and teacher have valiantly attempted to carry the best of the white man's civilization to other races, much of their effort was overshadowed during the course of subsequent economic and military developments.

Another reason given for enlarging the boundaries of older nations was the surplus population argument. As modern science lengthened the life span of the human race, the birth-rate exceeded the death-rate in a ratio of three to one. As portions of these surplus populations sought their fortunes in recently opened territories, it was natural that the parent nation should wish to place her protecting care over them. This sometimes involved countries in devious diplomatic procedure which occasionally ended in war or at least laid the basis for dangerous future disputes.

Perhaps the most far-reaching effect of modern imperialism was on the foreign policy of the industrial nations of Europe. Before World War I, even the solution of domestic issues and the rise and fall of cabinets were dependent upon a popular foreign policy, subscribed to by shipping magnates, exporters, financial and banking interests, and a patriotic working class.

The naval and military rivalries of the pre-war period may be largely laid to this world

South African Diamond Mine. This is the Bulfontein Mine of De Beers Consolidated, near Kimberley

race for raw materials and wider markets. Naval bases, coaling stations, and efficient merchant marines were necessary factors in modern economic imperialism. Political intervention and annexation were simply the next logical steps in the process.

BRITISH ACQUISITIONS IN AFRICA

European imperialistic spirit was intensified during the nineteenth century, and the vast continent of Africa became the scene of international rivalry. Great Britain had acquired Cape Colony, Natal, and a few possessions on the west coast early in the century. These acquisitions proved to be convenient bases for further expansion.

One of the chief agents of British African imperialism was Cecil Rhodes, who hoped that some day Great Britain would possess the southern half of the continent. Rhodes also dreamed of a Cape-to-Cairo railway to connect Egypt with the southern colonies. Clever business maneuvers, with the support of

South African Train climbing through a mountain pass on the route from Capetown to Johannesburg

Scene near Cairo. The tombs of the caliphs outside the city walls of the Egyptian capital. (Paul's Photos)

Egypt, where the monuments of man forty centuries ago look down on the changing modern scene

The Suez Canal near Port Said. Opened in 1869, the canal came under British control in 1875. (Pix)

British naval and military forces, enabled him to extend English influence over numerous native kingdoms in South Africa which soon became British protectorates and then colonies.

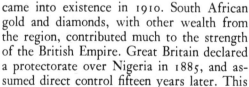

Cecil Rhodes, British "empire builder" in Africa. (Brown Bros.)

The Boer republics, the Transvaal and the Orange Free State, were acquired after a stubborn war from 1899 to 1902. General Botha then started a movement to unite Britain's colonies in South Africa, and the Union of South Africa came into existence in 1910. South African gold and diamonds, with other wealth from the region, contributed much to the strength of the British Empire. Great Britain declared a protectorate over Nigeria in 1885, and assumed direct control fifteen years later. This

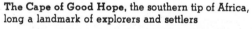

The Cape of Good Hope, the southern tip of Africa, long a landmark of explorers and settlers

fertile region was added to British possessions only after overcoming the opposition of France and Germany.

British interests in India made it advisable to secure control over Egypt, an area in which France was also interested. Disraeli managed to buy enough of the stock of the Suez Canal to establish British control. Then, when Ismail Pasha, the extravagant ruler of Egypt, defaulted on British and French loans, the two countries cooperated in exercising a joint control from 1879 to 1883. France was induced to withdraw from Egypt in return for a free hand in Morocco. France and Great Britain almost came to blows in the contest for the Sudan region. Military forces were sent by the two countries to Fashoda, where the inferior French detachment was compelled to retire.

British supremacy in Egypt, secured after a display of force, was more or less firmly established by Lord Cromer who was virtually dictator of the region until a short time before World War I. Many reforms were introduced, but the Egyptian natives were not reconciled to foreign domination.

British and French missionaries made the first pronounced advances into the East African region. The British East Africa Company had been formed and proceeded to establish a firmer foothold in the area. The French were eliminated when they were given a free hand in the island of Madagascar in return for giving up their claims on East Africa. Germany and Britain induced the Sultan of Zanzibar to grant them a coastal strip of territory. It was only a short time before both nations had extended their holdings into the interior. In a treaty (1890) Britain and Germany came to final agreement with the former acquiring Uganda, Nyasaland, and Zanzibar. The English government bought out the British East African Company, and protectorates were proclaimed over the colonies in 1894–1895. Once again Britain had emerged with the lion's share.

FRANCE

France, like England, was a possessor of African territory before 1870. Several small holdings along the western coast were claimed by the French nation, and French Algeria in the extreme north had been acquired in 1830. These areas were taken more by accident than deliberate imperialism. Algeria provided a good excuse for further North African conquests by France.

Tunis, a small area just east of Algeria, was overrun with foreign speculators, traders, money lenders, and concession seekers after 1860. France, England, and Italy vied with one another for control of the tiny territory. France loaned the reckless Bey (ruler of Tunis) large quantities of money, and, when disorder appeared in the area, the French creditors always had a good reason for entering and occupying the territory by force. In 1881 the Bey, under pressure, signed a treaty which amounted to French occupation of his country, and two years later France established a protectorate over the region.

Italy had hoped to gain the Tunisian territory and was indignant when France assumed control of it. When the Triple Alliance was renewed in 1887, Italy got Germany to support her in an effort to curb further French acquisitions in Northern Africa.

France moved next into Morocco, a territory to the west of Algeria. The French contended that protection for her valuable colony of Algeria was necessary, hence Tunis and Morocco had to be acquired as buffer colonies.

It so happened that other European nations enjoyed a rather prosperous trade with Morocco and would not give it up without a struggle. However, Delcassé, the French minister, was determined to add the territory to the French African empire. He assured Italy that France had no interest in Tripoli and Cyrenaica and would leave Italy to do what she wished there. Spanish support was won by offering that nation the northern and southern extremities of Morocco, if she would agree to leave the rest to France.

Revolts in Morocco furnished the necessary incident for French intervention and occupation. However, in the previous bargaining, Germany had been ignored, and it proved to be a grievous error. Germany insisted on the status quo with equal trade privileges to all in Morocco. When the German Kaiser landed at Tangier in 1905, he made this view plain.

France could not afford to risk war with Germany, and so a conference was held at Algeciras in 1906, in which a suitable, but only temporary agreement was reached. The Bank of Germany and the Bank of France were to have partial control of Moroccan finances. Concessions and contracts for public works, such as railways, were to go to the most favorable bidder. Frenchmen and Spaniards were to organize and train the Moroccan police.

France, thus reassured, continued the gradual conquest of the region. A revolt at Fez, the capital, furnished the necessary pretext for occupation by the French army in 1911. Germany responded by sending a cruiser to Agadir, more as a bluff to force concessions from France than for any other reason. Germany was obstinate and would have been ready to declare war on France had not the latter been assured of British support. Morocco was finally conquered by French troops and a protectorate proclaimed in 1912.

The struggle for possession of the Sudan region was no less intense than those previously mentioned. The great French dream was to connect by an unbroken strip her West African possessions of Senegal and Guinea with her eastern holding of Somaliland on the Red Sea. The French hoped to take over Abyssinia, but Italian interests prevailed there, much to British satisfaction. Although thwarted in its designs on the Sudan, France received a strip of territory which connected her Congo possession with the Nile River, thus providing access to the great waterway of Africa.

France had succeeded in carving for herself the second largest empire in Africa. The total area of her colonies on that continent was many times the area of the French nation in Europe. The success of her imperialistic policy was second only to that of Great Britain.

Scene at the Berlin Conference of 1885 on African affairs

BELGIUM

Belgium, despite her inferior size and power, carved out an unusually large slice of territory on the Dark Continent. To Henry Morton Stanley must go much of the credit for the establishment of the Belgian domain in Central Africa. Sent by his employer to search for David Livingstone, the English missionary-explorer, Stanley penetrated the wilds of Central Africa, the part now designated as Belgian Congo. He succeeded in his objective of finding Livingstone, but, more important, he had discovered another rich area unexploited by European nations. Upon his return to Europe he was employed by Leopold, king of Belgium, who had become interested in Africa.

Henry Morton Stanley explored the Congo

Stanley was sent back into the Congo in 1879. Leopold's professed altruism or humanitarianism was soon supplemented by his realizations of the possibilities of making profit from the Congo region. However, his project did not go unopposed. France entered a protest backed up by Germany and Britain. This led

David Livingstone, missionary and explorer

to the Berlin Conference of 1885 on African affairs. The fourteen nations attending agreed on freedom of navigation on the Congo and Niger, abolition of slavery and the slave trade, and the neutrality of the Congo Basin.

The Congo region was transformed into the Congo Free State (1885) with Leopold as sovereign. Measures were taken by the Belgian authorities to introduce European civilization, irrespective of the dislike of the native inhabitants. What began as a humanitarian venture became a cold-blooded business proposition. The system followed by Leopold was that of granting concessions to corporations which would exploit and develop the Congo region. The Belgian king was given liberal dividends out of the profits of these various corporations. Control over the Congo was transferred to the Belgian government in 1908, and the Congo Free State became Belgian Congo, a colony. The region had many natural resources, but labor was a problem.

PORTUGAL'S POSITION

The Portuguese had touched the fringes of Africa during the early period of discovery and exploration in the late fifteenth century. However, Portugal had not established any definite foothold in the form of settled colonies. These early claims were emphasized when the great scramble for African territory took place after 1870. Mozambique, later Portuguese East Africa, and Angola on the west were areas claimed by the Portuguese.

Although Portugal's possessions in Africa were not highly valuable, they were the object of international connivance by Britain and Germany. It was assumed that Portugal, being a weak rival or contestant in Africa, could be easily pushed aside. Germany desired to acquire parts of the Portuguese colonies to complete her great *Mittelafrika* scheme. She had actually signed a secret treaty with Britain in 1898 providing for the division of the Portuguese colonies. It was hoped that Portugal would sell her territories, but such was not the case. As late as 1913 a new pact between Germany and England was drawn up, whereby it was decided to divide Portugal's colonies regardless of what she, as the owner, might have to say. The plan fell through, and Portugal continues to hold her African territory.

GERMANY'S LATE ARRIVAL

Germany's late entrance into the development of Africa was a cause for considerable international friction. Under the guidance of Bismarck, Germany had been busy with continental European affairs. The German Chancellor's system of alliances occupied his time in the hope that his nation would be the supreme power in Europe. However, neither Bismarck nor the German people could resist the rising tide of imperialism. Pressure from the merchant class of Germany was a factor in converting Bismarck to imperialism. This took place some time after 1875, and it was not until the middle of the next decade that Germany secured a foothold in Africa.

Lüderitz, a German merchant, had landed in Southwestern Africa between the British settlements of Walfish Bay and Cape Colony. Great Britain was alarmed. Meanwhile, Bismarck decided to take Lüderitz and company under German protection. However, the German flag was not officially hoisted above African soil until the explorer, Nachtigal, landed in the vicinity of the Gulf of Guinea (1884). The German explorer had taken territory which was the beginning of what later became the Togoland and Cameroons of the German empire in Africa. About this same time, Flegel, another German apostle of imperialism, was losing the race for Nigeria which was taken by Great Britain. Germany began to push southward from her initial foothold in Togoland and Cameroons until the territory, later known as German South-West

Africa, had been acquired. However, she was not satisfied with what she had taken.

At approximately the same time that the Germans were taking parts of West Africa, a native son, Carl Peters, was extending German influence in Eastern Africa. A German East African Company was formed under protection of the home government. It began operations in the vicinity of Zanzibar and Tanganyika territory. The English also had their eyes on this region; hence an agreement of some sort had to be made. Each nation secured from the Sultan of Zanzibar, a strip of territory along the coast of East Africa. It did not take the two nations long to extend their territory inland a considerable distance. They finally came to a definite settlement by which the British nation was to take Kenya and Uganda, while Germany took over the Tanganyika territory.

It was after this acquisition that the German desire for a *Mittelafrika* empire became very pronounced. She now had eastern and western territories to connect, which, if accomplished, would form a continuous strip from ocean to ocean across South Central Africa. However, the British stood in the way of such a project. Germany, nevertheless, succeeded in extending the Cameroons inland to Lake Chad, having acquired a slice of the French Congo as compensation for French ascendancy in Morocco. Germany also acquired a narrow strip of territory which extended inland to the Zambesi River.

Considering her rather tardy arrival, Germany acquired an impressive empire in Africa. However, it was not enough to satisfy the extreme nationalists and imperialists of the "Fatherland." A nation as great as Germany must certainly get more than that! The result was that they turned to other parts of the world in order to make up for lost time in the African partition.

ITALIAN AFRICA

Italy became interested in acquiring African territory largely as a result of French acquisitions in the northern part of that continent. The Italians hoped to rise to the level where they could be considered one of the major powers of Europe, if not of the world.

Decidedly nationalistic and almost financially bankrupt, Italy entered the expensive game of imperialism. Her attention was first centered upon the insignificant territory of Tunis on the northern coast of Africa. However, as previously shown, France intended to take this territory. Despite Italy's joining the Triple Alliance, she could not bring enough pressure to bear to prevent French acquisitions in northern Africa. This old wound inflicted by France was healed some time later, when that nation gave Italy a free hand in the desert-like regions of Tripoli and Cyrenaica. This bargain was of importance because it tended to dissipate Italy's loyalty toward her allies, Germany and Austria.

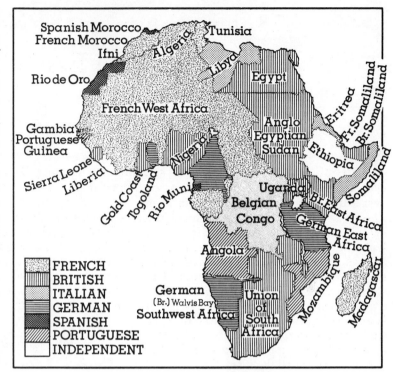

The Partition of Africa by the European Powers

Before proceeding into Tripoli, Italy had seen the expediency of securing promises of support from other nations. One by one she made secret bargains or agreements with the great powers. The process of "peaceful penetration" was begun, and before long the region was dominated by the Italians. Atrocity stories were made use of to spur the Italian nation into action. Internal disorder was a menace to Italian interests. While European nations focused their attention upon the Moroccan crisis in 1911, Italy took advantage of the situation. A sharp ultimatum was sent to Turkey, which claimed the territory. Italy could not wait and openly declared war on the "sick man" of Europe. The Turco-Italian War resulted in an Italian victory. The territory desired was annexed by a bold stroke of imperialism. Italy never did get her money's worth out of this great sand pile in Northern Africa. However,

it did tend to satisfy the intense nationalistic spirit of the Italian people.

In Eastern Africa also, Italy was forced to fight to gain the territory she desired. Eritrea, a small coastal area just north of Abyssinia, had been acquired about 1880. About nine years later Italian Somaliland, to the southeast, was taken. The next territory to which Italy turned was Abyssinia, the link between the two areas mentioned above. When the Italians began a policy of forceful penetration, they soon discovered their mistake. King Menelik and his Abyssinian subjects dealt the Italian army a stinging defeat at Adowa in 1896. Needless to say, the Abyssinian kingdom retained its independence. Italy abandoned her Abyssinian project, but never forgot the incident.

The Italian ventures into Africa were costly. The return on the original investment has been very small, generally speaking. Gratification over becoming an imperial power was probably the greatest reward for the Italian nation.

73. Imperialism in the Near and Middle East

RUSSIAN AMBITIONS

THROUGHOUT MOST of the nineteenth century Russia cast longing eyes toward those parts of the East which, roughly speaking, include the Balkans, Asia Minor, and even the Arabian peninsula. Turkey, an imperial power in Asia and Europe, which owned this land, would be the victim of the Russian aggression. The great dream of uniting all the Slavic peoples under Russian leadership must be kept in mind to understand Russian imperialism in the Near East. Desire to trade and gain access to the seas of the world dictated the persistent and almost traditional attempt to acquire Constantinople, the key to the door which connects the Black Sea with the Mediterranean. Possession of land in Western Asia was necessary to protect Russian interests around the Black Sea.

The treaty of San Stefano in 1878 gave Russia territory in the Balkans and also, by the creation of independent states, greatly weakened Turkey. The Congress of Berlin later that year, however, checked the momentum of the Russian imperialistic machine. England, France, and Austria opposed any scheme whereby the big Slavic nation would acquire the larger share of the spoils, if and when the time came to divide the territory of the disintegrating Ottoman Empire.

Russian dreams and ambitions were thwarted, but only temporarily. The settlement at Berlin did not heal the sore spot; instead, a new one appeared when Austria was given the administration of Bosnia and Herzegovina.

For some years there was no great disturbance or conflict in the Balkan area. Germany had cultivated a friendship with Russia which lasted until Bismarck's successors departed from his skillful policy of mollifying the Czar's foreign office. They launched the Berlin-to-Baghdad Railway project, which threatened Russian plans. The extension of German influence in the Balkans and Turkey could not be tolerated. The railroad might be the tonic which would revive the "sick man" of Europe. For economic and strategic reasons Russia could not, under any circumstances, agree to this stroke of German imperialism. Russia now joined with France and England in opposing German designs in the Near East.

ANGLO-RUSSIAN RIVALRY IN THE MIDDLE EAST

Russia had also directed her attention to the Middle East, that area including Persia, Afghanistan, and India. Nourishing the hope of obtaining a warm seaport outlet here also, she intrigued in the direction of the Persian Gulf. However, Britain felt that the road to India must be guarded at any price.

The Russian advance southward began shortly after the middle of the nineteenth century. By the late 1870's Russia appropriated such Central Asiatic lands as Turkmenistan, Bokhara, Khiva, and others, and began to encroach upon the northern borders of Persia and Afghanistan. If the Russian giant stepped across the Afghanistan mountain barrier, India would be seriously menaced. A crisis arose in 1884–1885 when Russia capitalized on British preoccupation with the Boers of South Africa to drive the Russian wedge still deeper in Middle Asia. Russia had gradually absorbed the Central Asian khanates. Merv was occupied in 1884, and in 1885 an attack by Russian troops on Afghan forces at Penjdeh, a small frontier town, brought Britain and Russia to the verge of war. This crisis was ended by negotiation in 1886.

By the year 1906, it was imperative that Russia and England decide the issue. Britain had announced that she would resist the establishment of a naval base on the Persian Gulf by any European power. England had recently formed a friendship with France and the latter was Russia's ally. Furthermore, Russia had not fully recovered from the defeat by Japan in the previous year. The new Russian foreign minister, Isvolsky, favored alliance rather than conflict with Great Britain. These factors led to a more friendly and equitable agreement in 1907. Afghanistan was left to British supervision; Tibet was established as a buffer state remaining nominally independent, but actually under a considerable British influence; and Persia was to be divided into three zones. The northern zone was to be left to Russian exploitation, the southern zone to Britain, and a neutral zone in the center open to both. Disorder within the divided nation soon followed and was used by Russia as a pretext for further extension of control in the zone allotted to her. Persia recovered a semblance of independence after World War I.

THE BERLIN-TO-BAGHDAD AXIS

As a result of her German alliance, Austria was opposing Russia in the Balkan area at this period. Germany under William II did not seem to fear France and Russia. When Germany decided to advance into the Balkan and Turkish areas, Austria was ready to cooperate. The alliance with Austria-Hungary became the cornerstone of German foreign policy. If Austria should become the dominant power in the Balkans, then the chances of building the great German railroad through that area would be aided. Thus, Germany stood behind the activities of her ally in the Balkan area, although at times restraining her more ambitious friend.

Bismarck, earlier, had been of the opinion that the entire Balkan area was not worth the "bones of a single Pomeranian grenadier." After he had left office, German policy was reversed, and the idea of a Berlin-to-Baghdad railroad was seriously considered. The emperor was an imperialist whose friendly missions to Turkey paved the way for the German project. The Turkish Sultan welcomed such a development; foreign capital was welcome in his almost bankrupt country. Turkey was soon overrun with bankers, missionaries, investors, and military men, in fine, all the typical elements of imperialism. The railway concession became a contract in 1903 and the project was launched upon turbulent waters. It is interesting to observe that French and British banking interests assisted the German promoters in the gigantic undertaking. However, Great Britain as a nation soon made it known that she opposed such a project. It would be a menace to the Suez Canal and the route to India. The French government at first appeared to lend support, for this project might divert German attention from Morocco, upon which France had designs.

Temporary agreements were finally reached

Cars and Station on the Baghdad Railway, which was one of the issues in pre-World War I diplomacy. Built by German companies, the road was regarded by the British and Russians as a threat. (Ewing Galloway)

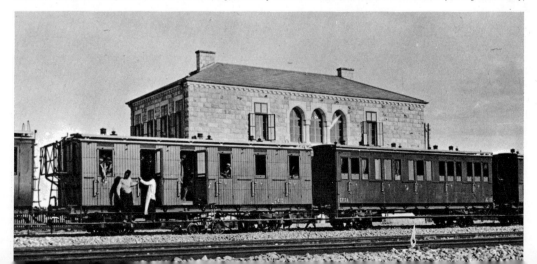

in regard to the Baghdad railroad project. Russia ceased to oppose it in return for German recognition of Russia's right to northern Persia. France sold her interest in the railroad and was given a free hand by Germany to receive concessions for railways in northern Anatolia and Syria. British opposition was overcome when Germany promised not to establish a terminal on the Persian Gulf except by English permission. Germany also recognized the priority of British interests in Mesopotamia. However, the French nation turned against the scheme when a possible threat to her Syrian concessions seemed imminent. Russia actually remained opposed to the German project and may have convinced France of the inexpediency of supporting it.

RISE OF BALKAN NATIONALISM

The Balkans from the beginning of the nineteenth century had indicated a developing consciousness of nationality. At the Congress of Berlin several Balkan states were granted their complete or partial autonomy. Nationalistic sentiment arose within the recently formed nations, which were dissatisfied with the peace settlement in 1878. Fearing European intervention, the Sultan played one nation against the other in an effort to maintain his position and avoid further loss of territory from the outside. The states of the Balkan peninsula, in the meantime, were growing in national strength, and the Austro-Russian rivalry for the control of these small nations was becoming more acute.

In 1908 occurred the Bosnian explosion. When the Young Turk nationalist revolution broke out, Austria took occasion to annex Bosnia and Herzegovina. This annexation was a direct violation of the terms of the treaty of 1878 which had placed the administration of the two provinces under Austrian control but reserved the sovereignty of Turkey over them. Little Serbia realized that hopes of incorporating her kinsmen into a greater Serbian kingdom and of securing an outlet to the sea were lost if the seizure were permitted to stand. So the Serbs were loud in their protests and appeals for aid to their big Slav brother, Russia.

Not yet recovered from the Japanese War and the subsequent civil conflict, Russia had to soothe Serbian anger. The storm blew over, but Serbia never forgot. The incident served to increase international hatreds. Austria, backed by Germany, became bolder. Russia felt some sympathy for Serbia, and realized that her influence over the Balkan states might not weather another refusal for aid. Serbia was inflamed, while England and France were interested spectators, not knowing just when a storm would break.

The Balkan states soon realized that the plan of the Young Turks was to dominate the people of Macedonia and Thrace, the only Balkan territories left to Turkey. These lands were coveted by the new nations for immediate expansion. They saw that co-operation in united resistance to Turkey was the best method by which to secure their objectives. The Turco-Italian War of 1911 provided a good opportunity to strike at the common enemy. The result was the formation of the Balkan League. A concerted attack upon Turkey was planned and an arrangement for division of the spoils was made. The War on Turkey began in 1912 and ended victoriously within a few weeks. The Ottoman Empire suffered further dismemberment.

The victory of the Balkan states had international implications. Because of the ascendancy of Serbia there was an increase in Russia's prestige. On the other hand, the defeat of Turkey served to weaken the position of Austria and Germany in the Near East. Austria was now more determined than ever to block Serbia. In this she had the backing of Germany and Italy, while Russia and France continued to throw their support in favor of the little Slavic kingdom.

The Balkan League was split asunder immediately after winning the war, because the victors could not agree upon a division of the spoils. Bulgaria was the victim of a concerted attack by her late allies. Turkey joined the allies, recovered some lost territory, and upon the conclusion of hostilities the extent of Bulgaria's boundaries was diminished.

The two Balkan Wars served to increase the size of those states. Holdings of Turkey in Europe were reduced to an insignificant quantity. The wars served to intensify nationalism and stimulate the ambitions of the states involved. The Austro-Serbian rivalry was a forecast of trouble in the future.

BRITAIN'S PRIZE IN THE MIDDLE EAST

The British nation held India, the richest prize of imperialism. The industrious Robert Clive deserves much credit for gaining India

Clive of India

for Britain in the middle eighteenth century. The East India Company was the agency administering and governing India during the great expansion of British control in the seventeenth, eighteenth, and early nineteenth centuries. In 1773 Parliament had provided for the appointment of a governor-general and a few years later set up a commission to supervise the Company. But on the whole, the Company, not the government, was responsible for the establishment of British India. By 1850 the Company found that order could be maintained only by use of military force. Continued annexations by the English only provoked the fear and hatred of the Indian

princes and their subjects. The Sepoys, native soldiers employed by the East Indian Company, mutinied in 1857. The rebellion was widespread and put down only after a great loss of life. This incident proved to the British government the necessity of assuming direct control and the Company ceased to function. In 1876 the Queen of England became Empress of India.

Indian reaction to British imperialism resulted in the rise of a nationalistic spirit. Previous to English occupation, there was no unity in India. Britain had made it a nation but at the expense of antagonizing the natives, who preferred their own habits and cultures. The movement for self-government in India started in the decades preceding World War I. Britain turned a deaf ear to such demands, but had to face a more intense native movement in that direction later, under the leadership of the popular Mahatma Gandhi.

India was regarded as Britain's most valuable colony, and around it evolved most of the elements of British foreign policy. Protection of this prize possession was the reason or excuse offered for British occupation and erection of spheres of influence in such areas as Egypt, Persia, and Afghanistan. These buffer states protected India on the west. To protect the eastern border, Burma was seized and annexed to India after 1880.

The problems of internal order in India continued to plague Britain. No small part of the general dissatisfaction of the Indian people was due to their diversity of interest. The Moslems looked to Turkey rather than England for aid; the Hindus, to the nationalist movement for their salvation; and the Christians preferred continued British domination. Thus did their religious affiliation affect their politics. Equally important was the breakdown of the caste system. The lowest castes threatened to leave the Hindu religion which had imposed the caste system on Indian society. The struggle in India indicated that the old Oriental social order was breaking down under the influence of Western social and economic ideas. Events in India after World War I, and the granting of independence, will be discussed in a subsequent chapter.

74. Imperialism in the Far East

REOPENING OF CHINA

THE FAR EASTERN areas offered a more fertile field for imperial expansion than did some of the areas previously discussed. The vast population of countries such as China and Japan would furnish an excellent market for European goods. Economic gain, more than any other motive, provided the incentive for imperialism on this distant horizon.

Napoleonic wars in Europe caused English commerce in Asiatic waters to outstrip all rivals. The East India Company of London became the champion of requests by Westerners for expanding trading opportunities at Canton and at other ports. The Chinese provincial authorities resisted these requests the more vigorously because of the ever increasing supplies of opium being smuggled into the kingdom.

Missions led by Macartney in 1794, and Amherst in 1816, attempted to secure better conditions for British trade, but they were rebuffed. When the trade monopoly of the English East India Company was rescinded in 1833, the interests of commerce in the Far East became the concern of the British government.

Upon the confiscation of a quantity of opium in 1839 and the refusal of the Chinese to make good the loss, the British withdrew to Macao. Events led to hostilities which have been named the Opium War. Peace was restored in 1842. Great Britain gained Hong Kong, which she still retains, an indemnity of $21,000,000, equality in diplomatic treatment, establishment of a regular tariff, and freer access to Chinese markets through the opening of five ports, including Canton and Shanghai. By this last provision, the English were performing a service for other occidental merchants as well as for themselves.

An American envoy, Caleb Cushing, negotiated an important treaty with the Chinese commissioner in 1844. This convention permitted natives to teach their language to foreigners and allowed foreign officials, instead of Chinese courts, to try civil and criminal cases involving their own citizens. This last concession is called extraterritoriality. In addition, missionaries might rent land and build churches and hospitals in treaty ports.

Soon it became apparent that the attitude of Chinese officialdom had not been altered merely because it had lost battles. Again, in 1857, war was undertaken by the English

Caleb Cushing made U. S. treaty with China

and French. For the second time, China was defeated by modern arms. Eleven more ports were opened to Western manufactures, and foreign envoys were permitted to reside in Peking, the capital. The contracting of coolie labor and the importation of opium were to be legalized and controlled, and greater freedom was given to missionary enterprise. France became the special protector of the Catholic Church in China.

Yankee clipper ships with their clouds of canvas, as well as vessels of other nations, soon frequented the treaty ports of China. Shanghai began to grow toward its later position as the world's fifth largest port.

OPENING OF JAPAN

The Japanese archipelago lay directly in the principal route of the growing trans-pacific traffic. American whalers had for years complained of the severe treatment meted out to shipwrecked crews by the Japanese. An American commercial mission and a naval expedition, in 1837 and 1846 respectively, failed to open relations with the islanders. Finally, in 1854, Commodore Matthew Calbraith Perry combined tact with a display of Western technology and naval strength, and obtained a treaty from the *bakufu* (Japanese military government). This treaty gave an American consul the opportunity to reside at Shimoda; three ports were to be open to American trade, subject to Japanese intermediaries. The first American consul, Townsend Harris, a gifted diplomat, secured additional privileges.

The lessons with which China was becoming slowly and forcibly impressed, were learned quickly by the Japanese. The Chinese example had always proved useful to Japan, but even more decisive as a factor was the characteristic energy of the islanders—the energy which an exposed location and stimulating climate had conditioned. Japanese statesmen recognized the superiority of Western methods, especially of Western guns. They set about to build ships, factories, and munition plants for themselves, in accordance with the successful Western methods.

Japan's planned development of the next eighty years was threefold: first, to throw off the domination of Western powers; then, to gain recognition as a great power herself; and finally, to become supreme in the Far East.

The first change for Japan was domestic. Realizing that a united front must be presented against external threats, the shogun (military ruler) resigned and in 1868 the emperor, with primacy restored, became political and spiritual ruler in Yedo, renamed Tokyo, or Eastern Capital. Taking the charter oath, the emperor stated that "knowledge shall be sought for all over the world, and thus shall be strengthened the foundations of the imperial polity."

The Iwakura mission was dispatched to the United States and Europe in 1871 to study methods in the Western world and adapt them to Japanese conditions and needs. In the same year, political feudalism was ended by the establishment of prefectures instead of daimiates (feudal states). Universal military service was inaugurated in the following year; navy yards were built, telegraph and railroad lines constructed, factories erected. At all times full use was made of the knowledge gained by Western civilization in centuries of trial and error. This economic revolution was limited to heavy industries mainly. To the old aristocracy of family was added that of wealth,

Commodore Perry meeting the Japanese imperial commissioners, 1854

and students of the subject are correct in ascribing aspects of economic feudalism even to twentieth century Japan.

Almost immediately Japan became diplomatically active. Although still chafing under extraterritoriality herself, she made in 1871 an unsuccessful attempt to impose the identical system upon China. Ironically enough, Japanese statesmen succeeded in this respect at the conclusion of the first Sino-Japanese war—within a year after a treaty was signed with Great Britain anticipating the abolition of extraterritoriality in Japan by 1899! On February 11, 1889, the new constitution was promulgated. It was a document framed by experts, foremost among whom was Prince Ito, who put into practice those ideas gained by study abroad, particularly in imperial Germany.

THE IMPENDING DISSOLUTION OF CHINA

China was entering a period in which she became a sorrow to her friends and a prey to her enemies. The Manchu rule was waning, and only by the erratic and autocratic vigor of Tzu Hsi, who became dowager empress and actual ruler until 1908, did the dynasty persist.

This was a period of jealous competition and acquisition by Western nations. They did not hesitate to force agreements upon the Chinese by naval demonstrations. The construction of railroads and other public works strengthened foreign control of the revenues.

In the 1860's, Spain and France began encroachment in Tongking in the South of China; by 1874 France had become "protector" of all Annam in that region. The British simultaneously acquired Lower Burma and by 1886 annexed the upper portion of the kingdom. Thus England was in a position to gain influence in Tibet, a process becoming apparent by 1900. Russia in 1860 was awarded the Maritime Provinces on China's northern border, in return for playing the role of "honest broker" in the peace negotiations of that year. A decade later the czar's men secured territorial cessions in the northwestern region of Ili, to the west of their earlier acquisition.

JAPAN AND CHINA

Meanwhile the Japanese imperial government was making rapid strides at home, and by playing one nation against another was achieving diplomatic victories. The United States, Japan's best friend until the twentieth century, signed a treaty in 1878 recognizing tariff autonomy. A decade later the oriental nation secured from Mexico its first modern treaty on a basis of equality. Japan won complete administrative independence in 1911 after the abolition of all external limitations on tariff regulation. But progress in this direction was too slow for the growing Japanese confidence and ambition.

Japan was interested in Korea, that peninsula over which China had exercised a vague suzerainty since long before the sixteenth century. In 1873 Japan had been on the verge of war with the Chinese Empire over conflicting policies in Korea. The Korean court vied with that of Peking for the questionable distinction of being one of the world's most corrupt regimes. On July 23, 1894, the Japanese took advantage of China's uncertainty to depose Queen Min in Korea and establish a regency. Two days later war broke out.

At the time, the outcome of the hostilities was by no means a foregone conclusion. There had always been an awesome respect for "China's teeming millions." Missionaries viewed them all as potential converts; merchants saw in them future customers; and military experts dreaded the distant day when modern Chinese legions would shake the earth. But China's weakness soon became apparent. The Empress Dowager had recently spent naval appropriations for the reconstruction of the Summer Palace. The army was still composed of Manchu Bannermen equipped with antiquated weapons.

Japanese forces launched a smashing attack which culminated in the victory of Pingyang and the defeat of the Chinese navy on the Yalu River. The war dragged on, however, with Japanese overrunning part of southern Manchuria and investing Talienwan (now Dairen) and Port Arthur. At the latter place the populace was massacred on a large scale.

As a result of the Treaty of Shimonoseki (April, 1895), China's humiliation was clear to the world. The once powerful empire was forced to recognize the independence of Korea, to pay an enormous indemnity, and to cede to Japan the Liaotung Peninsula, Formosa, and the Pescadores Islands. Japan herself was economically shaken by the war, and the worst fears of her statesmen were realized when notes from Russia, Germany, and France obliged her to relinquish claims to the Liaotung Peninsula in exchange for an addition to the indemnity. The Japanese accepted this reversal with bitter calm, resolving upon a policy of "watchful waiting."

BREAKUP OF CHINA

Aside from military inferiority in 1894–1895, China had to borrow further from foreign banks in order to pay the price of defeat. Now, as the ancient Chinese Empire began to crumble, every Western power attempted to get a share, and only mutual jealousies prevented the whole of China from being divided into spheres of influence. There was a scramble for railway rights, money loans, and sundry concessions. France started new competition by securing railway privileges in Yunnan, a southern province.

Germany, imitating the French reputation as a protector of Christians, took advantage of the murder of two German missionaries in Shantung to demand a ninety-nine year lease of Kiaochow and an area of fifty kilometers around that port. In the same month (March, 1898) Russia was granted a twenty-five year lease of Port Arthur and the tip of Liaotung Peninsula, much to the irritation of Japan, which had been forced to return this region to China only four years earlier. In April, France occupied Kwangchowan, and in June and July, Great Britain enlarged her hold on the Kowloon Peninsula opposite Hong Kong and raised the Union Jack over Weihaiwei, a port across the gulf from Port Arthur.

The United States, which as yet had not completely occupied all of its available land, was the only great nation which made no territorial capital out of China's predicament. Her big-brother attitude toward China continued and with some misgivings, toward Japan. Nevertheless, the United States at this time became an imperialistic Pacific power by acquiring the Philippines during the war against Spain. Secretary of State John Hay proposed in 1899 the Open Door doctrine of equal economic opportunity and maintenance of the territorial and political integrity of China. In view of the fact that a satisfactory balance of interests had been temporarily achieved, Japan and the European powers subscribed to this agreement.

John Hay proposed "Open Door" in China

THE BOXER REBELLION

Thus was China "saved" from the outside, but it was only natural that the degradation of Manchu power would result in antiforeignism and in plots against the dynasty from the inside. Many pre-existing secret societies redoubled activity, and Tzu Hsi, the Empress Dowager, was clever enough to divert popular antipathy from the administration to the "barbarians." Finally, in 1900, the wave of violence called the Boxer Rebellion engulfed aliens living in various parts of China. An allied force relieved foreigners in Peking and imposed a humiliating peace upon China. The government was forced to pay an excessive indemnity, reconstruct missionary property, inaugurate a ministry of foreign affairs at Peking, and permit a fortifiable legation quarter at the capital.

THE REVOLUTION OF 1911

Rulers of China, especially the wily old dowager, Tzu Hsi, realized that the Manchu Dynasty was in sore need of rejuvenation. Most of the ensuing reforms were either too hurried or ill advised. The ancient system of examinations was abolished, and a state apparatus of instruction, overlooking widespread missionary education, was instituted. Two decrees were issued with the purpose of more thoroughly assimilating the Manchus in the body politic. Provision was made for the suppression of opium production and consumption within ten years. A foreign language college was established; outstanding debts were reorganized. None the less, many improvements did not progress far beyond the imperial red pencil.

Chinese students in considerable numbers, especially since the dawn of the century, had emigrated for higher education in Japan, Europe, and the United States. By the year 1911, when ferment and leadership in China were both strong, there was growing an agitation for constitutional government. In spite of imperial promises that a limited monarchy would be conceded by 1917, the death of Tzu Hsi and the emperor Kuang Hsü in 1908 and the succession of the infant Pu Yi (Hsuan Tung) further weakened the imperial faction.

Revolution broke out in 1911, and, under the leadership of Dr. Sun Yat-sen, the Nationalist

Tzu Hsi, dowager empress of China

forces succeeded in a rapid military campaign to force the abdication of the emperor on February 12, 1912. Stronger hands were needed to undertake the empire's administration, but there was a question whether the Nationalists could supply the leadership to unify all the rival military and political forces.

China was in danger of losing still more territory, since English and Russian penetrations were threatening Tibet and Mongolia, respectively. In 1913 both buffer areas were divided into "inner" and "outer" regions, and autonomy was granted by China to the more remote parts.

President Sun Yat-sen had by this time made way for a new chief executive, Yuan Shih-kai. Under his administration the Chinese republic gained recognition by the United States and other powers. China's willingness to enter World War I on the side of the Allies was at first discouraged by Japan, who opposed a strongly equipped Asiatic army which might rival her own. Only in 1917 did the Chinese republic follow the United States into war against the Central Powers, and its aid consisted for the most part in furnishing Chinese coolies for manual labor in France.

The significance of the Chinese revolution should not be either neglected or overemphasized. It was to be expected that the Chinese would not make a complete break with their imperial past, and yet the political tradition of the people was not unmixed with a democracy which contributed some foundation for a new era, born in confusion, confronted by aggression, but possibly achieving eventual control and renascence.

ANGLO-JAPANESE ALLIANCE

While China was becoming somewhat more democratic, though at the same time more confused and weakened, Japan was becoming

more autocratic, centralized, and stronger. In the latter half of the nineteenth century England and Japan began to regard Russia as a common enemy. At first they saw no advantage in an alliance, but the czar's continual search for a warm water port brought the two island governments to act to-

Yuan Shih-kai, president of China, 1913–16. (Brown Bros.)

gether. The first Russo-Japanese friction, aside from the growing pressure of Russia in the north since the eighteenth century, came in Korea where agents of both nations competed for concessions and royal favor. In 1896–1897 the situation was somewhat eased by Russian withdrawal from Korea for the consolidation of her interests in other parts of China.

By the year 1901, however, Russian agents were again active in South Manchuria and in Korea. The situation became critical in 1902 when Russian troops, dispatched during the Boxer trouble, were not withdrawn as agreed. Japan, Great Britain, and other recent allies protested in vain to St. Petersburg. Finally on January 30, 1902, an Anglo-Japanese alliance was signed recognizing that Great Britain's principal interests lay in China while virtually a free hand was accorded Japan in developing her "peculiar" interests in Korea. If either of these powers were attacked by two or more powers, the other would give assistance. Theodore Roosevelt's administration practically committed the United States as a silent partner to this pact. Thus fortified, Japan maintained a positive policy and by February 10, 1904, war had developed between the empires of Japan and Russia.

RUSSO-JAPANESE WAR

In this Russo-Japanese war the Russian fleet was quickly bottled up in Port Arthur which, after a bloody siege, capitulated on the first day of 1905. Nipponese land forces on the Korean peninsula met with even more rapid triumphs, but the abundant resources of Russia might well have told in the end had not communications broken down and had not revolts disturbed the czar's domains. Both countries accepted President Roosevelt's proposed mediation, and the treaty was consummated at Portsmouth, New Hampshire, in September, 1905. Although parts of it were unsatisfactory to Japan, the treaty clearly indicated that there was now another great power with which to reckon in the Far East. Japan's paramount position in Korea was recognized, and she acquired the Russian rights to Port Arthur, the tip of the Liaotung

Peninsula, the southern half of Sakhalin, and the railroad connecting Port Arthur with Changchun.

Until delimitation was agreed upon, South Manchuria, in spite of the Portsmouth guaranty of China's sovereignty and the Open Door, became the arena of Russo-Japanese conflicting interests. From 1905 until World War I, the Japanese developed remarkably their industries, merchant marine, and military machine. Korea was annexed outright in 1910, and further penetration of southern Manchuria was pushed chiefly by the South Manchuria Railway and its affiliates.

By 1905 the renewal and strengthening of the Anglo-Japanese alliance had safeguarded Japan against a Russian war of revenge. Then a series of treaties, secret and open, actually cemented a new understanding with Russia. A second renewal of the agreement with England was signed in 1912 and bolstered the latter against the saber rattling of Emperor William II. It also set the stage for Japanese participation with the western Allies in World War I.

FRANCE IN INDOCHINA

To compensate for their loss of India, the French imperialists had moved farther eastward into the large peninsula which juts out from southeastern China. A foothold had been obtained in this area by France during the reign of Louis XIV but little more was done during the next hundred years. Concerted efforts in this direction were not made until, in the reign of Napoleon III, French admirals took matters into their own hands. A combined Franco-Spanish naval expedition set out in 1857 to avenge the death of a missionary. The French forced the emperor of Annam to accept a treaty granting to them three provinces of Cochin China and certain commercial privileges. Murder of Christian missionaries in the kingdom of Cambodia to the north furnished the necessary pretext for another French advance, and the ruler of that territory was forced to grant concessions. France now had Cochin China and Cambodia, forming a continuous compact block of territory in the southeastern tip of the peninsula.

Japanese and Russian representatives with Theodore Roosevelt at Portsmouth, N.H., during negotiations ending the Russo-Japanese War. (Bettman Archive)

Some complications arose between France and China, with the result that a war ensued between those two nations in the 1880's. France exacted concessions in the form of reduced tariffs and recognition of rights to certain sections. Thus France secured a rather large portion of the Indochina Peninsula. French Indochina was populous, with fertile soil and a generous endowment of natural resources. In commercial returns to France, it was, of all French colonies, second only to Algeria.

THE PACIFIC ISLANDS

The numerous islands of the Pacific Ocean, with their widely divergent cultures, furnished another arena for the operation of nineteenth-century imperialism. Prior to that time, many of the islands had been overrun or conquered by Asiatic peoples, but nothing substantial had been done in the way of economic development.

The islands now composing the East Indies group had been the goal for which European nations strove in the early period of discovery and exploration. The spices of this region had a wide demand in Europe. The Dutch began a systematic exploitation of the islands following the expulsion of the Portuguese by the Dutch East India Company during the seventeenth century. The islands were lost during the Napoleonic wars, but they were returned to Holland in 1818. As was so often the case, the area was ruled first by a commercial company and later passed under direct control of the home government. By 1941, the Dutch East Indies comprised an area almost sixty times that of Holland.

Some schools were erected and the natives were given the rudiments of an education. However, in most of these areas it was thought not feasible to educate the native population beyond a certain level. The Dutch actually tried to keep the islanders from becoming too Europeanized.

BRITISH ACTIVITY IN THE PACIFIC

The Pacific islands did not attract British attention until the nineteenth century. Some of her explorers had touched several of the larger islands, claiming them for England. As a matter of fact, most of the islands—even Australia and New Zealand—were considered of little value.

The period of aggressive imperialism in the Pacific began about 1870, and was often ushered in unconsciously by missionaries who, in their efforts to civilize the natives, were sometimes slain. Such an atrocity would furnish the necessary incident for punishing the offending natives by forcing them to concessions or by actually taking their territory from them. Traders were protected and avenged in about the same manner. Britain annexed the Fiji Islands in 1874. Shortly afterward Borneo and Papua, two large islands north of Australia, were invaded by the British; North Borneo was annexed while Papua was divided among several powers.

In the last years of the century there developed considerable international rivalry for coaling stations among these islands of the Pacific area, and it seemed as though the first European nation to land on an island took possession and claimed ownership.

Germany had become interested in the Pacific islands for commercial reasons, a trading station having been established in the Samoan island group. Commercial companies were organized and German imperialism made a debut in the Pacific. Part of New Guinea was annexed, and so were other small islands in the vicinity.

In the Samoa Islands, Germany encountered as her two strong rivals the United States and Great Britain. Each nation had secured certain privileges and refused to give ground. A crisis was reached in 1889 when Germany was about to take the islands by force. England and America also had warships in the area, but the hand of fate prevented battle, for a hurricane separated the warships. Within a short time a three-party agreement for supervision of the islands was reached. Britain withdrew in 1899, leaving Germany and the United States to divide the territory.

French imperialists had little success, if any, in the Pacific, although a few islands were acquired, among which may be mentioned New Caledonia, New Hebrides, and Tahiti.

75. American Imperialism

GROWTH OF AMERICAN IMPERIALISM

BY THE TREATY OF PARIS, 1783, the United States reached westward as far as the Mississippi River. A young energetic nation had come to realize its possibilities. From that time on there was a continuous expansion movement westward. The United States was destined to control the territory from the Atlantic to the Pacific. It was a natural and logical expansion in the minds of American leaders.

The Louisiana Purchase, in 1803, exerted considerable influence upon the young nation, which was rapidly developing an expansion complex, sometimes defined as "manifest destiny." The northern provinces of Mexico were acquired by the United States (in return for $15,000,000 and the assumption of certain claims) as a result of the Mexican War.

The war against Mexico (1846) gave the United States territory bordering upon the Pacific. With the battle cry of "Fifty-Four Forty or Fight," the Americans were stubborn and insistent enough to gain the Oregon Territory by an agreement with Great Britain. Only a small strip of land remained to be acquired before continental United States would make a complete picture for the map makers. This was done when the Americans paid a liberal sum for the minute Gadsden

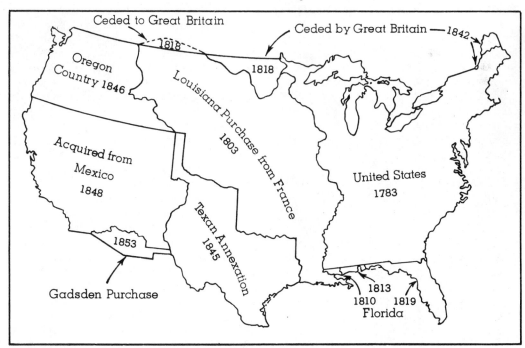

U. S. territorial expansion before 1860—the continental boundaries as they are today

Purchase along the present southern boundary
of the state of New Mexico.

"SEWARD'S FOLLY"— THE ALASKAN PURCHASE

The first territorial acquisition by the
United States beyond its regular boundaries
was Alaska, purchased in 1867. Secretary of
State William Seward was an avowed ex-
pansionist, and a sincere believer in "manifest
destiny." He thought that the United States
should control the entire North American continent with a national capital at Mexico City.
Seward believed that Alaska would furnish
another door on the Pacific through which to
enter the Far East, where the trading possibilities were known but not extensively exploited.
Seward's wisdom was borne out, for Alaska's
resources are worth many times its purchase
price of $7,200,000.

ANNEXATION OF HAWAII

In this same post-Civil War decade, the
Hawaiian Islands were an object of American
interest. They were first used as a whaling
station and a convenient rendezvous for trading

King Kalakaua of the Hawaiian Islands with his
advisors. In 1887 the king gave the United States
the right to maintain a naval base at Pearl Harbor

expeditions into the Pacific area. It was soon discovered that the islands could produce sugar on
a large scale. American sugar planters became numerous, and in 1875 they signed a
treaty with the United
States by which Ha-
waiian sugar was ad-
mitted free of duty into
the United States ports.

About ten years later,
the United States was
granted the right to
maintain a naval station
on the islands and virtu-
ally controlled the eco-
nomic and political sys-
tem. Foreign capitalists

Liliuokalani, queen of
Hawaii, dethroned in
1893.(Ewing Galloway)

organized a government under Sanford B. Dole,
a son of an American missionary living there.
The support of the American sugar planters
and the presence of United States marines
made possible the establishment of a government. A treaty providing for annexation by the
United States was signed in 1893, but, when
President Cleveland came into office, he refused to carry it out. Cleveland's successor,
McKinley, favored annexation, especially
when acquisition of the Philippines added to
the strategical value of the Hawaiian group.

Hawaii receiving the news of its annexation

The Battle of Manila Bay, May 1, 1898. Commodore Dewey and his squadron of four cruisers and two gunboats steamed into Manila Bay at midnight and opened fire at dawn. The Spanish fleet was shattered

The islands were annexed in 1898. Investment of American capital and exploitation of the natives continued and were mainly responsible for the economic development of the islands. The penetration and subsequent annexation of Hawaii was a true stroke of expansion.

WAR WITH SPAIN

Interest in the annexation of Cuba had almost become a tradition in the United States since colonial times. The United States for strategical reasons could not allow another nation to acquire Cuba. Americans preferred to see a weak nation like Spain in control, but in case of Spanish withdrawal they felt that the United States should assume the responsibility. Especially, before the Civil War, many Southern leaders wanted to annex Cuba.

Enterprising Americans had seen the opportunities for trade. Cuba was ridden with internal disorder, in spite of Spain's promises. American sugar and tobacco interests demanded that political stability be maintained on the island.

A war for Cuban independence broke out in 1895. The cruelty inflicted upon the natives by the Spanish generals made excellent newspaper headlines in the growing "yellow" dailies in the United States. The Cuban natives appealed for help to the United States, where they maintained an active propaganda machine.

The blowing up of the United States battleship *Maine,* in Havana harbor, stirred American spirit to a higher pitch. McKinley could no longer withstand the pressure of propaganda and public sentiment, and the United States declared war (April, 1898). The American navy was ready, having been built up by secretaries of that department for over a decade, while the army, on the other hand, was not prepared to engage in a major conflict.

Admiral Dewey, victor at Manila Bay

The war itself was short-lived, lasting but three months. The Spanish Pacific fleet was defeated by Commodore Dewey of the United States Navy, at Manila in the Philippine Islands. The Spanish West Indies fleet was defeated, and the American troops were victorious in the land battles in Cuba and Puerto Rico. In the land fighting in Cuba Theodore Roosevelt became well known as commander of the "Rough Riders."

In the treaty, Spain gave up Puerto Rico to the United States, while Cuba was given independence. The United States took over the Philippines until they should be ready for in-

The Capture of El Caney by American troops, July 1, 1898, during the Spanish American War

dependence, and Spain was given $20,000,000. It took many times that amount to pacify the natives and set up a stable government in the islands. William H. Taft was the first civil governor of the Philippines. Native participation in government gradually increased, and by the Jones Act of 1916 the Filipinos were given a voice in their affairs.

CIVILIZING MISSION OF THE UNITED STATES

It may be truthfully said that American imperialism was of benefit to the Philippines. The "civilizing mission" of the American nation was fulfilled to a great degree in that spot on the globe. Modern buildings, railroads, and schools adorn the islands where before a semijungle existed. The desire for independence by the Filipinos was the most serious problem to be faced by the United States and was not solved until after World War I. Of course, American interests were not solely altruistic; business enterprises made extensive investments in the islands.

Hawaii, Guam, and Wake Island also entered into American policy in the Pacific. The Hawaiian group was of importance from an economic point of view as well as being one of the strongest naval bases of the United States. Aside from Hawaii and the Philippines, the Pacific islands owned by the United States were maintained mostly for strategic reasons. With these possessions, most of them dating from the Spanish War, the United States became an imperial power, with worldwide interests.

VENEZUELA, EUROPEAN POWERS, AND THE UNITED STATES

Following the revolt of the Spanish-American colonies, the United States enunciated the Monroe Doctrine in 1823. This provided a barrier to European expansion on the American continents. It was a move in the direction of self-defense by the United States, by keeping foreign intruders from establishing menacing strongholds on the western continents.

The boldest assertion of the Monroe Doctrine came in 1895. Venezuela and Great Britain had long been at odds over the boundary between British Guiana and Venezuela. The discovery of gold in the disputed territory led both sides to press their claims vigorously. President Cleveland believed Britain was the aggressor, and his Secretary of State, Olney, sent Britain a note declaring that the United States' fiat was practically law on the American continent. For a time there was a war scare, but the matter was arbitrated and most of the British contentions declared valid.

In 1902, Venezuela figured in another incident involving European countries. Great Britain, Germany, and Italy, endeavoring to collect defaulted debts and secure reparation for injuries to their nationals, established a blockade of Venezuelan ports. The powers disavowed territorial desires and any intent to violate the Monroe Doctrine. Nevertheless, President Theodore Roosevelt was uneasy over the situation and supported Venezuela's request for arbitration. The blockading powers agreed, and the Hague Court decided, in 1904, in their favor. Roosevelt later declared he had forced Germany to agree to arbitration by threatening to send Dewey's fleet to Venezuelan waters. There is no evidence for this story.

THE BUILDING OF THE PANAMA CANAL

American imperialism next turned in a positive direction in the acquisition of the Panama Canal Zone (1900–1903). The United States had wanted an isthmian canal for over fifty years. At the turn of the nineteenth century, there seemed to be an opportunity to realize this ambition. Great Britain enjoyed, by treaty rights, the privilege of joint ownership and joint control. Because of her command

Theodore Roosevelt on one of the steam shovels used in digging the Panama Canal. (Underwood-Stratton)

of the sea, joint control would have meant English control. Finally in 1901, after repeated urgings, England in a new treaty agreed to cancellation of the joint provisions, and the United States was left to carry on the work.

Colombia, of which Panama was part, refused to sell canal rights to the United States. Native politicians hoped to make an additional profit upon the expiration of the contract given the French company which had made an unsuccessful attempt to dig a canal. Panama revolted, and American troops, taking a far from neutral attitude under Roosevelt's direction, prevented Colombia from putting down the insurrection. Panama declared its independence and made a treaty with the

Making the great Culebra Cut of the Panama Canal

United States, selling a perpetual lease of the canal zone for $10,000,000 plus an annual payment of $250,000. An American treaty with Colombia had been ignored. Work was begun in 1907, and the canal was completed in 1914. Theodore Roosevelt wanted the canal primarily because of its strategic value. Although later admitting that he took Panama, he had previously justified his action on the ground that such a project would benefit the world in general.

THE ROOSEVELT COROLLARY

During the canal negotiations Roosevelt announced his corollary to the Monroe Doctrine. It claimed for the United States the right to intervene whenever one of the Latin-American nations was faced with the problem of internal discord and disorganization. Roosevelt believed that, unless the United States was willing to assume this responsibility, it had no right to prohibit Europeans from protecting their rights in America.

The corollary was itself applied in this first decade of the twentieth century, when some of the Latin-American countries were in financial difficulties. Santo Domingo, an island republic in the Caribbean, had difficulty in meeting foreign debts. It was probable that one of the European nations might seize customhouses to do its own collecting, or take territory as compensation for the debts. The United States forestalled this possibility by taking charge of Dominican finances and making arrangements to pay foreign creditors. Thus, the American government assumed the duty of collecting debts for foreigners, although, of course, it was primarily in self-interest, for its own security, and for the maintenance of the principles of the Monroe Doctrine.

In the Central-American republic of Nicaragua there was a similar situation. The Nicaraguan government was unstable, and there was general disorder in the country. American and European interests were endangered. The logical step was intervention. United States Marines occupied the territory, the Nicaraguan government was reorganized and customs revenues were collected and supervised by American officials. This practice finally resulted in the establishment of a financial protectorate over that Central-American nation. American loans to Nicaragua have been numerous. The Central-American republics have been made to understand that granting of concessions to foreign nations will be frowned upon by the United States.

In fairness to the United States, it should be pointed out that under its supervision the customs collections were made with greater regularity and fewer losses, the debts were repaid, and the financial position of the various Latin-American states was much improved.

THE UNITED STATES AND MEXICO

In a discussion of the Latin-American interests of the United States one must certainly include Mexico, for that nation was one of the most tempting morsels for imperial conquest in the areas to the southward. Mexico is endowed with an abundance of rich resources among which is oil. Extensive investment by Americans in Mexican mines and oil fields was not undertaken until Porfirio Diaz became ruler of the country. During his administration he encouraged the entrance of foreign capital, and British and American investors indulged in a race to exploit the country. However, not an inch of territory was taken from Mexico.

When Díaz left office, things took a turn in the opposite direction. Internal disorder was widespread. Governments fell one after another. Bullets replaced ballots in Mexican elections. The United States refused to recognize anything but a constitutional form of government. President Wilson openly opposed American financial imperialism in Mexico, and favored a policy of nonintervention or "watchful waiting." However, when Huerta, the Mexican general, refused to respect the American flag, it was considered an insult and an encroachment upon "national honor" of the United States. The bloody raids of Pancho Villa along the border of Texas caused the United States to send a military expedition into Mexico to punish the outlaw. What might have become an imperialistic conquest ended in a peaceful evacuation by the United States.

76. Prewar Nationalism

EARLY NATIONALISM

NATIONALISM, the consciousness of unity among a people, was brought to the surface by the French Revolution. The French cry of *la patrie*, the fatherland, reverberated throughout Europe, inspiring the widespread struggles for national independence. In its early stages this patriotic philosophy was an ally of liberalism. The greatest exponent of early nationalism was Mazzini, the liberal Italian revolutionary. Among the liberal nationalists there was no trace of the intolerance and hatred which were to disturb the peace of the world by the end of the nineteenth century.

Nationalism was emphasized in many spheres of activity. Verdi, Wagner, Gounod, and Rimsky-Korsakov incorporated the spirit of their countries in their music. The poetry of Körner, Uhland, Leopardi, and Mickiewicz glorified the fatherland. The interest in the national role was evinced by historians. Scholars in many nations collected the documents of their early history. Niebuhr, Ranke, Stubbs, Froude, Guizot, and Michelet wrote extensively about the national history of their respective countries.

In some cases nationalism was beginning to assume an ominous form. Friedrich List advocated a type of economic nationalism based on the protective tariff which has been disturbing the world till the present day. On the whole, however, the nationalism from 1815 to 1870 was of a beneficial type. It promoted patriotism but not jingoism. The interest in national well-being did not necessarily lead to hatred of other nations. One factor in this situation was the fact that the early national movements were either directed against an outside ruler or were for national unification.

NEW FORMS OF NATIONALISM

The seizure of Alsace-Lorraine by Germany in 1871 was a symptom of the changing spirit of nationalism, which was assuming a malignant form. It was becoming the tool of conservative and reactionary forces. Not only were the rights of national minorities disregarded, but often the attempt was made to destroy the foreign elements. Forcible "Germanization" of the Poles in Germany, "Russification" of the vast numbers of non-Russians in Russia, and "Magyarization" of non-Magyars in Hungary, were indications of the rising spirit of national feeling.

The economic liberalism of the early part of the century was changing. Free trade was giving way to economic nationalism. Tariffs, bounties, and quotas were used to protect and foster national industry and commerce. The reason for this shift was the increasing industrialization of the European countries. As they developed industries, they became competitors of other nations for trade within their own borders and in other regions.

The new nationalism was one of the causes of imperialism—the domination of non-European peoples by the European nations. Nationalism was becoming international in its influence and scope.

Another indication of the changing spirit

could be seen in militarism. Before 1793 armies were, in the main, composed of professional, volunteer soldiers. After that date, conscript armies became more numerous. Universal, compulsory military training made possible the huge modern armies.

The schools were learning to sing a new hymn of hate. Textbooks such as those of Treitschke preached the new gospel of national hatred. In France, Maurice Barrès encouraged the hatred of Germany, while Germany taught her sons to distrust France. Nationalism meant not only love of fatherland, but also dislike for the foreigner.

The subject of national pride assumed an important role in international affairs. When a conflict arose between two nations, neither would yield for fear of losing "face." Thus unnecessary friction was generated. The "incidents" which preceded World War I provide innumerable instances of the perverse influence of national pride.

IMPERIALISM

The nations, such as Germany and Italy, which were left out of the imperialistic race felt that they had been seriously mistreated, and constituted another source of national friction. No European nation could feel itself a power without a colonial empire to bolster its national esteem. Italy spent billions of lire conquering the barren wastes of Tripoli and Cyrenaica, all for the sake of national prestige. Under Bismarck's leadership, Germany became a colonial power. Other secondary powers spent more on colonies than they received from them.

The effects of imperialism were not confined to overseas territories, but were very evident upon Europe itself. Most nations under the impetus of an intense nationalistic spirit strove to build up an empire which would serve, among other things, to enhance their power and prestige upon the European continent. Regardless of relative size and strength, each nation strove for "a place in the sun." In other words, an impressive empire was a requisite for greatness. The diplomatic success of one nation at the expense or embarrassment of another often produced an extremely tense

situation, thus giving rise to international rivalries and jealousies. The so-called "dangerous incidents," of which the Balkan and Moroccan crises are excellent examples, illustrate this fact.

It was in the years just preceding World War I that economic competition became acute. With the speeding-up process of industry, it was almost inevitable that economic competition among the various nations of Europe would be intensified. Each country desired to remain as self-sufficient as possible, trading for the most part with its own colonies, and at the same time erecting tariff barriers to shut out foreign goods. This great rivalry for the domination of foreign markets also jeopardized the peace of the world.

INTERNATIONAL TENSIONS

Within each nation, at this same time, a highly efficient military machine was being developed. Colonies, in many cases, had to be acquired by the use of military force. Then, to protect such colonies, a large navy was required. Competition in armaments arose in part as a result of this great wave of economic imperialism.

Imperialistic rivalries were brought to a near crisis when several European nations cast longing eyes toward the Near East. As Germany began her drive to the eastward, the other powers kept a close watch. Austria-Hungary continued her efforts to dominate the Balkans, but at the expense of incurring Russian and Serbian animosity. England and France, for strategic reasons, opposed any plan whereby one nation or an allied group should be allowed domination of this coveted area. Each nation watched the other suspiciously. It seemed as though certain ones were restraining themselves against their will. Two hostile camps were pitched for battle even before the actual outbreak occurred. So strained was the situation that any minor indignity or atrocity threatened an irruption which would involve all Europe. The intricate system of alliances and secret agreements made it almost certain that a war would be widespread.

Thus imperialism had much to do with the creation of a very tense situation. Sportsmanship and international ethics were scarcely considered in the contest among nations. No European power was really satisfied with what it had, for each wished to extend its economic and political influence still farther. Such an acute stage had been reached that a slight or sudden move by one of the nations in the direction of an enlarged imperialistic policy was likely to create a new crisis. The war feeling was everywhere dominant. This psychological element cannot be too strongly emphasized. Thus, in a sense, imperialism, bolstered up by militarism, had set nations on a fighting edge.

RADICALISM IN FRANCE

While English liberalism was continuing the gradual growth which had characterized it for almost a century, liberal groups on the Continent were experiencing greater difficulties and were working toward more radical ends. The bloody suppression of the Paris Commune had struck the progress of French Socialism a hard blow. The ablest leaders were killed or exiled, and the laws against them hampered any serious reorganization of the party. However, feelings ran high concerning the methods used in suppressing the Commune, and it was not long before the popular sentiment of the radicals was manifested in a new Socialist party.

But the leaders had taken new counsels in their exile, and had resolved to take direct action, as they called it, rather than to trust too strongly in political measures to effect a revolution. Strongly influential in this movement was Georges Sorel, who formulated the theory of what is called Syndicalism.

Trade unions, legalized in 1884, formed themselves into a large union in 1895, called the *Confédération Générale du Travail*, and by merging with the system of labor employment agencies, in 1902, the Syndicalist movement was formed. Briefly, Syndicalism holds that political action is futile in a bourgeois controlled state and that war on the capitalists is the only way to bring about a revolution. Therefore, the capitalists should be urged to withdraw from the field as quickly as possible, and, if they would not withdraw, they should

be forced to go by acts of violence. Sabotage, the injury of machinery or delay of production, was to be the chief weapon, with the general strike as a last resort. The general strike was to be a complete cessation of work on the part of all workers, thus paralyzing the industry of the entire country. Disease and starvation would finally compel the capitalists to capitulate.

Syndicalism had a strong effect on Socialism, making it more aggressive, and at the same time more progressive. Those Socialists who favored political methods instead of a long and possibly annihilating class war supported a less reactionary program. Two leaders, Jean Jaurès and Jules Guesde, who favored slightly different interpretations of the Marxian theory, united their forces in 1905. Socialism of the less violent type made great progress in France, electing almost one-fifth of the Chamber of Deputies by 1914.

BOULANGER AND DREYFUS INCIDENTS

Opposition served to infuriate the monarchists, who attempted by more or less secret means to inflame the people against the Republicans. General Boulanger, a popular soldier, appeared for a time to threaten the government, but he finally succumbed to panic and, when charges were preferred against him, fled the country. This attempted usurpation strengthened the Republican party.

The clash of feelings engendered by nationalism, strong anti-Semitism, and hatred of Germany was illustrated in the Dreyfus Case. Captain Alfred Dreyfus, a French army officer, of Jewish birth and a native of Alsace, was, on flimsy evidence, accused of treason. He was tried and convicted in 1894 and sent to prison on Devil's Island. In 1896 the new chief of the intelligence service, Colonel Picquart, discovered evidence that pointed to a Major Esterhazy as the real traitor. Picquart was promptly transferred to Tunis and Esterhazy was tried and acquitted by court martial. However, the affair became a public issue after Émile Zola's bitter denunciation of the government's actions in the case and the discovery that some of the evidence against Dreyfus had been forged. By now France was divided into two camps: Dreyfusards, those wanting to maintain the republic; and anti-Dreyfusards, the army and many Royalists and Catholics— interested in restoring the monarchy. In 1899 the highest French court set aside Dreyfus' conviction, but he was again found guilty by a court martial. However, he was pardoned. After the Dreyfusards accumulated new evidence, the highest court again set aside the court martial verdict. Dreyfus was then rein-

Captain Dreyfus (left) and Emile Zola, who figured in the Dreyfus Case, which divided France

stated in the army, and promoted to major. Colonel Picquart, who had been forced out of the army, was also reinstated and promoted to brigadier general. The Dreyfus Affair left bitter feelings for many years in France. Proof of Esterhazy's guilt came to light in 1930 when the papers of the German military attache were published.

The Anticlericalism which the Republicans had made one of their strong points in 1879 lingered throughout most of French politics up to the war. The issue had been established by Léon Gambetta, of the middle class party, and revolved about the unwillingness of the taxpayers to support a church which taught doctrines inimical to their political sentiments. The clergy, it cannot be disputed, was strongly monarchial in sympathy and figured largely— though usually unobtrusively—in the Boulanger and Dreyfus incidents.

CHURCH AND STATE

The Concordat of 1801, established between the Church and Napoleon I, provided that the state would pay the salaries of the clergy, while all ecclesiastical appointments would be made with the approval of the state. Thus the Church and state were inseparable. The anticlerical movement resulted in several changes. In 1886 primary education was made compulsory and public schools were set up, free from religious control, and supported by the state.

For many years Anticlericalism served to unite the various republican and lower middle class elements, but, with the passage of laws which struck at unauthorized religious bodies, came the final separation of Church and state in 1905. The clergy were given some slight concessions, which enabled them to keep active, but their political power was broken.

With their influential enemies out of the way, the various republican elements could afford to quarrel, and their bloc became disrupted. Thus arose some of the power of the Socialists. But World War I, which affected all Socialism adversely, soon overwhelmed French Socialists who were as nationalistic as other party groups when the crisis came.

SOCIALISM IN GERMANY

The formation of the German Empire in 1871 was an important new fact for the Great Powers to contemplate. Chancellor Bismarck was able to keep the nation happy and unified by subordinating class interests as much as possible to national interests. He accomplished this end by granting to each class a certain amount of privilege or ameliorating legislation, while keeping them all subordinate to his main policy.

The formation of a strong Socialist party in Germany explains why Bismarck aided the workers so materially. The Socialist party was stronger in Germany than in any other nation, not excepting France, and though meeting with bitter opposition from the Chancellor, it flourished and agitated for radical measures.

The formation of the Socialist party in Germany was due largely to the efforts and personality of Ferdinand Lassalle, and the cooperation of Wilhelm Liebknecht and August Bebel. Lassalle had a wide success in northern Germany, forming a party in 1863 which was called the General Workingmen's Association of Germany. In 1875 it was merged with Lieb-

A Wagon Train of the 1840's. Prairie schooners or canvas-topped wagons came into use in the 1830's, but wagon trains were not common until after 1840. They served as overland freight and passenger convoys, convenient for the protection afforded against Indian attacks. They were replaced by stagecoaches and railroads.

"The Image Peddler," by Francis W. Edmonds, a genre painting showing an aspect of the daily life of 19th-century Americans. The peddler sold knickknacks, small pieces of sculpture, wood carvings, and toys. Although the workmanship varied in quality, these novelties brought some beauty to people on the frontier.

The General Store on the Frontier. The local store was a center of activity for the towns and villages of early America, both in settled areas and on the frontier. Currency was scarce and trade was by barter. Miscellaneous items, from crackers in barrels, to household wares and yard-goods, were available to the settlers.

A Wilderness Court and Presiding Judge. In the early days of the republic the court system was loosely organized and served by circuit-riding judges and lawyers. Florid oratory and rhetoric took precedence over closely reasoned argument. Decisions were often a combination of sentiment and personal interpretation.

P. T. Barnum's "Museum," New York, 1842. This great showman caught the public's fancy by sensational advertising and strange exhibits. Tom Thumb, the midget, was popularized by Barnum. Barnum became famous for his circus, which he billed as "The Greatest Show on Earth." It later joined with Ringling Bros. circus.

A Union Pacific Train, Kansas, 1870. The transcontinental railroad had just been completed and it was possible to travel by rail from coast to coast. Stage lines and wagon trains were replaced by this new means of transportation, and the wilderness became part of civilization. Settlement followed at a fast pace.

The Klondike Gold Rush, 1896. Gold was discovered in Canada just east of the Alaskan border. From 1897 to 1898 the rush was on. This picture shows prospectors preparing to cross famous Chilkoot Pass to reach the upper Yukon. 1900 was the peak year of the rush when $22 million worth of gold was produced.

The Charge up San Juan Hill, July 1, 1898. The Rough Riders led by Colonels "Teddy" Roosevelt and Leonard Wood, took the hill on foot. As a result the American forces won the heights of Santiago, Cuba, and captured the city. The Spanish-American War group of volunteer cavalry won national fame for Roosevelt.

knecht's and Bebel's group to form a united party, called the Social Democratic Party of Germany.

The platform of this party was in general Marxian, though in many particulars it deviated from that dogmatic standard. State ownership of the means of production was to be accomplished through extending individual rights and privileges, which eventually would result in political supremacy for Socialists. Freedom of the press, freedom of person from arbitrary arrest, freedom of assembly, free education, freedom to form unions, and universal suffrage were some of their demands. Soon they were able to elect members to the Reichstag, and inevitably they encountered the opposition of the most influential man in Germany.

BISMARCK AND THE SOCIALISTS

Bismarck had long been alarmed at the spread of doctrines so contrary to his program, and in 1878 he took advantage of an attempt on the life of the emperor to pass laws aiming at the extinction of German Socialism. A law which was intended to prevent all open expression of socialistic opinion or doctrine was passed immediately, with a penalty of arrest and exile for those who broke it. Martial law was invoked against the Socialists. The measure provided that it was to be in force for four years, and was re-enacted in 1882 and 1886.

The Socialists, notwithstanding, continued to spread their doctrines. Although many of their papers and magazines were suppressed, others, smuggled into the country, took their place. Where one Socialist was arrested and exiled, two more arose. They continued vigorously to denounce working conditions in the empire, and, aided by a depression, rallied more converts than ever before to their cause.

Bismarck, clever diplomat that he was, turned to methods more practical than those he had used previously. In the decade of the 1880's, he put through several pieces of social and labor legislation. To be sure, the workers paid for their own insurance and the middle class, troubled very little by pressure on their pocketbooks to finance social measures, offered no serious opposition. Bismarck was able to retard the growth of Socialism by aiding the industrialists and merchants with high tariff barriers which seemed to improve the economic status of the country.

FALL OF BISMARCK

Nevertheless, there remained a strong Socialist party in Germany. When William II ascended the throne in 1888, he resented Bismarck's leadership. The Iron Chancellor was compelled to resign in 1890, and William II attempted to deal with the Socialists in his own way. His early policy included social legislation planned to undermine the leadership of prominent Socialists. This purpose was defeated by his relaxation of the decrees against socialistic propaganda. The Socialist party became influential in the Reichstag before World

Bismarck, the Iron Chancellor of Germany

War I, and, although it had opposed war as a method of settling international disputes, it offered no objection to the invasion of Belgium.

THE GOLDEN AGE BEFORE THE WAR

Despite the growth of strong nationalism and the rumblings of conflicting imperialisms, the quarter century before the outbreak of World War I is, to many historians and writers, a golden age. It was a period of peace, unbroken by any major war. Technological development was spectacular, and it was the age in which most of our present day scientific information was classified and disseminated. Art, music, and literature were experiencing brilliant developments, and it seemed to many as if the civilized world was moving into a bright new day of shared knowledge and international co-operation. In western Europe this seemed especially so, for here travel barriers were almost unknown, and the middle and upper classes moved with almost complete freedom from one country to another. But the peace was the lull before the storm.

77. The Coming of the War

THE GREATEST TRAGEDY in modern history is the failure of man to substitute right for might in international relations. The advance of civilization has in reality increased the dominance of might. One wonders why men still resort to weapons to settle disputes between nations, when peaceful means are available. A study of Europe's condition in 1906 helps us to answer the question. There existed a feeling among the nations that it was dishonorable to submit to any form of outside control. In addition there were economic and imperialistic rivalries.

This ill-feeling was increased by the revival of the old mercantilism which taught that each nation must protect and promote the economic interests of its own citizens, even by force if that should be necessary. Further, each was eager to gain as much power as possible to gratify its nationalistic pride. It was inevitable, therefore, that fear and hatred should permeate Europe.

FORMATION OF ALLIANCES

With the certainty fixed in their minds that this clash of interests would ultimately result in war, the statesmen of the various countries of Europe looked about them for allies. Their negotiations were secret, and the masses of the people never knew when or why they might be plunged into a war to aid an ally. Through this secret diplomacy Europe became divided into the two camps of Triple Alliance and Triple Entente.

The Triple Alliance was constructed through the crafty diplomacy of the great German, Bismarck. In 1879 he concluded a treaty with Austria, and in 1882 Italy joined to make a triple alliance. Russia, too, signed a secret treaty of alliance, and England was friendly, though not officially allied. France stood alone, faced by this formidable combination. Then Bismarck was dismissed in 1890. Almost immediately Germany's position weakened. The young kaiser failed to renew the Russian alliance. The czar succumbed to the blandishments of France, and in 1892 became her ally. In 1904, England signed a secret agreement, or *entente*, with France, which was almost as binding as a formal alliance. Three years later England made a similar agreement with Russia. So came into existence the Triple Entente.

TESTS OF THE ALLIANCE SYSTEM

The balance of power between the two systems seemed to be even. True, Italy had made a secret bargain with France in 1902, but Germany's military power more than made up for this maneuver. Neither side was certain that it could defeat the other; so there was much nervousness and tension. Each group believed it necessary to keep up with the opposing one by continually increasing armaments.

In such a charged atmosphere the slightest spark could set off the explosion. Four times a dangerous crisis arose. Each time it was settled, but each was more serious than its predecessor, and each tested the strength of the alliance system. The Algeciras incident in Morocco in 1906, the second Morocco crisis in 1911, and the Balkan wars of 1912 and 1913, all served not only to point to the catastrophe to come, but also played their part in preparing the way, for they intensified the spirit of hatred and rivalry.

In the eight years that had intervened between the first Moroccan crisis and the apparent settling of the Balkan struggles, the danger of a war between the Triple Alliance and the

Triple Entente was constant. Yet it had always been avoided. To the optimists this seemed to indicate that such a war would never come. As the bells tolled the end of 1913, those who saw only the surface claimed that the balance of power was so even that war could not happen. Also, they believed that the causes for international ill-will had been removed. Germany, eager for her "place in the sun," seemed satisfied with her gains in Africa and Turkey. France had achieved her aim in Morocco. The Balkans had quieted down. International tribunals of peace had been created.

It was only the lull before the storm. Actually, the European powers were feverishly preparing for war. Millions of dollars were being poured into weapons of death, for discerning statesmen knew that war would come in the very near future. Probably, it would result from the clash of Teuton and Slav in the southeastern corner of Europe.

THE DANGER SPOT IN EUROPE

The Balkans have been well termed the "powder keg" of Europe. Inhabited by turbulent and violent people of many nationalities, they were a favorite field for rivalries between Austria, Germany, and Russia in the long twilight of the Ottoman Empire.

Russia's primary interest in this region was to keep open the Straits of the Bosphorus, for if they were closed Russian trade and shipping would be bottled up in the Black Sea. So the czar's empire cultivated friendship with the small Balkan nations, whose Slavic blood made them closely akin to Russia.

German and Austrian designs in this region were political and economic. Austria looked forward to controlling the entire peninsula. By putting the Balkans under the hegemony of the Triple Alliance powers, and with the friendship of Turkey, Germany and Austria would hold a position of advantage over Russia and could dominate central Europe. Accordingly, Germany made overtures to Turkey, and obtained the concession of the Berlin-to-Baghdad railway.

The most difficult obstacle in the way of German-Austrian success was Serbia. Occupying a key position on the line of the proposed railway from the North Sea to the Persian Gulf, she forestalled all attempts to create German hegemony over the Balkans. Either German-Austrian plans must be given up, or Serbian opposition must be destroyed.

Thus, the two alliance systems faced each other, with the little Balkan nation of Serbia the focal point of discord. Only a concerted effort by the nations of Europe could avert immediate war.

SUMMER—1914

The pistol shots of a Bosnian assassin produced the crisis. Archduke Francis Ferdinand

The Last Few Minutes of Peace. Archduke Francis Ferdinand and his wife leaving the senate house in Sarajevo just before their assassination by a Bosnian student. The shooting touched off World War I. (Acme)

of Austria and his commoner wife were visiting the Bosnian city of Sarajevo. Heir to the throne of the Hapsburgs, Francis Ferdinand was a symbol of the tyranny so hated by all Slavs. Several young Slavic students slipped into the city prepared to murder the archduke. The assassins were armed with bombs and pistols taken from a Serbian government arsenal by a staff officer who was a leader of the group. One of the youths, Gavrilo Princip, succeeded in killing both Francis Ferdinand and his wife while they were riding through the streets on June 28, 1914. The actual assassination was the result of one of the decisive accidents of history. The irresolute Princip had let the archduke's car go by, but the chauffeur made a wrong turn and was forced to back up, past the point where the assassin was standing; this time he shot.

THE AUSTRIAN ULTIMATUM

For a moment statesmen were filled with consternation. Then the storm broke. Austria, highly excited, charged without real proof that the Serbian government was supporting the murderers. Here was an excellent chance to reduce Serbia to complete dependence and so end the Slavic menace on the southern borders of the empire, and open a clear way for Austrian supremacy in the Balkans. Therefore, a month later Vienna sent a note to Serbia making ten humiliating demands and giving only forty-eight hours for an answer. The gist of this ultimatum was such that, if Serbia complied, she would give up certain rights of government and become more or less an Austrian dependency.

Without doubt, Austria did not expect Serbia to yield, and the ultimatum was to be an excuse to declare war upon its rejection. Germany, without knowing the Austrian plans or the contents of the note, had given its promise to stand by her ally in the punishment of the assassin, a promise referred to as Germany's "blank check" to Austria. Hence, immediately after presentation of the ultimatum, Germany publicly announced the whole-hearted support of Austria. England and France, anxious to keep peace, urged Serbia to send a satisfactory reply. Humbled,

the Serbs accepted all but two of the demands, and offered to have these two arbitrated by The Hague Tribunal. Meanwhile, they appealed to Russia and were promised support.

To all the other nations the menace of war was dreadful. Frantically the statesmen sought a way to keep Austria and Russia apart. They knew that as soon as the first shot was fired they would all be involved. The lines had been so clearly drawn, the alliances so firmly welded.

THE LAST DAYS OF PEACE

The British proposed a conference of the Powers at London which should demand the cessation of all military activities by Austria, Russia, and Serbia. France suggested that they should all bring pressure to bear at Vienna and St. Petersburg to compel peace. To all suggestions Germany was at first cold; but when she saw that the war could not be localized in Serbia, but would involve all Europe and that the redemption of the "blank check to Austria" would mean having to fight France, Russia, and even Great Britain, she hastily changed her tactics and began urging Austria to negotiate the dispute. But the pressure on Austria slackened momentarily as the military party in Berlin insisted on war, and Britain's suggestion for a conference was rejected.

As expected, Austria found Serbia's reply unsatisfactory and declared war on Serbia on July 28, 1914. Russia began partial mobilization and the news of this action led the German General Staff to insist that the foreign ministry of William II decide on war or peace, for if war came, Germany should strike before Russia and her ally France. Germany, therefore, threatened war unless Russia ceased mobilizing. The czar's war department did not desist from its course and, when Russia refused, Germany declared war. Meanwhile Germany had sent France an ultimatum asking whether, if Russia and Germany went to war, France would aid her ally. France did not reply, and, to avoid appearing as the aggressor, delayed her declaration until Germany had actually declared war and invaded Belgian territory. France's position in the minds of her officials was simple: she must support her ally Russia, and the people upheld the government's action.

England's attitude was uncertain at this stage. The cabinet was divided, with the majority against England's taking part in a continental war. Parliament was not in session, and public opinion seemed opposed to participation. Lord Grey, the foreign minister, became more and more concerned as the realization of the meaning and obligations of the secret ententes and promises he had given France became clearer. But would the other members of the cabinet, let alone the British people, permit a declaration of war over a Balkan squabble, or for the defense of France?

At this point, German troops began marching through Belgium in direct violation of the treaty signed by six great European Powers in 1839, guaranteeing Belgian neutrality. In order to gain a quick victory over France, the Germans had believed themselves compelled to make this breach of international law. The British people knew that German possession of Belgium meant danger to Great Britain for "Belgium is a pistol aimed at the heart of England." The emotional appeal of invasion of little Belgium by powerful Germany was not overlooked. Lord Grey and the Cabinet decided to make this action a cause for war. Germany was called upon to live up to the terms of the treaty of neutrality or face England's declaration of war. Germany refused, and when the British ambassador asked for his passports the German Chancellor bitterly remarked that according to England's statement she was going to war "just for a scrap of paper."

THE OUTBREAK OF WAR

Although Austria mobilized on July 26, and bombarded the Serbian capital three days later, the more important phase of World War I began August 3, when the first German troops crossed the Belgian border. This long-planned movement of the German army seemed to take the French staff by surprise. According to the Entente plans, France was to attack the German army along the Franco-German border in Alsace-Lorraine, while Russia kept the other half busy in the East. These plans were disrupted when almost the entire German army poured through the neutral and relatively unfortified territory of Belgium. At great sacrifice to themselves, the Belgians resisted at the forts of Liége and Namur. Nevertheless, eighteen days later the huge army marched into northern France ahead of schedule.

The French Marshal Joffre maneuvered his armies in the Alsace-Lorraine region, withdrawing men and sending them northwest to meet the advancing Germans, and took up a position south of the Marne River. For four days the French, with the small English and

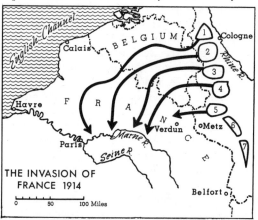

THE INVASION OF FRANCE 1914

The German 1st and 2d armies wheeled south short of Paris, a fatal abandonment of the Schlieffen Plan

German troops crossing boundary line into France in 1914 after overcoming stalwart Belgian defense

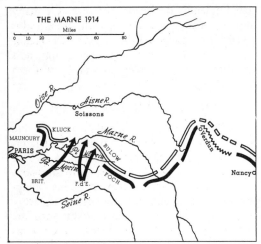

Maunoury's attack, ordered by Gallieni, led Kluck
to draw back, creating a gap between him and Bulow

Machine Gun in position on Western Front in 1914.
This weapon helped bring about trench warfare

Belgian armies, fought the famous Battles of
the Marne, so critical that the defenders of
the gate to Paris were sent out in taxicabs
and on bicycles. Aided by the British these
emergency troops rushed into a gap between
parts of the German army and almost isolated
one section. The entire German line had to
be withdrawn northward to the Aisne River.
The quick conquest of France was prevented.

The Germans hastened to extend their
lines northwestward to include the French
channel ports most important for the landing
of English troops. But the English succeeded
in turning the German right flank northward
to the Belgian coast near Ypres.

TRENCH WARFARE

Both armies were so strung out that they
had to entrench themselves for defense. This
marked a turning point in the war. Instead of
fighting with compact masses of movable
troops, the nations were facing each other in a
line six hundred miles long, from the Channel
to the Swiss frontier, in positions easy to
hold but difficult to capture. Instead of armies
of a few hundred thousand men, entire populations were involved, millions in the trenches,
millions working in home bases, and the
various countries completely concerned with
providing men and supplies. Western Europe
was in a state of siege.

RESOURCES FOR A LONG WAR

Under these conditions, staying power was
what counted. Germany had a standing army
of 820,000 men which could be expanded by
mobilization to over five million. During the
war she mobilized a total of eleven million
men. In addition, she had the armies of Austria
and Turkey. Their men were already trained
by a universal conscript system, well disciplined, and had leaders who were probably
the most efficient in the world. On the side of
the Allies, the huge Russian army, the largest
in the world, was slow, poorly officered, and
very ill-equipped for modern war. England
had a small standing army and no trained
conscripts of the type produced by the compulsory military service of the Continent.
France was better off in respect to men,
mustering seven and a half million during the
war. Germany had an advantage in fighting
on French soil, with some French munition
factories inside her lines. Because of their
middle location, the Central Powers were
able to transfer troops quickly from east to
west over their efficient rail system, while the
Allies were cut off from each other by sea.

Once the war had settled into trenches, the
Allies had more reason for hope. Direct
military advantage such as strategic plans,
prepared armies, and an internal position

German artillery in action in France. Stable conditions of warfare encouraged use of big guns

might be less important than other factors in a long war. Britain and her empire could eventually train a large army. The British navy ruled the seas, enabling her to blockade and starve Germany, while England and France could supply themselves from neutrals across the water. England's great industrial machine, product of a century longer growth than that of Germany, was thus spared the ravages of war, and after a year was tuned up to supply munitions as rapidly as Germany's

more specialized factories. Even more important, Britain and France could buy in quantity from the United States, and pay by vast borrowings in that country. Without Britain's manufactures to make up for her lost coal and iron region—both to supply her armies and to maintain Allied borrowing power—France would have been swamped.

To paralyze London, that world center of trade, finance, and industry, Germany had two weapons: the Zeppelin and the submarine. The airships had little effect on the London populace, but the submarine was more effective in threatening England's food supply, a most vital point, for England was more dependent than other nations on overseas trade. England was much like a great city dependent upon country areas over the sea, while Germany had enough agricultural and raw materials to make her self-sufficient in a short war.

THE EASTERN ALLY

While western Europe was tightening its belt for the costliest war in history, the Russians were discovering that their old system of enslaved peasantry and corrupt aristocracy could furnish neither good officers, good soldiers, nor adequate supplies. At first their "steam roller" army was able to invade Galicia while the Austrian army was weak-

German Submarine U-53. Craft of this type sank hundreds of thousands of tons of Allied ships

Huge German Zeppelins of this type crossed the English Channel in bombing raids on England

ened by unsuccessful
fighting with the Ser-
bians. In the north,
against East Prussia,
their operations were
of some value to the
French, for the influ-
ential landowners there
demanded of the Berlin
government protection
of their farms. This
was accomplished by
withdrawing men from
the Battle of the Marne,

**Hindenburg, German
World War I leader**

and the British and French, penetrating the
weakened spot, won the battle.

German armies under generals Hindenburg
and Ludendorff, however, soon won a great
victory over the Russians at Tannenberg, advancing far into Russia to threaten Petrograd
by spring, 1915. In the same year, under the
German general, von Mackensen, Austria re-

trieved all of Galicia and Russian Poland
besides. Bulgaria, thereupon, joined the Central
Powers in the hope of winning territory lost
in the last Balkan War, and assisted in conquering Serbia and Montenegro.

The Allies launched a naval and land attack
upon Turkey in the Dardanelles to render aid
to Russia on the Black Sea. They also began
ventures at Salonika, in parts of Armenia, and
in Mesopotamia. All involved great waste of
manpower and all failed. The Allies were
struggling desperately to keep the Central
Powers from completely smashing Russia.
If Russia collapsed all might be lost for the
Allies.

Moving a heavy gun during the fighting in Rumania, August 17, 1917

THE SPREAD OF THE WAR

In September, 1914, the Allies had agreed
not to withdraw separately from the conflict.
They used diplomacy in other directions.
Neutrals were offered rich rewards for join-
ing them. Though Turkey went over to the
Central Powers at the beginning as an enemy
of Russia, Japan joined the Allies, quickly
taking over German interests in China.
Portugal, bound by an old treaty to assist
England, joined in November.

The Central Powers were unable to hold
Italy to her alliance with them since her interests conflicted with Austria's. In the spring of
1915 she accepted the Allies' promises of
enough Austrian, Balkan, Greek and oversea

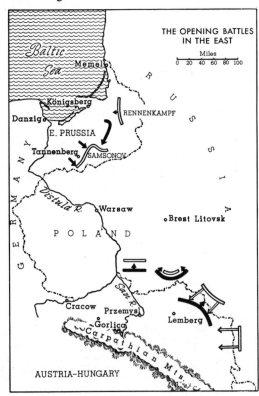

The Eastern Front in 1914–15

Farman Pusher Bombing Biplane used by the French in World War I. A 1916 photograph

territory to give her control of the Adriatic and Aegean seas.

The Allies received a setback when Bulgaria joined Austria in the fall of 1915 following von Mackensen's success against Russia. The Central Powers, by this alliance and by a final conquest of Serbia and Montenegro under von Mackensen, had control of the whole of the Balkans. The Berlin-Baghdad connection was an accomplished fact, at least territorially.

THE EARLY WAR ON THE SEA

Sea control was of vital importance in World War I. At the outset, Germany possessed the second finest fleet in the world, and Austria had a small fleet and port on the Adriatic. Neither fleet, however, dared leave its harbor in the face of superior Allied sea power. Britain thus was able to declare a blockade of the North Sea, including neutral Holland and Denmark. As usual, the United States protested the high-handed breach of neutral rights, but as usual the rights of neutrals were ignored.

Germany suffered greatly from the blockade. She could not pay for the huge costs of the war if she could not sell her manufactures as formerly. Where could she get food now that all her manpower was drawn from the fields into the tremendously enlarged and all-engulfing war? She had to rely on what could seep through Holland and Denmark.

England destroyed Germany's warships at sea systematically; one fleet was destroyed in the battle of the Falkland Islands, and various

lone commerce raiding cruisers were captured or interned in neutral ports. The giant *Vaterland*, world's largest vessel, interned in New York, was later renamed *Leviathan* and employed by the Americans to transport troops. Most of Germany's merchant marine suffered a similar fate, and thus her foreign markets were lost to the British and Americans.

COLONIAL LOSSES

Worse yet, Germany's colonies lay undefended at the mercy of the Allies. As early as August, 1914, the colony of Togoland fell to French and British invasions. Kamerun surrendered early in 1915. German South-West Africa was finally conquered by the famous Boer generals Jan Smuts and Louis Botha. German East Africa held out until 1918, but the German Pacific islands and Far Eastern possessions had fallen to the New Zealanders and the Japanese respectively by the end of 1914.

General Smuts, who took South-West Africa. (Karsh—Ziff Davis)

Turkey suffered too, losing Cyprus and Egypt to England's sea strength. The early failures of the Allies at the Dardanelles, Salonika, and Mesopotamia were recouped later, in operations described in the next Chapter.

JUTLAND AND SUBMARINE WARFARE

In the Battle of Jutland, May 31, 1916, Germany's High Seas Fleet, commanded by Admiral Scheer, met the British Grand Fleet, under Admiral Jellicoe. A running battle, at first between battle cruiser squadrons, ensued, and the British lost heavily. In the main action, the Germans lost several vessels before Scheer abruptly broke off the fight. In the darkness and mist the German fleet succeeded in escaping back to its base. The British lost 3 battle cruisers, 3 cruisers, and 8 destroyers; the Germans lost 1 battleship, 1 battle cruiser, 4 cruisers, and 5 destroyers.

Battle of Jutland, May 31, 1916. Results were indecisive, but the German fleet withdrew. (Paul's Photos)

In spite of Jutland's indecisive character, it helped convince German leaders that the British blockade could be broken only by submarine action against British commerce. Surface raiders, especially the *Emden*, the *Wolf*, and the *Karlsruhe*, had inflicted some damage on Allied shipping, but submarines were far more useful, because they could slip through the Allied patrols with relative ease. However, if the German submarines dared to obey international law and warn carriers of contraband before torpedoing them, they were in great danger of destruction by British armed vessels, some flying neutral flags. The U-boats, therefore, had begun sinking all suspicious vessels without warning. This campaign gave promise of ultimately starving England into submission. However, the United States, the only powerful nation not in the war, protested strongly over the sinking of the British *Lusitania* which was carrying American passengers. A year later, in May, 1916, Germany finally agreed to warn merchant vessels, fearing lest the United States join the Allies. Britain could not be starved, while Germany was virtually in a state of siege.

Submarine Warfare. The sinking of the great passenger liner "Lusitania," above, without warning, on May 7, 1915, aroused great American indignation. Lives lost were 1,198, including 128 Americans. (Acme). Left, torpedo from a German submarine striking a merchant vessel. This remarkable photograph, made in October, 1914, was taken from the U-boat which fired the torpedo. (International)

78. The Last Two Years of World War I

THE WESTERN FRONT

BY THE END OF 1916 a virtual stalemate existed on the western front. The prolonged German attacks at Verdun had failed to achieve any definite decision, although they had worn down the French forces so seriously that they were unable to participate on a large scale in the Allied offensive on the Somme. This battle, which raged from July 1 to November 18, was therefore primarily a British operation. After an intensive bombardment, the British advanced on a front of 15 miles toward Bapaume. But the assault bogged down, and in one day the British lost about 60,000 men. Small gains were made in the succeeding months, partly due to the first use of the tank, but eventually the offensive foundered in the mud and rain. The casualties on both sides were enormous: the British, 420,000; the French, 194,000; the German, 440,000.

Changes in command preceded the operations in 1917. Hindenburg, with Ludendorff as quartermaster general, succeeded von Falkenhayn as chief of staff of the German field armies. Nivelle succeeded Joffre as commander in chief of the French armies. Nivelle's plans for a great offensive toward Laon were delayed by disagreement between him and Haig, the British commander, who favored an offensive in Flanders, and by a German withdrawal to stronger positions, fortified as the Hindenburg Line. Neverthe-

Marshal Joffre, the "Victor of the Marne"

less, the Allied offensive began in the spring of 1917. In the Battle of Arras the British advanced four miles but failed to achieve a breakthrough despite the Canadians' capture of Vimy Ridge. Nivelle's own offensive in Champagne failed, with heavy losses. Discontent and mutiny spread in the French army until 16 corps were affected. Discipline was restored when Pétain replaced Nivelle in May, and decided to keep to the defensive until the arrival of American reinforcements.

The collapse of Nivelle's offensive gave Haig, the British commander, the opportunity to embark on a drive into Flanders. He hoped to roll up the German right flank and destroy the submarine bases on the German coast. A surprise attack on Messines ridge in June, 1917

British howitzer hidden in the woods

Camouflaged French railway howitzer

British Trenches near Ypres, one of the famous battlefields of British troops in World War I

was successful, but his main assault, in the third battle of Ypres (or Passchendaele), failed to achieve a breakthrough and cost the British about 400,000 men. In the latter part of the year the Allies achieved some small successes at Verdun, Malmaison, and in the Battle of Cambrai, the first great tank raid. But the overall effect was indecisive.

CAPORETTO

In the fall of 1917 Germany decided to heed the appeals of war-weary Austria, and help her knock Italy out of the war. Ludendorff could spare only six divisions, but with nine Austrian divisions they were launched on Oct. 24, 1917, against the Italians in the weak Caporetto sector. A breakthrough was at once achieved, and the Italian front collapsed. The Italian commander, Cadorna, only saved the

wreckage of his army by a hasty retreat, first to the Tagliamento, and then to the Piave, leaving over a quarter of a million prisoners in the enemy's hands. He was replaced by General Diaz, and fortunately for the Italians the enemy had been surprised by the extent of their success. Unwilling to stop short, they tried to push on without the necessary resources and communications. Thus the Italians were able to reknit their line and hold it on the Piave although they had lost 600,000 men.

UNRESTRICTED SUBMARINE WARFARE

With the situation on the western front still a stalemate, and the British blockade gradually sapping Germany's strength, German leaders came to the conclusion that British supremacy on the sea had to be broken at any cost. They decided on unrestricted submarine warfare as the means. If the raw materials, food, and munitions flowing into Great Britain from overseas could be cut by sinking 600,000 tons of shipping a month, it was felt that in six months England would have to yield. Already, in the last months of 1916, the German submarines were destroying 300,000 tons a month. By the beginning of 1917 Germany had 120 submarines, and on January 31, she notified the United States that unrestricted submarine warfare would begin on the following day. At first the underseas campaign met with great success, and in April 875,000 tons of shipping were destroyed, more than half of

CAPORETTO 1917

Arrows show the directions of German-Austrian drive that hurled the Italian army back to the Piave

German submarine forced to surface by U.S.S. "Fanning." Crew scuttled vessel, then surrendered

The War Message: President Woodrow Wilson addressing Congress April 2, 1917, and calling for a declaration of war by the United States against Germany. (Acme)

it British. Increased antisubmarine measures, especially the introduction of the convoy system, cut down the losses, however, and by the beginning of 1918 the Allies were building more tonnage than was being destroyed.

AMERICA'S ENTRY INTO THE WAR

From the outbreak of the war, President Wilson apparently felt that the United States could sooner or later step in as a mediator. Officially, the policy was one of neutrality, but the sympathies of the country and the administration were soon on the Allied side. In 1916 Wilson was in negotiation with both the Central and Entente powers, and in December he suggested the belligerents state

The Draft of 1917. Secretary of War Baker drawing the first number called in World War I. (Acme)

their terms for peace. Both sides had stated their terms, and the President, feeling the Allies would soon be unable to continue the war without American aid, was continuing his efforts for a "peace without victory," when Germany announced her new submarine policy. The United States government severed relations with Germany on Feb. 3, 1917. Several American ships were sunk soon after, and the Zimmerman note, intercepted by the British secret service, revealed German plans against the United States. Wilson asked for a declaration of war, and on April 6, 1917 the United States entered the struggle against Germany.

THE BALKANS AND THE MIDDLE EAST

On August 27, 1916, Rumania, encouraged by Allied promises of territorial gain and by the apparent weakness of Austria, declared war on Germany and Austria-Hungary. But her army failed against the German, Austrian, and Bulgarian forces directed by the capable von Mackensen and von Falkenhayn. Soon Rumania was overrun, and her territory furnished valuable oil and grain for the Central Powers.

In the Middle East the British captured Baghdad, on March 10, 1917. Encouraged by the Allies, the Arabs had revolted against the Turks in the previous year. This rising had been in danger of collapse, but the danger was averted by a young British archeologist-soldier, Col. T. E. Lawrence. Brilliantly unconventional and gifted with a magnetic personality he organized the Arab efforts so that the flame of revolt spread through a thousand miles of desert. After a failure in Palestine, the British, under a new commander, Allenby, seized Beersheba, broke through the weakened Turkish center, captured Jaffa, and in December took Jerusalem. Further advance was delayed because Allenby had to send large contingents to France. But in September,

T. E. Lawrence, who organized Arab revolt

1918, in the Battle of Megiddo, the British broke the Turkish line near the Mediterranean and, aided by the Arabs under Lawrence, went on northward to Damascus and Aleppo. The new Turkish sultan then appealed for an armistice, which was concluded, on the Allies' terms, on Oct. 30, 1918.

END OF THE EASTERN FRONT

The disappearance of Russia from the war occurred in 1917. In March, 1917 the long repressed hatred of a corrupt and inefficient regime, merged with disgust with the war, resulted in a revolution which forced the abdication of the Czar. The moderate groups which assumed charge of the government had little success, and in May the government was succeeded by another, more leftist. Its leader,

Camouflage in World War I. U. S. Negro troops moving along a road camouflaged by Germans

U. S. Troopship Convoy, "George Washington" in van. Photo taken May, 1918, on an escorting ship

Kerensky, urged the troops to carry on the war, but in October he was overthrown by the Bolsheviks of the extreme left, who established their rule under Lenin and Trotsky. They speedily sought and concluded an armistice with Germany, in December. Three months later they accepted Germany's drastic terms. The Germans had already begun a wholesale transfer of troops from the eastern to the western front.

THE WESTERN FRONT IN 1918

The Allies began the year 1918 by stating their war aims (British war aims and Wilson's "Fourteen Points"), which depended on military victory. But the prospects looked grim when the Germans, disillusioned with their submarine campaign, staked everything on a decision in the west before the Americans arrived in great force. On March 21, Ludendorff launched a crushing offensive against

German troops moving to the front, April, 1918, during Ludendorff's great Spring offensive

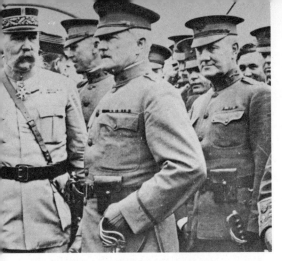

Marshal Foch and General Pershing on the latter's arrival in France, June 13, 1917

Chateau-Thierry: American supply wagon passing through the town after U. S. troops retook it in 1918

the British Fifth Army, which had been weakened because the attack was expected elsewhere. The Germans drove deeply into the British line, and in the crisis General Foch was named to coordinate Allied operations on the western front. A second German blow delivered south of Ypres opened up a wide breach in the British line, but Ludendorff lacked reserves to take advantage of the situation. Then, in the Third Battle of the Aisne, the success of a diversionary attack on the French to draw their reserves from Flanders, took both Ludendorff and the French by surprise. The Germans took Soissons and reached the Marne, but in June the French, aided by an American division at Chateau-Thierry, managed to break the German advance. Ludendorff attacked again at Rheims, but little progress was made. On July 18, Foch ordered a counterattack in which nine American divisions took part. The Germans

were forced back over the Marne, and the French retook Soissons. The Allied counteroffensive frustrated Ludendorff's plans for an attack in Flanders, and enabled Foch to take the offensive.

The Allies now went over to a sustained offensive. In the Battle of Amiens and the second battles of the Somme and Arras, the British and French pushed the Germans back to the Hindenburg Line. The American forces pinched out the St. Mihiel salient. Foch now aimed to cut the main German lateral railway with an American force driving through the Argonne and a British thrust in the Cambrai-St. Quentin sector. Pershing, the American commander, had pushed one third of the way to his objective when, in mid-October, he was forced to suspend operations and reorganize because of heavy casualties. The other attack was more successful, and by October 5, it broke the Hindenburg Line.

American Troops of the 2d Division in action in a shattered wood on the Meuse-Argonne front, 1918

British Tanks lined up in preparation to support troops in an attack on the Hindenburg Line

Airplane Squadron in flight in World War I, when air power first became an important military factor

Bristol Fighter airplane, Mark IV, used by the British on the Western Front in 1918

THE WAR IN THE AIR

Although the airplane was regarded primarily as useful for observation at the outset of the war, air raids were made as early as December 24, 1914, when a single German airplane dropped a bomb on Dover. The first Zeppelin raid was made Jan. 19, 1915, over Yarmouth and King's Lynn; four persons were killed. The heaviest raid of the war was an airplane attack on London, June 13, 1917, when 160 were killed and 432 injured. During the war, 94 raids were made on Britain, 56 by Zeppelins and 38 by airplanes; there were 2 in 1914, 23 in 1915, 28 in 1916, 30 in 1917, and 11 in 1918. There were a total of 202 airship sorties and 452 airplane sorties. The total amount of bombs dropped on Britain during the entire war was 280; total casualties were 1,413 killed and 3,408 injured.

The first heavy bombing of troops occurred in 1915; in the Battle of Loos 5 tons of bombs were dropped, and at the Somme, 300 tons. According to the air theory of the day, the primary objective of airplanes was to direct artillery fire; observation missions were put first, with combat and pursuit missions (to retain air supremacy) second, with bombardment and communications as other missions. Popularly, combat missions and the exploits of individual fliers were stressed. A pilot who destroyed five enemy airplanes was rated as an ace. Popular heroes were Richthofen for Germany, Fonck for France, Bishop for Canada, McCudden for England, and Rickenbacker and Luke for the United States.

The Air Service of the American Expeditionary Force was separated from the Signal Corps in May, 1918. American airplane crews flew more than 35,000 combat hours, all of them in 1918 and most of them in foreign-made aircraft.

Thousands of balloons were used during the war for directing artillery fire and observation. Their use was stimulated by the relatively stable conditions of trench warfare. Continuous observation of the same sector enabled observers to detect even slight changes in enemy positions. Fighter aircraft and antiaircraft guns protected the balloons, which were generally placed from two to four miles in rear of the line of trenches.

NAVAL WARFARE IN 1917 AND 1918

Except for the submarine and convoy operations described above there was little sea

British Grand Fleet, controlling sea approaches to Germany, forced enemy to adopt submarine warfare

The Western Front, World War I. Scenes along the 600-mile line of trenches and field fortifications that ran from the Belgian coast to Switzerland. Above left, American tank crews of the 311th Tank Center moving up to action in the Meuse sector, France. Above right, a shell bursting in front of a French trench near Rheims. Right, American troops moving through Chateau-Thierry, which they occupied during the Second Battle of the Marne, July 15–August 7, 1918. Below, a trench scene about 1916; note the rifle-grenade, a much used weapon in the war. Below right, "Calamity Jane," a 155 mm. howitzer, which fired the last American shot of World War I

Armistice delegates of the Allies outside the railway car in which the armistice of 1918 was signed. (International)

After the armistice the German High Seas Fleet surrendered to the British at Rosyth. In June, 1919, at Scapa Flow, the German ships were scuttled by their crews. American naval forces sustained very slight losses, and were engaged primarily in convoy, patrol, and mine-laying operations.

THE COLLAPSE OF THE CENTRAL POWERS

The success of the Allied drive coincided with the news of the surrender of Bulgaria, following a drive by the Serbs and the French. Fearing for his army, Ludendorff asked the German government to appeal for an armistice. This was done on October 3, and although Ludendorff now became more optimistic as his lines held, the bad news had spread through Germany and crumbled the will to resist. Austria, menaced by a successful Italian advance, sued for peace on October 28, and Turkey capitulated on October 31. The American advance, resumed on November 1, went on smoothly. On November 4, revolution broke out in Germany. The Kaiser was forced to abdicate, and on November 11 the German representatives signed armistice terms designed to make Germany helpless and ensure the acceptance of peace terms. Six hours later the last shots were fired, thus ending the war at the eleventh hour of the eleventh day of the eleventh month of the year 1918.

fighting in the last two years of the war. A British light cruiser attack off Heligoland was beaten back in November, 1917. In an attempt to block the German submarine base at Zeebrugge, on the Belgian coast, the British, in a desperate attack, ran three old cruisers in and sank them in the canal entrance.

Allied Generals in ceremony at Metz when General Pétain received the baton of a French marshal. Left to right: Marshal Joffre; Marshal Foch; Field Marshal Haig, Great Britain; Gen. Pershing; Gen. Gillain, Belgium; Gen. Albricci, Italy; Gen. Haller, Poland

79. The Making of Peace

BULGARIAN REVOLT

ONE OF THE MOST immediate and important results of World War I was the wave of revolutions that swept over eastern Europe. Peoples that had been dominated by foreign powers or by an aristocratic ruling class for centuries asserted their autonomy by overthrowing their old governments. Thus, Bulgaria, Turkey, and the Austro-Hungarian Empire underwent radical changes.

After initial successes against Rumania, the Bulgarian army was beaten back behind its own borders in September, 1918. The morale of the people was already low, and a clamor for peace arose. The government yielded and Bulgaria withdrew from the war at the end of the month.

Meanwhile, Alexander Stambulinsky, the Bulgarian peasant leader who had been imprisoned for his opposition to the war, was released. He made his way to the front, got control of the army, and declared a republic. The old King Ferdinand was driven out, but his son, Boris, was crowned. Stambulinsky was loyal and agreed to this new arrangement. Shortly afterward he became prime minister when the Peasant party came into power.

TURKISH DEVELOPMENTS

The people of Turkey had welcomed the armistice with joy; but their hostility was aroused when the Allies occupied large parts of their country. Turkey's great general, Mustapha Kemal Pasha, became the leader of the budding nationalist movement. He gained control of the central government at Constantinople (Istanbul) in 1920, and refused to accept the terms of the peace treaty offered by the Allied Powers.

Kemal was forced to retreat to Anatolia, in Asia Minor, where he established a republic that had the support of the people. His military victories over the invading Greeks in the subsequent years soon had the Allies concerned

Mustapha Kemal, first president of Turkey

lest their opposition to him lead to a new great war. They agreed to treat with him as an equal to the sultan. Then the latter was driven out by the Nationalists, and on October 1, 1922, the Republic came into complete control. Kemal was elected president, but was actually a dictator. So died the Ottoman Empire, for centuries the scourge of Christian Europe.

DEFECTIONS IN THE AUSTRO-HUNGARIAN EMPIRE

For many years the Austro-Hungarian Empire of the Hapsburgs had included numerous races, all under the autocratic domination of a small German and Magyar ruling class. But defeats and dissatisfaction of the soldiers at the front, and privations at home, led to rebellious movements among the subject nationalities.

These revolts first came into the open with the Corfu Manifesto of July, 1917, which proclaimed the union of the South Slavs. In 1918 a Congress of the Oppressed Nationalities of Austria-Hungary agreed that all the subject peoples would work together to establish their own national states.

The first new nation to emerge was Czechoslovakia. The Allies had aided thousands of Czechoslovakian soldiers to desert Austria.

Thomas Masaryk, organizer of Czech independence, and first president of Czechoslovakia

Then they recognized the existence of a Czechoslovakian state, with headquarters at Paris. After Austria's collapse in October, 1918, a republic was proclaimed at Prague. In order to preserve his crumbling domain, the Austrian emperor offered to transform the empire into a federation of nations, but it was too late. The Yugoslavs proclaimed their independence, but internal disagreements prevented the firm establishment of the new state. The Peace Conference at Versailles finally created the Kingdom of the Serbs, Croats, and Slovenes with the king of Serbia at its head.

Meanwhile, Hungary went through the throes of several revolutions. With the collapse of the Hapsburg monarchy, middle class nationalists obtained control of the government and established a republic. They were soon displaced by a socialist labor government. The country was torn by internal anarchy and endangered by the occupation of foreign troops, so the Socialists had to unite with the Communists to keep in power. Finally the latter, led by Béla Kun, gained complete domination and set up a Soviet republic in March, 1919.

The House of Hapsburg, rulers of Austria for centuries, had reached the end of its career. On November 11, 1918, the last of the line abdicated, and an Austrian Republic was established the next day. Austria was destined to suffer grievously. Because of desperate economic conditions, there was much internal strife, but the republican form of government persisted.

REVOLUTION IN GERMANY

The most surprising of the waves of revolution that swept over Europe in 1918 was that which overthrew the German empire. In 1914 the Kaiser's Germany had been proud and mighty with millions of loyal citizens. In 1918 it disappeared almost overnight, while its once proud and powerful ruler rushed into exile.

In the enthusiasm of 1914 all the German political parties had joined in supporting the war. The first flush of unity soon vanished and the opposition reappeared. As the years dragged by, the German people began to feel the effects of the war, and complaining became common.

In 1917 the Social Democratic party had called attention to this discontent by demanding democratic reforms and peace. Of course, they were unsuccessful then, but they had convinced many that only an armed revolt could free the nation from the grip of the old aristocracy. This belief spread to the men in the trenches and on the battleships—men who were discouraged, hungry, and tired of the mad slaughter.

When the western front collapsed, the Kaiser suddenly awoke to his dangerous predicament. He appointed the liberal Prince Max of Baden as chancellor, permitted Socialists to enter the cabinet, and tried to make Germany a parliamentary monarchy. But William II was doomed. The people were determined that he should abdicate and that a republic be established.

The first revolutionary blow was struck at the end of October by the sailors who mutinied against the order to attack the British fleet. The mutiny spread to the cities, where it became a revolution of the workers. Reveling in their power they cried, "Down with the Kaiser! Long live the Republic!"

At first William was stubborn. Then he discovered that the army, previously the bulwark of the monarchy, refused to fight in his defense.

William II, exiled German Kaiser, at his home in Doorn, Holland, where he lived until his death

American Troops Entering Germany. This is a unit of the Third Army. Maj. Gen. H. T. Allen commanded the American occupation forces in Germany after World War I; they held part of the Rhineland. American occupation ended in Jan., 1923. (Brown Bros.)

The Social Democrats, now in power, set November 9, 1918, as the deadline for the Kaiser's abdication. On that day, at two o'clock in the afternoon, they proclaimed the Republic from the steps of the Reichstag. That night a special train sped westward across the border to Holland and safety. Aboard was the Kaiser, William Hohenzollern. Imperial Germany was no more.

The Moderate Socialists, in power now, announced that a constitutional assembly was to be elected by universal suffrage. This proposal was vigorously opposed by the communistic Spartacists, who demanded that all power should be in the hands of Workers' and Soldiers' Councils. Riots followed and the provisional government was forced to crush the Spartacists by force. Elections were then held in which the Moderates were victorious.

In February, 1919, a National Assembly met at Weimar, elected Friedrich Ebert president, and proceeded to draft a new German constitution. Commonly called the "Weimar Constitution," it was signed Aug. 11, 1919. It established a parliamentary democracy headed by a president. Real executive power was vested in a chancellor and cabinet. The president was given the fateful power to dissolve the Reichstag and suspend constitutional guaranties in periods of national emergency.

ACHIEVEMENT OF POLISH INDEPENDENCE

Although Poland had ceased to exist as a nation after 1795, the memory of their great past was ever present among the Polish people. The oppressions of their hated foreign rulers, Russia, Prussia, and Austria, only increased the desire for freedom. Their opportunity came with World War I.

The man of the hour was Marshal Josef Pilsudski—Poland's George Washington. This great soldier had plotted for years against Russia. When the war broke out he enlisted in the army of Austria because that nation had

Marshal Pilsudski led in Polish independence movement and was afterwards dictator

treated his people better than Russia or Prussia had. But after Russia collapsed and Germany refused Polish independence he turned against the Central Powers. Imprisoned in Germany he was released after the revolution there. He returned to Warsaw and proclaimed himself head of the Polish Republic.

In this struggle for freedom, the Poles had the active support of the French, who wanted to erect a buffer state between Russia and Germany. Also, President Wilson had advocated in his Fourteen Points the creation of an "Independent Polish state" with access to the sea and an international guarantee of its independence and territory. Fired by this encouragement, the Poles rallied to the standard of Pilsudski, and Poland once more took its place in the family of nations.

ALLIED PEACE AIMS

With victory a new spirit entered into the hearts of the people of the Allied Powers. Save for America, all were eager for reparations and territorial gains at the expense of the vanquished foe. When the terms of the peace became known, many felt that they were not sufficiently severe, and that their nations had not been granted enough of the spoils of the victory. Elation turned to disillusionment, and in some great Allied countries the heads of the government were repudiated.

Italy, especially, felt she had been cheated of her rightful share. She had entered the war primarily to gain certain definite additions of territory promised her by secret treaties with England, France, and Russia. When the Versailles Conference failed to meet all her demands, Italy was willing to use force. Thus she seized the city of Fiume and occupied parts of Albania. Italy failed, however, to achieve her aims in Africa and the Mediterranean. The resulting humiliation and disappointment led directly to the Fascist seizure of power in 1922.

The sentiments of the British people were revealed in the Khaki elections of 1918. Politics had been "adjourned" in Great Britain during the war, and by the time it was over, elections had not been held in eight years. That astute politician, Lloyd George, sensed the feeling of the people. He appealed to the country on a platform that called for punishment of German "war criminals" such as the Kaiser and ranking officials, and full payment of the Allied war costs by the defeated powers. The result was a sweeping victory for his group.

France had suffered more than any other nation from the war. Much of it had been fought in her territories and the devastation was beyond imagination. As early as 1914 the French government had promised to reimburse its citizens for all losses caused by the war. When Clemenceau failed to convince the Allies at the Peace Conference that Germany should be made to pay all the costs of the conflict, he lost much popular support. Shortly afterward, when the time came to elect a new French president,

The Palace at Versailles, June 28, 1919, as Allied representatives approached it to sign the treaty ending World War I. Built for Louis XIV, Versailles was the residence of French kings, 1682–1793

The Big Four, the Allied leaders who made most of the important decisions at the Versailles Peace Conference, 1919. Left to right: Premier Vittorio Orlando of Italy; Prime Minister David Lloyd George of Great Britain; Premier Georges Clemenceau of France; President Woodrow Wilson of the U. S. (Brown Bros.)

Clemenceau was rejected though he desired the position.

THE PEACE CONFERENCE

After much quibbling it was decided that the Allied and Associated Powers should gather at Versailles in January, 1919, to negotiate the peace. The defeated nations were not represented, for they were to have no part in determining the terms of the treaty. The Russians, too, were unrepresented. The greatest statesmen of the thirty-two victorious nations were all there, besides a host of unofficial delegates. But the "Big Four," Clemenceau of France, who was chairman, Woodrow Wilson of the United States, Lloyd George of Great Britain, and Orlando of Italy, dominated and controlled the negotiations.

Faced with the desolation caused by the late conflict, the victors were determined to end forever the danger of a recurrence of such events. But they were also intent on getting reparation for the damage done by the enemy. Only Woodrow Wilson opposed this, for he believed that the Central Powers had already suffered to their utmost capacity. He had thought the Allies would make his Fourteen Points the basis of the settlement. They did become the basis, but were modified by the requirements of reparation and security.

Wilson's Fourteen Points included demands for freedom of the seas, reduction of armaments, adjustment of colonial claims, evacuation of Russia and the Balkans, readjustment of the Italian borders, formation of national states in Austria-Hungary and Turkey, national self-determination in the Balkans, an independent Poland, and the formation of a League of Nations. This last was closest to Wilson's heart. He saw it as a world wide organization of nations, united for the common welfare of all.

PUNISHMENT OF GERMANY

On May 7, 1919, the completed treaty was handed to the representatives of Germany, who had only recently arrived. The Germans were shocked at its harsh terms. They refused to sign, claiming that it did not live up to the Fourteen Points. But Clemenceau, the Tiger, who had seen France humbled in that very building in 1871, was implacable. He threatened a French invasion of Germany on June 21 unless they accepted. At the very last minute the hopeless Germans submitted to the terms. So was concluded the Treaty of Versailles, June 28, 1919, almost five years after Austria's declaration of war against Serbia.

It was intended to reduce the Reich to the status of a minor power, and so remove forever

Friedrich Ebert, first president of Germany, held office from 1919 until his death in 1925. (Acme)

the threat on France's eastern border. France won back Alsace and Lorraine. Large territories were awarded to Poland. Germany lost twelve per cent of her population and her most important natural resources. Her colonies were taken away and divided among the victors. Millions of dollars' worth of machinery and livestock were taken to replace what the Kaiser's armies had destroyed in Allied countries. Above all, the treaty demanded the payment of billions of dollars over many years as reparation for the cost of the war. The exact amount was so huge that it was left to be determined later. The treaty declared that Germany was responsible for all the damage of the conflict because she had started it. Finally, to keep the Reich from rebuilding its military power, the treaty limited her armed forces to 100,000 men and a tiny navy, abolished compulsory military service, and forbade a union with Austria, except by unanimous consent of the League of Nations.

TREATY OF ST. GERMAIN

The treaty with Austria takes its name from St. Germain, near Paris, where it was signed. It had been drawn up during the Versailles negotiations, and was presented to the Austrians on June 2, 1919. It reduced Austria from

an empire of 30,000,000 people to a tiny, land-locked state of 6,500,000. The rest of her vast territories were divided up among her former subject peoples and Italy. The army was reduced to 30,000 men, the entire navy confiscated. Reparations were to be made though the amount was not stated. Further, Austria, like Germany, had to permit international trade to go through its important rivers with no interference. Austria finally signed on September 10, 1919, after bitter but vain protests.

Shortly before this date Bulgaria was presented with her treaty, which she signed at Neuilly-sur-Seine in late November. Bulgaria's military and naval forces were drastically reduced, though she lost comparatively little territory. Yet the result was that Bulgaria became one of the weaker Balkan states.

TREATY OF THE TRIANON

The signing of the Treaty of the Trianon with Hungary was delayed until June 4, 1920. This was because of the turbulent political situation in that country, mentioned above. Béla Kun's communistic republic had dissolved, after five months, before the onrush of invading Rumanian troops. A Rumanian occupation had followed and not until late in 1919 was a firm government re-established. The Hungarians fought desperately against acceptance of the treaty for it meant they would lose 12,-000,000 inhabitants and 90,000,000 square miles of land. In the end, however, they submitted to the inevitable terms.

CONCESSIONS TO TURKEY

The last of the peace agreements to be concluded at Paris, and the only one never ratified, was that with the Ottoman Empire, signed at Sévres on August 10, 1920. The rise of Kemal Pasha and his refusal to accept the treaty have already been described. With the complete victory of the Kemalists in 1922, the Allies were compelled to recognize the new regime. They invited Turkey to a peace conference at Lausanne, Switzerland. Here the Turks gained practically all of their demands, being the only defeated power to take active part in drawing up a peace treaty. They recovered all the purely Turkish areas that had been under foreign

Legend:
- Areas Ceded by Germany
- Former Area of Austria-Hungary
- Areas Ceded by Bulgaria
- Areas Demanded from Turkey by Treaty of Sevres but Regained by Treaty of Lausanne
- Area Seized by Poland from Lithuania (1920-1923)
- Areas Lost by Russia

Territorial Changes in Europe, 1914–26

control. No restrictions were placed on their military or naval forces, nor were reparations demanded. They did agree to permit free passage of all foreign vessels through the Straits of the Dardanelles and to demilitarize its shores. The pact was signed July 24, 1923.

DISSOLUTION OF THE HAPSBURG ESTATE

The Conference at Versailles regarded itself as "the executor of the Hapsburg estate." The many heirs were grasping and quarrelsome, and the statesmen at Paris had to intervene to settle many boundary disputes. After much argument and investigation, new frontiers were drawn which attempted to include as many peo-

ple of the same racial stock as possible within the same nation. A plebiscite was held where there was reasonable doubt as to whose were the just claims in a specific area.

Not all of the boundary fixing was limited to the Balkans. With the breakup of Romanov Russia, the subject races in the Baltic provinces declared their independence. Because the Bolsheviks believed in national self-determinism they made no attempt to reconquer these regions. So Finland, Estonia, Latvia, and Lithuania became republics. The peace conference handed over to the new Poland some Russian territory that was indisputably Polish. Poland attempted to extend this by military force. This resulted in war with Russia in which Poland, with French aid, succeeded in gaining part of the disputed territory.

Despite the efforts of the Allies, Europe was still far from being organized into purely national states. Therefore, provisions to protect minorities were included in the peace treaties, and special pacts were made with Poland, Czechoslovakia, Rumania, Yugoslavia, and Greece.

THE LEAGUE OF NATIONS

Included in all the major peace treaties was the Covenant of the League of Nations. Largely the product of Wilson's idealism, it was an attempt to prevent future international war. All civilized nations of the world were invited to join at the start, except Russia, Mexico,

The League of Nations headquarters in Geneva, Switzerland. It cost $9,369,000, not including interior furnishings. Much of the money was given by John D. Rockefeller. After World War II the buildings lay empty and unused, a monument to the futility of the League's attempt at international organization. (Acme)

Costa Rica, and the defeated powers. These could join later. The League's headquarters were to be at Geneva, and meetings were to be held at stated intervals. All members were to send delegates to an Assembly, and a Council of representatives of the five great powers— England, the United States, France, Italy, and Japan—and four other nations, was to be formed. The members agreed to submit all international disputes to the arbitration of the League. If any member disregarded a decision, the Council could recommend collective military or economic action (sanctions) against the offender. The League was charged with coordinating the labor and social welfare activities of its members, and with registering all future treaties.

Further, it was entrusted with certain specific duties, such as the administration of the Saar Valley and Danzig. Also, each nation that had received any portion of the colonies of Germany or Turkey, was declared a "Mandatory"

of the League. This meant that the new ruling nation had to report regularly to the League and be responsible to it for a good administration.

Tired of the madness of war, eager to preserve the fruits of their triumph, the Allies had great hopes for the League. They realized that cooperation had won the war, and they believed that cooperation would keep the peace.

All the nations concerned ratified the Versailles Treaty, with the exception of the United States. The disillusioned American people of nineteen twenty feared that the League would entangle their country in European affairs. Politics, too, played a part, for the Republicans were elected to control of the Senate, and helped prevent ratification. Separate treaties were made with Germany, Austria, and Hungary in March, 1921. This defection of the United States struck a severe blow at the League, which suffered grievously in international influence as a result.

80. The Russian Revolution

BACKGROUND OF THE REVOLUTION

D URING WORLD WAR I a great revolution occurred in Russia. It came about from a variety of causes—economic, social, psychological, and military. Although serfdom was abolished in Russia in 1861, the lot of the peasant improved but little. At the beginning of the twentieth century the peasants still lacked any of the civil liberties, and with the rest of the lower classes in Russia they had no political rights. Poverty was widespread among them, and few owned land.

Russia as a whole remained predominantly agricultural, but a growth of industry and trade took place in the cities in the latter half of the nineteenth century. Because of the continued influx of impoverished peasants, working conditions in the factories were generally poor. The laboring groups became more and more revolutionary. Their attitudes found expression in new radical parties, especially the Russian Social Democratic Party. This group, organized in 1881, split soon after 1900 into the Mensheviks, who believed in cooperating with bourgeois groups to achieve social reforms, and the Bolsheviks, who advocated violent armed rebellion.

Revolutionary discontent increased after the defeat of the Czar's forces in the Russo-Japanese War. The prestige of the government was undermined and a wave of strikes took place. At the end of October, 1905, Czar Nicholas II capitulated and made some concessions. He granted the demand for a national assembly, or Duma, and freedom of speech and of assembly and practical manhood suffrage were promised. These grants did not satisfy

Nicholas II, Czar of Russia, 1894–1917

the more extreme revolutionists, and fierce fighting took place, but the army finally suppressed the uprising.

A period of reaction now set in. The Duma was assembled, but the government practically nullified much of its legislation. New electoral laws nullified the promise of universal suffrage. Discontent was growing during the period 1907-14. There were many strikes and some riots.

With the declaration of war by Germany on Russia in 1914, a complete change took place in the Russian internal situation. Members of most political groups, including many Socialists, accepted the war as a national crusade, and Russia presented a united front to the foe. But the military disasters in the summer of 1915 changed the temper of the people. They discovered that their troops were badly equipped, that their military leaders were

Grigori Rasputin, the "mad monk," influenced Russian royal family. (Acme)

being outgeneraled, and that food and ammunition were scarce. Rumors of treason, corruption, and bribery abounded. Even the emperor and empress fell under suspicion; at the Imperial court the dark and sinister figure of Rasputin, the "mad monk," held sway, dominating the royal family, cashiering commanders and ministers, and directing state affairs.

The Duma and other public organizations made despairing efforts to save the country. Rasputin was assassinated in December, 1916, but the grief of the emperor and empress and the elaborate funeral they ordered for the monk, served to alienate public sympathy still more. Starvation and misery spread in the Russian cities, bread riots broke out, and the masses were aroused. Then the Duma leaders took a revolutionary step and attempted to assume direction of the mass protest by forcing the Czar to abdicate, on March 16, 1917.

However, it is a mistake to believe as so many people do that the Soviet government immediately and directly succeeded the czarist government. Actually, the first revolutionary government of Russia in March, 1917, was the provisional government of Prince George Lvov, who was succeeded as prime minister in July, 1917, by Alexander Kerensky, and it was Kerensky's provisional cabinet that was overthrown in November by the Communists, then known as the Bolsheviks.

Kerensky, first head of the provisional regime. (Acme)

WHAT THE MASSES WANTED

Two chief needs dominated the revolution of March, 1917. One was an age-old desire of the peasants, who constituted a vast majority of Russia's population, for more land than was at their disposal. The other was the people's overwhelming longing for peace.

The provisional government either did not understand the importance of these two desires clearly enough, or, understanding them, did not know how to deal with them adequately. Prince Lvov, the first head of the provisional government, represented Russia's liberal bourgeoisie who, on the whole, wished to satisfy the desires of the masses but not at once. Kerensky, who was to the left of Lvov and who served as Lvov's minister of justice and later minister of war and navy, assumed premiership on July 20, 1917, when the pressure

"Storming the Winter Palace" in the November Revolution. An artist's conception. (Sovfoto)

of the radical elements became unbearable for Lvov. His program, however, differed little from Lvov's. In the summer of 1917 he was losing precious time, failing to solve the land problem in the spirit which his own party, the Socialist-Revolutionaries, recommended. Even as peasants throughout Russia were taking law into their own hands by seizing estates of landlords and monasteries, Kerensky claimed the problem was so complex that special commissions had to study it first and work out practical ways of dividing land.

Hearing of the spontaneous division already going on, peasants in uniform forsook the front by the hundred thousand. These deserters hurried home to their villages, afraid to miss their share of new acreage. The universal desire for peace was thus enhanced by the desire for land. But Kerensky insisted on the prosecution of the war to ultimate victory. Part of the blame rested on the Western Allies who, failing to comprehend the extreme war fatigue of the Russian people, repeatedly called on the provisional government to carry on the war against the Central Powers.

THE RISE OF LENIN

The only political group in Russia which understood the true temper of the masses was the Bolshevik faction of the Social-Democratic party. Until April 16 it, too, had marked time or spent it in meaningless oratory. But on that date Vladimir Ulyanov, better known under his revolutionary pseudonym of Nikolai Lenin, arrived from his Swiss exile. His ultra-

Nikolai Lenin haranguing a crowd in Petrograd in the early days of the Communist revolution

American Troops at Popoff, Russia in July, 1919, during the Allied intervention

radical program pleased the German high command which therefore facilitated his return to Russia by allowing him (with a group of his co-revolutionists) to travel through Germany in a sealed car. Later this led to charges against Lenin and his aides that they were paid agents of German imperialism. It is clear, however, that whether or not Lenin accepted money from the German imperialists in addition to those travel facilities, he did this in order to use the German imperialists and not to be used by them.

For the moment their and his aims coincided, indeed. German generals wanted Russia to be weakened internally and withdrawn from the war. Lenin wanted an end of the war for Russia, so that the guns of the Russian soldiers could be turned against what he termed as domestic foes and exploiters of the Russian masses. Wars between nations, according to him, were predatory; a civil war against the owning classes, first of Russia and then of the entire world (including the Central Powers), would be good. "Peace to the huts, war upon the palaces," was his slogan. He agitated for a social revolution and a dictatorship of the proletariat and thought these could be won without a long civil war. He pictured the uprising as thorough, victorious, and brief.

TWO UPRISINGS

An ill-advised attack upon the Austro-German troops, ordered by Kerensky as minister of war on June 29, ended in a complete failure. This touched off new disorders through-out Russia, the most serious of which was an uprising of Bolshevik-led workers and soldiers in Petrograd on July 17-19. The uprising collapsed, and Lenin and Gregory Zinoviev (one of his chief aides) escaped into hiding. Other Bolshevik leaders, among them Leon Trotsky and Leo Kamenev, were arrested. They were subsequently released by the provisional government.

From his hiding place in Finland, Lenin urged his party to organize a new revolt. This was finally timed for the meeting of the All-Russian Congress of Soviets in early November. At two o'clock in the morning of November 7, 1917, the Bolshevik revolution began. Soldiers, sailors, and workers seized the main governmental and communication centers in Petrograd, and the ministers were besieged in the Winter Palace. Only a handful of officer candidate trainees and a battalion of women-soldiers defended the palace. Kerensky escaped just before the palace was captured.

The Bolshevik party seized power and formed a revolutionary government in the name of the Soviets, headed by Lenin and Trotsky. On November 8 it proclaimed the nationalization of land and the award of it to the peasants free of charge. On Nov. 23 the new Soviet government abolished ranks and other social distinctions; on the 27th it issued a decree on workers' control in industries. Peace negotiations with the German and Austrian governments were begun on Dec. 2 at Brest-Litovsk. A treaty with humiliating terms to Russia was signed on March 3, 1918.

Leon Trotsky, People's Commissar of War, reviewing the Red Army. Trotsky was later exiled. (Acme)

Russia surrendered to the Central Powers, for their disposal, Finland and the Aland Islands, the Ukraine, Russian Poland, Lithuania, the Baltic provinces (later forming Latvia and Estonia), and Russian Armenia. Only the defeat of the Central Powers in the West eight months later freed Russia from the yoke of this treaty. But even the collapse of Germany in November, 1918, did not bring Finland, the Baltic states, a large part of Poland, and certain areas in Transcaucasia back into Russia, now that Russia was communist.

THE CIVIL WAR

Instead of ushering the much-desired peace, the Soviet revolution caused a civil war, which dragged on from the winter of 1917 to the spring of 1921. In the spring of 1918 British, French, American, and Japanese troops were landed on the various shores of Russia to help the Russian Whites (anti-Soviet forces) because these promised to rally Russia back into the war on the Allied side. After the war's end in Nov., 1918, this foreign intervention continued for a time because Lenin openly challenged the existing socio-economic order of the entire world. He and his government agitated and plotted against private capitalism and for communism everywhere. In Russia, the Soviets nationalized banks, factories, stores, mines, land and many other forms of private property as one of the first steps toward socialism and communism. In March, 1918, the Bolsheviks changed their party's main name to Communist. It became Russia's only legal party, all other parties being outlawed by

Lenin's government, their leaders and many of their members shot or jailed on orders of the Cheka, the new organ of terror established by the Soviet government. In March, 1919, the Communist International was founded by Lenin to foster world-wide revolt against the owning classes.

The varying fortunes of the civil war at one time (early autumn of 1919) brought White armies within some 100 miles of Moscow and but a few miles of Leningrad. The Soviet government seemed to be tottering on the brink of utter defeat. Yet in the course of 1920 the Soviets won a complete victory on all fronts, and for these reasons:

(1) While there was throughout Russia a tremendous amount of dissatisfaction with the Bolsheviks and their ruthless methods, the opposing or White forces represented another extreme of brutality and their slogans lacked even the attractiveness of the Red mottoes. The Whites were mainly reactionaries who wished to restore Czarism if not the ex-Czar Nicholas II himself (who, with his entire family, was executed by the Soviets at Ekaterinburg, in the Urals in July, 1918). Wherever the Whites won their temporary victories, they returned the expropriated land to landlords and punished the peasants for having taken that land.

(2) The peasants, although disliking the Reds for their policy of requisitioning food supplies and other such measures, rallied to the Reds' support when the Whites plainly revealed their program of returning the land to its old owners.

(3) The workers of Russia, although numerically small, acted resolutely on their belief in the high-sounding slogans of revolutionary justice and equality coined by the Bolsheviks.

(4) Foreign intervention was resented by many non-Bolsheviks as well, on purely patriotic grounds. And foreign intervention itself was feeble and indecisive, as the foreign governments responsible for it were faced by postwar troubles and unrest at home. Consequently, foreign troops were withdrawn from the strategic theaters on Russian soil (in the south of Russia especially) long before the civil war's conclusive battles were fought between the Whites and the Reds.

81. Fascism in Europe

EFFECTS OF THE WORLD WAR

THE EFFECTS of the first world war were vast. The four-year reign of destructiveness cost hundreds of billions of dollars. The United States alone spent a million dollars for every hour from its entrance into the war to six months after the armistice. The destruction of ships and cargoes, and the devastation of vast areas of prosperous country by the ravages of war, added to the frightful loss. It is impossible to calculate how much material wealth was lost through converting factories and machines from useful production to the manufacturing of war materials.

Human losses were even greater than this material destruction. Ten million soldiers were killed. Twenty millions were wounded, and six million were reported missing. The human cost did not stop there. The rest of the sixty million who fought in the holocaust carried mental pictures which had profound physiological and psychological consequences. Civilians also suffered from starvation, disease, and violent death. At least thirteen million civilians perished during the conflict.

The war, however, freed many of the subject peoples of Europe whose national feelings had made them chafe under foreign rule. The transfer of the Baltic states from Russian hegemony, the union of Slavs in Yugoslavia, the return of the Transylvanians to their fellow Rumanians all calmed prewar national hatreds, as did the carving out of Czechoslovakia in Central Europe. Poland gained her independence after generations of division and subjection; and Tyrol, with its many Italians, was transferred from Austria to Italy. With each change, however, new nationalistic problems resulted. For example, instead of Italians chafing under German rule in Tyrol, the German inhabitants of the same region now chafed under Italian rule. The vindictiveness of certain of the victorious nations carried territorial changes far beyond proper national bounds, and laid the basis for new hatreds and restlessness. German sections of Austria were transferred not only to Italy but also to Czechoslovakia, and East Prussia was cut off from Germany by the establishment of the Polish corridor, although its people were more German than Polish. Hungary was embittered by the loss of many of her people to surrounding nations, and Italy and Yugoslavia quarreled sharply over their claims to the Adriatic port of Fiume.

PREPARING THE GROUND FOR ITALIAN FASCISM

Confusion and instability characterized the life of Italy in the years after the Armistice. There were numerous strikes and class wars; lands and factories were seized and the prevalence of profiteering helped to develop extremely high living costs. In the midst of these critical symptoms, the government remained passive. Particularly bad was the situation under the ministry of Giolitti, an old time liberal, who believed that the sole function of the state was the maintenance of order. During his term of office class warfare became widespread;

factories were taken over by the workers and managed by the proletarian leaders with little success. With strife and disorder rampant, the moderate elements came to be thoroughly distrustful of the existing government. Eyes were now turned to the rising Fascist movement.

The Fascists, who at first were mostly discontented war veterans, had grown rapidly since their organization in 1919. Their program emphasized direct action, glorified nationalism, and the power of youth, and called for the suppression of Socialism and Communism. The new movement was welcomed, under the existing circumstances, by the alarmed middle and upper classes, and many of them joined the Fascist leader, Mussolini, a prewar Socialist. The prestige of this nationalistic party was enhanced in the upper and middle classes by the manner in which it broke the general strike of August, 1922.

The confidence of the Fascists increased with their numbers, and at a great review of the Black Shirt (Fascist) militia in Milan in October, 1922, Mussolini demanded that five most important cabinet posts be given to his organization. He threatened, in case of refusal, to lead the Fascists in a march on Rome. The premier temporized, offering them a few seats in the cabinet, but his proposals were refused. Finally, the stalemate was broken by Mussolini's lieutenants, who began forcibly to take over control of local and provincial governments, and began the threatened march on Rome. In the face of this open defiance of authority, the premier asked the king to proclaim martial law throughout the land. But Victor Emmanuel, afraid of civil war, himself performed the act that ended democratic Italy by asking Mussolini to form a new cabinet. Mussolini, who was not with the marchers, came to Rome by train, demanded and received dictatorial powers from the Parliament, and began the Fascist regime in Italy.

Victor Emmanuel III, Italian king, 1900–1947, made Mussolini premier

FASCISM VICTORIOUS

The first step taken by the victorious Fascists was to gain control over all local and provincial offices. This done, they proceeded to "Fascistize" the Parliament: no criticism of Fascism was to be allowed, no other parties were permitted to exist, the Fascist party was given the dominant place in the administrative hierarchy, and democratic parliamentary government was scrapped for an absolute dictatorship. By a series of laws passed in December, 1925, the assumption of power by Mussolini, already accomplished, was legalized; he was given more dictatorial powers, freedom of the press was abolished, non-Fascist editors were forced out, oaths of loyalty were required of university professors, and the central government was accented as against the local units. In carrying out this program terroristic methods were used as well as the armed force of the Black Shirt militia.

The mechanics of the new regime were relatively simple. The premier exercised supreme power, and cabinet ministers were responsible to him alone. The real sovereign of Italy was this premier, Il Duce (the Leader). The Fascist Grand Council, established by law in December, 1928, was the coordinating agency of the

Black Shirt Leaders just before the march on Rome. On the left are Italo Balbo and Mussolini

government. It met only on call of Il Duce, and its members were appointed by and subject to him. The Fascist militia, which aided Mussolini in his rise to power, undertook various political and social functions, although it remained primarily a fighting force, the bulwark of the Fascist regime.

Benito Mussolini, 1883–1945, Italian dictator and founder of Fascism

The Fascist party, which, under its leader, controlled the government, became a closed corporation in 1925. New members were added only from the ranks of its junior organizations: The *Balilla*, for boys from six to fourteen years old, the *Avanguardia*, for those from fourteen to eighteen years old, and the Young Fascists, eighteen to twenty years of age. At twenty, the Young Fascist was admitted to the Fascist party. As in Russia, the dominant party comprised but a small part of the population.

FASCIST ACTIVITIES

The state was one huge organism according to Fascist doctrines, and in line with this idea a number of acts were passed which really made Italy into a great corporation. Syndicates of workers and associations of employees were set up; they were coordinated by the government which had supervision over all the economic interests of the state. In April, 1927, the Charter of Labor was proclaimed which established the theoretical rights and privileges of workers and their syndicates, but in actual fact the state retained the dominant voice. In 1928 the Italian legislative body was made representative of the various economic interests of the state rather than of geographical districts. By 1937 the Council of Corporations, which represented all of the Italian syndicates, was changed into a group of national corporations, controlling lower ones. At the top, centralizing and controlling all economic and political activities, stood Il Duce, who occupied a position of almost arbitrary power.

During the Fascist regime the relation of the Papacy to the nation of Italy, one of the most perplexing questions in Italy, was settled. The existence of the popes as voluntary prisoners in the Vatican area after Rome was taken from the control of the Papacy in 1870 had created a puzzling situation, but the whole problem was settled in 1929 by an accord between the Papacy and the Italian government. The pope was given a small piece of territory in Rome, which was to be a separate, sovereign state. The Papacy recognized in return the Italian government and gave up its claim to Rome. On the other hand, the government agreed to enforce the Canon law within its territory, to establish compulsory religious education in Italy, and to recognize the various Catholic societies. By financial agreement, the Papacy was paid almost $100,000,000 as a settlement of all its territorial claims. The Papacy, on its part, agreed not to interfere in any manner in the political affairs of the state.

In the first years following the accession of the Fascists to power, Italy concentrated on internal development rather than colonial expansion. Her existing colonies were developed economically, but it was not until 1935 that Italy attempted to add to its colonial area. For some time Mussolini had eyed the independent,

Mounted Royal Bodyguard of the Emperor of Ethiopia, who was defeated by the Italians in 1936

rich, and unexploited native African state of Ethiopia. A slight skirmish on the frontier, probably incited by the Italians, was seized as the pretext for Italian occupation of the country. In a short, sharp, undeclared war, the modern Italian munitions and the excellent training of Il Duce's legions proved too much for the poorly equipped troops of the Ethiopian emperor, Haile Selassie. A steady advance resulted in the seizure of the capital, the flight of the emperor, and the annexation of the territory, although guerrilla warfare between the Italian occupants and the hardy natives of the hill country continued through 1937. Victor Emmanuel was proclaimed emperor of Ethiopia and economic development of the territory began. The entire conquest was carried on so rapidly that the application of economic sanctions against Italy by the League of Nations proved to be ineffective, and, after the annexation of the country, they were lifted.

POLITICAL DISORDERS IN GERMANY

The severe depression in Germany following the war led the middle classes to distrust the new republic that was set up at Weimar, and as a result there occurred between 1920 and 1923 a series of attempted revolutions by various groups. Aided by high military officers, there was a movement to re-establish monarchy in Germany in May, 1920. The attempt failed, largely due to resistance by the German working classes. Monarchists, however, engaged in anti-Republican activities and began a campaign of systematic terrorism. The Republican authorities replied to these acts of violence by suspending constitutional guarantees and enacting a law designed to thwart revolutionary maneuvers. But these were only half-hearted reprisals, and the monarchists and nationalists continued to promote discontent and disorder. Emboldened by this, another group under General Ludendorff and Adolf Hitler attempted to seize power in an advance from Bavaria, the famous "beer-hall *putsch*," but this attempt was a complete failure.

There were operating during the following five years, 1926-1930, a number of factors tending to bring about the downfall of constitutional government in Germany. From the left there was violence by the Communists and Socialists against the Republic, and from the right was the threat of the influence of the old Junker families. There was also loss of prestige by the German legislative body, the Reichstag, which suffered from the multiplicity and rigidity of political parties. Real power during the period was slipping into the hands of various economic associations, especially the Federation of German Industries, representing "big business," and the German Trades Union Federation, representing the workers. Under this system it was inevitable that agreements behind the scenes should replace ordinary legislative processes, and the importance of the Reichstag steadily declined in the eyes of Germans.

Organized labor, a pillar of the Republic, too, had grown weaker as a result of the inflation of the early 1920's. This decline strengthened the industrial and agrarian interests that were hostile to it. The increasing significance of the German bureaucracy was also a factor of importance. With the decline of the Reichstag many of its functions were taken over by the bureaucracy which in all important political questions was an ally of the German middle class. Economic depression gave the coup de grâce to the Republic. Without the depression the Republic might have survived.

THE SIGN OF THE SWASTIKA

The National Socialists, or Nazis, profited the most as a result of the operation of these factors. This group, led by Adolf Hitler, had a program which appealed to people during a time of humiliation and depression. Like the Italian Fascists, whose methods Hitler followed, they were extremely nationalistic, seeking to unite all Germans in Europe. They also advocated many social and economic re-

Adolf Hitler, just before he became chancellor

Chancellor Hitler explaining his new policies to the Reichstag and President von Hindenburg, March 21, 1933

forms, such as abolition of all unearned income, nationalization of certain trusts and stores, agrarian reforms, shifting of tax burdens to the rich, and a guarantee by the government of employment for all citizens. As an emotional appeal to certain groups, they began a persecution of Jews, whom they did not count as citizens. By 1930, this program had come to appeal to so many classes of the German people—youth, professional classes engaged in competition with the Jews, business men, peasants, and white-collar classes—that in the election of that year the Nazis acquired 107 seats in the Reichstag, an increase of ninety-five. This, however, was not enough to control the government.

DER FUEHRER

So critical did the situation become in 1930-1931, that the government found it necessary to resort to emergency decrees to try to save the country's financial basis. Although the aged Hindenburg defeated Hitler for the presidency in the 1932 election, the Nazi leader displayed organizing strength. In a new election to the Reichstag, the party captured 230 seats, the largest number obtained by any group though not a majority. A parliamentary stalemate resulted. Another election did not change the situation greatly, and after the failure of two short-lived cabinets, Hindenburg asked Hitler to form a cabinet. The new chancellor immediately called for a new election. In a campaign marked by strong-arm methods against their opponents, suspension of all constitutional liberties, and red-baiting, the Nazis managed to gain control of the Reichstag by acquiring 52 per cent of the popular vote. At its first session an act was passed giving Hitler dictatorial powers for four years.

Der Fuehrer, "the Leader," as Hitler now came to be called, thereupon set out to make of Germany a totalitarian state like Italy. Parliamentary government was practically done away with in all the German states, and the Nazis were given control of all administrative posts. The Nazi, like the Fascist in Italy, was made the only legal political party, and it was decreed that the formation of any new ones would constitute high treason. Propaganda and force were used to maintain the Nazis in control. Freedom of the press and of speech was abolished and all opposition ruthlessly suppressed.

The task of coordinating German industry and commerce proved easier than that of nationalizing religion to conform to Nazi policies. Many religious, internationalist, and pacifist societies were dissolved. An uneasy truce resulted from an agreement between Hitler and the Papacy by which the religious freedom of the Catholics was to be guaranteed. Attempts were made to gain control of the thinking and social policies of the various Protestant groups. New fanatical sects arose, sponsored by Nazis, which called themselves German Pagans or German Christians and sought to eradicate what they called the Jewish theology behind Christianity. Some even sought to revive the old Norse gods.

Self-sufficiency or "autarchy" became the cry in foreign trade. Imports were rigidly restricted, German-made goods were forced on the market internally and externally, and materials for armaments received import priorities. Huge construction programs were started to eliminate unemployment. Service in labor battalions became compulsory for the young. A German Labor Front was created, incorporating all labor unions and including both employers and workers as members; this was rigidly controlled by the state.

In the fall of 1933 Germany withdrew her representatives from an international disarmament conference and announced her withdrawal from the League of Nations, on the ground that Germany had not been treated on an equal basis. Most important of all was Germany's abrogation of the Treaty of Versailles. The war-guilt clause was denied, further reparation payments ceased, production of armaments and the size of the army were increased beyond treaty provisions.

German leaders demanded the return of the colonies their nation forfeited in accepting the provisions of the Treaty of Versailles. Nazi sympathizers were organized into clubs and parties in the neighboring states and even North and South America. In 1936 the Nazi army marched into the demilitarized Rhine zone. Neither the League of Nations nor individual nations took strong action.

In February, 1938, Hitler called Chancellor Kurt von Schuschnigg of Austria to a conference at Berchtesgaden, a border town. The result of this conference was the inclusion of two Nazis in the Austrian cabinet. Schuschnigg chose to resist further encroachments, and ordered a referendum on Austrian liberty to be held on March 13. That election never took place, for on March 11 the German army moved into Austria unhindered. Two days later Hitler personally entered Vienna and declared Austria a part of the Third Reich.

Under the Nazi regime, German industry expanded and unemployment was eliminated because of many public works, development of armament factories, and the enlargement of the army. There was, in fact, a labor shortage by 1939, and the country exhibited an appearance of prosperity and unity.

A National Socialist Parade in Nuremberg

82. Democracies and Dictatorships—the Struggle for Security

FRANCE AFTER WORLD WAR I

THE FIRST TASK of the French government after the war was reconstruction. Over one-eighth of its area was devastated by shot and shell, by pillage and military sabotage. Industry and mining were practically wiped out in the northern part of the country, and hundreds of villages were in ruins. It was decided that private losses should be recompensed by the state. To accomplish this purpose, gigantic loans were floated by the government to be repaid, partially at least, by German reparations payments.

Raymond Poincaré, French statesman

The collection of reparations did not keep up to schedule. French leftists began to favor moderation of exactions from Germany, bitterly denouncing the government's policy, and in the elections of 1924 they won decisively. This leftist cabinet, which was soon in financial difficulties, was forced to resign and a crisis ensued. Under the premiership of Poincaré, a National Union ministry restored the financial competence of the nation by balancing the budget and stabilizing the value of the franc. Gradually France regained economic health as a result of Poincaré's policies and as industry and agriculture recovered from the war. In the parliamentary elections of 1928, his program was heartily endorsed, and all conservative and moderate parties increased their strength.

Poincaré resigned in 1929 because of ill health, and for a number of years ministerial instability characterized the Republic. Nationalistic Right and Socialist Left conflicted continually. Economic questions played a large part, as depression spread over the world. In 1935 the pendulum swung sharply to the left, and a Popular Front government, composed of all radical groups, was formed under Léon Blum as premier. The new government stood definitely committed to gradual socialization in France. The Blum government lasted until the summer of 1937, when the refusal of the upper chamber to grant him extraordinary financial powers resulted in a change in nominal leadership of the government, with Chautemps becoming premier.

GREAT BRITAIN
1919-1937

The Lloyd George coalition cabinet, under which England had finished the war, won a sweeping victory at the polls in December, 1918; but when the ministry was reconstructed, it reflected the dominant strength of the Conservative element in the coalition. Depression and unemployment were important problems which the new government had to face: various palliative measures were employed, but there could be no permanent solution until shipping and industry revived. The strength of the Conservatives made them restless under the leadership of the Liberal Lloyd George, and in 1922 they seceded from the coalition. In the ensuing election they gained a complete victory, although the Labor Party made a remarkable gain, winning 142 seats.

Faced with continued unemployment, Baldwin, the new Conservative premier, decided to abandon England's traditional free-trade policy for one of protection. He took the issue to the country, and, although the Conservatives retained the largest number of seats in the House of Commons, they no longer were able to command a majority over all others. The people had definitely rejected protection; so Baldwin resigned, and, having the support of the Liberals, Ramsay MacDonald formed Britain's first Labor government. In the election the Labor party had increased its membership in Parliament by fifty.

The *de jure* recognition of Russia and trade treaties with that country alarmed the Liberals, who soon joined the Conservatives in opposing MacDonald. No longer having the support of a majority of Parliament, he was forced to call new elections, which resulted in a sweeping Conservative victory. Baldwin again became premier, inaugurating a period of Conservative ascendancy.

Unemployment, industrial disputes, and the stagnant condition of trade were problems remaining for the Conservatives, whose time in office lasted for five years, the legal limit of one Parliament. In the general election of 1929, they stood on their record and presented a program which was economically conser-

Stanley Baldwin, British prime minister

vative and moderate in foreign policy. Labor, which presented a program of gradual socialization, won the largest number of seats, although it did not obtain a majority, and, again with the support of Liberals, Ramsay Mac-

Ramsay MacDonald, first Labor prime minister

King George V and Queen Mary entering the city of London during his Silver Jubilee celebration

Donald became prime minister for the second time.

But, in 1931, financial difficulties caused MacDonald to sponsor reduction of unemployment relief, splitting the party. With a group of National Laborites, some Liberals, and the Conservatives, MacDonald formed a coalition cabinet, called the National Government. In a new election that year, with the National Government advocating protective policies, it was overwhelmingly victorious. Most of its huge majority were Conservatives, who dominated the new cabinet. Under the National Government the nation began to emerge from the depression.

The Conservatives remained in control of the government and in 1935 Baldwin took over the duties of prime minister, while MacDonald remained as an honorary member of the cabinet for another year.

The Baldwin cabinet remained in office after an election late in 1935. During the next two years, the main concern of the English government was rearmament. Patriotism and national loyalty were called upon to support measures strengthening the army, navy, and especially the Royal Air Force.

THE ABDICATION OF EDWARD VIII

In 1936, King George V died and was succeeded by his eldest son, the Prince of Wales, who became Edward VIII. Edward wanted to make the role of king more active than had become customary in recent years. Perhaps the most important issue became his decision to

The Duke and Duchess of Windsor in Paris after the Duke had abdicated as British king. (Acme)

King George VI and his family at his coronation ceremony in the spring of 1937

marry an American divorcee, Mrs. Wallis Warfield Simpson. Clerical, official, and public resentment blocked him, but rather than change his mind, he abdicated in December, and was succeeded by his brother, the Duke of York. Stanley Baldwin resigned in 1937 and was replaced by Neville Chamberlain.

Several important changes occurred in other parts of the British Empire during the postwar period. Southern Ireland became internally independent with the establishment of the Irish Free State in 1922. In 1931 the Statute of Westminster defined the legal status of elements in the Empire. Under this act the Dominions, together with Great Britain, were to be considered equal and independent members of the British Commonwealth of Nations, held together only in the person of the king and by the sentimental ties of nationality. The Government of India Act of 1935 gave local autonomy to the 11 provinces of India and provided for an All-India Federation governed by a central legislature under the British viceroy.

SPAIN

Torn by labor disputes and disturbed by regionalism and separatism, Spain presented a picture of unrest during the war and postwar years. Ministerial instability was increased by the interference of army officers in political affairs. Failure of Spanish efforts to subdue Morocco added to the national discontent and led to the establishment of a military dictatorship under Primo de Rivera. He attempted to improve economic conditions; but his disregard

for constitutional government and inability to eliminate corruption alienated most of the populace. He suddenly resigned in 1930 and left the country.

King Alphonse's efforts to satisfy the country met little success, and the desire to establish a republic increased rapidly. In April, 1931, when elections showed the strength of the Republican element and a revolution was threatened, Alphonse left for France after suspending the exercise of the

Primo de Rivera addressing Spanish troops. (Acme)

royal power. A republic was proclaimed, a constitution drawn up, and numerous reforms instituted. Education was secularized, church property taken over by the state, and the land owned by the former king and the higher nobles was confiscated without compensation and distributed to about a million farmers.

Opposition to the Republic soon developed; both Rightists and Leftists caused trouble. In 1932 a royalist uprising was suppressed, and in 1933 a radical revolt broke out but soon collapsed. The election of 1933 revealed a marked Conservative tendency, and, as successive cabinets leaned more and more to the Right, the Left parties became dismayed and rose in revolution. The insurrection was bloody but short, and was so definitely sup-

659

Destruction in Madrid from Rebel bombardment. Note Loyalists giving Communist salute. (Acme)

pressed that Conservatives and Moderates were left in a strong position.

In 1936, however, radical groups scored heavily at the polls, and a popular coalition government took charge. A rebellion broke out, inspired by army officers, the large land-holders, and perhaps by the Church. The latter two groups opposed the land policy of the government, while the first objected to the retrenchments made in the overly officered army; and, supported by Moorish troops, the Rebels advanced rap-idly. However, defenses were hastily established by the Loyalists, and the insurgents failed to capture Madrid.

As the war devel-oped, foreign elements became prominent on both sides. A Non-In-

Generalissimo Franco, Spanish Civil War vic-tor. (International)

tervention Committee of European Nations was set up, with important countries proclaiming neutrality and establishment of a blockade of the Spanish coast to prevent war materials from reaching either side. It was unsuccessful and foreign soldiers formed a large proportion of both armies.

Russians, and Leftists of all nations, wished to aid the government while Germany and Italy began systematically to reinforce Gen-eral Franco, the Rebel commander. Thousands of Italian and German troops and implements of war were sent to aid him, and Russia and

Leftists of other countries helped the Loyalists. In March, 1939, the Loyalists surrendered, and Franco's position was secure.

NATIONAL DEVELOPMENT AFTER THE WAR IN SOVIET RUSSIA

The first problem of the Bolshevists, after defeating the White Counter-Revolution and the assisting armies of the Allies, was to unify the territories which were left to Russia. During the early days of the Red Revolution many regions on the fringes of the old czarist empire had become self-governing. Some of these were gradually absorbed in the Soviet republic already set up in Russia proper. After various negotiations, in 1922 there was pro-claimed a new federation called the Union of Soviet Socialist Republics. In form the gov-ernment was federal, but in fact it was a highly centralized arrangement, with local governments having only limited powers. Fundamental authority was given to the central government, although the "cultural autonomy" of the local states was encouraged.

In its nature the new Russian government was a distinctly class government. The suffrage was sharply limited to citizens over eighteen years of age who were "productive workers," soldiers, sailors, and the wives in these groups. All private merchants, those who hired labor for profit, clergy, former czarist officials, and persons with an income not earned by their own labor, were barred from voting or holding office.

The administration of justice in the Union was characterized by the cataloguing of po-litical crimes as most serious. Capital punish-ment was reserved for only embezzlement and counter-revolutionary attempts, while personal crimes received but light sentences, the penalty for murder being but ten years' imprisonment. Freedom of speech and of press were nonexistent in Russia. Opposition was suppressed ruthlessly, and as in Italy and Germany only the official party was permitted to exist.

The Communist party in Russia was in reality an extra constitutional government. Although it included less than seven million members out of Russia's one hundred and sixty millions of people, it controlled practically all offices. It was rigorously organized, from local cell to central committee, and included only active workers with a definite goal. Like Fascism, the party relied on militant youth organizations to provide future leadership.

More far-reaching than the changes in the political system was the revolution in Russian economics effected by the Bolshevists during the early years of their regime. Prevention of capitalist "exploitation" of workers, and state ownership of all lands, forests, and minerals, as well as all means of production and distribution, were fundamental concepts. In line with this belief, the government, immediately after the November Revolution, took over all the land. In the following May peasants were ordered to deliver to the state, at a confiscatory price, all grain over and above a minimum for family use and seed.

But the peasants had thought that land nationalization meant that they themselves would take over the great estates of the crown, church, and nobility, so they now resisted the Bolshevist attempts to take away the grain. Although they used armed force at times, the peasants' most effective weapon was the passive policy of reducing crops. As a result, Russia was brought to the verge of famine. The Communist experiment was breaking down in the handling of its agricultural problem. Faced with the loss of their power as famine and discontent spread over the land, the Bolshevists, under their leader, Lenin, instituted changes in their original economic system.

THE NEW ECONOMIC POLICY

This New Economic Policy (NEP) as it was called, allowed the peasants to rent land, hire workers for assistance, and to sell their produce to private traders, who were allowed to operate freely. While the land still was owned by the state, peasants were allowed permanent possession, as long as they used it. The NEP extended to industry too, as it returned small factories to private enterprise. Taken altogether, the NEP was a definite reaction from extreme theoretical communism

back to a measure of capitalism, under, of course, a certain amount of state control.

With the inauguration of the NEP, trade and agriculture shook off their lethargy, and in the economic rise that followed, there began to appear again various classes of farmers. Those who profited most from the new plan and who became prosperous farmers or kulaks stood in contrast to the middle and lower classes of peasants. The kulaks hired farm hands, rented land of their poorer fellows, and received growing profits. This was a cause for alarm to the Soviet officials. From the outset the kulaks had opposed Soviet policies especially that of land socialization; and now this class which was hostile to the existing regime, was benefiting the most from the NEP. To remedy this situation the government decided to embark on a more systematic and ruthless plan of land socialization.

THE FIRST FIVE-YEAR PLAN

The new policy was embodied in the first Five-Year Plan, a comprehensive program of development for the entire nation. Agriculturally, its aim was expansion of state and collectivized farms. Some advance was made the following year in this direction, but in 1930 more drastic methods were used to extend collectivization. Brigades of workers were sent to the country to enforce the government's decrees, and the kulaks were treated harshly. Their property was confiscated, and they were forbidden to join any collective farms. In reprisal the kulaks shot Soviet officials, slaughtered their own cattle, and burned granaries in an attempt to gain their ends by again causing national famine. The government retaliated with severer methods, executing many of the kulaks, and by March 55 per cent of all peasant land had been collectivized.

At this juncture the government modified its policy by organizing artels, collective farms where certain possessions remained as private property. This was a concession to the middle class peasants who had sided with the kulaks in complaining against the government. The artels contracted with the government to furnish all produce over the needs of their members; but the peasants opposed this policy. Government prices were still lower than market prices, so there was little incentive to increase their output. The government and the peasants often differed, too, as to how much constituted their "needs." Even in 1931, a famine year, the government made heavy exactions, for which it gave, according to the peasants, too little. In the following year, 1932, the peasants resisted passively, refusing to sow enough grain, letting it rot, or hiding it. As a result, the 1932 harvest was light, but the government rigorously exacted the fulfillment of its contracts. Famine, disease, and death resulted, and from one to two million people were estimated to have perished.

To alleviate peasant hostility, the government again changed its policy that winter. It instituted a grain tax, the amount of which was to be decided before planting. The provision permitting peasants to keep all of the surplus over the tax appealed to the profit motive and in consequence the harvest of 1933 was plentiful and by the end of the year 70,000,000 peasants were included in 200,000 collective farms comprising 75 per cent of the cultivated area.

The first Five-Year Plan had an industrial aspect also. It aimed at developing a Western industrial economy in Russia by the building of factories, railroads, and highways, and by creating better living conditions. It sought to transform the people culturally by establishing libraries, eliminating illiterates, and popularizing music. This plan was officially declared completed in December, 1932. It was followed by a second Five-Year Plan which aimed at developing lighter industries and complete literacy. Schools, under the plan, were made active Communist agencies, especially in discrediting all religion.

CHANGE IN POLITICAL POLICY

In political affairs a definite change occurred in 1924 after the death of Lenin. Trotsky and Stalin, leaders of the Bolsheviki during and after the Revolution, each attempted to assume the leadership of the Party. Stalin believed in the more moderate policies of gradual acquisition of peasant land and the concentration on internal affairs, while Trotsky believed in the immediate acquisition of the peasants' holdings, and in aggressive attempts to foment world revolution. Stalin was victorious and Trotsky was ousted from the Comintern and exiled in 1929. This conflict between Stalin and Trotsky was felt not only in Soviet Russia, but among Communists throughout the world. It came to the fore in 1936 and 1937 with the famed trials for treason of former leaders of the party. Kamenev, Zinoviev, and Radek were among the many who spectacularly confessed to the charge of plotting with Trotsky to assassinate Stalin and overthrow the Soviet Union. In the course of the purges, thousands of persons were shot and hundreds of thousands sent into slave labor in Siberia or elsewhere.

In June 1937, eight Soviet generals, including Marshal Tukhachevsky, were convicted of high treason and executed. This was followed by a renewed wave of purges and death sentences of numerous senior officials.

NEW CONSTITUTION

By 1936 the government of Joseph Stalin felt that the first stage of Revolution had been completed—the dictatorship of the proletariat had firmly established the new Soviet state. Therefore a new constitution was promulgated in December of that year. Under it, the supreme authority resided in the Supreme Council of the Union. It was divided into houses with equal powers. One house, the Council of the Union elected by direct universal suffrage, had representatives apportioned according to population. The other house, the Council of Nationalities, had its members chosen by the highest soviets of the republics and regions in the Union.

Appointed by the Supreme Council were the administrative and executive heads of the government, who were collectively known as the Council of People's Commissars. These officers were similar to the cabinet members of other democratic governments, but there were additional Commissariats.

Local government, as previously, was carried on by distinct rural and urban soviets. Education was free and compulsory for all children in the Union. Complete equality for men and women was stressed.

Though the Constitution of 1936 was avowedly democratic, the one-party system, the ruthless suppression of opposition to the Communist party, the strict censorship, and the government propaganda machine all united to nullify many of the constitution's provisions, including those guaranteeing civil liberties.

THE SEARCH FOR SECURITY

After the horrors of World War I, it was natural that European countries, especially the victorious nations, would be desirous of achieving security by various means. Security was interpreted by the Allies, as well as the newly created states of Central Europe, to mean the maintenance of the *status quo* as outlined by the Versailles Treaty. The creation of a League of Nations was considered an effective method of guaranteeing the much desired security.

France was particularly interested in safeguarding her new prestige in Europe and made various diplomatic efforts to bring about mutual peace agreements. She succeeded in getting an international commission to classify certain vague points in the League Covenant, dealing with the definition of an aggressor and the exact means to be taken to discipline an aggressor. The "Geneva Protocol," as the resulting agreement was called, failed because of opposition from England. France sought further security by concluding a defensive military alliance with Belgium in 1920, and other alliances with Poland, Czechoslovakia, and finally, in 1935, with Russia.

The cooperation of the French diplomat, Aristide Briand, and the German foreign minister, Gustav Stresemann, brought about the ratification of the Locarno Pact, in which Germany renounced any attempt to obtain modification of her western boundaries by the use of military force. Another important step in the search for security was the signing by almost every nation of the world of the Kellogg-Briand Pact for the outlawing of war. None of these treaties, however, successfully solved the international problems in Europe, for the vanquished nations continued to press

Aristide Briand, who sought French security. (Underwood & Underwood)

for a revision of the Versailles Treaty, while France and her late allies remained hostile to any plan which might deprive them of their spoils of the war.

In central and eastern Europe fear of the return of the Hapsburgs and alteration of the *status quo* established by the peace settlement led to moves for collective security. Yugoslavia, Rumania, and Czechoslovakia formed the "Little Entente" which they bulwarked by treaties with Italy and France. The countries bordering on Russia made agreements to support each other in opposition to any projects of annexation by the USSR, while Russia, in return, sought to establish a group of buffer states between her and the great capitalistic nations of the West, especially that of Nazi Germany. Poland, which had been close to France, immediately after the war developed friendly relations with Germany, although after the triumph of Hitler, the Poles, alarmed at the Nazi threat, began to look toward France again.

Diplomatic efforts were not the only ones tried to preserve peace in the postwar period. Force of arms continued to be relied on heavily, and great armament programs reminiscent of prewar days were drawn up, although there were attempts to limit them. Naval arms of the great powers were put on definite ratios in the Washington Arms Conference in 1921, but ten years later fear and distrust had developed to such an extent that the Paris and London Naval Conferences ended with virtually nothing accomplished, and finally Japan announced that she was abrogating the Washington Treaty, which permitted her only three capital ships to five for both England and United States. Attempts to limit land armaments ended in failure, too, with the breakup of the Geneva Disarmament Conference. Throughout Europe remained the problem of reconciling security and disarmament.

83. The Republican Decade and the New Deal

UNITED STATES REJECTION OF THE LEAGUE

THE COVENANT OF THE LEAGUE OF NATIONS was made part of the Treaty of Versailles and heartily supported by President Woodrow Wilson. Chances for the approval by the United States of the Covenant and Treaty sank sharply when the Democrats under Wilson suffered a heavy defeat in the Congressional elections of 1918. Control of both Houses of Congress, Democratic for six years, fell to the Republicans.

The Senate, in 1919, rejected the Treaty and Covenant contained therein, both in their original form and with amendments proposed by Senator Lodge of Massachusetts. President Wilson, who had suffered a nervous breakdown from strain and overwork in a national tour to gain support for the treaty, declared that he would again appeal to the country, presumably in the presidential campaign of 1920. But again the Senate rejected the treaty, 49 in favor to 35 against, less than the two-thirds required to approve under the Constitution.

THE RAILROADS AND INDUSTRIAL UNREST

An act of Congress in 1918 provided that the utilities which were being used for government purposes, must be returned to their owners within twenty-one months after the end of the war. Thus, in the summer of 1919 the telephone, telegraph, and cable lines were handed back to private ownership, but by the end of the year the railroads were still in the hands of the government, and no plan had been drawn up for their restoration to private owners.

Some people wished to leave the operation of the railroads in the government's control, and Director-General McAdoo asked that the twenty-one-month period be lengthened in order to study the question more deeply. Congress, however, did not approve of his suggestion, and also refused to adopt the so-called "Plumb plan," in which the railroad workers would obtain a part in the management of the roads.

In February, 1920, Congress passed the Esch-Cummins, or Transportation Act, one of the most complicated pieces of American legislation in modern times. This act repealed the Sherman Anti-Trust Law as it applied to railways, and encouraged their consolidation into "systems" instead of individual companies. Despite the opposition of the workers themselves, who insisted that the bill was very unfair to labor, President Wilson signed it, and a few days later the railroads were back in the hands of their former private owners.

America was the scene of much labor unrest and industrial quarrels in 1919 and 1920. During the war labor and capital had joined hands to such an extent that Samuel Gompers, then president of the American Federation of Labor, promised that labor would not strike during the time of war production.

But after the war had ceased, there was a spread of strikes from coast to coast. The reasons given for this labor trouble were the return of the troops to civilian life, the rising cost of living, and the general disorder resulting from the emergency years of the war in which the natural course of political and economic affairs had been severely disarranged.

The most important of the labor troubles of these years was the great coal strike which began on November 1, 1919. Almost a half-million men in the bituminous coal fields laid

Warren G. Harding, 29th president, 1921–23. (Harris & Ewing)

down their tools and demanded a 60 per cent increase in wages and the guarantee of a minimum of thirty hours of work a week. However, as America was still technically at war with Germany, the President had the power to regulate the fuel supply, and his administrator compelled the men to settle the strike which a few months later brought the miners a wage increase of 27 per cent.

PROHIBITION AND WOMAN SUFFRAGE

Another important event of those years immediately following the war was the amendment prohibiting the manufacture and sale of intoxicating liquors. In December, 1917, after many states had already gone "dry" during the war, Congress approved and later the states ratified the Eighteenth Amendment to the Constitution. It went into effect in 1920.

Also, in the late summer of 1920, the Nineteenth Amendment to the Constitution was ratified. This act removed sex as a basis for suffrage disqualification. Many states had at first refused to consider ratification of this proposal, but after a difficult and exciting battle led by the women's organizations, the measure won out, and thus 8,000,000 more voters were added in 1920.

"RETURN TO NORMALCY"

Chicago was the scene of the Republican nominating convention in June of 1920. On the tenth ballot, much to the surprise of the country at large, a "dark-horse" candidate, Senator Warren G. Harding of Ohio, was chosen. The vice-presidential nomination went to Governor Calvin Coolidge of Massachusetts, who had come into the public attention by decided action in the interest of the public safety in a strike of Boston policemen in 1919.

The Democratic convention, meeting in the same month at San Francisco, had an even more trying contest. Finally, on the forty-fourth ballot, Governor James M. Cox of Ohio was chosen.

Strangely enough the problems of war and foreign policy did not affect the election so much as domestic questions such as taxation, labor disputes, the high cost of living, and, especially, popular reaction against "Wilsonism." The election was a Republican landslide. Harding and Coolidge won the entire North and West and even made inroads into the traditionally "Solid South" by carrying Tennessee. The electoral vote was 404 to 127, and the Republicans totaled 7,000,000 more popular votes than their opponents. The Republicans also greatly increased their majorities in both houses of Congress.

The new Republican administration had many serious problems to face. A depression, which began late in 1919, was very pronounced during 1920, and a real crisis was evident. This financial crisis, of course, was world wide and the direct result of the ravages of war. In the fall of 1920 prices had fallen so rapidly that a delegation of farmers and producers visited the capital to ask for direct relief. Their pressure resulted in the creation of a more efficient national budget system, an emergency tariff, and a loan of $2,000,000,000 to the farmers and producers.

President Harding's views on the League of Nations were directly opposed to those of President Wilson's. America, according to his policy, should keep out of any alliance with other nations, but would be glad to see the European countries live in harmony. Meanwhile, America was still technically at war with Germany, although all fighting had ceased three years earlier. Congress passed an act in July, 1921, which declared the war over, and offered peace terms to Germany and Austria, which nations agreed to them the next month.

THE WASHINGTON CONFERENCE

Harding, evincing his interest in world affairs, invited an international conference to meet in Washington in November of the same

Charles Evans Hughes, secretary of state under Harding; he was later chief justice. (Karsh–Ziff Davis)

year to discuss naval disarmament, especially in the Pacific area. Great Britain, France, Japan, Holland, Portugal, Belgium, China, and Italy were present, and representing the United States were Secretary of State Hughes, former Secretary of State Elihu Root, and Senators Lodge and Underwood.

Although the time for disarmament was excellent, and the people were in a mood that earnestly reflected peace, there were many difficulties in the way of success. That the conference did accomplish as much as it did was attributed to Secretary Hughes, who had been made permanent chairman. He at the start suggested that for the next fifteen years there should be no further building of ships, and that the navies of the United States, Great Britain, and Japan should scrap their old battleships and large ships being built.

There was a great deal of deliberation over these questions, and the agreements finally adopted, although less extensive than Hughes had hoped for, were most certainly favorable to peace so far as naval warfare was concerned. The most important result was the establishment of a naval quota for the Great Powers. England, the United States, and Japan were placed on a 5:5:3 ratio, respectively; while France and Italy each received a quota basis of 1.75 in relation to the first three Powers. Perhaps the most significant agreement was the Nine-Power Pact safeguarding the territorial integrity of China and island possessions in the Pacific. Japan's frequent and flagrant disregard of this pact laid her open to serious international indictment.

In the summer of 1923, while visiting Alaska, President Harding became ill of ptomaine poisoning, and died at San Francisco, August 2, 1923. His death was followed by the revelation of several political scandals.

COOLIDGE AS PRESIDENT

Vice-President Coolidge was administered the oath of office as president by his father in his Vermont home, soon after news of Harding's death. Coolidge was a quiet, efficient man of simple tastes. He announced his intention of retaining the cabinet and administrative program of the late President.

The first scandal inherited by Coolidge from the Harding administration involved the misappropriation of more than $200,000,000 in the administration of the Veterans' Bureau. A second exposure revealed the secret leasing, by Secretary of the Interior Albert B. Fall, of naval oil reserves in Wyoming (Teapot Dome) and in California (Elk Hills). Secretary Fall was later found guilty of accepting a bribe, and Attorney-General Daugherty and Secretary of the Navy Denby were forced out of the cabinet, although they were not convicted of any crime. Actually, the Teapot Dome lease itself was invalidated on technical grounds, and not for any fraud, and H. F. Sinclair, president of the oil company involved, was acquitted of conspiracy. But, because the newspapers had already tried and convicted the men charged, in their columns, and because the Senate investigation was pushed vigorously in an attempt to discredit the Republican administration, Teapot Dome has become a synonym for graft in government.

Coolidge got along no better with Congress than did the previous executive, and in fact even many of the Republicans refused to concur with his policies. He tried to kill the Bonus Bill in 1924 and Congress passed it over his veto. He proposed Mellon's system of taxation and Congress disapproved of it. As a matter of fact, in almost every phase of administration Coolidge and Congress were at loggerheads.

Calvin Coolidge, 30th president of the U. S., 1923–29. (Bachrach)

Coolidge was more popular with the common people than with the legislators, as the 1924 presidential campaign proved. At the Republican nominating convention, which met in Cleveland in June, Coolidge won on the first ballot, by the overwhelming vote of 1065 votes, with only 34 for La Follette and 10 for Hiram Johnson. Charles G. Dawes of Illinois was nominated as vice-president when Governor Lowden of the same state declined.

The Democratic nominating committee met in New York in the same month. A bitter battle ensued between William G. McAdoo and Governor Alfred E. Smith of New York. Finally after one hundred and three ballots, John W. Davis of West Virginia was nominated. Governor Charles W. Bryan of Nebraska was nominated as vice-president.

Charles Gates Dawes, vice-president from 1925 to 1929. (E. L. Ray)

Another complication of the 1924 presidential election was the formation of an independent Progressive party by Senator La Follette, a former Republican, who attacked Coolidge for his treatment of the farmers. La Follette was named as the candidate for president, and Senator Burton K. Wheeler of Montana as vice-president. The Socialist party endorsed this ticket. Although it was expected that this group would carry several western states they won only La Follette's home state, Wisconsin.

Coolidge's victory was almost as decisive as had been Harding's in 1920. He won 35 states and 382 electoral votes. The Democrats won only twelve southern states. Thus, Coolidge, who came to the White House through death, was made president through election, by a sweeping personal victory.

COOLIDGE PROSPERITY

The four years of the Coolidge administration were the most prosperous in the history of the nation. International problems were not numerous, and domestic affairs were at a peak of production and increase in the national budget. Coolidge has been called the "business man's president," and it is true that under his administration corporations and industries were almost completely free of any restrictions and control. Coolidge believed in laissez faire economics, that is, allowing business as much freedom as possible, with a minimum of government supervision.

The only exception to the general spread of prosperity was that ever present farm problem, as the country seemed to be growing richer at the expense of the farmers. The rise of local and state taxes after the war, and the rising prices for farm implements placed a great burden upon the farmer. For three years, from 1924 to 1927, the "farm bloc" in Congress urged measures to help the farmers. President Coolidge vetoed the McNary-Haugen farm bill a second time in the spring of 1928. The farmers believed that the president was doing this in the interest of business as opposed to them, and a storm of protest arose.

On the whole, though, in spite of the exposures of the Harding administration, the four years of the Coolidge administration were among the most prosperous in American history. Industry, the stock market, real estate, and commerce were soaring to new heights. President Coolidge reduced taxes and expended some of the excess income on government engineering projects. During his administrations, the automobile and the radio became common in the United States.

FOREIGN POLICY

United States' participation in foreign affairs was relatively unimportant during Coolidge's regime. There were slight conflicts with Mexico and Nicaragua which the government finally conciliated both by a show of force and by diplomacy. A factor which acted for peace and understanding with these countries was the Sixth Pan-American Congress which met at Havana in 1928. A world conference held at Geneva in 1927, at Coolidge's suggestion, for further naval armament reductions, resulted in failure. America signed the Briand-Kellogg Peace Pact in 1928, a treaty which, sponsored jointly by Briand of France and Secretary of State Kellogg, pro-

Herbert Hoover, 31st president of the United States, 1929–33. (Harris & Ewing)

posed to outlaw war and settle all disputes peacefully.

Another important element that contributed to prosperity was the increasing interest in aviation. The growth of this industry, which by World War II had billions of dollars in investments, was stimulated by Charles A. Lindbergh whose nonstop flight in the *Spirit of St. Louis* from New York to Paris in May, 1927, aroused the interest of the entire world. Polar expeditions were begun as a result of aviation improvements and Admiral Richard E. Byrd was thus enabled to explore heretofore unknown Antarctic areas.

CAMPAIGN OF 1928

The presidential campaign of 1928, as compared with the campaigns of the preceding eight years, was cool and orderly. President Coolidge, when asked whether he intended to be a candidate for re-election, issued his famous statement: "I do not choose to run." Herbert Hoover, then Secretary of Commerce, was chosen as the Republican candidate for president on the first ballot. Senator Charles E. Curtis of Kansas was

Wall Street, New York, financial center of the nation, during the stock crash, Oct. 29, 1929. (Acme)

named as his running mate. The Democrats proposed almost a half-dozen candidates, but Governor Alfred E. Smith won the nomination, also on the first ballot, with Joseph T. Robinson of Arkansas as candidate for the vice-presidency.

Hoover swept the election, carrying forty states and capturing 444 electoral votes to Smith's 87. The Republicans again returned a substantial majority to both houses of Congress.

In October, 1929, the stock market crashed, ending a wave of speculation. The panic resulted in a general curtailment of industrial production, widespread business and banking failures, and accelerating unemployment. Hoo-

Lindbergh's Return to New York City after his solo flight across the Atlantic. (Acme)

"The Bonus Army" in Washington in 1932 to demand cash payment of veterans' bonuses. (Acme)

ver's efforts to deal with the situation included: the creation of the Reconstruction Finance Corporation to assist banks and business concerns in financial difficulties; establishment of the Federal Home Loan bank; and legislation extending Federal credit to states and cities. However, economic conditions became worse, and the number of unemployed rose to about 11,000,-000. Hoover was handicapped when his party lost control of the House in 1930.

Inauguration of President F. D. Roosevelt, in 1933. Chief Justice Hughes is shown administering the oath of office to the new president. (Acme)

THE NEW DEAL

In 1932 the Democrats nominated Governor Franklin D. Roosevelt of New York for president and Congressman John Garner of Texas for vice-president. The Republicans renominated Hoover and Curtis. To the voters the great issue was the depression, which was blamed on the party in power. The Democrats, calling for a "New Deal," easily won the presidency and control of Congress.

The new President acted quickly on: the early repeal of Prohibition and the complementary boom of the distillery industry; a devaluated dollar; expanded government services, such as the National Industrial Recovery Act, the Agricultural Adjustment Administration, the Works Progress Administration, the Home Owners Loan Corporation, the Reciprocal Tariff Act, and many others. He created a direct relief agency for families who were impoverished because of the depression, and a Civilian Conservation Corps for young men who could not find jobs.

Great engineering projects, such as the Hoover Dam and the Tennessee Valley development, were continued, while construction was begun on Grand Coulee and Bonneville Dams on the Columbia River. Public works were pushed, and a high relief budget continued.

At executive behest, Congress passed the

W. P. A. Relief Project in New York, one of the many financed by public funds for the jobless. (Acme)

Grand Coulee Dam, world's most massive masonry structure, was begun as a relief project in 1933

Wagner Labor Disputes Act in June, 1935. Its machinery was used with varying success in the labor disputes of the next year. The Guffey Coal Stabilization Act set up a commission to establish a code regulating the industry. A Farm Credit Act, the Frazier-Lemke Farm Mortgage Act, later declared unconstitutional, and the Agricultural Adjustment Act of 1935 made further attempts to alleviate the suffering in the drought-stricken farm areas. The Social Security Act of 1935 established a system of old age insurance and pensions.

Roosevelt, in sponsoring the Public Utility Holding Act, made an effort to regulate the extensive holdings of public utility companies. A banking act made permanent a government plan of insuring bank deposits up to $5,000. Another measure which caused much protest from the more conservative propertied groups, was the Wealth-Tax Act, increasing the surtaxes on annual incomes of $50,000 and over.

ELECTION OF 1936

In the presidential campaign of 1936, the anti-Roosevelt forces redoubled their attacks upon the administration. It is estimated that 80 per cent of the press was editorially opposed to the New Deal. Nevertheless, President Roosevelt, unanimously nominated for re-election, swept aside the Republican nominee, Gov. Alfred M. Landon of Kansas, in the greatest landslide of American history, winning 27,000,000 popular votes, with 508 electoral votes, and carrying forty-six out of forty-eight states.

Beginning early in 1937, President Roosevelt campaigned for a reduction in the power of the Supreme Court, which had declared several major New Deal laws unconstitutional. This, again, met with opposition, and Roosevelt was forced to modify his stand, although he did effect some important changes in the Federal judiciary.

Recovery from the depression was irregular during this period and lagged considerably behind that made by other nations. The recovery was rapid from 1933 to 1936, although interrupted by minor recessions. A severe recession led to a drop in business activity of 27% in 1937. The drop continued into 1938; thereafter, the threat of war, and then the outbreak of World War II, sharply stimulated American industry.

FOREIGN POLICY OF ROOSEVELT

Intensely concerned with internal economic questions, while every nation was striving frantically to solve its own depression problems, the United States displayed little activity in foreign affairs in the early portion of Roosevelt's first administration.

The London Economic Conference of 1933, called to consider the stabilization of world currency, failed in its objectives because of Roosevelt's refusal to cooperate. *De jure* recognition was accorded Soviet Russia in November of the same year.

As the pressing problems at home were relieved, the government turned more attention to questions of foreign policy and trade. Reciprocal trade treaties were negotiated with several Latin-American and European countries. The McDuffie-Tydings Act in 1934 provided for the complete independence of the Philippines by 1944. The Platt Amendment, which had always been resented by Cuba as an infringement on her sovereignty, was abandoned.

America's traditional desire to remain neutral in foreign conflicts resulted in the Neutrality Act of 1935. As renewed and amended in 1936, the Act provided that American economic relations with belligerent countries would be severed and the lives and property of its citizens would not be protected by the government, when the president declared that a state of war existed between two or more countries. The Act of 1935 was invoked in the Italo-Ethiopian War, and under the Act of 1936 a state of war was declared to exist in Spain.

In a speech at Chicago in October, 1937, Roosevelt declared that the peace-loving countries should impose a moral quarantine on aggressor nations. The unfavorable reaction to this speech and the sharp depression of 1937 led the President to abandon active international cooperation until war broke out.

84. Latin America Between Wars

AMERICAN REPUBLICS IN THE WORLD SCENE

THE TWENTY LATIN-AMERICAN REPUBLICS emerged from World War I with their material possessions enhanced. The war demand for their products, together with the large scale investment of foreign capital, produced a period of economic, social, and political progress between the years of 1919-1929 which was unparalleled in Latin-American history. Nor had these republics had to pay the price exacted of other nations for their advancement in this period. Only eight of them had declared war on Germany; five had severed diplomatic relations; and seven remained neutral during the whole conflict. Numbered among those seven were three of the greatest powers in Latin-America —Mexico, Argentina, and Chile.

In the field of pacific settlement of Latin-American disputes, the record of the League of Nations was one of monotonous failure. In 1920, the League was called upon by Peru and Bolivia to settle the Tacna-Arica dispute. When a third Latin-American republic protested, the League decided this was a private matter and not within its competence. In 1921, Panama and Costa Rica were on the verge of a war over a boundary dispute. But while the Secretary-General of the League of Nations, of which both were members, cabled for information, the American Secretary of State, Charles Evans Hughes, intervened and the conflict was settled. In the undeclared war between Bolivia and Paraguay over the Chaco boundary, the League once again proved ineffective as an agency of pacific settlement.

MODIFICATION OF THE MONROE DOCTRINE

With the failure of the United States to enter the League of Nations, the Latin-American states became apprehensive of the meaning of the Monroe Doctrine which was incorporated into Article 21 of the League Covenant. Not only did Honduras, El Salvador, Costa Rica, and Mexico ask for a redefinition of the Covenant from the Geneva forum, but also at successive Pan-American conferences the question was persistently raised and persistently evaded.

The answer remained in doubt until the United States, in pursuit of its "good neighbor" policy, declared first at the Montevideo Congress of 1933, and at the Buenos Aires Conference of 1936, that the preservation of the Monroe Doctrine was to be shared in by all states, and not maintained by the United states alone. This appeased Latin-American feelings, and in 1938 a Pan American conference at Lima adopted a declaration of mutual protection against outside aggression.

ECONOMIC DISTRESS AND DICTATORSHIPS

Profound internal changes appeared in Latin America in the decade from 1919 to 1929. Prices and standards of living rose. Public utilities were built, educational facilities were increased, the arts were cultivated, industries were established, and a certain amount of labor legislation was passed. Political habits became less unstable. Wherever military disorders occurred, they were generally of short duration.

Then came the depression. In the years that followed, much of the progress made by the Latin-American states seemed to be wiped out. Foreign markets disappeared. In Cuba, for instance, exports were cut in half. Everywhere military authorities rose to challenge the civil government. Dictators bid for power. The standard of living of the masses was depressed. The rifle squad rather than the ballot box distinguished most of Latin-American politics. The triumph of the semi-Fascist dictators is reflected in the fact that in 1937 possibly three Latin-American states, Colombia, Chile, and Mexico, could be described as republics. The strength of the dictators is further reflected in the hostility to liberalism shown by most of the Latin-American representatives at the League of Nations. When they refused to seat the Loyalist Spanish government on the Council of the League of Nations in 1937, they indirectly extended their hand to General Franco.

TOWARD STABILITY IN MEXICO

In the midst of all these upheavals in Latin America, Mexico appeared to be following a relatively peaceful road. This country emerged from World War I with Carranza as its president. The revolutionary forces which swept him into office had also formed a constitution which sought in Article 27 to nationalize the subsoil of the Mexican Republic. The objective of this clause was to check the foreign ownership of its minerals, the main wealth of Mexico. American and British interests, who owned most of the mines of Mexico, protested against the Article, charging that it was confiscatory in nature.

So concerned was the United States with the interpretation of this article, that when Álvaro Obregón in 1920 was constitutionally elected president of Mexico, both Wilson and Harding withheld recognition of the legitimacy of his government. Finally in 1923, the Mexican Supreme Court rendered a decision holding that the article in question was not retroactive and hence it was not confiscatory. This meant that all foreign holdings acquired prior to the adoption of the Constitution would remain in private hands, but that no mineral or oil concessions could be acquired in the future. The decision of the Mexican Supreme Court removed the impediment from the recognition of the Obregón government. The working relation between Obregón and the American government thereafter was so close that when a revolt against his leadership broke out in the last year of his term of office, Obregón received arms from American arsenals to suppress the revolt.

In 1924 Plutarco Calles was elected president of Mexico in the first peaceful election in fifty years. Calles had been nominated by the National Revolutionary party. So powerful had this party become that mere nomination was equivalent to election. In 1928, Obregón was elected to succeed Calles, but was assassinated a few days later, before he took office. This left Calles virtual dictator of the National Revolutionary party. He was able to choose his own presidents and they responded to his advice.

Álvaro Obregón, during the few days between his election as Mexican president and his assassination. Right, Mexican leaders in 1934. (International). Left to right: Gen. Almado; President Rodriguez; President-elect Cárdenas; Secretary of War and Navy, Gen. Quiroga. (Acme)

Plutarco Calles arriving in the United States in 1936 after his deportation from Mexico for opposing President Cárdenas. Below, President Vargas of Brazil welcoming U. S. President Roosevelt, who visited Brazil Nov. 27, 1936, on his way to the Pan American Peace Conference. (Acme Photos)

In June of 1933, Calles announced through the National Revolutionary party a six-year plan for Mexico which, if enacted, would bring about changes in Mexico without violating private interests. It was in essence a program emphasizing better education, minimum wage laws, agrarian reforms and public works. The plan was approved by the National Revolutionary party in December of the same year and it fell to President Lázaro Cárdenas, elected in 1934, to put the plan into effect. In pursuit of this policy, Cárdenas took steps to secure minimum wage laws, to fix the price of certain commodities, to forbid child labor, and to protect women in industry. By the constitutional amendment of October, 1934, his government established the basis of a new educational system by forbidding church-sponsored education. This revived the conflict between the government and the Catholic Church.

In 1935, there came a split between Cárdenas and Calles. The latter, accustomed to having his presidents listen to his advice, never expected Cárdenas to push through the six-year plan. Charging the president was confiscating property, Calles set himself up in opposition to the existing government. The radical section of the labor movement, the peons, and the army supported Cárdenas in the struggle, and Calles was forced to leave the country.

The government confiscated foreign oil properties in 1938, and agreed later to gradual reparation.

DICTATORSHIP IN BRAZIL

The strong man of Brazil after 1930 was Getulio Vargas. This energetic leader was compelled to face a number of serious political problems, including disastrous civil war. Although Vargas succeeded in consolidating his power, communistic propaganda grew in disturbing proportions. Political revolts and unrest in Brazil's twenty states created a precarious condition which was not conducive to economic development. On November 10, 1937, President Vargas assumed dictatorial powers in an attempt to make his country a corporate state, somewhat similar to the totalitarian states of Europe. Vargas announced that payments on the principal and interest of foreign indebtedness would cease temporarily while the government put its finances in order. The new constitution provided for a consultative council on national economy composed of representatives from workers' and employers' organizations. Legislative power was to be exercised by a chamber whose membership was proportioned to the population. A federal council of thirty members was to act in an advisory capacity. These sweeping changes apparently had the approval of the various states and the support of the army.

ARGENTINA

Argentina persisted in its policy of neutrality after the United States entered World War I in 1917. The government was then under the guidance of a radical *caudillo*, Dr. Hipólito Irigoyen. Argentine industry prospered under the stimulus of war demands, and although there was a brief period of depression when hostilities ceased, economic progress was resumed under the presidency of Alvear from 1922 to 1926. Irigoyen's party enacted a social program which was far advanced, but these promising measures were not carried out as thoroughly as their proponents expected.

Irigoyen was re-elected in 1928, but his support had dwindled. The continuance of economic distress was partly responsible for the revolution of 1930 which placed José Francisco Uríburu in power for a brief time. Augustín P. Justo succeeded to the presidency in 1931 after a military coup, and for a time Argentina was unstable politically. In 1937, Roberto M. Ortiz, a conservative, was elected president.

Argentina continued to be a prominent contender for the economic and political leadership of South America. Its statesmen were especially jealous of the economic strength of the United States, although British, German, French, and Italian influences were prominent. Brazil, traditionally suspicious of Argentina, was the only Latin-American nation capable of challenging Argentine leadership.

TURMOIL IN PERU AND CHILE

Peruvian history after World War I continued its troubled course. Augusto B. Leguia was president from 1908 to 1930, with exception of the four-year term of José Pardo from 1915 to 1919. The Tacna-Arica dispute, long a dangerous contention, was settled in 1929 with a division of the two provinces between Peru and Chile. Leguia's dubious financial arrangements contributed to his downfall in 1930, and Luis M. Sanchez Cerro headed the

government until his assassination in 1933. The administration of Oscar Benavides, who succeeded Cerro, opened with a serious dispute over the Leticia corridor which was finally settled amicably.

The presidency of Juan Luis Sanfuentes in Chile, which began in 1915, promised to carry forward the program of the "Democratic Republic." Sanfuentes promoted public works, encouraged a merchant marine, reorganized public administration, and improved conditions in the army and navy. These beneficial measures were interrupted by World War I and the resulting loss of Chilean markets in Europe, especially for its nitrates. Chile, with a large German population, favored the Central Powers, but sentiment veered toward the Allies by 1917. This change in attitude was attended by an increased trade with Europe. A prominent figure, both in Chile and abroad, was the historian Augustín Edwards, who became president of the League Assembly in 1922.

Arturo Alessandri was elected president in 1920. Internal unrest prevented the completion of his reform program, and in 1925 Colonel Ibáñez forced Alessandri from office. An election in the same year seated Emiliano Figueroa, who had the honor of instituting fiscal reforms recommended by the Kemmerer Commission. Ibáñez again seized power in 1926 and remained in control until a revolution in 1931 caused him to flee. Alessandri was recalled to the presidency in December, 1932. He was followed in 1938 by Pedro A. Cedra, the Popular Front candidate.

THE AGE OF GÓMEZ IN VENEZUELA

Venezuelan history after 1908 was the story of a remarkable dictatorship under Juan Vicente Gómez. Although this *caudillo* died in 1935, at an advanced age, he impressed his personality upon Venezuelan politics for nearly thirty years. His dictatorship had many cruel features, such as arbitrary imprisonment, exile, and confiscation of property. Gómez allowed two other presidents to serve during his dictatorship, but he was the real ruler. During Gómez' regime, foreign nations began the development of Venezuela's great oil fields. Political disturbances were few.

85. Events in Africa and the Far East

AFRICA

IN AFRICA, the fate of the blacks and the Arabs after World War I ran along different paths. While the black peoples, as represented by the Ethiopians, had none of the national cohesiveness which makes for effective national organization, the Arabs in the northern strip of Africa had varied success in developing patterns of government. These Arab peoples, along with their kinsmen in Asia proper, emerged from World War I to find their dreams of a greater Arab state frustrated. Sporadic disturbances demonstrated their reaction to disillusionment. One of the most successful of these Arab uprisings occurred under the leadership of Abd-el-Krim who led his Riffian warriors in Spanish Morocco and so effectively defeated the Spanish that by 1923, Spanish control was limited to the coast line. From his success in Spanish Morocco, Abd-el-Krim turned to French Morocco and repeated his successes there. It required the combined forces of Spain and France under Marshal Pétain finally to force Krim to lay down his arms in 1926.

Great Britain made a wise move in 1922 by granting a measure of independence to Egypt. For all practical purposes Egypt still remained a British protectorate, with British control over international affairs and foreign investments within the country. In August, 1936, a new Anglo-Egyptian Treaty was signed. Egypt was declared independent but in alliance with Great Britain for at least 20 years. British troops assumed the obligation of guarding the Suez Canal as an international interest, and joint Anglo-Egyptian administration was established in the Sudan. In 1937 the age-old system of capitulations (treaties granting foreign countries jurisdiction in Egypt over their nationals) was ended, a convention having been concluded by Egypt with each of the countries involved. In the same year Egypt became a member of the League of Nations.

JAPANESE MILITARISM AFTER WORLD WAR I

The ability of Japan to carve out an empire for herself in the two decades of postwar history can be understood in terms of its internal politics. The Japanese military and naval imperialists were to play the leading role in empire building. Japan had emerged from the war with a full grown military machine. She had successfully imposed on her feudal society the techniques of western industry without losing one of the basic concepts of her feudalism—an intense patriotism and deification of the emperor. Two parties controlled Japan: the Minseito party, representing the industrialists; and the Seiyuki party, representing the feudal land barons and army leaders. Wherever conflicts occurred within Japan, the parties to the conflict lined up not as conservatives but rather as civil or military authorities. The army repeatedly challenged the authority of the civil government after 1929, and by acts of terrorism and propaganda often was able to intimidate the civil authorities.

The world depression of 1929 heightened the power of the military class, for it brought in its wake an attempt to recapture shrinking markets at the expense of depreciating the yen at home. As cheap Japanese goods flooded the world markets, the Great Powers of the West were aroused against this threatening competition. The implied threats to Japan in this hostility enabled the army to pose as the rallying-point for the Japanese. Wherever possible, as in China, the army offered by force of arms to carve out a monopolistic market for Japanese products. It was with this objective in mind that the army entered upon its program of conquest in China.

HOSTILITY OF THE PACIFIC POWERS

With the aggressions of 1931, the leading world powers demonstrated their reluctance to risk a war for defense of whatever interests they may have had endangered in the areas occupied by Japan. The United States, as the champion of the "Open Door" policy in China, announced through the Stimson Doctrine that it would not recognize any territorial acquisitions made by Japan contrary to existing treaties and pacts. This position was rephrased by the League of Nations and caused Japan to withdraw from the League.

Not content with having aroused all the Pacific powers of the world by its invasion of China, Japan sought to have the London Naval Agreement of 1930 modified so as to give her naval parity with Great Britain and the United States. When this demand was refused, Japan denounced both the Washington and London agreements and started a naval race with her more wealthy competitors in the Pacific. Domestic and international affairs led to an alliance between Japan and Germany in November, 1936. When Italy joined the alliance one year later, some observers believed that the three countries had formed a united front against all non-Fascist states.

THE CHINESE REPUBLIC

Two principal factors may be discerned in the history of China since 1919: a struggle against internal chaos, and an effort to retain its existence as a nation in the face of the threats of the Great Powers. Confronted on the east by Japan and on the west by Russia, China was the stake for which these countries evolved the grand strategy of their "power politics." The effect of that strategy on the internal and external affairs of China, linked to the chaos into which the country plunged after the overthrow of the corrupt Manchu dynasty in 1911, raised more than academic doubts whether the twentieth-century Chinese would endure to prove again the maxim that China

The tomb of Sun Yat-sen, on the slopes of Nanking's Purple Mountain. (Keystone)

has always absorbed her conquerors.

The period of internal turmoil following the overthrow of the Manchu dynasty came to a head in the years after the close of World War I. Sun Yat-sen, the father of the Chinese Revolution, had formulated three principles for the unification of China: People's nationalism, People's democracy, and People's livelihood. When the presidency of the new Chinese Republic, born of Sun Yat-sen's efforts, passed to the opportunist, Yuan Shih-kai, Sun retired to Canton. There he organized the Kuomintang, or people's party, which was committed to the introduction into China of the economy, technology, and political democracy of the West. The opportunist Yuan died in 1916, and as he started on the road to the eternal reward for his corruption, the feudal war lords of various Chinese provinces began to fight with one another for the control of the central Chinese government at Nanking. They turned for support to the belligerent big brothers of the Far East, Japan and Russia.

In 1921, while the struggle between the war lords continued, Sun Yat-sen was engineered into the presidency of the Republic by a rump

Sun Yat-sen, founder of the Chinese Republic. (Acme)

parliament meeting in Canton. In the face of constant threats to his existence by the militarists, Sun turned to Russia for assistance. The Russian aid was personified by Michael Borodin who arrived from Moscow in 1923. The alliance between Soviet Russia and the Kuomintang, which was effected by Borodin and Sun, brought immediate results. The Kuomintang was reorganized on the same pattern as the Russian Communist party. The new Chinese army was trained by Russian officers. In 1924, the Chinese Communists, hitherto excluded from the Kuomintang, were absorbed into Sun's party. On the eve of Sun Yat-sen's death in 1924, there had been planted the seed of a new China.

CHIANG KAI-SHEK

The alliance of the Kuomintang with Soviet Russia sharpened the conflict within China. What had begun as an antiforeign, Chinese nationalism soon evolved into a conflict between the bourgeoisie and proletariat within China itself. After Sun's death, Chiang Kai-shek, with the assistance of Borodin, established himself as the successor to Sun by assuming control of Canton. With the Soviet-Kuomintang alliance still operating effectively, Borodin and Chiang set forth to unify China by force in a campaign which was both antiforeign and anticapitalist.

Although this campaign against the northern war lords yielded them the Yangtze River Valley and the city of Shanghai, it caused a disagreement between Borodin and Chiang. Chiang had been willing to use Russian aid for the purpose of gaining control of China, while Borodin had been willing to use Chiang for the purpose of making China communist. Now, with success at hand, they had little more use for each other. In the break that followed, Chiang called to his side all the militarist and anti-communist forces. And despite the denunciation of his activities by Sun Yat-sen's widow, to whom he was related by marriage, Chiang proceeded to purge Shanghai and Canton of both Russian and Chinese Communists. Borodin returned to Russia, and in the face of new disorders, Chiang also retired for a year. He returned in 1928 and set up a personal dictatorship in Nanking which he had wrested from the control of Chinese Communists.

JAPANESE CONQUEST OF MANCHURIA

Through the cooperation of several Chinese war lords, all of China seemed to come under a semblance of unity centering in the dictatorship of Chiang. The Kuomintang, now controlled by Chiang, soon set itself up as the single political party of China. But rival factions within the single legalized party, and the

Chiang Kai-shek, president of China and generalissimo of its armed forces during most of the second quarter of the 20th century. He is shown with his wife, the former Mayling Soong. (Acme)

impossibility of bringing independent war lords and provincial governors under complete control, led to a series of civil disturbances which represented a constant threat to Chiang's life as well as to the life of his Nanking government.

The close of World War I had found Japanese forces occupying all of Manchuria, eastern Siberia, Shantung, and Northern Sakhalin. But the pressure of the victorious Red Russian army and of the Western powers forced her to disgorge the part of China she had swallowed. By signing the Nine Power Treaty in 1922, Japan committed herself to respect the territorial integrity and administrative entity of China, as well as the "Open Door" policy.

But Japan was only temporarily reconciled to nonintervention in China. Internal pressures for Chinese and Manchurian markets, the aggressive demands of her military fanatics, and antiJapanese boycotts in China convinced Japan that she must conquer Manchuria. A bomb explosion on the Japanese controlled South Manchurian Railway gave the Japanese expansionists the pretext they wanted. Japa-

Henry Pu Yi, last emperor of China and emperor of Manchukuo

nese forces attacked Mukden at once on September 18, 1931, a date regarded by some observers as marking the beginning of World War II. Despite protests from the United States and the nations of the League, Japan completed her conquest by 1932 and set up the puppet regime of Manchukuo. In the same year, Japanese troops landed and attacked Shanghai far to the South. A truce followed by which Japan evacuated the city.

JAPANESE AGGRESSION, 1936-1941

Japanese pressure on China did not cease. Her troops were active all along the northern borders of China and she demanded an increasing number of privileges within China itself. In 1936, agitation among his followers and the semi-independent war lords forced Chiang-Kai-shek to resist more strongly Japanese encroachments. Japan then resorted to open attack and invasion. Late in 1937, her troops captured Shanghai and began fanning out over the whole coastal area of China. The main Chinese forces under Chiang moved into the interior. Peiping and Nanking fell to the Japanese who thereupon proclaimed a "New Reformed Government of the Republic of China" in 1938. Chungking, far to the West, became the capital of Chiang's nationalist or Kuomintang government. In Northern China, a communist regime remained independent of both Japan and the Kuomintang and at odds with both.

Japanese troops in Shanghai after their capture of the city in 1937. China lost almost all her large cities in 1937 and 1938, but thereafter held the Japanese until World War II. (Acme)

86. Munich and the Outbreak of War

THE DESTRUCTION OF ALLIED POLITICAL POWER

BEFORE HITLER unleashed his armed might on the nations of Europe, he, together with his friend, Mussolini, disarmed the democracies morally and politically. The decade of the thirties saw a long series of psychological defeats for the Allies, of which

the dismemberment of Czechoslovakia was the worst. After Italy had conquered Ethiopia and intervened in Spain, she was compelled to take a less dominant role in the Balkans and Central Europe by the expanding Nazi state. France, unsupported by Britain in the East of Europe, just as Britain was unsupported by her in the Ethiopian crisis, continually lost influence and trade among the nations which had been tied to her since the first world war. German influence penetrated these areas, and Austria, Hungary, Yugoslavia, Bulgaria, Rumania, and Greece swung from the French orbit into the Nazi sphere of influence.

In speech after speech, Hitler denied having any claims to French territory or aggressive designs toward England. He tried in every way possible to divide his Eastern opponents from his Western ones in order to avoid the great mistake of the German strategy of the first world war, the war on two major fronts. He almost succeeded in his plan.

THE SUDETEN PROBLEM

Beginning in 1937, Germany began actively to foster the agitations of the German population of the Czech Sudetenland for self-determination. Hitherto, this German minority in Czechoslovakia had been one of the best treated minorities in Europe. Its three million people had representation in the Czech parliament and had many rights of local autonomy.

But Konrad Henlein, the German Sudeten leader, wanted complete local rights, which the Czech government refused to grant.

Although in March, 1938, Hitler pleased all the powers by announcing he had no interest in Czechoslovakia, a few weeks afterward he began to threaten to intervene to protect the rights of the "persecuted" Germans. The Czechs mobilized; French, British and Russian support seemed to be forthcoming. The Czech government made further concessions to the Sudeten Germans just short of complete independence. Henlein was not satisfied. A Russian proposal to the French to guarantee Czech security was not accepted.

THE CHAMBERLAIN MISSIONS

On September 15, 1938, Prime Minister Chamberlain of England flew to Berchtesgaden to confer with Hitler. There the Fuehrer declared that Germany would fight, if necessary, to free the Sudeten Germans. Chamberlain returned to England and consulted with the British cabinet and French representatives. They decided that the French and British nations were unprepared and unwilling to go to war to save Czechoslovakia. A minority of British and French opinion were convinced that Hitler could not be appeased under any circumstances and that a strong front should be made regardless of the consequences. But official French and British policy won and, judging by the indications of popular approval which followed, public opinion in the democracies was not ready to go to any lengths.

Thereupon, on September 19, the Czechs were notified of the joint decision and advised to surrender the Sudeten area to Germany. When President Benes of Czechoslovakia tried to delay this catastrophe, the Western powers brought pressure on him to consent. He had to choose between the loss of true Czech independence and war without allies, save possibly Russia. He accepted the terms.

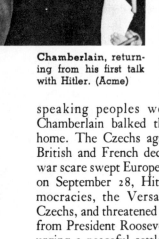

Chamberlain, returning from his first talk with Hitler. (Acme)

Chamberlain again flew to Berchtesgaden to tell Hitler that the Czechs would give in, but found that Hitler had now upped his demands to include territory in which German-speaking peoples were in the minority. Chamberlain balked this time and returned home. The Czechs again mobilized, and the British and French declared their support. A war scare swept Europe. In a belligerent speech on September 28, Hitler denounced the democracies, the Versailles Treaty, and the Czechs, and threatened to mobilize. A message from President Roosevelt, two days previous, urging a peaceful settlement, seemed to have no effect. Chamberlain still sought desperately for further negotiations, for he had no desire to go to war over what he still considered a local matter. At the behest of Mussolini, Hitler finally agreed to a conference.

THE MUNICH AGREEMENT

On September 29 and 30, 1938, Chamberlain, Daladier (the French Premier), Hitler and Mussolini met at Munich to decide the fate of Czechoslovakia, and indirectly that of Eastern Europe. Czechoslovakia, the victim, was left out, as was Russia, for the leaders felt that an Allied-Axis compromise would be impossible with the Soviets present. Germany received those parts of Czechoslovakia inhabited mainly by Germans. Poland and Hungary also received small pieces of Czech territory. In certain areas, internationally administered plebiscites were arranged to determine whether the inhabitants wanted to join Germany. Altogether Czechoslovakia lost some 30 per cent of her land and population. Britain and France guaranteed the new Czech frontiers.

The conference adjourned, and Chamberlain, back in England, declared he had secured a "peace with honor." But the peace was not secure for many weeks. Now helpless, Czechoslovakia fell prey to Germany. Slovakia became an independent state under German influence early in 1939. Hungary seized all of Sub-Carpathian Ruthenia with Hitler's approval. Finally, although he had declared that Munich represented his "last territorial demand," Hitler sent German troops into Prague, the Czech capital, on March 15. The Western Allies protested and stepped up rearmament.

The Allied concessions at Munich cost them Eastern Europe and, as events turned out, probably the loss of any possibility of Russian sup-

Participants in the Munich Conference, which decided that the Sudetenland should be transferred from Czechoslovakia to Germany. Left to right: Prime Minister Chamberlain of Great Britain; Premier Daladier of France; Chancellor Hitler; Premier Mussolini and Count Ciano, Italy

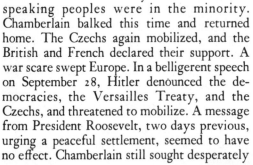

German Troops entering Danzig in September, 1939. Hitler's demands on Poland with respect to Danzig were a factor in the precipitation of World War II

port against Hitler. The Czechs had a strong army and a well fortified border running through the Sudetenland. Their Skoda works produced large quantities of munitions and armaments. The Czech mountains formed a natural barrier between Germany and Southeast Europe. The Czech democracy was disciplined and solidly behind its leaders. With the complete occupation of the land by the Nazis, all these things were lost to the Allies and all Eastern Europe was opened to German penetration. The Polish plains lay open before Hitler. The agricultural resources of the Balkans supplied Germany with foodstuffs, and the oil of Rumania was more accessible.

The Russo-German Pact. Stalin and Von Ribbentrop shaking hands after signing the Soviet-German treaty of 1939. (Acme)

DEMANDS ON POLAND AND DANZIG

Hitler moved without pause. German troops occupied part of Lithuanian Memel. Germany signed treaties with Rumania and Slovakia, then announced a German-Italian military alliance. The German-Italian Axis was joined by Spain and Hungary in an anti-Comintern Treaty against Communism. Italy invaded Albania and made it a protectorate.

Simultaneously, Hitler began a war of nerves against Poland. He demanded the city of Danzig and the right to build a railroad and highway connecting West and East Prussia across the Polish corridor south of Danzig. He offered in return to sign a guarantee of the new Polish frontiers. The Polish government sought desperately for assurances from France and England to resist German demands, but, being bitterly anti-communist, refused a British suggestion to arrange also an alliance with Russia. Still, in March, 1939, Britain and France guaranteed the Poles their support. A month later, Hitler denounced the German-Polish nonaggression pact of 1934. The Poles refused to back down and again the Allies reaffirmed their pledges of support.

THE RUSSO-GERMAN PACT

In the spring of 1939, France and England began negotiations with Russia for an alliance against Germany. They hoped to disarm Russian suspicions about the intentions of the Western nations and to repair the chasm that had opened between the parties when the Russians were left out of the Munich Conference. On the other hand, the Germans, too, had been carrying on negotiations with the Russians, ostensibly for trade purposes. But on August 23, it was announced to the startled world that Russia and Germany had signed a ten year treaty of nonaggression and friendship. The

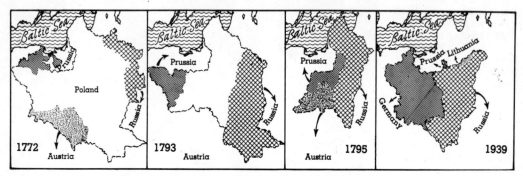

THE FOUR PARTITIONS OF POLAND

Poland, after the partition of 1795, ceased to exist as a nation until it was recreated at the end of World War I. Invasion by the German and Russian armies in 1939 resulted in the fourth partition of the country

parties agreed to submit to a peaceful resolution any disputes which might arise.

Hitler had accomplished the aim of German grand strategy in Europe. He had established security on the Eastern Front and could turn now to dealing with the West. Chamberlain's attempts to turn Germany to the East had boomeranged with disastrous effects.

THE FINAL STEPS TOWARD WAR

Hitler now was prepared to deal roughly with Poland and her Western Allies. A last chance was presented France and England to abandon Poland, for, without Russian support in the East, Poland could not be expected to last very long in a struggle alone with Germany. Britain and France stood firm, however, proposing that the issue should be settled by negotiation. Hitler denounced their position and insisted on a settlement with Poland on his terms.

Ignoring various appeals for peace from the Pope and others, Hitler refused general negotiations on the Polish question. He offered to guarantee the peace in Western Europe, with the implied condition that he would then be given a free hand in the East. This Britain refused to do and signed a mutual assistance pact with Poland. Hitler denounced the behavior of Poland and declared that German minorities in Poland were being persecuted.

At the last minute, Hitler said that he would discuss these questions with a Polish representative with full power to come to an agreement, providing that the Polish plenipotentiary arrived by August 30. Fearing that under such conditions, a Polish representative would be forced to give in on all points, the Poles neglected to meet the deadline. The German Foreign Office informed the British Ambassador that such neglect constituted rejection of any German terms which might have been offered. The Poles, on August 31, offered to negotiate directly. On the same day, Mussolini offered to arrange another four-power conference. France and Britain accepted but asked that Poland be included in order to avoid a repetition of the Munich Pact. On the same evening, the German radio broadcast to the world a set of terms which it asserted it required from Poland. The terms appeared to be considerably less rigorous than those demanded in private negotiations. German Foreign Minister Ribbentrop is reported to have told the British Ambassador that Germany contemplated serving no ultimatum with threat of force.

These events of the last hours of peace were without hope, for the armies of Germany were already on the march. In the dawn of September 1, 1939, German forces invaded Poland. There was no declaration of war. Hitler claimed that he acted because of Polish violations of the German frontier. Britain and France issued an ultimatum to Germany, stating that, unless German troops were withdrawn from Poland, a state of war would exist between them and Germany. On September 3, France and Britain declared war.

87. The War to Pearl Harbor

SCOPE OF THE WAR

Wᴏʀʟᴅ Wᴀʀ II began on a single front in Poland. It increased in size and ferocity until practically every nation in the world was involved in it and there were many fronts. The Polish campaign became only one in a series of vast campaigns in many areas. Finland, Norway, Holland, Belgium, France, North Africa, East Africa, Russia, Yugoslavia, Greece, Crete, and Italy all became the scenes of violent battles between the axis and allied forces. And in the Far East, bloody struggles took place in China, Hongkong, Singapore, the Netherlands East Indies, the Philippines, New Guinea, and many islands of the South Pacific. Those were the principal battle places for the land armies, at all times assisted by the air and sea forces of the combatants. In addition, naval battles occurred in places as remote from one another as the South Atlantic and the South Pacific, the Indian Sea and the North Sea. And in the air, vast armadas of fighters and bombers added a new dimension to warfare. The skies above France and the Low Countries, above England, Russia, Italy, and Japan, and finally above Germany were host to clouds of aircraft, intent upon destroying not only armies but also the industrial centers of the enemy.

The Siegfried Line. Aerial view of part of the defense system built along the western German border

GRAND STRATEGY IN THE BEGINNING

With only Poland, France, and England to contend with in the first stage of the war, Hitler's strategy was first to annihilate Poland before the Allies could intervene effectively, and then to turn the full German might on the Western Front. This differed from the German grand strategy of World War I when the German general staff planned to hold the Eastern Front while crushing France in the West. On the other hand, Allied strategy aimed at holding off German pressure on the Polish front long enough for English and French forces to launch an attack against the Siegfried Line in the West.

THE DEFEAT OF POLAND AND RUSSIAN INTERVENTION

Long preparation and efficient organization characterized the German plans on the Polish front. Swarms of aircraft and panzer units broke through the main Polish defenses with crushing force, followed by the main body of the German infantry and artillery. The shattering of the Polish lines broke the Polish armies into small pockets of resistance which were isolated and then methodically wiped out by the Germans. Within a month after the crossing of the frontier, all effective resistance ceased. Then, by prearrangement, German troops halted along a boundary in central Poland and Russian troops poured into the Eastern part of the country. Poland was wiped out as a political entity.

Polish Surrender. Polish troops awaiting arrival of Germans after the capitulation of Warsaw. (Acme)

Late in the year, while the Allies were preparing for the German onslaught in the west, Russia sought territorial concessions from Finland, especially in the neighborhood of Leningrad. Impatient at the progress of negotiations, Russia attacked Finland in November and by the end of December had conquered strategic areas which were conceded to it under duress by the Finns in a treaty of March, 1940. World opinion availed nothing against what Russia believed to be necessary for its national security against a possible war with Germany. In fact, the Soviet armies went on to occupy Latvia, Lithuania, and Estonia.

THE FATE OF DENMARK AND NORWAY

Both Denmark and Norway had succeeded in maintaining neutrality in World War I, but were less fortunate in 1940. Denmark was a rich and useful agricultural land with some strategic importance to control of the North Sea. Norway provided excellent shelter for submarine bases and well located sites for air fields. Both nations were caught completely by surprise. Denmark capitulated immediately. In Norway, a traitorous faction or "fifth col-

umn" led by Quisling served as another arm of the German war machine and brought that country to disaster in two months. The Norwegian army was able to mobilize only 30,000 men before the German forces invaded the country by sea and air. German naval power and troop transports were protected by complete air superiority. Some 12,000 Allied troops were landed to assist the Norwegians in their defense but were compelled to withdraw to the far north from where they were evacuated by sea to England. By the middle of June Germany held complete control of Norway.

THE BATTLE OF FRANCE

But by then, the main theater of war had already shifted to the Lowlands and France, where, on May 10, the Germans launched a series of gigantic attacks designed and destined

Vidkun Quisling on trial in 1945 on charges of treason against Norway during the German invasion in 1944. He was declared guilty and executed. (Acme)

to wipe out the Allies in Western Europe. German strategy again as in 1914 aimed at out-

Belgian refugees passing British soldiers moving up to meet the German attack on the Lowlands. (Acme)

The Evacuation from Dunkirk. British and French soldiers waiting on the dunes for transport to England and safety. In one of the great feats of military history, 330,000 men were withdrawn from the Continent in spite of persistent German assaults. British fighter aircraft covered the beaches and the boats used in the operation. (British Combine)

flanking the main Allied defenses by cutting around through the Low Countries (the so-called Schlieffen Plan). This time Holland as well as Belgium was invaded. Preceded again by the "fifth column" of saboteurs and native traitors, terrific air bombardment of strategic areas, and the dropping of thousands of paratroopers to take and hold vital points, the German tanks and armoured vehicles broke through the main Dutch and Belgian defenses and overran the countryside.

The large forces of the Dutch and Belgians were split asunder and demoralized. Within a week the Dutch surrendered. France and England rushed troops to the aid of Belgium. There they engaged the German columns pushing southwest but were unable to prevent German troops from reaching the English Channel. The surrender of all Belgian forces to the Germans by King Leopold in the last days of May rendered critical the whole Allied position in the North. Evacuation of all British troops from the continent was imperative. Choosing the port of Dunkirk and utilizing every available boat, the British managed to rescue the main body of the Allied troops, numbering some 330,000 men.

THE FINAL STAGES

The German drive was relentless. There was scarcely a pause between the destruction of the Lowlands and the final battles in France. Between May 10 and June 3, the German forces had occupied all of Belgium and Holland and pressed South into France. The Maginot Line, into which the French had poured their military resources between wars, lay stretched out between Sedan and the Swiss

Franco-German armistice of 1940 was signed in the Forest of Compiègne in the same railway car in which the armistice ending World War I was signed. (Wide World)

Paris During the German Occupation. Life went on much as usual. Note the German signs pointing the way to hospitals. (Pix)

the French fleet, the bulk of which had been destroyed by the British off Oran, Algeria, on July 3, to prevent its falling into German hands. The French Republic was abolished and a totalitarian regime substituted.

General De Gaulle, who had correctly predicted the strategy of the battle of France, escaped to England where he formed a Free French group to continue the struggle alongside England. In 1943, he formed the Committee of National Liberation, became recognized as the leader of the French under-

Gen. Charles De Gaulle. (Karsh—Ziff Davis)

ground resistance against the Nazis and led French troops in the invasions of 1944.

border, useless to the French. They needed but did not have the kind of mobile, mechanized brigades that might have plugged the holes in the Allied lines where the German

Marshal Pétain

tanks had plunged through. Reynaud replaced Daladier as Premier of France and he appointed Weygand as Chief of Staff in place of Gamelin. It was far too late. German mechanized columns fanned out everywhere; Paris fell on June 14, Cherbourg on June 18, Brest on June 20, and the Maginot Line was abandoned on June 16. Italy declared war on France on June 10. Pétain replaced Reynaud as Premier and asked Hitler for terms of an armistice. The severe German terms were accepted and an armistice signed on June 22 at Compèigne. The Germans were to occupy the North and West of France. The cost of occupation and huge war reparations were to be paid by the French.

Pétain set up a new French government at Vichy which, although it did not declare war against England, declared its policy as collaboration with Germany. It maintained control of its African colonies and a few elements of

THE BATTLE OF BRITAIN

As the Nazis invaded the Low Countries Chamberlain resigned as Prime Minister and was replaced by Churchill, who had been alert for many years to the Fascist threat to England. In a famous speech to the Commons, Churchill declared, "I have nothing to offer but blood, tears, toil, and sweat . . . Our policy?

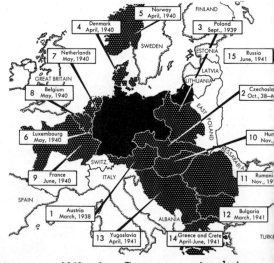

Europe in 1941, when German expansion during World War II had reached its greatest extent

686

Reichsmarshal Goering, German air force chief, interviewing a squadron commander just returned from a raid on England. (Acme)

British 4.5-inch antiaircraft gun battery during a night raid, 1940. (Acme)

It is to wage war by land, sea, and air . . . Our aim? It is victory." Britain renewed its determination to fight on. With the end of the summer, Goering's air force turned on England with full fury. Hundreds of bombers and their fighter protection journeyed to and fro across the channel carrying loads of bombs to blast British industry and communications and to weaken by continuous assault the morale of the people. London suffered great damage throughout for residential areas were not spared. Many other cities were severely damaged.

But the expected decline in British strength failed to appear and the Luftwaffe began to suffer enormous losses of planes from the Royal Air Force fighters and ground antiaircraft. By the middle of September, 1940, it appeared to

the Germans that they would not be able to harm England sufficiently to warrant launching a sea-borne invasion from the Continent. The air attacks therefore were reduced in number although they continued throughout the war.

WAR IN THE BALKANS

The movement of the war shifted then to the Mediterranean and the Balkans. Russia, foreseeing a German move to the Southeast, seized Bessarabia-Bukovina in June, 1940. The Axis forced Rumania to make further territorial concessions to Hungary, already an Axis satellite, and when unrest spread through the rest of Rumania, Hitler ordered in the German army in October. Bulgaria decided to collaborate with the Axis. That winter, Italy attacked Greece but her forces made little headway in

The German Air Assault on London, 1940. After failing to knock out the British fighters, the Germans concentrated their air attacks on London. For a month the city was pounded by daylight raids. In October, the Germans turned to night raids and began to attack other cities also. Londoners used subway stations as air raid shelters, below. Some of London's bomb damage is shown, right. (Acme Photos)

German Occupation of Greece. Trucks and other military equipment drawn up on the Acropolis. (Pix)

The African Campaign. British tanks racing over the North African desert in 1940. (International)

the mountains of the northwest. When Yugoslavia appeared reluctant to join the Axis, Germany declared war on her on April 6 and at the same time went to the aid of Mussolini in Greece. Both countries were conquered within the month by the Germans, and the British expeditionary force which had been sent to aid the Greeks was forced to evacuate. The island of Crete came next. In the first full-scale invasion of a major objective by air-borne troops, the Germans captured the island from its British defenders.

CONTEST FOR THE MEDITERRANEAN

The loss of Crete weakened the British position in the Mediterranean. Strain on the British lifeline to the Orient, which was already large owing to Italy's strategic position astride the Mediterranean, was increased. The Near East, gateway to the Orient and possessor of vast oil resources, lay exposed.

Marshal Montgomery

In the spring of 1941, Britain countered German successes in the Balkans by sending troops into Syria, Iran, and Iraq.

Farther west, the war in Africa moved back and forth from Tripoli to Egypt. In September, 1940, Italian forces drove 75 miles into Egypt. A British counterattack in December recovered more than the Italians had gained and

took large numbers of prisoners. German help was forthcoming in 1941 and the British were again pushed into Egypt. Finally, in 1942, the British under Montgomery defeated the combined German and Italian forces in the Battle of El Alamein and drove them deep into Libya. In early 1943, the attack resumed in connection with the newly arrived Allied forces in Algeria and the Axis forces of Rommel were forced into Tunis, where the vast majority capitulated in May, 1943.

THE DISAPPEARANCE OF AMERICAN NEUTRALITY

When the Axis was finally defeated in Africa, America had already been at war for a year and a half, and American ships, planes, and men were already locked in combat over the whole globe. The story, however, should be told from the beginning. When war broke out in 1939, the United States had more stringent neutrality laws than any nation on earth. It was hoped that the country could avoid future wars by scrupulous neutrality.

But the circumstances of wartime events caused an almost immediate change in policy. Congress, on the request of the President, modified the Neutrality Act to allow shipment of munitions to Britain and France. The disasters to Allied arms in the spring of 1940 in Norway and Western Europe brought increased alarm to American opinion. The feeling grew that the United States could not allow the British Isles to be occupied by the Germans. In a bold move, President Roosevelt negotiated with the British to give them 50 destroyers immediately in

The First Peacetime Draft in U. S. History. Secretary Stimson drawing the first number. (Acme)

Shipbuilding During World War II. America's enormous production capacity is evident here

exchange for long-term leases on British bases in the Caribbean which would be useful for protecting the American coast and the Panama Canal.

Rearmament came next. The President asked and received from Congress authorization to spend an extraordinary appropriation of $1,000,000,000 on arms. A defense council was created to coordinate war production, and American factories began to work day and night to turn out planes, tanks, and ships. The Selective Service System was established in the fall and for the first time in American history American men were drafted for the army in peace time. The object was to create an army of four million men. The National Guard units of the 48 states were incorporated into the Army of the United States.

Domestic issues, which had been submerged in the growing crisis in foreign affairs, appeared briefly in the presidential campaign of 1940. The Republicans nominated a dark horse, Wendell L. Willkie of New York, for president and Charles McNary for vice-president. Willkie was a liberal corporation lawyer, originally from Indiana, and was strongly internationalist in views. The Democrats, shattering a precedent prevailing since Washington's time, nominated President Roosevelt for a third term. Much of the campaign centered over this issue of the justification for a third term. Willkie also accused the Democrats of inefficiency, waste, and regimentation in running the government. The Democrats stood on the Roosevelt record. The results gave Roosevelt 54.9 per cent of the popular vote and 449

electoral votes to Willkie's 82. After the election, foreign affairs monopolized the attention of the people of the country.

Early in 1941, Roosevelt asked Congress for legislation making possible the equipping of the Allies with vastly greater armaments than was possible under a policy of cash and carry. The result was the Lend-Lease Act which authorized the President to sell, transfer, lend, or lease ships, airplanes, and other war materials to nations whose independence the President deemed vital to the security of the United States. Lend-Lease ended American neutrality although America was not yet in the fighting war. Between March, 1941 and July, 1945, such aid amounted to over 42 billions of dollars in equipment and foodstuffs.

GERMAN ATTACK ON RUSSIA

Frustrated in his hopes of invading England,

Russian Motorized Column set on fire before it was abandoned to the advancing Germans. (Acme)

689

Pearl Harbor. U. S. battleship "West Virginia" burning after the Japanese attack, Dec. 7, 1941, left. (Acme). Above, the U. S. destroyer "Shaw" exploding after being hit by the Japanese. (Wide World)

Hitler again turned to the East. Ignoring his nonaggression pact and gathering his immense forces of tanks, planes, and men, he launched a surprise assault on the Soviet Union on June 22, 1941 along a front of 2000 miles. The Nazi divisions cut through the Russian defenses and drove deeply into Russia. Victory after victory was won, but, despite German calculations, the key cities of Leningrad and Moscow did not fall. Russia was tremendously weakened by the end of 1941 but not crushed. On the other hand, having failed in their first violent attacks to destroy the Soviets, the German armies were stretched far forward in hostile territory. Supply problems multiplied, a harsh winter set in, and the Russians began to launch counter-attacks.

PEARL HARBOR

Across the world in the Orient, relations between Japan and the United States were steadily deteriorating. The militarists took com-

plete control of the Japanese government in October 1941 and were bent on eliminating all American and European influence in the Orient and extending Japanese control throughout the area. Tojo, an enemy of the United States and friend of Hitler, became Premier. In November, Kurusu was sent to the United States to continue discussion of the dispute over Japanese ambitions in China. The United States demanded a pledge of Japanese nonintervention in neighboring states. At dawn on December 7, while Japanese-American negotiations were still under way in Washington and without warning, a Japanese war fleet launched a devastating attack by carrier-based planes against American ships and shore installations at Pearl Harbor in the Hawaiian Islands. U. S. forces began retaliation, and on December 8, Congress declared war on Japan. Britain followed the American action on the same day. On December 11, Germany and Italy declared war on the United States.

America Goes to War. Right, President F. D. Roosevelt asking Congress to declare war on Japan, Dec. 8, 1941. (Press Assoc.). Below, the President signing the resolution declaring a state of war. (Acme)

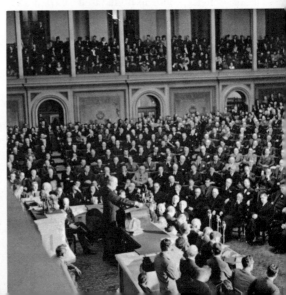

88. Destruction of the Axis

THE MARCH OF NIPPON

JAPAN WAS PREPARED for war and struck a series of fast blows. Pearl Harbor, while it completely aroused America for the long and arduous war ahead, resulted in the temporary crippling of the Pacific fleet of the United States. Japanese forces soon seized Guam, Midway, and Wake Islands as well. The Philippine Islands were taken over after bitter fighting against isolated American forces under MacArthur on Bataan Peninsula. Hongkong and Thailand surrendered, and the Japanese moved on to capture Malaya and Singapore, which was supposed to be impregnable. By the end of winter, they had taken over the Dutch East Indies with their resources of tin, oil, and other vital raw materials. Rangoon, in Burma, fell in March, and by May, 1942, all Burma was occupied. India was threatened, and the Burma Road which had brought American materials to the Chinese Nationalists was cut. American aid to China was

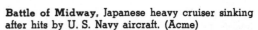

thenceforth flown in and American air bases were maintained in China. In the Southeast Pacific, the Japanese occupied New Britain, The Solomons, and New Guinea.

Japan now dominated an area several times greater than that of the United States, with a population of almost half a billion. Almost all of the world's rubber and most of its tin were in Japanese hands, not to mention vast oil resources. The task of organizing such a large and scattered empire was too much for the Japanese in the short time allowed them before the United States began to counterattack.

THE UNITED STATES STRIKES BACK

American reenforcements were rushed to the aid of threatened areas. The Philippines could not be helped, but Alaska, the Hawaiian Islands, and Australia were defended successfully. Thus the limits of Japanese expansion to the North, East, and South were determined.

Burma Road, part of which is shown here, was China's chief supply artery, 1939 to 1942, when it was cut. (International)

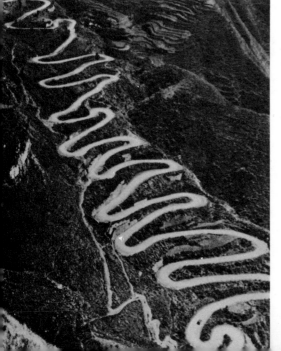

Battle of Midway, Japanese heavy cruiser sinking after hits by U. S. Navy aircraft. (Acme)

The strengthened American navy won two important victories in the Battles of the Coral Sea and Midway. In both engagements, American carrier-based aircraft caused major damage to the Japanese fleets involved. In August, 1942, American marines landed on Guadalcanal in the Solomon Islands in the first of the bitter island-jumping amphibious operations that came to characterize the war in the Pacific. Bitter fighting continued in the Solomons throughout the year and well into 1943. Defeat of Japanese naval units in a crucial engagement helped to establish American control in the area.

THE WAR IN EUROPE

Meanwhile, in the European theater, American war materials were flowing into Britain and Russia. Allied strategy called ultimately for an invasion of Europe which had been converted into a gigantic fortress by the Germans. The timing of the invasion was not decided upon immediately but was postponed until events elsewhere presented a clearer picture. But the American air forces established many bases in England and, together with the British Strategic Bombing Force, began to hammer away at German industrial and communication centers. The devastating air attacks reached new heights in 1943 and continued at a peak until the end of the war.

VICTORY IN THE MEDITERRANEAN

On November 7, 1942, a combined American and British task force under General Dwight Eisenhower landed at several points

German submarines, four of which are pictured here, were the greatest threat to Allied commerce. Frequently they attacked in packs. (Acme)

First American troops in Europe during World War II are shown landing at a North Irish port. (Intl.)

Convoy to Great Britain, photographed from one of the escort ships, foreground. (British Combine)

American B-26 bombers attacking the railway marshalling yards at Namur, Belgium

Naval support to Allied troops in Sicily Campaign is given by guns of British battleship off Catania. The picture was taken July 17, 1943

Anzio Beach, where the Allies tried to break the stalemate in Italy by landing behind the German lines. Troops go ashore as an LCI, hit by German gun, burns

Raid on Ploesti, Rumania by B-24's. Note the flak and smoke from hits on the oil refinery

along the French North African Coast. Bringing the area speedily under control, the Allied forces moved eastward toward Tunisia. There, after a winter of severe fighting, they launched a drive in co-operation with the forces of the British Eighth Army advancing from Egypt and Libya. Caught in a giant pincers, the Axis armies in North Africa surrendered in May, 1943.

General Eisenhower, supreme Allied commander. (Acme)

The next step was designed to complete control of the Mediterranean and knock Italy out of the war. In a little over a month, a British and an American army landed in Sicily and swept the island clear of enemy forces. The invasion of Europe had begun. In September, the British and American armies landed in Southern Italy and began a hard struggle for mastery of the peninsula. Meanwhile, the long enduring regime of Mussolini was overthrown by an Italian group under General Badoglio, who was then appointed Premier by the King. He sued for peace and accepted Eisenhower's terms of unconditional surrender. Mussolini was imprisoned, but was later rescued by German paratroopers and placed in power in Northern Italy. The German army assumed complete control of Italy, and rushed troops to counter the Allied invasion in the South.

Fighting near Stalingrad. Russians counterattack in an effort to drive back German troops. (Sovfoto)

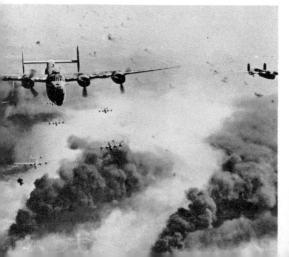

C-47's towing gliders to Normandy on Invasion Day, June 6, 1944

The Allied Fifth Army pushed slowly northward over rugged terrain. The winter of 1943-44 was spent in bloody battle before Cassino. The following year saw advances made up to the rim of the Po Valley. Rome was liberated. Finally, in April 1945, the Allied offensive forced an unconditional surrender of all German troops in Italy. Mussolini was executed by Italian partisans.

THE WAR IN RUSSIA

The Germans, despite the employment of three million well equipped troops, were not able to knock Russia out of the war in their great offensives of 1941. Russian winter counterattacks recovered about one-fifth of the German gains and relieved pressure on Moscow. In June, 1942, the Germans renewed their attacks but shifted the weight of operations to the South, in which direction lay the huge oil resources of the Caucasus. They swept forward to the Caucasus mountains in the far South but were stopped at Stalingrad in the southeast. A fierce struggle ensued for the city and after months of battle the Germans in the city were surrounded and forced to surrender.

Germany could never revive from this blow. The Russians went on the offensive and recaptured most of the territory the Germans had won during the year. In 1943, the Russians drove into the Ukraine and cleared much of the territory around Leningrad. A German offensive of that year had only local successes.

While the Allies were landing in France in 1944, another great Russian offensive was launched which recaptured most of occupied Russia and much of Poland. Rumania, Bulgaria, and Finland surrendered to the Soviets. The Baltic states were occupied in the winter and Russian troops reached the gates of Budapest, capital of Hungary, in early 1945. The final Russian offensive drove straight through the Polish plain along the same route as the Germans had come in 1939. In April the Red Armies entered Berlin and a few days later met the Allied forces advancing from the West.

THE WAR IN WEST EUROPE

The year 1944 dawned over a vast panorama of invasion preparations in England. Huge quantities of materials were readied in dozens of depots throughout England. The air forces

Crossing the Channel. Part of the Allied task force that invaded Normandy on "D-Day"

Canadian infantry and equipment of the 3d Division on a Normandy beach, June 7, 1944

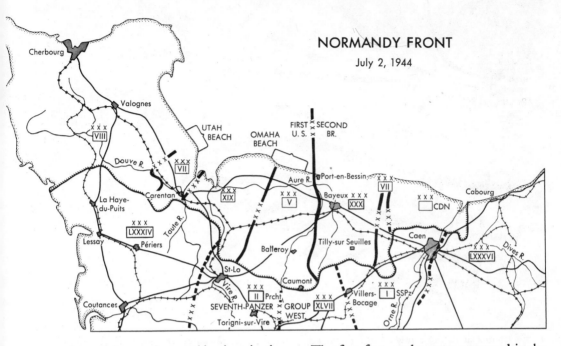

NORMANDY FRONT
July 2, 1944

stepped up their assaults on objectives in the German defense wall. After weeks of aerial preparations, the greatest war armada ever mustered on earth crossed the narrow seas between England and the continent, preceded by showers of parachute troops at key points. The Allied High Command under Eisenhower had selected Normandy as the point of invasion, and there thousands of troops landed on June 6 in the face of heavy opposition.

The first few weeks were consumed in the consolidation of beachheads and the capture of the port of Cherbourg. At the end of July, a major offensive against the Nazi defenses was begun. While the British engaged large bodies of German troops in the north, American mechanized divisions broke through in the south and turned the Germans' flank. In a series of lightning engagements and thrusts, the armies of Generals Hodges and Patton liberated vast stretches of French territory. The whole German line collapsed. Meanwhile, the Allies had landed the Seventh Army in Southern France and it raced northward, overcoming

Air attacks on German transport helped Allies

Liberation of Paris. People celebrating Allies' arrival scatter as a sniper opens fire

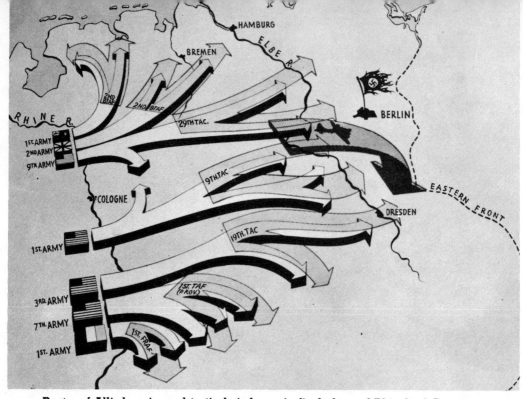

RHINE R.

HAMBURG

ELBE R.

BREMEN

2ND BTAF

2ND BTAF

29TH TAC.

BERLIN

1ST ARMY
2ND ARMY
9TH ARMY

COLOGNE

9TH TAC

EASTERN FRONT

1ST ARMY

19TH TAC.

DRESDEN

3RD ARMY

1ST TAF (PROV)

7TH ARMY

1ST ARMY

1ST FTAF

Routes of Allied armies and tactical air forces in final phase of Rhineland Campaign

moderate German resistance. By September, the Germans had been driven out of France except for a belt along the northeast border stretching from the Saar to Switzerland. Most of Belgium was liberated.

While the Allies were preparing for a winter of continuous pressure against the German lines and a spring offensive to follow, Germany struck with all the might she could still muster against a weakly defended section of the American line in the Ardennes Forest. The German aims were to capture the great city of Antwerp and to split the Allied forces in two. The initial impact of the German onslaught wrought havoc in the divisions facing them. A bitter American defense at St. Vith, which was later abandoned, and at Bastogne, which resisted successfully until relieved, delayed the German timetable. Allied elements in the north were placed under Montgomery by Eisenhower, and Hodges and Patton regrouped and drove into the German bulge from the south. Slowly the Germans were driven back toward their original positions. In this Ardennes Counteroffensive, or Battle of the Bulge, they broke up the Allied campaign plans, but at a cost that proved fatal.

GERMAN COLLAPSE

When spring came, the western Allies had gathered men and materials for a last gigantic assault designed to carry the democratic forces into the heart of Germany. Their first attacks carried them up to the Rhine, destroying practically all of the organized German divisions remaining. The Rhine Bridge at Remagen was captured intact by an American patrol and the American forces swept into central Germany on a wide front. British forces crossed the Rhine into the north of Germany. In the last

The Remagen Bridge, a lucky foothold across the Rhine, furthered Allied advance into Germany. (Acme)

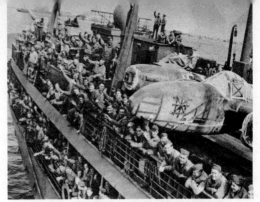
Troopship to Australia. American troops and war materials arriving in Australia, May, 1942

Marshal Goering removing a decoration during processing at prison camp at Augsburg

days of April, they contacted advance Russian elements from the east and both groups took up positions along boundaries marked out in advance by their leaders. In the south, the American Seventh Army made contact with the allied forces in Italy by way of Austria and the Brenner Pass.

The death of Hitler by suicide was reported from Berlin on May 1. Other high Nazis either perished or were taken prisoner. Goebbels poisoned himself and his family. Goering was captured, and later committed suicide while awaiting execution. Admiral Doenitz took command and surrendered unconditionally to the Allies on May 8, 1945.

THE DEFEAT OF JAPAN

In 1944 the tempo of American victory in the Pacific war was stepped up. Arms and men were now available for the exhausting job of taking innumerable, fiercely defended and widely scattered Japanese positions. Tactics emphasized split-second coordination of land, sea, and air forces. After the Solomons came New Guinea; then came New Britain. The Gilbert Islands, the Marshall Islands, and the Marianas were conquered in amphibious operations. Tarawa, Kwajelein, Eniwetok, Saipan,

Iwo Jima, and Okinawa were the bloody stepping stones in the strategy aimed to bring American forces to the very door of the Japanese home islands. Farther west, forces under General MacArthur landed in the Philippines and completed their reconquest by July, 1945.

All was being readied for the final landings in Japan itself. American B-29 bombers in large numbers attacked Japanese industrial targets daily. Japanese shipping was swept from the seas. Then, on August 6, 1945, an American airplane, flying high above the important city of Hiroshima in Japan, dropped a bomb on which America and Allied collaborators had spent years of work and billions of dollars in development. It was called "the atomic bomb" and it worked with astounding effect. Hiroshima was almost completely leveled. After three days, a second bomb was dropped on Nagasaki. In all, some 200,000 persons were killed or wounded by the two bombs. On August 8, Russia declared war on Japan and sent its troops into Manchuria. But the Japanese leaders waited no longer; they accepted Allied terms and surrendered the nation to MacArthur aboard the battleship *Missouri*.

German surrender of forces in northern Europe. Marshal Montgomery is reading the terms

Army weapons troops move in from the beach after their landing on Leyte Island in the Philippines

U. S. Capture of Iwo Jima. Marines celebrating the raising of the U. S. flag. (Acme)

Atomic bomb explosion at Nagasaki, photographed eight miles away. The cloud top is at 40,000 feet

World War II thus ended suddenly and dramatically. The effect of modern weapons of war was seen when Japan, once a militarily powerful nation, surrendered without a foreign soldier having set foot on the soil of her homeland.

LOSSES FROM THE WAR

The damage wrought by World War II was incalculable. The diversion of manpower to the huge armies and navies, and the switch of most productive facilities to making implements of war form an element of cost which can hardly be measured. But in human lives, the full meaning of the worst war in history is evident. Total American casualties numbered over a million of whom more than a quarter of a million were killed. The British Empire lost a slightly larger number, France slightly less, although the million and a half French prisoners of war brought the total French casualty list of killed, wounded, missing, and prisoners up to over the two million mark. In both Britain and France many thousands of civilians were killed in air raids. Poland lost a million men in war

and five million civilians of whom three million were Jews.

Germany lost almost 10 million men, killed, wounded, and missing. Civilian casualties from bombing were high. The Soviet Union lost more than all the Western powers put together, an estimated 12 million persons. Chinese estimates of deaths attributable to war from 1931 to 1945 were around two million, not including heavy civilian losses from starvation and maltreatment. Japanese deaths were about 450,000 soldiers and 260,000 civilians.

Many millions of persons throughout the world lost their homes through bombings and battle damage. Some 38 million persons were driven from their homes in Russia alone. Many lands were laid waste and countless livestock and personal property were destroyed. The Allies lost 21,000,000 tons of shipping. Japan lost 6,000,000 tons, Germany and Italy almost all their shipping. Allied expenditures to conduct the war were estimated at $560,000,000,-000, of which the United States contributed $287,000,000,000; costs of the war to the Axis were estimated at $445,000,000,000.

Okinawa. Marines awaiting the result of explosion in a Japanese cave position

Japanese surrender terms are signed by General MacArthur aboard the "Missouri." (Press Assoc.)

89. Postwar Nations

WAR AIMS AND PEACE AIMS

EARLY IN THE WAR, as soon as it became apparent that America had acquired a stake in Allied victory, concern over the war aims of the Allies developed. In August, 1941, before Pearl Harbor but after America had abandoned her policy of neutrality, President Roosevelt met Prime Minister Churchill aboard an American cruiser in mid-ocean. There they issued a joint declaration which became known as the Atlantic Charter. In it they pledged to seek no new territories as a result of the war, to allow all peoples the right of self-determination, to foster free world trade, to pursue the war to the complete destruction of nazism, and to work afterward for world peace and disarmament.

On January 1, 1942, the Declaration of the United Nations was promulgated by the United States, Great Britain, the Soviet Union, and China. All Allied nations were invited to become signatories and by the end of the war in Europe forty-seven had done so. The Declaration bound the parties to pursue the war against the Axis, including Japan, until complete victory and to follow the policies of the Atlantic Charter.

The next important international meeting was a council of war between Roosevelt and Churchill with their staffs, held at Casablanca, Northwest Africa, January, 1943. It was here that they decided to demand the "unconditional surrender" of the Axis and to launch invasions of Sicily and Italy.

Toward the end of the year, the United Nations Relief and Rehabilitation Administration (UNRRA) came into being. It was an emergency organization to feed and clothe the war devastated areas of the world as they were liberated from the Axis. It was a true international organization, operating under a single executive head and including personnel from a number of nations. It was liquidated in 1947, after the United States, which was providing the bulk of UNRRA'S funds, withdrew its support, chiefly because of the amount of aid going to Communist-dominated areas. The United States then embarked on a unilateral program of foreign relief, culminating in the European Recovery Program (Marshall Plan).

At the same time as UNRRA was being formed, important political conferences were taking place in Moscow, Cairo, and Teheran (Iran). The American, British, and Russian foreign affairs chieftains met in Moscow and, together with the Chinese ambassador, signed a declaration on November 1 pledging the pursuit of the war until the unconditional surrender of Germany and proposing the establishment of an international organization as soon thereafter as possible.

Later in the same month, Roosevelt, Churchill, and Chiang Kai-shek met in Cairo, Egypt, to prepare plans for the defeat of Japan. They declared that Japan would be stripped

World War II Ended in a schoolhouse near Reims, France—victory for Allies over Nazis. (United Press)

Yalta Conference "Big Three"—Churchill, Roosevelt, and Stalin. Yalta decisions that resulted in expansion of Russian sphere of influence were later severely criticized by some. (United Press)

of all territory which she had ever taken by imperialist aggression. From Cairo, Roosevelt and Churchill continued on to Teheran where they were met by Stalin, and here the Allies exchanged information on their strategy in Europe and promised to work together in peace as in war.

A year passed and then, shortly before the war in Europe ended, Roosevelt, Churchill, and Stalin met once more, this time at Yalta in the Russian Crimea. Vital decisions affecting the future of Europe were made. The division of Germany into four zones was planned, following that nation's surrender. A central control commission was projected to unify treatment of Germany. The punishment of war criminals, destruction of the German general staff, and the rooting out of nazism were agreed on. A method of settling German reparations questions was devised. Provisional boundaries for Poland were settled. Free elections in all liberated countries were promised.

The United Nations General Assembly opened its seventh session in its permanent headquarters

And finally the parties decided to call a conference at San Francisco in April, 1945, to prepare a charter for the United Nations; in providing for the conference it was agreed in advance that in the United Nations organization, each major power would have a veto on any course of action it found undesirable. The Soviet Union promised to enter the war against Japan two or three months after the defeat of Germany in Europe. The transfer of South Sakhalin Island and the Kuriles to the U.S.S.R. was arranged.

THE UNITED NATIONS

In April, 1945, 51 nations convened in San Francisco and drew up the Charter of the United Nations. They worked on the basis of proposals outlined in an international conference at Dumbarton Oaks, six months before. On June 26 the Charter was completed and signed by 50 nations. On October 24, it had 29 ratifications and went into effect. Headquarters were set up in New York.

The structure of the United Nations consisted of the General Assembly in which all members were represented on equal terms, the Security Council in which the five big powers, the United States, Soviet Union, France, China, and the United Kingdom, wielded the major influence, and the Secretariat which was the administrative organ of the United Nations. Threats to the peace were made the particular concern of the Security Council but no effective action could be taken against a big power member in the face of its veto. Russia saw fit from an early date to use the veto to block action unfavorable to its interests.

Such use of the veto power was thought by many to impair the possible effectiveness of the United Nations.

The old League of Nations facilities were given to the United Nations. The Permanent Court of International Justice was joined to the new body, as was the International Labor Organization. Former League mandates were transferred too. A new home was built for the organization in New York City.

The United Nations faced a world which was drastically changed as a result of the war.

Europe, which had always been the home of the great powers, lay in waste and ruin. The United States had become the greatest power the world had ever seen. Her military and productive achievements outweighed those of the nations of western Europe put together. As a result of six exhausting years of war, during part of which she had stood alone against the Axis powers, Great Britain no longer held the position in world affairs she once had. Germany's might had been destroyed completely. France's role had diminished, and Italy was no longer a great power. In Europe only Russia had emerged stronger, and she was now classed with the United States as one of the "Big Two" of world politics.

New areas of the world moved toward the centers of power.

Europe Today

The South American countries were strengthened, partly because of their relatively untouched position during World War II, and also because of their technical development and population growth. Ordinarily, in the United Nations, they sided with the United States against the Soviet powers. However, the Argentine dictatorship of Juan Perón pursued a ruggedly independent course of action, domestically and internationally although facing ever-increasing unrest among churchmen, navy and other officials, and the people. In British Guiana the incumbent elected government was denounced as Communist and forcibly removed by British troops in 1953. In Bolivia, a revolutionary junta seized power in 1952 and nationalized the highly important tin mines.

In 1954, a revolt led by army elements in exile overturned the pro-Communist government of Guatemala. Colonel Castillo Armas became provisional president on July 8th. A population and economic boom was occurring in a number of places in South America, and was especially apparent in Uruguay and Venezuela.

Nations in the Near East, the Middle East, and the Far East came into prominence in the postwar period. Various African countries,

Berlin Airlift. U.S. aircraft with food and supplies being unloaded at the Russian-blockaded city

too, developed toward nationalism. The historical troubles of Europe took root everywhere in the world. From the scene of the destruction of nazism in Germany to Tokyo in the Far East, to the southern tip of Africa and over to Argentina, continual strife and agitation centered about problems of nationalism, democracy, rights of the poor and oppressed, and struggles for economic development.

WESTERN VERSUS EASTERN EUROPE

Germany was split into four zones of occupation according to plans made at Yalta and confirmed at a meeting of Truman, Churchill, Attlee, and Stalin at Potsdam, Germany, in August, 1945. Later, the American, British, and French zones were combined. The only common meeting ground of the four occupying powers was in Berlin, where a four-power government was set up. In 1948, a succession of incidents in Germany and elsewhere led the Russians to attempt to evict the other three powers from Berlin. This they did by cutting off all land communications between Berlin and the Allied zones to the west. Supplies had been going to the people of the Allied-controlled parts of Berlin through Russian-controlled territory. The Americans and British replied by setting up an "air lift." This stupendous operation lasted 10½ months, until the Russians lifted the unsuccessful blockade.

To aid economic recovery of West Germany, the Western Allies gradually relaxed their earlier demands for a harsh peace. In 1949 the German Federal Republic was established in West Germany. The new state was made a full partner in the European Recovery Program, and in 1950 it voted to become a member of the Council of Europe. It was granted permission to rearm within the framework of an Allied agreement. In May, 1955, the last vestige of foreign control over the Federal Republic was removed.

Formation in 1949 of the East German Republic in Soviet-occupied Germany completed division of the prewar Reich and separated the agricultural east from the industrial west. In June, 1950, East Germany ratified the Oder-Neisse River line as its eastern boundary, thus ceding 39,000 square miles of territory to Poland.

Austria enjoyed a happier fate than Germany. For various reasons, the four powers had managed to maintain a much more peaceful occupation government there than in Germany; to some extent Austria was regarded as more a pawn than a partner in Nazi crimes; also Germany was a more important target of control. In May, 1955, the four occupying powers signed a treaty of peace with Austria, ending the long occupation.

The victorious Allies had cooperated in the early stages of the German occupation, but they very soon fell out over Russian efforts to expand her influence in Europe. By 1948, in eastern Europe, from the Arctic to Greece there stretched a belt of Russian satellite nations. Poland, Rumania, Bulgaria, Hungary, and Yugoslavia were in the grip of the Communist Party. Czechoslovakia, after a period of neutrality and democracy, fell victim to a Communist conspiracy and joined the others. Greece was torn by civil war for three years until in 1949 American military and economic aid under the Truman Doctrine enabled the government forces to halt Communist guerrilla activity. In 1954, Greece, Turkey, and Yugoslavia signed a 20-year military pact.

EUROPEAN COMMUNISM

Internal conflicts developed in Communist countries. Frequent purges of high officials occurred. Yugoslavia broke sharply with the Soviet Union and, under Marshal Tito, continued an independent dictatorship known as "Titoism."

An "iron curtain" which restricted trade and information lay between the nations of

Eastern and Southern Europe and the Western European countries that had resisted Communist efforts to gain control. Through gifts, loans, and the Marshall Plan, the United States led the Western Powers in a "cold war" against Russia. The three most important cooperative developments in Europe were the European Coal and Steel Community, the European and American cooperation for military defense, and the development of European federation plans.

The **Permanent NATO Council** met in Paris to implement the effectiveness of NATO. (United Press)

The European Coal and Steel Community, which grew out of the Schuman plan (so-called for the French minister who promoted it), began operation on August 10, 1952, when its High Authority or executive agency met at Luxembourg. France, West Germany, Italy, Belgium, Luxembourg, and the Netherlands agreed to the control of the coal and steel of their countries by international authority for a period of 50 years. The High Authority became the governing body of the Community which, in addition, consisted of a Council of Ministers, a Common Assembly, and a Court of Justice. The Authority was empowered to impose taxes, control and finance modernization and improvements in the industries, increase production, adjust prices, remove trade barriers, and improve wages and working conditions.

The same countries that formed the Community joined in a European Defense Community for mutual defense against possible Soviet aggression and for collaboration with the North Atlantic Treaty Organization. The latter agency was founded largely at the instigation of the United States and included, besides that country and the six Community nations, Canada, Britain, Denmark, Norway, Iceland, Portugal, Turkey, and Greece. Elaborate plans were made to develop NATO with the ultimate objective of establishing a force of all arms sufficient to defend effectively the Western portion of the continent against any Eastern aggression. A supreme headquarters was established in 1951 with Eisenhower as commander-in-chief. The Supreme Headquarters, Allied Powers in Europe (SHAPE) progressed with difficulty. The Korean conflict slowed American aid. The French were troubled by

the thought of German rearmament and withheld full adherence to the European Defense Community. Problems associated with internal command responsibilities and organizational matters arose. Finally, strong Pacifist, Socialist, and Communist opposition slowed defense preparations. Only partial preparedness was accomplished.

Then in 1954 and 1955, plans for the common defense of Western Europe suffered an abrupt reversal and almost as abrupt a success. The French National Assembly in August, 1954, rejected the European Defense Community Treaty because the rearmament of Germany might again threaten France. For the moment, the anti-Soviet front seemed about to collapse. Then a new plan was brought forward by the French, approved by the United States, Great Britain, and Germany, and on December 30, 1954, the French National Assembly approved the crucial idea of rearming Germany within a West European Union. The West European Union came into existence in May, 1955. Members of the Union, besides France and Germany, were Belgium, the Netherlands, Luxembourg, Italy, and Great Britain. Germany also became a member of the North Atlantic Treaty Organization.

In 1952, the Common Assembly of the European Coal and Steel Community established a committee to draft a treaty of European Political Federation.

EUROPEAN DEMOCRATIC POLITICS

The international struggle over Communist expansion caused repercussions within Western European nations. In France and Italy, Com-

Sir Winston Churchill opens a car door for Queen Elizabeth as she leaves a party at the premier's home on his last night at No. 10 Downing St. (United Press)

munists made especially strong efforts to take over national leadership. But despite their great strength in labor unions and among poor farmers, they were unable to achieve parliamentary majorities in either country, and could not remain members of coalition governments after brief periods of shared power following World War II.

At times it seemed as if they might have their opportunity when non-Communist factions in several countries were at loggerheads. Governments changed in England, with tiny pluralities at the polls; yet the Communist vote diminished. The postwar French government was characterized by great instability, but the many different coalition ministries were able to avoid Communist participation in the government. The strong agitation by the extreme rightist Rally of the French People, led by Charles deGaulle, did not throw the central, moderate parties into hopeless confusion. The Italian center element maintained control despite the bare majorities that could be mustered by the Christian Democratic party in Parliament after the 1953 elections. The promise and fact of American aid assisted these and other Western European countries in combating Communist demands. The Reds gradually lost their following. Between 1945 and 1955 the trend

Prime Minister Eden
(United Press)

of politics and elections in Western Europe went generally against the Communists.

Great Britain underwent a seesaw electoral struggle between the Labour and Conservative parties after the war. The Labour party won a decisive election in 1945, then a close election in 1950, and lost to the Conservative party in 1951. Churchill again became prime minister and the Socialist program of nationalizing key industries, and social and medical services was halted. On Feb. 6, 1952, King George VI died, and Elizabeth II succeeded to the throne. Her Coronation took place on June 2, 1953.

On April 5, 1955, Winston Churchill resigned, because of old age, as Prime Minister, amidst universal acclaim, and was succeeded by Anthony Eden. The Conservatives strengthened control of the government in an election in May, 1955.

AFRICA

The so-called "dark continent" lighted up after World War II and revealed in abundance the problems upsetting peace and orderly development in the historically better-known parts of the world. The European-Arab belt of countries along the Mediterranean and North Atlantic shores erupted constantly in nationalistic displays. Highly dissatisfied with the unequal role granted them by the French government, French Morocco, Algeria, and Tunis were the scenes of riots, assassinations, and strikes against the government. In Northeast Africa, Egypt unilaterally abrogated its treaties which gave England bases and control of the Suez Canal and its approaches. On July 23, 1952, an army junta led by Gamal Abd el Nasser revolted, seized Cairo, and named General Mohammed Naguib head of state. King Farouk was forced into exile and a Republic proclaimed. A vigorous cleansing of the official ranks of the country followed. After unsuccessful efforts at shaking free of Nasser's control, Naguib was removed from office in November, 1954, and Nasser became premier in name as well as in fact. From 1953 on, Egypt put great pressure on the British to withdraw from Egypt. Finally, on October 19, 1954, assured of Egyptian cooperation in any wartime emergency, the

British signed a pact agreeing to evacuate the Suez canal zone by June, 1956.

To the south of Egypt in the vast domain that had been the Anglo-Egyptian Sudan, elections were conducted among the scattered inhabitants to determine whether they would prefer independent status, British protectorship, or union with Egypt. The Egyptian Nationalists won easily and England moved out of yet another sphere of influence. In middle Africa, a broad belt of Negro territories and colonies were in varying stages of self-rule. The Belgian Congo, rich in many minerals and crops, enjoyed great economic prosperity under colonial rule; few signs of resentment were evident among the prosperous and technically advancing natives. The Gold Coast elected its first self-governing parliament in June, 1954. But far across Africa to the East, serious disturbances occurred in Kenya colony, where native terrorists, called the *Mau Mau*, struck against the British and British-oriented natives. Ruthless measures were taken against the *Mau Mau*, and the bitterness engendered among British and native Kenyans by the experience probably precluded a prompt evolution of the territory toward self-rule.

Far to the south, in the Union of South Africa, where the anticolored government of Daniel Malan ruled, riots and widespread passive resistance among Hindus, colored, and Negroes obstructed Malan's repressive program and caused concern throughout the British Commonwealth. Member nations such as India could not tolerate racism in another Commonwealth member. Malan and his co-leaders were determined to pursue their nationalistic program at the cost of breaking all ties with England, a course of action which was bitterly opposed by most South African settlers of English descent.

THE NEAR EAST ARAB STATES

During and immediately after World War II, Syria, Lebanon, and Transjordan cut almost all ties with European powers and set out upon their own courses as United Nations members. Syria won freedom from France in a series of semivoluntary steps in 1941, 1944,

and 1946. Its republican form of government was soon dominated by a military junta. The pattern of liberation in Lebanon followed the Syrian pattern. However, the Lebanese government escaped serious troubles of succession in its early years. With Syria and other Arab powers, it took part in the unsuccessful war to dislodge the Jews from Palestine.

Transjordan, unlike Syria and Lebanon a constitutional monarchy in form, was from 1929 to 1946 under the direct protection of Great Britain. British officers commanded its military forces which included a well-equipped "Arab Legion." In March, 1946, a treaty between Britain and Transjordan declared the independence of the kingdom, and His Highness the Amir Abdullah became king. A bicameral legislature with an elective lower house and an upper house appointed by the king was instituted. In 1949 the country became the Hashemite Kingdom of Jordan, and in 1950 it annexed central Palestine. Abdullah was assassinated in 1951. The reign of his son, Talal I, was terminated by parliament in 1952, upon medical recommendation, and Hussein, son of Talal, became Jordan's king.

ISRAEL

The most striking and important development out of World War II in the Near East was the growth and attainment of independence of the Jewish state of Israel. Composing a large part of what had been the ancient land of Palestine and had been a British mandate since 1920, the new state represented the final triumph of the Zionists' dream.

The Zionist movement, compounded of religious, cultural, and nationalist feelings, gath-

Birth of a Nation. Premier Ben-Gurion of Israel reading the proclamation declaring the existence of the new state of Israel. (United Press)

ered strength slowly during the nineteenth century. The Balfour Declaration of World War I led Zionists to believe that England would sponsor a Jewish national home in Palestine at the end of the war. This in fact did not happen because Great Britain was also deeply committed to Arab interests. It was the shocking treatment of the Jews of Central and Eastern Europe that made the new state immediately possible. Determined to win by diplomacy or violence a place for the Jews who survived the methodical slaughter by the Nazis, the Zionists pressed their cause. Immigrants were smuggled into the country in excess of the small quota set by the British, arms were imported and concealed, an underground military force was organized, and the Jewish National Council set itself to take over the duties of government.

The United Nations, successor to the League of Nations as controller of mandated territories, took upon itself the task of so dividing Palestine as to provide an independent Jewish State and an independent Arab State. Neither Jews nor Arabs would tolerate the plan of partition proposed by the U.N. boundary commission. Great Britain, harassed by underground tactics and the barbs of international opinion, gave advance notice to all parties and terminated her mandate over Palestine on May 15, 1948.

On the same day, the Jewish National Council proclaimed the new state of Israel, elected Dr. Chaim Weizmann, a famous scientist, as president, and appointed David Ben-Gurion to head the government. The United States, Soviet Russia, and many other powers recognized immediately the legitimacy of the new nation. The 700,000 Jews of Israel girded themselves to face the attacks of Egypt, Transjordan, Lebanon, Syria, and Saudi-Arabia, who sent their armies into Palestine in May. Fierce fighting began, but was temporarily halted by a truce managed by the United Nations. Israel retained all and a little more than had been provided by the boundary commission in the way of territory. The Arab nations, finding they could not destroy the new state and faced with domestic dissension as a result of their defeats, accepted the U.N. proposal to negotiate peace with Israel. Armistices were signed early in 1949. Israel, with a newly-elected constitutional government, undertook to solve the staggering problems of building a modern prosperous state in a land that had once been a desert. In 1949, it became a member of the United Nations. Fresh border disputes between Israel and individual Arab state erupted every few months thereafter. An Arab blockade and embargo damaged Israel's trade. But some progress was being made on a plan to harness the Jordan River to provide water and power for Israel and its neighbors; it was possible that such an economic community might bring about a general easing of tension in the area and the United States pushed hard to accomplish it.

IRAN

Iran had long been a poverty-stricken, underdeveloped pawn of international politics. During World War II it was strategically important in providing access from the sea to supply lines to the southern Soviet Union. Vast quantities of American war materials were shipped across Iran to the Soviet Union for the Eastern European front. Awakened by military events, increased contacts with the outside world, and the ideas of nationalism alive in the Near East, Iranian politics were critically agitated. Communists, Nationalists, and pro-Western forces struggled for power.

In April, 1951, the party of Mohammed Mossadegh achieved control of parliament and voted to nationalize the Anglo-Iranian Oil Company, whose rich holdings were the largest enterprise in Iran. Anti-British riots accompanied the move, and oil production dwindled to nothing. In the face of international opposition, the properties involved were

Abadan Refineries, which were shut down when Iran nationalized the Anglo-Iranian Oil Company

manned by Iranians, and Mossadegh adamantly opposed British plans for restoration or compensation. In 1953, Mossadegh was overthrown by partisans of the Shah and tried for treason against the monarchy. He was sentenced to prison and the new government began discussion of the oil problem with England. On August 5, 1954, Iran signed a contract with an International Oil Consortium representing eight major world oil companies providing for settlement of the claims of the Anglo-Iranian Oil Company and for the development and management of Iran's oil resources according to a formula that divided profits several ways.

INDIA, PAKISTAN, AND CEYLON

In 1947 a century of agitation for independence brought free dominion status within the British Commonwealth to the world's second most populous country. India was freed of all but a tenuous voluntary affiliation to the British Crown. The Constituent Assembly of India, successor to the old Indian Legislature, assumed the lawmaking powers for the new government in August, 1947. Under the constitution of 1948, there were created a President, a Council of Ministers headed by the Prime Minister, a Council of States, a House of the People, and a Supreme Court. In 1949 India became an independent republic, but remained within the Commonwealth.

Jawaharlal Nehru, India's Prime Minister

The former provinces of India assumed a form of government resembling that of the American states. Certain powers were allocated exclusively to the central government, others to the state governments, and a number could be concurrently exercised by both. For example, currency, defense, communications, and foreign affairs were assigned the federal government, while health, land questions, judicial administration, and education were entrusted to the states. Power over matters like labor conditions, criminal law, and insurance was concurrent.

Since India had even before the second world war acquired large independent powers, she had become a member of the United Nations during the war. The independence movement gathered strength in the struggle, and, although India contributed a great amount of supplies, manufactures, and men to the British cause, it was the express understanding of both British and Indian leaders that Allied victory would be followed immediately by full independence for India. Mahatma Gandhi, revered leader of the Indian nationalist movement and head of the Indian Congress party that dominated Indian politics, was assassinated in 1948 and, by his own designation, Pandit Jawaharlal Nehru succeeded to his position of leadership.

Nehru, a western-educated socialist, became prime minister. Together with a small group of associates, he became the effective ruler of the new state whose internal difficulties and overcrowded population promised to present its rulers with continuous crises. The efforts of the new government were directed several ways. They began to reorganize more efficiently the hodge-podge of local jurisdictions which history had presented to modern India. Education had to be extended to millions of persons more if the people were to have any active hand in the democratic election structure that was enacted into law. Industrialization, speeded up by two world wars, had to be continuously accelerated if the standards of living of the population were to be raised even minutely. The bitterness of the religious question had to be reduced, and peace had to be made with Pakistan to stop the possibility of a recurrence of the bloody massacres among Hindus and Moslems in 1948. The first parliamentary elections were held throughout India in 1951–52. The Congress party retained control of the government and repeated its successes in the elections of 1955. Indian foreign policy in this period caused great concern in America inasmuch as Nehru plotted a diplomatic course that seemed perilously pro-Communist.

Pakistan, the second large nation created out of British India, was much more friendly

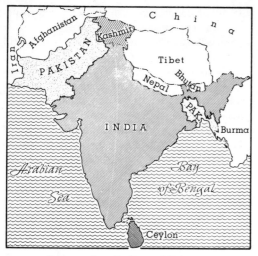

Independent India and Pakistan

the Philippines came into being on July 4, 1946, in a spirit of friendship with the United States. Since 1934, the islands had been preparing for their eventual complete liberty. In that year, the United States Congress gave them commonwealth status after having governed them as a territory since acquiring them from Spain in 1899. The constitution that had been adopted in 1935 served the new government of 1946 as well. Its twenty million citizens had suffered greatly under the Japanese occupation for three years during World War II, and faced many problems of reconstruction.

Manuel Quezon was elected first president of the Philippine Commonwealth in 1935. He held office during most of the second world war; Sergio Osmena, the vice-president, succeeded to the presidency upon Quezon's death in 1944. In 1945, Manuel Roxas was elected first president of the independent republic but died and was succeeded

Ramón Magsaysay, Philippine Nationalist leader, the republic's third president. (United Press)

by Elpidio Quirino before completing his term. In 1946 occurred the complete withdrawal of American sovereignty. A treaty with the United States in 1947 allowed free trade between the two nations for eight years and a reduced scale of tariffs until 1974. In 1947, the United States was allowed to lease for 99 years five major and 18 auxiliary bases for its armed forces in the Far East.

to the United States and received military and technical aid to combat Communist influence. Pakistan had been given separate existence because its preponderant Moslem population feared discrimination at the hands of the more numerous Hindus if they were included in the new free India. Like India, Pakistan's 70,-000,000 inhabitants received their independence in 1947. The country became a Dominion of the British Commonwealth also, and Ali Jinnah took the post of governor-general while Liaquat Ali Khan became prime minister. Ali Jinnah, the "Gandhi of Moslem India," died in 1948. Pakistan became a member of the United Nations in 1947.

Ceylon, lying off the southeast tip of India, received fully responsible status within the British Commonwealth in early 1948. Like India and Pakistan, freedom came after a gradual evolution toward self-government. The six and a half million inhabitants of the country, mainly Buddhist in religion, produced large quantities of tea, spices, and oils for the world markets. British connections with the island remained close following its receipt of independence; defense and foreign affairs were conducted cooperatively.

THE FAR EAST: THE PHILIPPINES

In marked contrast to the bloodshed that greeted the Israelite republic, the Republic of

The political leadership of the islands after the war had lived through foreign domination, enemy domination, and wars. They knew the problems of the people and were realistic in treating with other nations. Carlos Romulo, for example, became president of the United Nations Assembly. In 1953, after a vigorous campaign against corruption in government, Ramón Magsaysay, Nationalist leader, became the third president of the Philippine Republic. He vigorously pursued a campaign against Communist-led Hukbalahap guerrillas and was successful in curbing them.

BURMA, MALAYA, AND THAILAND

Burma is peopled largely by Mongolians and derives much of its culture from India. But it is isolated from both China and India and has developed independently of those countries during most of modern history. A series of battles between the British forces and the Burmese royal levies resulted in the annexation of all Burma to the British Empire between 1826 and 1886. It was governed as a province of India later on and then separated from India in 1937

From 1942 to 1945 the country was occupied by Japanese forces. When the British returned late in 1945, they met an insistent demand for independence from most of the political factions of the country. In 1947 a constitution was adopted. In 1948 full independence was granted Burma, which refused even the status of an independent dominion within the British Commonwealth. In the same year, Burma joined the United Nations.

Malaya itself was undergoing rapid change. The British had taken over Singapore early in the nineteenth century and gradually extended their control over nine sultanates of the north under treaties of protection. Under the British, exports of tin and rubber to the western world increased enormously and the population became diversified. In 1947, there were 2,400,000 Malayans, 1,900,000 Chinese, and half a million Indians in Malaya. The different races lived together amicably but with little tendency to amalgamate; racial tensions have developed from time to time. The Malayans suffered from the Japanese invasion and occupation, and welcomed back the British at the end of the war.

The war had, however, intensified nationalism, and the British, for this reason as well as because they thought the number of governments too large for so small an area, proposed a new centralized constitution. The Malayan leaders opposed centralization with the result that the Federation of Malaya was formed in 1948 to replace the centralized 1946 Union. Under the new form, a High Commissioner was given powers on behalf of the British Crown and the Sultanates. He has a federal executive council and legislative council. Important powers remain with the local rulers and their councils. Singapore is outside the federation. From 1948 to 1954 British and Malayan constabulary and troops fought many difficult skirmishes with Communist rebels.

Thailand, formerly Siam, enjoyed considerable prosperity in the postwar period under its military-dominated monarchy. The government pursued an anti-Communist policy that favored the United States. Its geographical position in the middle of the Indochina Peninsula exposed its population to strong Communist influences from the North and East, so that many observers foresaw difficulties in its maintaining independence of action.

INDONESIA

The most important of the new southeast Asian countries was Indonesia. Some 70,000,-000 persons of various linguistic and cultural subgroups inhabited Java, Sumatra, Borneo, Celebes, Timor, Bali, and the many other islands of the Netherlands East Indies at the beginning of the second world war. Java alone contained 40,000,000 inhabitants. The Dutch first arrived in the islands in the late sixteenth century and dispossessed the Portuguese traders they found there. Gradually they extended their control over the vast area and consolidated it. In the early twentieth century, following general world practice, the Dutch began to allow a greater measure of local autonomy to the Indonesians.

The pace toward self-government, while it pleased many Indonesians and brought many reforms to the islands, was not swift enough for some of the Indonesian leaders. During this period the Nationalist party was suppressed and Soekarno, its leader, jailed. When the Japanese defeated the British and Dutch in southeast Asia, republican sentiment mounted, and the Japanese promised independence to Indonesia for cooperation in an "Asia for the Asiatics" program. Soekarno was freed and he and other leaders collaborated with the Japanese in return for ultimate independence.

Just before Japan's surrender, the Japanese turned over the country to the Indonesians who proclaimed their independence and prepared to resist Dutch rule. Soekarno was joined by Sjahrir, who had fought against the Japanese, and both insisted that the Dutch acknowledge the new government. The Dutch tried to reinstate their position by negotiation and by force. Neither succeeded. While they controlled key ports and important plantations, they could not rest secure and large parts of the islands were in turmoil. World opinion pressed the Dutch to discontinue force.

Conferences in the Netherlands between the Indonesian and Dutch representatives agreed to the complete independence of the East Indies within a Netherlands Union under the nominal headship of the Dutch Crown. On December 27, 1949, the independence of the new Republic of United Indonesia was proclaimed at Batavia (now Jakarta) and Soekarno became the first president. Full control over huge amounts of the world's rubber, tin, oil, manganese, and copra passed to Indonesian hands along with full responsibility for the security and welfare of the people. On August 30, 1954, the remaining bonds between the Netherlands and Indonesia were dissolved by mutual accord. There remained to be settled the claim of Indonesia to western New Guinea, a large, underdeveloped, but potentially rich area over which the Dutch retained control.

JAPAN AND CHINA

Occupied by American troops after World War II, Japan served as the base for the conduct of the Korean War. The Japanese governments were generally favorable to American foreign policy, but the Japanese were restive under their subordination to a foreign power. On April 28, 1952, at San Francisco, the peace treaty, which had been signed by all participants in the war against Japan was officially handed the Japanese. The United States, under a separate security alliance, was authorized to maintain troops in Japan for the defense of the Far East against the Soviet Union.

Japan's prewar economic problems remained. Her great population found no outlet by emigration. Her manufactured goods lacked adequate markets and sources of raw materials were unavailable in some cases. Her natural trade area was China, but China was almost closed to trade because of the Korean War. Shipbuilding, in which Japan replaced the United States in 1952 as the second largest builder, helped reduce the gap between exports and imports. Still Japan required an additional billion dollars a year in export trade

In the elections of 1955, Premier Ichiro Hatoyama's Democratic party won 185 of the 467 seats in parliament and again played the chief role in a coalition government.

For three years after the end of World War II, Communist and Nationalist forces in China seemed fairly evenly matched. But during 1949, the Communists seized province after province and by the beginning of 1950, all that remained to the Nationalist armies of Chiang Kai-shek was the island of Formosa. Inasmuch as the moment of Communist triumph in China corresponded to a time of great tension between America and Russia, American politicians turned anxious attention to America's Chinese policy. Opponents of President Truman and Secretary of State Acheson condemned their failure to help Nationalist China in time. The administration countered that the Chinese Nationalist government had received and wasted much American aid. However, the United States did not recognize Communist China and gave as much aid to the Nationalist government on Formosa as could be absorbed by the limited facilities existing there. Furthermore, the United States placed Formosa under its military protection. Both of these steps were taken after North Korean Communists invaded South Korea.

The complete conquest of continental China by Mao Tse-tung's armies opened a new chapter in the history of power in Asia. China, the most populous nation in the world, now in Communist hands, bordered on the Soviet Union, Korea, Indochina, Burma, India, and Tibet. It overlooked a number of important and potentially Chinese-dominated nations. Throughout Asia and the islands of the South Seas, Communists took courage and plotted to duplicate the Chinese examples in their own lands. The Chinese Communists signed a long-term friendship and mutual aid treaty with the U.S.S.R. in February, 1950. By its terms China was to receive Russian industrial products and military aid in the event of attack by any foreign power. In fact, Russian aid in the form of military supplies, equipment, and training helped support the Chinese Communists in several ventures. They seized Tibet, though that vast and isolated territory proved of so little value that some troops were withdrawn in 1953. The Chinese also gave aid to Communists fighting the French and Indochinese in Indochina. Most important of all, they entered the Korean War and helped produce a stalemate that was of great disadvantage to the United States. Communist China's geographic position and its alliance with Soviet power placed it in an extremely advantageous position to incite, in a number of areas, small wars calculated to embarrass and drain the resources of America and Western Europe.

Chinese Communist Leaders Mao Tse-tung and Chou En-lai, with other government officials, review a May Day demonstration. (Eastfoto)

KOREA

On a peninsula off Manchuria lay two new nations divided by the 38 degree parallel of latitude, the republics of North and South Korea. At Potsdam in 1945, the United States, China, the U.S.S.R., and the United Kingdom had pledged a free, united, and independent Korea. When the Japanese surrendered, America and Russia decided on the 38 degree parallel as the dividing point between Soviet and American occupation forces. Later on the two regions were to be united under a democratic and free Korean government.

But the Soviet authorities insisted on a strict isolation of their area despite repeated American attempts to unite the land. In 1947 negotiations broke down, and the United States appealed to the United Nations to take up the matter. The Soviets then urged that both nations withdraw their occupation forces simultaneously in 1948. This was opposed by the United States as being an attempt to create a power vacuum in the country which then would be filled by the armed and Communist-led North Korea government.

After protracted diplomatic maneuvers in the United Nations, the United Nations Temporary Commission urged elections throughout Korea to found a new national government. The Russians refused to allow the United Nations to oversee such elections, and in May,

1948, the United States went ahead with elections in the South. The elected government adopted a constitution providing for a strong president, a prime minister appointed by him with the approval of the legislature, and a single chamber assembly. The United States turned over the administration of South Korea to the new government of Dr. Syngman Rhee.

At the same time, a newly elected (without neutral observers) Supreme People's Council of North Korea proclaimed the establishment of a Democratic People's Republic of Korea under Communist domination. The U.S.S.R. then declared it would recall all of its troops by the end of 1948, and at the end of the year announced that the last Soviet occupation forces had left North Korea. On December 12, 1948, the United Nations recognized the new government of South Korea, and, by implication, left the United States free to keep its forces in South Korea as long as there was danger that it would be overrun by the North Korean Communist army. However, the United States began reducing its forces, and in June 1949, the last U. S. troops (except for an advisory commission) sailed from Korea.

THE KOREAN WAR

Friction along the border between North and South Korea after U. S. forces left, erupted into open warfare on June 25, 1950, when North Korean Communist forces, led by armored columns, invaded South Korea. The lightly-armed southern troops offered relatively slight resistance as the northern forces swept southward. A cease-fire resolution passed by the United Nations Security Council

Korean Campaign. Men and equipment land on the beach at Inchon in 1950. (United Press)

was ignored. On June 27, President Truman ordered U. S. air and naval forces under Gen. Douglas MacArthur to the aid of the South Koreans. On the same day the U.N. Security Council, without Russia present, invoked military sanctions against North Korea. The United Nations condemned the aggression and on July 7 authorized the United States to establish a unified U.N. command in Korea. President Truman then appointed MacArthur as over-all commander of United Nations forces in Korea. British naval forces aided U. S. forces from the beginning, and later small detachments of British, Turkish, Philippine, and other nations' troops joined in the fighting. Russia and her satellites denounced the U.N. sanctions resolution as illegal.

On June 28, Seoul, the South Korean capital, fell. U. S. ground troops joined the fighting on July 5, but were pushed back as the South Korean retreat on the western portion of the front turned into a rout. Much of the North Korean success was due to excellent Russian-made arms, especially tanks, which were shipped to Korea in large numbers.

On July 15, after savage fighting, the North Koreans crossed the Kum River and soon had overrun the entire southwestern corner of Korea. By August 3, the U.N. foothold in Korea had been whittled down to an area in the southeast about 50 miles wide and 90 miles long. Further U.N. withdrawals took place until September, when MacArthur was able to launch a counteroffensive; the key operation was an amphibious landing at Inchon, high up on the west coast of Korea. Marines and U. S. Army troops, supported heavily by navy gunfire and widespread bombing and strafing by U. S. Air Force and Marine aircraft, reoccu-

pied Seoul, and smashed the main North Korean army between them and U.N. forces advancing out of the southeastern bridgehead. South Korean forces crossed the 38th parallel into North Korea and, after a wait of several days, MacArthur was authorized by the U.N. to advance across the line with all of his forces. The North Koreans were steadily pushed up the peninsula, their capitol, Pyongyang, was captured, and by October 26, the first South Koreans reached the Manchurian border.

President Syngman Rhee of the Republic of Korea. (United Press)

However, hopes for an early end to the conflict were jolted as Chinese Communist troops, armed with tanks and Soviet rocket weapons, crossed from Manchuria to the aid of the North Koreans. Late in November they launched a smashing attack into North Korea with hundreds of thousands of troops. They cut off some U.N. units and drove the Allied forces far down the peninsula to defense positions in the south. In January, 1951, Seoul was recaptured. In February the U.N. Assembly, despite Soviet opposition, charged Communist China with aggression in Korea. On April 11, President Truman relieved General MacArthur of his commands and recalled him to the United States on grounds that the general obstructed U.N. policies and military orders from the American Command in Washington. MacArthur, in an address to Congress, denounced U.N. inactivity, and American reluctance to

Communist Prisoners leave their compound on Koje Island. (United Press)

use more devastating attacks against the Chinese. Seoul was reoccupied on March 15. On July 8, 1951, U.N. and Communist officials held their first meeting at Kaesong to discuss an armistice. The talks lasted two years and seventeen days. The Korean War settled into intermittent conflict along a line roughly similar to the 38th parallel. On July 27, 1953, hostilities were halted after three years and one month of war. Prisoners of both sides were subjected to controlled persuasion by their home country to encourage their return. Only 21 Americans refused repatriation, whereas many thousands of Chinese and North Korean prisoners chose not to return to their homelands. Casualties totaled over a million, with those of the United States amounting to about 141,000, of which over 22,000 were dead. Casualties among the South Koreans were about twice that number. An uneasy peace prevailed in Korea, and the critical theater of war in Asia shifted southwest to Indochina.

INDOCHINA

French intervention in this southeastern protrusion of the Asian continent began in the seventeenth century. Before 1946, the 27,000,-000 inhabitants of the area were grouped into a French colony of Cochin China, and the French protectorates of Annam, Cambodia, Tonking, and Laos. When the Japanese finally ousted the French officials in 1945 after allowing them administrative powers during the earlier part of the war, they proclaimed the independence of the area. When the French returned in the latter part of the same year, they were met with demands for permanent independence. A compromise prevented complete and disastrous warfare, but hardly appeased the more insistent nationalists.

A Federation of Indochina was formed under a French High Commissioner that was composed of the Associated States of Vietnam, Cambodia, including Tonking, Annam, Cochin China, and Laos. Rice and rubber production began to rise to their prewar position in the Asian economy, but political relations between the French and the Indochinese nationalists were strained to the breaking point. Independence was promised, but the French argued that immediate freedom could only mean conquest of Vietnam by the Communists. From small beginnings at the end of World War II, Ho Chi Minh organized his Communist guerrillas into a major fighting force which reached its peak offensive strength in 1954. Aid came to them from Communist China. They caused the French greater losses and materiel expenditure relative to France's wealth than the Korean War caused the United States. The French forces received American material aid, and more direct intervention was threatened should China send troops into Vietnam.

As events proved, the Chinese did not have to send large forces to the aid of their Communist friends in Indochina. While the United States hesitated to give all-out help, the French position steadily deteriorated. On May 7, the French fortress at Dienbienphu fell to the Communists. French morale was dealt a staggering blow at home, and her allies in Indochina were disheartened. A clamor for peace arose. With the great powers standing by, the delegates of the French Union and Vietminh met at Geneva, Switzerland, and on July 21, 1954, signed a truce agreement. Vietnam was to be divided roughly along the 17th parallel into a North and South territory. North Vietnam was conceded to the Communists and the South to the French. Free elections for the whole country were promised for 1956. French influence over the reduced Vietnam government diminished while American influence rose. In 1955, Emperor Bao Dai, residing at the French Riviera, was overthrown by Premier Diem, who simultaneously dispersed various private armies and gave a measure of unity and order to the hard-pressed country.

French Soldiers with U.S. equipment made their last stand at Dienbienphu, Indochina. (United Press)

90. The World in the Atomic Age

A PRECARIOUS FAR EAST BALANCE

THE DISASTER that befell the French in Indonesia reacted against the whole American system of anti-Communist alliances. The free governments of the Far East were dismayed. Embarrassed at having arrived upon the Indochinese scene too late with too

little to win, the American government set about strengthening its alliances in the Far East. In September, 1954, it convened a South-East Asia Defense Conference at Manila. Present besides the United States were Britain, France, Australia, New Zealand, Pakistan, Thailand, and the Philippines. A collective Defense Treaty and Pacific Charter were signed, proclaiming the intention of the assembled nations to take immediate steps to repel any further Communist aggression against any non-Communist territory in Asia. They further pledged to engage in a program of mutual economic assistance to develop internal strength against communism among the free Asian nations. Secretary of State Dulles expressed pleasure at the agreements reached, but an unbiased observer could detect loopholes in the pact sufficient to let escape any frightened or unwilling partner.

Not to be outdone by the European and American powers, four neutralist Asian governments, led by India, called a conference at Bandung, Indonesia, which met between April 18 and 24, 1955. Present were representatives of 29 Asian and African nations that contained 1.4 billions of the world's people. A prominent figure at the conference was Communist China's President Chou En-lai. It was expected that the conference might develop strong criticism of the United States. In fact, colonialism was thoroughly castigated, for practically all of the participants had recently been subjected to European rule. But it was made clear that communism was regarded by many of those present as being also a potential imperialist and colonial force.

The assembled nations demanded that the U.N. give increased attention to the financial and trade needs of Asia and Africa. They voiced opposition to colonialism "in whatever form it may be." They urged greater cultural ties among the nations of the East. They supported a universal human rights declaration and deplored the repression of the colored races in South Africa. Self-determination of all peoples was acclaimed; the end of French rule in North Africa was demanded. They called for greater representation of Asia and Africa on the Security Council of the U.N., and for universal disarmament and the abolition of nuclear weapons.

The United States and its friends had feared that the conference might plead the Communist Chinese cause in Formosa, but the conference adjourned without taking a position on the issue. The political struggle over Formosa had reached its height about the same time as the conference met. Amid intensified Communist demands and threats against the Americans, who were protecting the island and its Nationalist Chinese defenders, Congress in January approved a resolution giving President Eisenhower discretion to act in defense of Formosa and the adjoining Pescadores Islands as he saw fit; presumably the Quemoy and Matsu islands, lying just off the Chinese coast, were also included in the discretion tendered the President. No fixed policy regarding these latter islands was announced. Secretary of State Dulles stated in February that the decision whether or not to defend these close-in areas depended on tactical con-

Chancellor **Adenauer** of Germany reached agreement on NATO terms with Premier Mendes-France. (United Press)

siderations regarding the defense of Formosa itself, to which the United States was firmly committed. Faced by the uncertainty of American reaction to aggressive moves, the Chinese Communists mobilized for attack, but paused indecisively on the threshold of war, not knowing what would happen. While this precarious balance prevailed into the Asian summer of 1955 — on a line from Korea to Formosa to Vietnam — important diplomatic moves in Austria and Germany, changes in the Soviet leadership, and talk of a meeting of Eisenhower and Bulganin focused world attention back upon the European theater of the Cold War.

AMERICAN POLITICS IN WAR AND PEACE

Some of the leaders who were cast into the role of saving world peace in 1955 were not world renowned in World War II. The top leadership of the United States, the Soviet Union, Great Britain, France, Italy, and Germany had changed; so had that of the Chinese mainland, of Japan, India, and Indonesia.

Men who had subordinate roles during the war had the principal responsibilities now. Domestic politics of the United States and the Soviet Union brought new leaders to the fore between 1945 and 1955.

In the presidential campaign of 1944, President Roosevelt was nominated for a fourth term. Senator Harry S. Truman, who had gained popularity for critical investigations of the war effort in industry, replaced Henry Wallace as the vice-presidential candidate. The Republicans nominated Thomas E. Dewey, racket-busting New York district attorney, for president and Governor Bricker of Ohio for vice-president. Roosevelt won by 3,500,000 votes, with 432 electoral votes to Dewey's 99. The conduct of the war was not an issue in the campaign.

On the eve of American victory in Europe, President Roosevelt was stricken with a cerebral hemorrhage in Warm Springs, Georgia, and within a few hours passed from unconsciousness into death. It was April 12, 1945, on the 83rd day of his fourth term of office. He was buried in Hyde Park, New York. Vice-President Truman succeeded immediately to the presidency and pledged his energies to the completion of Roosevelt's policies and the successful conclusion of the war.

The coming of peace brought a host of new problems before the American people. Domestic and foreign issues demanded constant attention. In the elections of 1946, the Republican party gained control of Congress for the first time since 1932. Soon after the election, price controls were abolished on all items except rents. The Wagner Act was replaced by the Taft-Hartley Labor Relations Act despite the bitter opposition of organized labor. Legislation included the Atomic Energy Act which established an Atomic Energy Commission composed of civilians whose task it was to organize, own, and operate the major facilities for the production of fissionable materials for conversion into atomic energy.

A second major legislative development of the first Truman administration was the Economic Cooperation Act of 1948, better known as the Marshall Plan. The Marshall Plan had its origins in the Truman Doctrine of

March, 1947, which announced that America would give economic aid to Greece and Turkey in order to help those nations withstand the threat of communism. Food, machinery, and military supplies were subsequently furnished both nations.

The Marshall Plan, presented by Secretary of State George C. Marshall, applied this principle to all the nations of Europe, to forestall economic and political chaos. It invited all nations who would cooperate in reconstructing Europe and reviving international trade to combine and submit their needs to the United States. The total needs were estimated by computing the amounts of food and equipment required in order to return the economies to their level of 1939. The Soviet Union and her satellite countries of eastern Europe refused to join the cooperating nations, contending that the real purpose of the Marshall Plan was to subject Europe to American imperialism. Thus, the plan turned into a series of agreements between the United States and the cooperating democracies of Western Europe. Principal beneficiaries of the aid were England, France, Italy, and Western Germany. Most of the funds were used to buy food and machinery from the United States. The program was directed by the Economic Cooperation Administration and the contracting countries had to satisfy certain American conditions in order to qualify for aid.

Former Presidents Truman and Hoover photographed at inauguration of Eisenhower and Nixon. (Wide World)

THE ELECTIONS OF 1948

In the face of domestic and foreign needs, American production on the farm and in the factory boomed to heights unprecedented in peace time. Still, demand outstripped supply for many commodities and prices soared to almost double their 1940 level in many cases. In his campaign for re-election in 1948, the President accused the Republicans of having brought about this inflation by removing price controls abruptly. He also attacked the Republican 80th Congress for wishing to remove protection from farm prices, for blocking public housing for veterans, and for discriminating against labor. He came out for a full program of guarantees of civil liberties, especially for the Negro people. But Truman's foreign policy was attacked as being anti-Russian and

for war by Henry Wallace, who deserted the Democratic ranks and formed a Progressive party with himself as candidate for president. Antagonized by the civil rights program, a number of southern Democrats deserted the Democratic party and formed the States' Rights party, popularly called the Dixiecrats, with Governor Thurmond of South Carolina as their candidate.

The Republicans again nominated Thomas E. Dewey for the presidency, with Governor Warren of California for vice-president. Dewey defended the record of the 80th Congress and asked for national unity. Furthermore, Wallace and Thurmond were expected to draw many voters from the Democratic ranks. In the face of almost universal predictions, Truman won a clear majority in the electoral college and was elected president in his own right. The Democrats, in addition, won control of the Senate and the House and retained their control by slim margins in the elections of 1950.

There ensued a period of embittered relations between Truman and Congress, where a Republican-Democratic coalition opposed the

President's "Fair Deal" program. The national emergency, brought on by the Korean War, inflicted unpopular restraints upon industry and consumers. The dismissal of General Mac-Arthur in 1951 diminished Truman's popularity. In the spring of 1952, the steelworkers threatened to strike and on April 8, the President ordered seizure of the steel industry. On June 2, the Supreme Court declared the seizure unconstitutional and a new strike began which did not end until July 24. Truman suffered great criticism because he refused to use the Taft-Hartley Act to prevent the strike. Various exposes of corruption among Democratic officials and of suspiciously pro-Russian action by Democratic officeholders of the past added to the tribulations of the administration.

THE ELECTIONS OF 1952

On January 7, 1952, General Dwight D. Eisenhower announced his willingness to accept the Republican nomination for the presidency if he were drafted. This put him in direct opposition to Senator Robert Taft, who was already in active pursuit of the nomination. The several months before the Republican convention brought out an intense struggle for support within Republican ranks by the Eisenhower and Taft forces. The Eisenhower candidacy triumphed, and Taft pledged his support in the campaign.

Meanwhile, President Truman announced he would not be a candidate for the Democratic party nomination, and several contenders appeared. Senator Estes Kefauver of Tennessee appeared the strongest in popular tests. The Democratic convention, however, selected Governor Adlai Stevenson of Illinois and nominated Senator John Sparkman of Alabama to run against Richard Nixon of California for the vice-presidency.

The personal popularity of Eisenhower, whose name had long been a household word, was enormous. Stevenson was relatively unknown. The Democrats were disheartened, and were disliked by many for the corruption that had been exposed in high places. The Korean War had been unpopular, and resentment was focused upon the Democrats. Eisenhower promised a prompt conclusion of

the war and a personal visit to the Korean front, if elected.

The results of the voting staggered the Democrats. Eisenhower carried 39 states with 442 electoral votes, while Stevenson carried 9 states with 89 electoral votes. A record total of 61,547,861 votes were cast for president. Eisenhower's total was 33,927,549 votes, or 55.4 per cent of the popular vote. The Republicans won control of the House and Senate, though by small margins.

Upon his inauguration Eisenhower appointed a cabinet which fired large numbers of Democratic officeholders, in some cases making inroads into posts recently classified as civil service. Stringent economies were forced on many governmental agencies. The armed forces budget was cut. Foreign policy remained unchanged, generally. Legislation to construct a waterway from the St. Lawrence River to the Great Lakes was passed. Tax burdens on many middle and upper-middle incomes were eased. President Eisenhower's appointee as Chief Justice of the Supreme Court, Earl Warren, joined all the other justices on May 17, 1954, in declaring that the maintenance of separate schools for whites and Negroes was unconstitutional.

In the November elections of 1954, the Democrats regained control of Congress and won 19 of the 34 elections for state governors. A dip in industrial activity and the absence of Eisenhower's name from the ballot accounted for most of the Republican losses. The new Congress nevertheless showed itself scarcely more disposed than the previous one to engage the President in political controversy.

Former President Truman took an active part in 1952 campaign supporting Adlai Stevenson. (United Press)

AFL's George Meany, left, and CIO's Walter Reuther ended rivalry with a "live and let live" agreement looking toward merger of labor groups. (United Press)

Of further significance to the approaching presidential elections of 1956 was the decision of the Congress of Industrial Organizations and the American Federation of Labor, America's two large federations of labor unions, to merge into a single organization. The presidency of the new group went to George Meany, head of the old AFL. The 27 vice-presidents provided for were divided up, 17 going to AFL leaders and 10 to CIO leaders. The joint statement of the parties to the merger declared that "both craft and industrial unions are appropriate, equal and necessary." It pledged that the new organization would bar Communists, eliminate corrupt unionism, and ban religious and racial bias in labor unions. The integrity of each affiliated union was guaranteed. From the junction, both greater bargaining strength and political power were expected to result.

THE SOVIET UNION

Across the world, the Soviet Union suffered its own kind of change of administration. On March 5, 1953, Premier Joseph Stalin died at the age of 73 of a cerebral hemorrhage. He had ruled the Soviet Union and its many satellites since 1924, and had been Premier since 1941. The Russian succession of government was accompanied by great uncertainty, and as had been expected, a purge. Stalin was succeeded by Gheorghi Maximilianovitch Malenkov, born in the Urals in 1902, a man who had

joined the Red Army in the Civil Wars in 1919 and had been a Communist party member since 1920. His background and youth were little known. He rose to great prominence as a member of the five-man Committee for Defense of the States, formed in June, 1941, on the occasion of the Nazi assault on Russia and numbering also Stalin, Molotov, Voroshilov, and Beria. Malenkov became chairman of the new Presidium of the Council of Ministers, the others being Lavrenti P. Beria, Molotov, Bulganin, and Kaganovich.

On July 10 the arrest of Beria, minister of internal affairs and chief of the Security (Secret) Police, was announced. He was accused, with several colleagues, of criminal and antistate activities aimed at gaining personal power and converting the U.S.S.R. to capitalism. Expelled from the Communist party and tried before the Supreme Court of the U.S.S.R., he was condemned and executed, along with his aides, in December, 1953. The indictment and judgment of Beria were ironically apt, considering his functions in the Soviet Union before his arrest. He was alleged to have confessed orally and in writing, and to have been proved to have engaged in treasonable activities against the U.S.S.R. for thirty-five years.

Just as it seemed that the Soviet leadership had settled into the saddle, the resignation of Malenkov was announced at a meeting of the Supreme Soviet, the parliament of the Soviet Union, in February, 1955. He confessed failure at solving the agricultural crisis and was reduced to a subordinate post. Bulganin became premier and Gheorghi Zhukov was named minister of defense. Most probably, Nikita Khrushchev, first secretary of the Central Committee of the Communist party, was then the strongest man in Soviet Russia. A change in policy was announced that favored greater emphasis upon

Premier Bulganin
(United Press)

the production of capital goods and building up heavy industry as opposed to consumer goods and industry.

ATOMIC POLITICS

The many disastrous wars, revolutions, riots, and other power struggles characterizing the world in the middle of the twentieth century were accompanied by the threat of almost un-imaginable general disaster contained in the development of atomic weapons. In 1949, four years after the explosion of the first American atomic bomb in Japan, the Soviet Union exper-imentally exploded its first atomic bomb. In 1952 the United States exploded a hydrogen weapon in a test at Eniwetok. Less than a year later, Malenkov indicated that Russia, too, possessed hydrogen weapons. The world could assume that each of the superpowers had amassed a considerable stock of atomic bombs of the earlier type, and were producing the enor-mously destructive H-bomb. Physicists esti-mated in 1953 that if cobalt were built around hydrogen bombs, the vast explosive force of the hydrogen would be accompanied by enor-mous radioactivity. The explosion of perhaps less than two dozen C-bombs might be suffi-cient to destroy all life on the earth's surface.

Considerations such as these prompted Pres-ident Eisenhower to reopen the question of international control of atomic energy in a speech to the United Nations in December, 1953. He stated that the United States' stock-pile of atomic weapons exceeded by many times the explosive total of all bombs or shells delivered or fired from all planes or guns in all

A Geyser of blinding light and smoke mushroomed up when the United States tested an H-bomb at Mar-shall Islands in 1952. (Civil Defense–United Press)

theaters of war in the whole of World War II. He declared that the United States would be prepared to release this destructive energy against an aggressor, but pleaded with the United Nations, and specifically with Russia, to join an international control of atomic en-ergy. He proposed a pool of atomic facilities for peaceful use in the underdeveloped world. He asked for creation of an international bank of fissionable materials in U.N. custody.

The settlement of the Trieste dispute be-tween Italy and Yugoslavia in 1954, the freeing of Western Germany in 1955, the signing of a peace treaty with Austria in 1955, the decla-ration by Russia of an end to the legal state of war with Germany, and the exchange of corre-spondence between Zhukov and Eisenhower, appeared as omens of a possible general peace; at least they contrasted sharply with the tense situation along the Eastern rim of Asia. Cast-ing a shadow over all thought of war as a means of settling problems were the uncertain but terrifying aspects of newly discovered armaments. In January, 1955, the *Nautilus*, America's atomic-powered submarine, made its first surface voyage. Intercontinental rock-ets armed with hydrogen-bomb warheads were almost ready for use. The Soviets were expanding a fleet of heavy bombers capable of attacking directly the United States.

The Chiefs of State of Britain, France, the United States and the Soviet Union met at Geneva, Switzerland, in July, 1955, to discuss

Austria is Reborn as nation at Belvedere Palace, Vienna. Among delegates were U.S. Secretary of State Dulles, at left end of table, and Russia's Molotov. (United Press)

Geneva Conference in 1955; left to right, Bulganin, Eisenhower, Faure, and Eden. (United Press)

Britain Leaves Suez as Maj. Gen. Edward Riou Benson initials agreement with Egypt. (United Press)

major problems such as unification of Germany, European security, disarmament, and breaking down of East-West barriers. While none of these issues were solved by the meeting there was a new atmosphere of friendliness and apparent willingness to cooperate. Specific settlements were left to future meetings of the foreign ministers. President Eisenhower offered exchange of military plans and aerial inspections of military installations and urged a lifting of the Iron Curtain.

TOWARD THE THIRD MILLENNIUM

Almost two thousand years have passed since the birth of Christ, and most of humanity lives under conditions close to those known to the carpenter of Nazareth. A stupendous material superiority has fallen into the hands of a few leaders of technically advanced, centralized powers. Both the United States and Russia have achieved signal successes in diplomacy, military affairs, and the consolidation of economic forces. The fate of hundreds of millions of people rested upon the decisions of these powers,

divided by a seemingly permanent and ineradicable line of hostility.

The world was marvellously shrunken. The jet plane, exceeding the speed of sound, could traverse the globe in hours. If the closeness of communication meant the spread of well-being, mutual respect, cultural exchange, increased travel, then the world would be most attractive. On the other hand, interdependence might mean that the fatal errors of a few men would bring universal destruction. Within nations, Socialist, Capitalist, and Communist theories vied with one another in a combination of forms, and nations passed from one ideology to another.

There remained the problems of human and social relationships and all the complex problems of adjustment that would enable mankind to pursue its proper course of development in the future. Whatever the ensuing events, it would be difficult for one to dispute the almost universal feeling that the second half of the twentieth century would be a great turning point for mankind.

The USS Nautilus, the first atomic-powered submarine, was launched in early 1954. (United Press)

A Selected Bibliography

BY PART AND CHAPTER

THE READER who is interested in pursuing further some of the events described in this book will find this bibliography useful. Several titles of well-known and well-recommended books are suggested for each part and chapter. Most of the suggested titles contain their own bibliographies and allow the reader to acquire an even greater acquaintance with the sources of history.

❦ With rare exceptions, titles are not repeated but placed only after the most relevant part or chapter. Therefore, in seeking further reading, it is best to look at the titles for the chapters above and below the one in which the reader is interested as well as the titles following the major section number.

General

ALLEN, FREDERICK A. *Big Change* (America 1900-1950), 1952.

American Peoples Encyclopedia, 20 vols., 1954.

American Peoples Encyclopedia Yearbooks, 1952 forward.

BARNES, HARRY ELMER. *The History of Western Civilization*, 1935.

BRUNN, GEOFFREY. *The World in the Twentieth Century*, 1948.

CHITWOOD, OLIVER P., OWSLEY, FRANK L., and NIXON, H. O. *The United States: From Colony to World Power*, 1950.

CREVEA, RAFAEL ALTAMIRA Y. *A History of Spanish Civilization*, 1930.

Dictionary of American Biography, 20 vols., 1928-1937.

Dictionary of National Biography (English), 22 vols., 1885-1901 (with supplements).

DURANT, WILLIAM JAMES. *The Story of Civilization*, rev. ed., 1950.

DUTCHER, G. M., AND ASSOCIATES (eds.). *A Guide to Historical Literature*, 1937.

EASUM, C. Y. *Half-Century of Conflict*, 1952.

Encyclopedia of the Social Sciences, 15 vols., 1930-1935.

FARROW, JOHN. *Pageant of the Popes*, 1950.

GOODRICH, LUTHER C. *A Short History of the Chinese People*, rev. ed., 1951.

HAYES, C. J. H., BALDWIN, M. W., and COLE, C. W. *History of Europe*, 1949.

HERMANN, PAUL. *Conquest by Man*, 1955.

HITTI, PHILIP K. *History of the Arabs*, 5th ed., 1951.

JAMES, HERMAN G. *The Republics of Latin America*, 1923.

LANGER, W. L. (ed.). *An Encyclopedia of World History*, rev. ed., 1952.

LARNED, JOSEPHUS NELSON. *The New Larned History for Ready Reference, Reading and Research; The Actual Words of the World's Best Historians, Biographers and Specialists*, 1928.

LATOURETTE, K. S. *Short History of the Far East*, rev. ed., 1951.

MORRIS, HENRY C. *The History of Colonization from the Earliest Times to the Present Day*, 2 vols., 1900.

NEVINS, ALLAN. *The Gateway to History*, 1938.

PINNOW, HERMAN. *History of Germany: People and State Through a Thousand Years*, 1933.

SEDGWICK, HENRY D. *A Short History of Italy, 476-1900*, 1905.

SEIGNOBOS, CHARLES. *The Evolution of the French People*, 1932.

SEIGNOBOS, CHARLES. *The Rise of European Civilization*, 1938.

The Statesman's Year-Book, 1864 to date.

TEGGART, FREDERICK J. *The Processes of History*, 1918.

THORNDIKE, LYNN. *A Short History of Civilization*, 1931.

TOYNBEE, ARNOLD JOSEPH. *A Study of History*, 3 vols., 1935. (Also available in one volume edition, abridged.)

VERNADSKII, GEORGII V. *Political and Diplomatic History of Russia*, 1951.

WELLS, HERBERT GEORGE. *Outline of History*, 1931.

WHITTLESEY, DERWENT. *Environmental Foundations of European History*, 1949.

Part I: THE ANCIENT NEAR EAST

General

BAIKIE, JAMES. *The Ancient East and Its Story*, 1929.

BREASTED, JAMES HENRY. *The Conquest of Civilization*, 1938.

BURY, J. B., COOK, S. A., and ADCOCK, F. E. (eds.). *The Cambridge Ancient History*, Vols. I-IV, 1923-26.

GLOVER, TERROT REAVELEY. *The Ancient World, A Beginning*, 1935.

HALL, HARRY R. H. *The Ancient History of the Near East, from the Earliest Times to the Battle of Salamis*, 1936.

OLMSTEAD, ALBERT TEN EYCK. *History of Palestine and Syria to the Macedonian Conquest*, 1931.

ROSTOVTSEV, MIKHAIL IVANOVICH. *A History of the Ancient World*, 2 vols., 1930.

TREVER, ALBERT AUGUSTUS. *History of Ancient Civilization*, 2 vols., 1936-39.

Chapter 1. The Land

GOLDENWEISER, ALEXANDER A. *Early Civilization*, 1932.

HOGARTH, DAVID G. *Nearer East*, 1902.

KLUCKHOLN, CLYDE. *Mirror for Man*, 1948.

LEAKEY, LOUIS SEYMOUR BAZETT. *Adam's Ancestors*, 1935.

MACCURDY, GEORGE GRANT. *Human Origins*, 2 vols., 1933.

SMITH, GEORGE A. *Historical Geography of the Holy Land*, 1894.

Chapter 2. The Prehistoric Near East

CHILDE, VERE GORDON. *New Light on the Most Ancient East; The Oriental Prelude to European Prehistory*, 1934.

MASPERO, GASTON CAMILLE CHARLES. *The Dawn of Civilization; Egypt and Chaldea*, 1922.

MYRES, JOHN LINTON. *The Dawn of History*, 1911.

Chapter 3. The Beginning of Recorded History

BAIKIE, JAMES. *A History of Egypt from the Earliest Times to the End of the XVIIIth Dynasty*, 2 vols., 1929.

BREASTED, JAMES HENRY. *A History of Egypt from the Earliest Times to the Persian Conquest*, 1919.

CAMERON, GEORGE GLENN. *History of Early Iran*, 1936.

DELAPORTE, LOUIS JOSEPH. *Mesopotamia; The Babylonian and Assyrian Civilization*, 1925.

JASTROW, MORRIS. *The Civilization of Babylon and Assyria; Its Remains, Language, History, Commerce, Law, Art and Literature*, 1915.

OLMSTEAD, ALBERT TEN EYCK. *History of Assyria*, 1923.

Chapter 4. The Time of the Patriarchs and the Judges

GRANT, ELIHU. *Orient in Bible Times*, 1920.

MASPERO, GASTON C. C. *Struggle of the Nations: Egypt, Syria and Assyria*, 1910.

MASPERO, GASTON C. C. *Art in Egypt*, 1912.

PERITZ, ISMAR J. *Old Testament History*, 1915.

STEINDORFF, GEORG. *Religion of the Ancient Egyptians*, 1905.

Chapter 5. The Last Thousand Years Before Christ

BLUNT, ALFRED WALTER FRANK. *Israel in World History*, 1927.

JONES, ARNOLD H. M. *The Herods of Judea*, 1938.

KENT, CHARLES F. *History of the Hebrew People*, 2 vols., 1896-97.

MASPERO, GASTON C. C. *Passing of the Empire, 850 B.C. to 330 B.C.*, 1900.

SYKES, SIR PERCY MOLESWORTH. *A History of Persia*, 2 vols., 1930.

Part II: THE ANCIENT MEDITERRANEAN WORLD

General

BURY, J. B., COOK, S. A., and ADCOCK, F. E. (eds.). *The Cambridge Ancient History*, Vols. V-XII, 1927-39.

FOWLER, WILLIAM WARDE. *The City-State of the Greeks and Romans*, 1895.

GLOVER, TERROT R. *Democracy in the Ancient World*, 1927.

ROBERTSON, JOHN CHARLES. *The Story of Greece and Rome; Their Growth and Their Legacy to Our Western World*, 1928.

ROSE, JOHN HOLLAND. *The Mediterranean in the Ancient World*, 1933.

SANFORD, EVA MATTHEWS. *The Mediterranean World in Ancient Times*, 1938.

Chapter 6. The Cretan Background of Greek History

BAIKIE, JAMES. *The Sea-Kings of Crete*, 1910.

EVANS, ARTHUR JOHN. *The Palace of Minos*, 4 vols., 1921-35.

GLOTZ, GUSTAVE. *The Aegean Civilization*, 1925.

HAWES, CHARLES H. *Crete, the Forerunner of Greece*, 1909.

Chapter 7. The First Stages of Greek Development

BOTSFORD, GEORGE W. (ed.). *Hellenic Civilization*, 1929.

BOTSFORD, GEORGE W. *Hellenic History*, 1930.

BURN, ANDREW R. *The World of Hesiod; A Study of the Greek Middle Ages, c. 900-700 B.C.*, 1936.

BURY, JOHN BAGNELL. *A History of Greece to the Death of Alexander the Great*, 1927.

GROTE, GEORGE. *A History of Greece*, 12 vols., 1925.

LAVELL, CECIL FAIRFIELD. *Biography of the Greek People*, 1934.

NILSSON, MARTIN P. *The Age of the Early Greek Tyrants*, 1936.

SEYMOUR, THOMAS D. *Life in the Homeric Age*, 1907.

Chapter 8. Development and Decline of the Greek City-States

DECOULANGES, NUMA FUSTEL. *Ancient City*, 1901.

FERGUSON, WILLIAM S. *Greek Imperialism*, 1913.

GARDNER, ERNEST A. *Greece and the Aegean*, 1933.

HASEBROEK, JOHANNES. *Trade and Politics in Ancient Greece*, 1933.

HOPKINSON, LESLIE W. *Greek Leaders*, 1918.

JAMES, HENRY ROSHER. *Our Hellenic Heritage*, 1924.

LAISTNER, MAX L. W. *A History of the Greek World from 479 to 323 B.C.*, 1936.

MURRAY, GILBERT. *History of Ancient Greek Literature*, 1897.

STOBART, J. C. *Glory That Was Greece: A Survey of Hellenic Culture and Civilization*, rev. ed., 1951.

VAN HOOK, EARNE. *Greek Life and Thought: A Portrayal of Greek Civilization*, 1930.

ZIMMERN, ALFRED E. *The Greek Commonwealth: Politics and Economics in Fifth Century Athens*, 1931.

Chapter 9. Alexander the Great and the Hellenistic Age

CARY, MAX. *A History of the Greek World from 323 to 146 B.C.*, 1932.

PICKARD-CAMBRIDGE, ARTHUR N. *Demosthenes and the Last Days of Greek Freedom, 384-322 B.C.*, 1914.

TARN, WILLIAM W. *Hellenistic Civilization*, 1930.

WILCKEN, ULRICH. *Alexander the Great*, 1932.

Chapter 10. Roman Origins and Early Conquests

BOAK, ARTHUR E. R. *A History of Rome to 565 A.D.*, 1929.

HAVELL, HERBERT LORD. *Republican Rome*, 1914.

HOMER, LÉON. *Primitive Italy and the Beginnings of Roman Imperialism*, 1926.

MOMMSEN, THEODOR. *The History of Rome*, 4 vols., 1911.

SCULLARD, HOWARD HAYES. *A History of the Roman World from 753 to 146 B.C.*, 1935.

Chapter 11. Roman World Domination

ABBOTT, FRANK F. *Roman Politics*, 1923.

FROUDE, JAMES ANTHONY. *Caesar: A Sketch*, 1932

HEITLAND, WILLIAM EMERTON. *Roman Republic*, 3 vols., 1909.

MARSH, FRANK BURR. *A History of the Roman World from 146 to 30 B.C.*, 1935.

Chapter 12. The Last Five Centuries of the Roman Empire

BAKER, GEORGE P. *Constantine the Great and the Christian Revolution*, 1930.

BURY, JOHN BAGNELL. *History of the Later Roman Empire from the Death of Theodosius I to the Death of Justinian*, 2 vols., 1923.

BURY, JOHN BAGNELL. *The Student's Roman Empire, 27 B.C.-180 A.D.*, 190?.

DIEHL, CHARLES. *The Byzantine Empire*, 1925.

FERRERO, GUGLIELMO, and BARBAGALLO, CORRADO. *A Short History of Rome*, 2 vols., 1918-19.

FIRTH, JOHN BENJAMIN. *Augustus Caesar and the Organization of the Empire of Rome*, 1903.

FRANK, TENNY. *An Economic History of Rome*, 1927.

FRANK, TENNY (ed.). *An Economic Survey of Ancient Rome*, 6 vols., 1933-40.

GIBBON, EDWARD. *The Decline and Fall of the Roman Empire*, 2 vols., 1932.

GOODENOUGH, ERWIN R. *The Church in the Roman Empire*, 1931.

GREENE, WILLIAM CHASE. *The Achievement of Rome: A Chapter in Civilization*, 1933.

ISH-KISHOR, SULAMITH. *Magnificent Hadrian*, 1935.

MARSH, FRANK BURR. *The Reign of Tiberius*, 1931.

PARKER, HENRY M. D. *A History of the Roman World from A.D. 138 to 337*, 1935.

ROSTOVTSEV, MIKHAIL IVANOVICH. *The Social and Economic History of the Roman Empire*, 1926.

Part III: EARLY INDIA AND CHINA

General

GOWEN, HERBERT H. *Asia: A Short History from the Earliest Times to the Present Day,* 1926.

STEIGER, GEORGE N., BEYER, H. O., and BENITEZ, C. *History of the Orient,* 1926.

WEBSTER, HUTTON. *History of the Far East,* 1923.

Chapter 13. The Pageant of India

ALLEN, JOHN. *The Cambridge Shorter History of India,* 1934.

LANE-POOLE, STANLEY. *Medieval India Under Mohammedan Rule, 712-1764,* 1903.

SMITH, VINCENT A. *The Oxford History of India, from the Earliest Times to the End of 1921,* 1928.

SMITH, VINCENT ARTHUR. *The Early History of India from 600 B.C. to the Mohammedan Conquest,* 1924.

SRINIVAS-AIYANGAR, P. T. *A Short History of India,* 1930.

Chapter 14. China and Its Dynasties

GOWEN, HERBERT H. *An Outline History of China,* 1936.

HIRTH, FRIEDRICH. *The Ancient History of China to the End of the Chôu Dynasty,* 1908.

LAMB, HAROLD. *Genghis Khan, The Emperor of All Men,* 1928.

LATOURETTE, KENNETH SCOTT. *The Chinese: Their History and Culture,* 1934.

WILHELM, RICHARD. *A Short History of Chinese Civilization,* 1929.

WILLIAMS, EDWARD T. *A Short History of China,* 1928.

Part IV: MEDIEVAL EUROPE

General

BOISSONNADE, PROSPER. *Life and Work in Medieval Europe,* 1927.

PAINTER, SIDNEY. *History of the Middle Ages, 284-1500,* 1953.

PREVITÉ-ORTON, C. W. *Shorter Cambridge Medieval History,* 2 vols., 1952.

RAND, EDWARD KENNARD. *Founders of the Middle Ages,* 1928.

SCOTT, JONATHAN F., HYMA, A., and NOYES, A. H. (eds.). *Readings in Medieval History,* 1933.

STEPHENSON, CARL. *Europe from the Second to the Sixteenth Century,* rev. ed., 1951.

THOMPSON, JAMES WESTFALL. *An Introduction to Medieval Europe, 300-1500,* 1937.

Chapter 15. Meaning of the "Middle Ages"

ADAMS, GEORGE BURTON. *Civilization During the Middle Ages, Especially in Relation to Modern Civilization,* 1922.

CRUMP, CHARLES G., and JACOB, E. F. (eds.). *The Legacy of the Middle Ages,* 1926.

TAYLOR, HENRY OSBORN. *The Classical Heritage of the Middle Ages,* 1931.

Chapter 16. The Germanic Kingdoms

ARRAGON, REGINALD F. *The Transition from the Ancient to the Medieval World,* 1936.

EMERTON, EPHRAIM. *An Introduction to the Study of the Middle Ages, 375-814,* 1916.

HASKINS, CHARLES HOMER. *The Normans in European History,* 1915.

LOT, FERDINAND. *The End of the Ancient World and the Beginnings of the Middle Ages,* 1931.

MOSS, HENRY ST. LAWRENCE B. *The Birth of the Middle Ages, 395-814,* 1935.

OMAN, CHARLES W. C. *The Dark Ages, 476-918,* 1928.

Chapter 17. Papacy and Church in the Early Middle Ages

BALDWIN, SUMMERFIELD. *The Organization of Medieval Christianity,* 1929.

CHEETHAM, SAMUEL. *History of the Christian Church During the First Six Centuries,* 1894.

FLICK, ALEXANDER C. *Rise of the Medieval Church and Its Influence on the Civilization of Western Europe from the First to the Thirteenth Century,* 1909.

ROBINSON, CHARLES H. *Conversion of Europe,* 1917.

WALKER, WILLISTON. *History of the Christian Church,* 1918.

Chapter 18. The Eastern Empire and Islam

ALI, SYED AMEER. *Short History of the Saracens,* 1921.

BAYNES, NORMAN H. *Byzantine Empire,* 1925.

GILMAN, ARTHUR. *The Saracens from the Earliest Times to the Fall of Bagdad,* 1887.

MOYLE, JOHN B. *Institutes of Justinian Translated into English,* 1906.

VASILEV, ALEKSANDR. *History of the Byzantine Empire,* 2 vols., 1928-29.

Chapter 19. The Carolingian Renaissance

EINHARD. *Life of Charlemagne,* 1880.

HASKINS, CHARLES H. *Normans in European History,* 1915.

HODGKIN, THOMAS. *Charles the Great,* 1897.

WELLS, CHARLES L. *Age of Charlemagne,* 1898.

Chapter 20. The Feudal System

DAVIS, WILLIAM S. *Life on a Medieval Barony: A Picture of a Typical Feudal Community in the Thirteenth Century*, 1923.

GAUTIER, LEON. *Chivalry*, 1891.

JENKS, EDWARD. *Law and Politics in the Middle Ages*, 1913.

PETIT-DUTAILLIS, CHARLES E. *The Feudal Monarchy in France and England from the Tenth to the Thirteenth Century*, 1936.

SEIGNOBOS, CHARLES. *The Feudal Regime*, 1926.

Chapter 21. The Holy Roman Empire and the Papacy

BRYCE, JAMES. *The Holy Roman Empire*, 1919.

STUBBS, WILLIAM. *Germany in the Early Middle Ages, 476-1250*, 1908.

THOMPSON, JAMES W. *Feudal Germany*, 1928.

Chapter 22. England and the Norman Conquest

COSTAIN, T. B. *The Conquerors*, 1949.

FREEMAN, EDWARD A. *A Short History of the Norman Conquest of England*, 1896.

OMAN, C. (ed.). *History of England, England Before the Norman Conquest*, Vol. I, *England Under the Normans and Angevins*, Vol. II, 1904-13.

RAMSEY, JAMES H. *Foundations of England, B.C. 55-A.D. 1154*, 2 vols., 1898.

Chapter 23. Feudal France

FUNCK-BRENTANO, FRANTZ. *The National History of France: The Middle Ages*, 1922.

GUÉRARD, ALBERT LÉON. *French Civilization from Its Origin to the Close of the Middle Ages*, 1920.

TILLEY, ARTHUR A. (ed.). *Medieval France*, 1922.

Chapter 24. The Crusades

ADENAY, WALTER F. *Greek and Eastern Churches*, 1908.

ARCHER, THOMAS A., and KINGSFORD, C. L. *The Crusades: The Story of the Latin Kingdom of Jerusalem*, 1895.

KREY, AUGUST C. *First Crusade: The Accounts of Eye-Witnesses and Participants*, 1921.

LAMB, HAROLD. *The Crusades*, 2 vols., 1934-35.

NEWHALL, RICHARD AGAR. *The Crusades*, 1927.

OMAN, CHARLES W. C. *History of the Art of War in the Middle Ages*, 2 vols., 1924.

Chapter 25. The Church Triumphant

FULTON, JOHN (ed.). *Ten Epochs of Church History*, Vols. V-VI, 1896-1900.

GASQUET, F. A. (CARDINAL). *Monastic Life in the Middle Ages*, 1922.

HARDWICK, CHARLES. *History of the Christian Church During the Middle Age*, 1872.

KREHBIEL, EDWARD B. *The Interdict: Its History and Its Operation, with Especial Attention to the Time of Pope Innocent III, 1198-1216*, 1909.

LEA, HENRY C. *Studies in Church History*, 1869.

PIRIE-GORDON, C. H. C. *Innocent the Great: An Essay on His Life and Times*, 1907.

WORKMAN, HERBERT B. *Evolution of the Monastic Ideal from the Earliest Times Down to the Coming of the Friars*, 1913.

Chapter 26. Medieval Culture

ADAMS, HENRY. *Mont-Saint-Michel and Chartres*, 1936.

COULTON, GEORGE G. (ed.). *Life in the Middle Ages*, 1930.

HASKINS, CHARLES HOMER. *The Rise of Universities*, 1923.

HASKINS, CHARLES HOMER. *The Renaissance of the Twelfth Century*, 1927.

JARRETT, BEDE. *Social Theories of the Middle Ages, 1200-1500*, 1926.

NEWTON, ARTHUR P. (ed.). *Travel and Travellers of the Middle Ages*, 1926.

POWER, EILEEN EDNA. *Medieval People*, 1924.

RASHDALL, HASTINGS. *The Universities of Europe in the Middle Ages*, 3 vols., 1936.

TAYLOR, HENRY OSBORN. *The Medieval Mind*, 2 vols., 1930.

THORNDIKE, LYNN. *A History of Magic and Experimental Science*, 4 vols., 1929.

WADDELL, HELEN JANE. *The Wandering Scholars*, 1934.

Chapter 27. The Medieval Towns

CLARKE, MAUDE VIOLET. *The Medieval City State*, 1926.

Medieval Towns, 36 vols., 1898-1923 (accounts of individual towns).

PIRENNE, HENRI. *Medieval Cities: Their Origin and the Revival of Trade*, 1925.

THOMPSON, JAMES WESTFALL. *An Economic and Social History of the Middle Ages, 300-1300*, 1928.

THOMPSON, JAMES WESTFALL. *Economic and Social History of Europe in the Later Middle Ages, 1300-1530*, 1931.

Chapter 28. European States in Transition

JOINVILLE, JEAN DE. *Saint Louis: King of France*, 1901.

EMERTON, EPHRAIM. *Medieval Europe, 814-1300*, 1894.

HASSALL, ARTHUR. *France, Medieval and Modern: A History*, 1918.

HENDERSON, ERNEST F. *History of Germany in the Middle Ages*, 1894.

HUTTON, WILLIAM H. *Philip Augustus*, 1896.
MCKECHNIE, WILLIAM S. *Magna Carta*, 1905.
RAMSEY, JAMES H. *Angevin Empire*, 1903, and *Dawn of the Constitution*, 1908.

Chapter 29. France and England in the Hundred Years' War

CHEYNEY, EDWARD P. *The Dawn of a New Era, 1250-1453*, 1936.
LODGE, RICHARD. *The Close of the Middle Ages, 1273-1494*, 1922.
LOWELL, FRANCIS CABOT. *Joan of Arc*, 1896.
OMAN, CHARLES W. C. *The History of England from the Accession of Richard II to the Death of Richard III, 1377-1485*, 1906.

ORTON, CHARLES W. PREVITÉ. *A History of Europe from 1198 to 1378*, 1937.
RAMSAY, JAMES H. *Genesis of Lancaster*, 1913; *Lancaster and York*, 2 vols., 1892.

Chapter 30. The Changing Church

CREIGHTON, MANDELL. *History of the Papacy from the Great Schism to the Sack of Rome*, 6 vols., 1901.
LEA, HENRY CHARLES. *A History of the Inquisition of the Middle Ages*, 3 vols., 1922.
SALEMBIER, LOUIS. *Great Western Schism*, 1907.
TURBERVILLE, ARTHUR S. *Medieval Heresy and the Inquisition*, 1920.

Part V: RENAISSANCE AND REFORMATION

General

HOLLINGS, MARY A. *Europe in Renaissance and Reformation, 1453-1659*, 1909.
LAMB, HAROLD. *Suleiman the Magnificent*, 1951.
LUCAS, HENRY STEPHEN. *The Renaissance and the Reformation*, 1934.
SYMONDS, JOHN ADDINGTON. *Renaissance in Italy*, 7 vols., 1887-1908.
TANNER, EMMELINE M. *Renaissance and Reformation, 1494-1610*, 1908.
WARD, A. W., and OTHERS (eds.). *The Cambridge Modern History*, 14 vols., Vols. I-IV, 1902-12.

Chapter 31. Essential Features of the Renaissance

BELLONCI, MARIA. *Lucrezia Borgia*, 1954.
HUDSON, WILLIAM H. *Story of the Renaissance*, 1912.
ROEDER, RALPH. *The Man of the Renaissance*, 1933.
SAINTSBURY, GEORGE E. B. *The Earlier Renaissance*, 1901.

Chapter 32. Renaissance Arts and Science

ALLEN, PERCY S. *Erasmus' Services to Learning*, 1926.
BURCKHARDT, JAKOB C. *The Civilization of the Renaissance in Italy*, 1929.
TAYLOR, RACHEL A. *Aspects of the Italian Renaissance*, 1923.
WOODWARD, WILLIAM H. *Studies in Education During the Age of the Renaissance*, 1914.

Chapter 33. Martin Luther and the Protestant Reformation

BAINTON, R. H. *Martin Luther*, 1950.
BEARD, CHARLES. *The Reformation of the Sixteenth Century in Its Relation to Modern Thought and Knowledge*, 1927.
JOHNSON, ARTHUR HENRY. *Europe in the Sixteenth Century, 1494-1598*, 1928.
LINDSAY, THOMAS MARTIN. *A History of the Reformation*, 2 vols., 1906-07.
SMITH, PRESERVED. *The Age of the Reformation*, 1930.
TAYLOR, HENRY OSBORN. *Thought and Expression in the Sixteenth Century*, 2 vols., 1930.

Chapter 34. Protestant Sects and Counter-Reformation

JONES, RUFUS M. *Spiritual Reformers in the Sixteenth and Seventeenth Centuries*, 1914.
PALM, FRANKLIN C. *Calvinism and the Religious Wars*, 1932.
TAWNEY, RICHARD H. *Religion and the Rise of Capitalism*, 1926.
THOMPSON, FRANCIS. *Saint Ignatius Loyola*, 1910.
TROELTSCH, ERNST. *Protestantism and Progress*, 1912.
WALKER, WILLISTON. *John Calvin, The Organizer of Reformed Protestantism, 1509-1564*, 1906.

Chapter 35. The Thirty Years' War

GARDINER, SAMUEL R. *The Thirty Years' War, 1618-1648*, 1903.
OGG, DAVID. *Europe in the Seventeenth Century*, 1931.

Part VI: EMERGENCE OF EUROPEAN NATIONS

General

WARD, A. W., and OTHERS (eds.). *The Cambridge Modern History*, 14 vols., Vols. V-VI, 1902-12.

Chapter 36. The Age of Charles V

ARMSTRONG, EDWARD. *Emperor Charles V*, 2 vols., 1902.

MERRIMAN, ROGER B. *Rise of the Spanish Empire in the Old World and in the New*, 3 vols., Vol. III, 1918-26.

Chapter 37. Consolidation of Royal Power in France

GRANT, ARTHUR J. *French Monarchy, 1483-1789*, 2 vols., 1925.

KIRK, JOHN F. *History of Charles the Bold, Duke of Burgundy*, 3 vols., 1864-68.

WILLERT, PAUL F. *Henry of Navarre and the Huguenots in France*, 1893.

WILLERT, PAUL F. *Reign of Louis XI*, 1876.

Chapter 38. The Age of Louis XIV

FARMER, JAMES. *Versailles and the Court under Louis XIV*, 1905.

HASSALL, ARTHUR. *Louis XIV and the Zenith of the French Monarchy*, 1895.

PERKINS, JAMES B. *France under Mazarin, with a Review of the Administration of Richelieu*, 2 vols., 1886.

PERKINS, JAMES B. *France under the Regency, with a Review of the Administration of Louis XIV*, 1892.

Chapter 39. Two Centuries of English Development

CREIGHTON, MANDELL. *Queen Elizabeth*, 1899.

FROUDE, JAMES A. *History of England from the Fall of Wolsey to the Defeat of the Spanish Armada*, 12 vols., 1899.

GARDINER, SAMUEL. *History of England from the Accession of James I to the Outbreak of the Civil War, 1603-1642*, 10 vols., 1901; *History of the Great Civil War, 1642-1649*, 4 vols., 1901; *History of the Commonwealth and Protectorate, 1649-1656*, 4 vols., 1903.

MACAULAY, THOMAS BABINGTON. *History of England from the Accession of James II*, 6 vols., 1913-15.

MERRIMAN, ROGER B. *Life and Letters of Thomas Cromwell*, 2 vols., 1902.

POLLARD, ALBERT F. *Henry VIII*, 1905.

TREVELYAN, GEORGE M. *England Under the Stuarts*, 1947.

Chapter 40. Prussia as a National State

ATKINSON, CHRISTOPHER T. *History of Germany, 1715-1815*, 1908.

BRIGHT, JAMES F. *Maria Theresa*, 1897.

MARRIOTT, JOHN A. R., and ROBERTSON, C. G. *Evolution of Prussia: The Making of an Empire*, 1915.

PARNELL, ARTHUR. *War of the Succession in Spain During the Reign of Queen Anne, 1702-1711*, 1905.

REDDAWAY, WILLIAM F. *Frederick the Great and the Rise of Prussia*, 1904.

Chapter 41. Russia Becomes a European Power

BAIN, ROBERT NISBET. *Slavonic Europe: A Political History of Poland and Russia from 1447 to 1796*, 1908.

PARES, BERNARD. *History of Russia*, 1926.

PLATONOV, SERGIEI F. *History of Russia*, 1925.

SCHUYLER, EUGENE. *Peter the Great*, 2 vols., 1884.

SEEGER, ELIZABETH. *Pageant of Russian History*, 1950.

Part VII: EXPANSION OF THE EUROPEAN WORLD

General

ABBOTT, WILBUR CORTEZ. *The Expansion of Europe: A Social and Political History of the Modern World, 1415-1789*, 1924.

DEVOTO, BERNARD. *Course of Empire*, 1952.

VILLIERS, A. J. *Monsoon Seas: Story of the Indian Ocean*, 1952.

Chapter 42. An All-Water Route to India

BEAZLEY, CHARLES R. *Prince Henry the Navigator: The Hero of Portugal and of Modern Discovery, 1394-1460*, 1895.

JAYNE, KINGSLEY G. *Vasco da Gama and His Successors, 1460-1580*, 1910.

MARTINS, JOAQUIM P. OLIVEIRA. *Golden Age of Prince Henry the Navigator*, 1914.

Chapter 43. The Search for "El Dorado"

GUILLEMARD, FRANCIS H. H. *Life of Ferdinand Magellan and the First Circumnavigation of the Globe, 1480-1521*, 1890.

MADARIAGA, SALVADOR DE. *Christopher Columbus,* 1949.
RICHMAN, I. B. *Spanish Conquerors.*
WATSON, ROBERT GRANT. *Spanish and Portuguese South America During the Colonial Period.* 2 vols., 1884.

Chapter 44. French Exploration and Settlement in the New World

BOLTON, HERBERT E., and MARSHALL, T. M. *Colonization of North America, 1492-1783,* 1920.
FISKE, JOHN. *Discovery of America,* 1892.
GIRAULT, ARTHUR. *Colonial Tariff Policy of France,* 1916.
MUNRO, W. B. *Crusaders of New France,* 1921.
THWAITES, R. G. *France in America, 1497-1763.*
WINSOR, JUSTIN (ed.). *Narrative and Critical History of America,* 8 vols., Vols. IV-V, 1884-89.

Chapter 45. English Colonies in the New World

ANDREWS, C. M. *Colonial Self-Government, 1652-1689.*

THWAITES, R. G. *The Colonies, 1492-1750,* 1910.
TYLER, L. G. *England in America, 1580-1652,* 1904.
WINSOR, JUSTIN (ed.). *Narrative and Critical History of America,* 8 vols., Vols. III, V, 1884-89.
WOOD, W. *Elizabethan Sea-Dogs.*

Chapter 46. The Development of the English Colonies

EGGLESTON, EDWARD. *Transit of Civilization from England to America in the Seventeenth Century,* 1901.
FISKE, JOHN. *Old Virginia and Her Neighbors,* 1897, and *Beginnings of New England,* 1889.
GREENE, E. B. *Provincial America, 1690-1740,* 1905.
OSGOOD, HERBERT L. *American Colonies in the Seventeenth Century,* 3 vols., 1904-07, and *American Colonies in the Eighteenth Century,* 4 vols., 1924-25.
PARRINGTON, VERNON L. *Main Currents of American Thought,* 2 vols., Vol. I, 1927.
WEEDEN, WILLIAM B. *Economic and Social History of New England,* 2 vols., 1891.

Part VIII: DECLINE OF EMPIRES

General

ABBOTT, WILBUR CORTEZ. *The Expansion of Europe, 1415-1789,* 1924.
ROSE, J. H. and OTHERS (eds.). *Cambridge History of the British Empire,* 3 vols., 1930.
WARD, A. W., and OTHERS (eds.). *The Cambridge Modern History,* 14 vols., Vol. VII, 1902-12.

Chapter 47. Europe in Search of Spice, Land, and Souls

LUCAS, CHARLES P. *Historical Geography of the British Colonies,* 7 vols., 1888-1923.
RICCI, MATTHEW. *Journals: China in the 16th Century,* 1954.
VAN LOON, HENDRIK W. *Golden Book of the Dutch Navigators,* 1916.

Chapter 48. The Age of Philip II

DAVIES, REGINALD T. *The Golden Century of Spain, 1501-1621,* 1937.
HUME, MARTIN A. S. *Spain: Its Greatness and Decay, 1497-1788,* 1899; *Philip II of Spain,* 1911; *Court of Philip IV: Spain in Decadence,* 1907.
PRESCOTT, WILLIAM H. *History of the Reign of Philip the Second, King of Spain,* 4 vols., 1904.

Chapter 49. France and England Struggle for World Dominance

BUFFINGTON, ARTHUR H. *The Second Hundred Years' War, 1689-1815,* 1929.
ROBINSON, HOWARD. *Development of the British Empire,* 1922.
SEELEY, JOHN R. *Expansion of England,* 1895.

Chapter 50. Grievances of American Colonies

ANDREWS, CHARLES M. *Colonial Background of the American Revolution,* 1924.
BEER, GEORGE L. *Commercial Policy of England Toward the American Colonies,* 1893; *British Colonial Policy, 1754-1765,* 1907.
EGERTON, HUGH E. *Causes and Character of the American Revolution,* 1923.
MCILWAIN, CHARLES H. *American Revolution: A Constitutional Interpretation,* 1923.
SCHLESINGER, ARTHUR M. *Colonial Merchants and the American Revolution, 1763-1776,* 1918.

Chapter 51. American War for Independence

ALDEN, JOHN R. *The American Revolution,* 1954.
BECKER, CARL L. *The Declaration of Independence,* 1922.

FREEMAN, D. S. *George Washington*, 5 vols., 1952.

FROTHINGHAM, RICHARD. *Rise of the Republic of the United States*, 1910.

JAMESON, JOHN F. *The American Revolution Considered as a Social Movement*, 1926.

NEVINS, ALLAN. *The American States During and After the Revolution, 1775-1789*, 1924.

Chapter 52. The Confederation and the Constitution

BEARD, CHARLES A. *An Economic Interpretation of the Constitution of the United States*, 1913.

FARRAND, MAX. *The Fathers of the Constitution: A Chronicle of the Establishment of the Union*, 1921.

HART, ALBERT B. *Formation of the Union, 1750-1829*, 1925.

McLAUGHLIN, A. C. *The Confederation and the Constitution, 1783-1789.*

PARRINGTON, VERNON L. *Main Currents in American Thought*, 2 vols., Vol. I, 1927.

Chapter 53. Early Years under the Constitution

ADAMS, HENRY. *History of the United States During the Administration of Thomas Jefferson*, 2 vols., 1930; *History of the United States During the Administration of James Madison*, 2 vols., 1930.

BABCOCK, K. C. *The Rise of American Nationality, 1811-1819*, 1906.

BASSETT, J. S. *The Federalist System, 1789-1801*, 1906.

BEARD, CHARLES A. *Economic Origins of Jeffersonian Democracy*, 1915.

CHANNING, E. *The Jeffersonian System, 1801-1811*, 1906.

CHINARD, GILBERT. *Thomas Jefferson: The Apostle of Americanism*, 1929.

LODGE, HENRY CABOT. *Alexander Hamilton*, 1917.

Part IX: ENLIGHTENMENT AND REVOLUTION

General

BOURNE, HENRY ELDRIDGE. *The Revolutionary Period in Europe, 1763-1815*, 1914.

FLICK, ALEXANDER C. *Modern World History Since 1775*, 1935.

GOTTSCHALK, LOUIS R. *The Era of the French Revolution, 1715-1815*, 1929.

STEPHENS, HENRY MORSE. *Revolutionary Europe, 1789-1815*, 1897.

WARD, A. W., and OTHERS (eds.). *The Cambridge Modern History*, 14 vols., Vols. VIII-IX. 1902-12.

Chapter 54. The Age of Enlightenment

HEARNSHAW, F. J. C. (ed.). *The Social and Political Ideas of Some Great French Thinkers of the Age of Reason*, 1930.

MORLEY, JOHN. *Voltaire*, 1923.

MOWAT, ROBERT B. *The Age of Reason*, 1934.

SEE, HENRI E. *Economic and Social Conditions in France During the Eighteenth Century*, 1930.

Chapter 55. The French Revolution

BARTHOU, LOUIS. *Mirabeau*, 1913.

BRINTON, CLARENCE CRANE. *A Decade of Revolution, 1789-1799*, 1934.

GERSHOY, LEO. *The French Revolution, 1789-1799*, 1932.

MATHIEZ, ALBERT. *The French Revolution*, 1928.

THOMPSON, JAMES MATTHEW (ed.). *French Revolution: Documents, 1789-94*, 1933.

WARD, REGINALD S. *Maximilien Robespierre: A Study in Deterioration*, 1934.

Chapter 56. The Napoleonic Wars

BAINVILLE, JACQUES. *Napoleon*, 1933.

BRINTON, CLARENCE CRANE. *The Lives of Talleyrand*, 1936.

FOURNIER, AUGUST. *Napoleon: a Biography*, 2 vols., 1911.

MADELIN, LOUIS. *The Consulate and the Empire*, 2 vols., 1934-36.

Part X: THE TRIUMPH OF NATIONALISM

General

ACHORN, ERIK. *European Civilization and Politics since 1815*, 1934.

CROCE, BENEDETTO. *History of Europe in the Nineteenth Century*, 1933.

DAVIS, WILLIAM S. *Europe Since Waterloo: A Non-technical History of Europe from the Exile of Napoleon to the Treaty of Versailles, 1815-1919*, 1926.

HAYES, CARLTON J. H. *The Historical Evolution of Modern Nationalism*, 1931.

MERZ, JOHN THEODORE. *A History of European Thought in the Nineteenth Century*, 4 vols., 1912-1928.

SCHAPIRO, J. SALWYN. *Liberalism and the Challenge of Fascism: Social Forces in England and France, 1815-1870*, 1949.

SCHAPIRO, J. SALWYN. *Modern and Contemporary European History, 1815-1934*, 1934.

SCOTT, JONATHAN FRENCH, and BALTZLY, ALEXANDER (eds.). *Readings in European History Since 1814*, 1930.

WARD, A. W., and OTHERS (eds.). *The Cambridge Modern History*, 14 vols., Vols. X-XI, 1902-12.

Chapter 57. Conservative Reaction in Europe

ARTZ, FREDERICK BINKERD. *Reaction and Revolution, 1814-1832*, 1934.

LUCAS-DUBRETON, JEAN. *The Restoration and the July Monarchy*, 1929.

PHILLIPS, W. ALISON. *Confederation of Europe: A Study of the European Alliances, 1813-1823*, 1919.

WEBSTER, CHARLES K. *Congress of Vienna, 1814-15*, 1919.

Chapter 58. The Age of Metternich

HERMAN, ARTHUR. *Metternich*, 1932.

MAY, ARTHUR JAMES. *The Age of Metternich, 1814-1848*, 1933.

PERKINS, DEXTER. *The Monroe Doctrine, 1823-1826*, 1927.

TAINE, H. A. *The Modern Regime*, 2 vols., 1931.

Chapter 59. Liberalism—The Creed of the Middle Class

BLEASE, WALTER L. *Short History of English Liberalism*, 1913.

BURY, JOHN B. *Idea of Progress*, 1920; *History of Freedom of Thought*, 1913.

FISHER, H. A. L. *Republican Tradition in Europe*, 1911.

HALEVY, ELIE. *History of the English People*, 2 vols., 1924-27.

MAURICE, C. E. *The Revolutionary Movement of 1848-49*, 1887.

MERZ, JOHN T. *History of European Thought in the Nineteenth Century*, 4 vols., 1897-1914.

ORTON, WILLIAM. *The Liberal Tradition*.

Chapter 60. Romanticism and Realism

BINKLEY, ROBERT C. *Realism and Naturalism, 1852-1871*, 1935.

BRANDES, GEORGE. *Main Currents in Nineteenth Century Literature*, 6 vols., 1923.

LECKY, WILLIAM E. H. *History of the Rise and Influence of the Spirit of Rationalism in Europe*, 2 vols., 1914.

LIPPINCOTT, BENJAMIN. *Victorian Critics of Democracy*, 1938.

ROGERS, ARTHUR K. *English and American Philosophy Since 1800*, 1922.

Chapter 61. A Century of Latin-American Development

CLEVEN, N. A. N. (ed.). *Readings in Hispanic American History*, 1927.

RIPPY, JAMES F. *Historical Evolution of Hispanic America*, 1932.

ROBERTSON, W. S. *History of the Latin-American Nations*.

WEBSTER, HUTTON. *History of Latin America*, 1936.

Chapter 62. England and the British Commonwealth of Nations

CARRINGTON, C. E. *The British Overseas*, 1950.

HALL, HESSEL D. *British Commonwealth of Nations: A Study of Its Past and Future Development*, 1920.

HALL, WALTER PHELPS. *Empire to Commonwealth*, 1928.

KEITH, ARTHUR B. *Responsible Government in the Dominions*, 1928; *Imperial Unity and the Dominions*, 1916.

Chapter 63. Nationalism in Continental Europe

DAWSON, WILLIAM H. *German Empire, 1867-1914, and the Unity Movement*, 2 vols., 1919.

GEWEHR, W. M. *The Rise of Nationalism in the Balkans, 1800-1930*, 1931.

HAYES, CARLTON J. H. *Essays in Nationalism*, 1926.

MUIR, RAMSAY. *Nationalism and Internationalism*, 1916.

ROBERTSON, CHARLES G. *Bismarck*, 1918.

ROSE, J. HOLLAND. *Nationality in Modern History*, 1916.

USHER, R. G. *Pan-Germanism*, 1913.

Part XI: GROWTH OF THE MODERN ECONOMIC ORDER

General

BOWDEN, WITT, and OTHERS. *An Economic History of Europe since 1750*, 1937.

CLOUGH, S. B., and COLE, C. W. *Economic History of Europe*, 1946.

DIETZ, FREDERICK CHARLES. *The Industrial Revolution*, 1927.

MUMFORD, LEWIS. *Technics and Civilization*, 1934.

OGG, FREDERIC AUSTIN. *Economic Development of Modern Europe*, 1935.

SEE, HENRI. *Modern Capitalism: Its Origin and Evolution*, 1928.

Chapter 64. Agricultural and Commercial Changes

DAY, CLIVE. *History of Commerce*, 1922.
HAMMOND, J. L., and B. *The Village Labourer*, 1920.
MACPHERSON, LOGAN C. *Transportation in Europe*, 1910.
SANFORD, A. H. *The Story of Agriculture in the United States*, 1915.
WEBSTER, W. C. *A General History of Commerce*, 1903.

Chapter 65. Industrial England

BEER, MAX. *History of British Socialism*, 2 vols., 1919-20.
BOWDEN, WITT. *Industrial Society in England Toward the End of the Eighteenth Century*, 1925.
CLAPHAM, J. H. *An Economic History of Modern Britain: The Early Railway Age, 1820-1850*, 1927.
MACGREGOR, DAVID H. *Evolution of Industry*, 1912.

Chapter 66. England in the Nineteenth Century

HOBSON, JOHN A. *Evolution of Modern Capitalism: A Study of Machine Production*, 1917.
HUTCHINS, B. L., and HARRISON, A. *History of Factory Legislation*, 1911.
ROTH, C. *Benjamin Disraeli*, 1953.
SMITH, ADAM. *The Wealth of Nations*, 1776.
TREVELYAN, GEORGE M. *British History in the Nineteenth Century, 1782-1901*, 1922.
WEBB, S., and B. *History of Trade Unionism*, 1920.

Chapter 67. Industrialism Comes to France and Germany

ARNAUD, RENÉ. *The Second Republic and Napoleon III*, 1930.
CLAPHAM, JOHN H. *Economic Development of France and Germany, 1815-1914*, 1921.
SOMBART, WERNER. *Socialism and the Social Movement*, 1909.

Part XII: THE UNITED STATES FROM 1815 TO 1917

General

ADAMS, JAMES TRUSLOW. *The Adams Family*, 1930.
BEARD, CHARLES A., and MARY R. *The Rise of American Civilization*, 1934.
CARMAN, HARRY J., and SYRETT, H. C. *History of the American People*, 2 vols., 1953.
COMMAGER, HENRY STEELE (ed.). *Documents of American History*, 1934.
DUNBAR, SEYMOUR. *A History of Travel in America*, 1931.
MCLAUGHLIN, ANDREW C. *A Constitutional History of the United States*, 1935.
SIMPKINS, FRANCIS B. *History of the South, 1820-1952*, 2nd ed., 1953.
TURNER, FREDERICK JACKSON. *The Frontier in American History*, 1935.

Chapter 68. Young America

BEVERIDGE, ALBERT J. *Life of John Marshall*, 4 vols., 1916-19.
FISH, CARL R. *The Rise of the Common Man, 1830-1850*, 1927.
OGG, FREDERIC A. *The Old Northwest*, 1921; *The Reign of Andrew Jackson*, 1921.
TOCQUEVILLE, ALEXIS DE. *Democracy in America*. 1946.

Chapter 69. Expansion, Sectionalism, and Slavery

MACY, JESSE. *The Anti-Slavery Crusade*, 1921.
STEPHENSON, NATHANIEL W. *Texas and the Mexican War*, 1921.
WHITE, STEWART E. *The Forty-Niners*, 1921.

Chapter 70. Civil War and Reconstruction

BOWERS, CLAUDE G. *The Tragic Era: The Revolution after Lincoln*, 1932.
COLE, ARTHUR CHARLES. *The Irrepressible Conflict, 1850-1865*, 1934.
DUBOIS, W. E. B. *Black Reconstruction, 1860-1880*, 1935.
FORD, HENRY JONES. *The Cleveland Era*, 1921.
HENRY, R. S. *The Story of Reconstruction*, 1938.
NEVINS, ALLAN. *The Emergence of Modern America, 1865-1878*, 1927.
NICOLAY, JOHN GEORGE. *A Short Life of Abraham Lincoln*, 1902.
PRATT, FLETCHER. *Ordeal by Fire, an Informal History of the Civil War*, 1935.
RANDALL, JAMES G. *Civil War and Reconstruction*, 1953.
SANDBURG, CARL. *Abraham Lincoln; the War Years.* 1952.
STEPHENSON, NATHANIEL W. *Abraham Lincoln and the Union*, 1921.
THOMAS, BENJAMIN P. *Abraham Lincoln*, 1952.

Chapter 71. Industrialization and Social Change

BEARD, CHARLES A. *Contemporary American History, 1877-1913*, 1918.
BUCK, SOLON JUSTUS. *The Agrarian Crusade*, 1921.
FAULKNER, HAROLD V. *The Quest for Social Justice, 1898-1914*, 1931.
HACKER, LOUIS MORTON. *The United States Since 1865*, 1934.
HENDRICK, BURTON JESSE. *The Age of Big Business*, 1921.

HOWLAND, HAROLD J. *Theodore Roosevelt and His Times*, 1921.

KEIR, ROBERT MALCOM. *The March of Commerce*, 1927; *The Epic of Industry*, 1926.

LINK, A. S. *Woodrow Wilson and the Progressive Era*, 1954.

MOODY, JOHN. *The Masters of Capital*, 1921.

MOODY, JOHN. *The Railroad Builders*, 1921.

THOMPSON, HOLLAND. *The Age of Invention*, 1921.

SCHLESINGER, ARTHUR M. *The Rise of the City, 1878-1898*, 1933; *Rise of Modern America*, 1951.

Part XIII: WORLD IMPERIALISM

General

GOOCH, GEORGE P., and MASTERMAN, J. H. B. *A Century of British Foreign Policy*, 1917.

HOSKINS, H. L. *European Imperialism in Africa*, 1930.

LANGER, WILLIAM L. *The Diplomacy of Imperialism, 1890-1902*, 2 vols., 1935.

LIPPMANN, WALTER. *Stakes of Diplomacy*, 1915.

MOON, PARKER THOMAS. *Imperialism and World Politics*, 1929.

Chapter 72. European Partition of Africa

HOSKINS, HALFORD L. *European Imperialism in Africa*, 1930.

JOHNSTON, HARRY H. *The Opening Up of Africa*, 1911.

WALKER, ERIC A. *A History of South Africa*, 1935.

YOUNG, GEORGE. *Egypt*, 1927.

Chapter 73. Imperialism in the Near and Middle East

MARRIOTT, J. A. JR. *Eastern Question: An Historical Study of European Diplomacy*, 1924.

TYLER, MASON W. *European Powers and the Near East, 1875-1908*, 1925.

YOUNG, GEORGE. *Nationalism and War in the Near East*, 1915.

Chapter 74. Imperialism in the Far East

BARNES, JOSEPH (ed.). *Empire in the East*, 1934.

OWEN, DAVID E. *Imperialism and Nationalism in the Far East*, 1929.

QUIGLEY, HAROLD S., and BLAKESLEE, G. H. *The Far East: An International Survey*, 1938.

SKRINE, FRANCIS H. *Expansion of Russia, 1815-1900*, 1903.

TREAT, PAYSON JACKSON. *The Far East: A Political and Diplomatic History*, 1935.

VINACKE, HAROLD MONK. *A History of the Far East in Modern Times*, 1936.

Chapter 75. American Imperialism

BAILEY, THOMAS A. *A Diplomatic History of the American People*, 1946.

BEMIS, SAMUEL F. *A Diplomatic History of the United States*, 1942.

RIPPY, J. F. *Latin America and World Politics*, 1938.

Part XIV: WORLD WAR I

General

CRUTTWELL, C. R. M. F. *A History of the Great War, 1914-1918*, 1934.

DAVIS, WILLIAM S. *Europe Since Waterloo: a Non-technical History of Europe from the Exile of Napoleon to the Treaty of Versailles, 1815-1919*, 1926.

EDMONDS, J. E. *A Short History of World I*, 1951.

GOOCH, GEORGE P. *History of Modern Europe, 1878-1919*, 1923.

LIDDELL HART, B. H. *A History of the World War*, 1934.

SEYMOUR, CHARLES. *Woodrow Wilson and the World War*, 1921.

SLOSSON, PRESTON W. *Europe since 1870*, 1935.

STAMWOOD, EDWARD. *Our Times, 1900-1925*, 1935.

Chapter 76. Prewar Nationalism

BARNES, HARRY ELMER. *The Genesis of the World War: An Introduction to the Problem of War Guilt*, 1929.

DICKINSON, GOLDSWORTHY L. *The International Anarchy, 1904-1914*, 1926.

EWART, JOHN S. *The Roots and Causes of the Wars, 1914-1918*, 2 vols., 1925.

FAY, SIDNEY B. *The Origins of the World War*, 2 vols., 1930.

SCHMITT, BERNADOTTE EVERLY. *Triple Alliance and Triple Entente*, 1934.

Chapter 77. The Coming of the War

DANE, EDMUND. *British Campaigns in the Nearer East, 1914-1918*, 2 vols., 1919.

FAY, SIDNEY B. *The Origins of the World War*, 1930.

HEADLAM, JAMES W. *History of Twelve Days, July 24th to August 4th, 1914. Being an Account of the Negotiations Preceding the Outbreak of War Based on the Official Publications*, 1915.

NEVINSON, HENRY W. *Dardanelles Campaign*, 1918.

PERRIS, GEORGE H. *Battle of the Marne*, 1920.

POLLARD, ALBERT F. *Short History of the Great War*, 1920.

PRIBRAM, ALFRED F. *Austrian Foreign Policy, 1908-1918*, 1923.

SCHMITT, BERNADOTTE EVERLY. *Coming of the War, 1914*, 2 vols., 1930.

WOLFF, THEODOR. *The Eve of 1914*, 1936.

Chapter 78. The Last Two Years of World War I

BASSETT, JOHN S. *Our War with Germany, a History*, 1919.

HAYES, C. J. H. *Brief History of the Great War*, 1920.

HOWLAND, CHARLES R. *Military History of the World War*, 2 vols., 1923.

MCMASTER, JOHN BACH. *The United States in the World War*, 2 vols., 1933-36.

MILLIS, WALTER. *The Road to War: America, 1914-1917*, 1935.

THOMAS, SHIPLEY. *History of the AEF*, 1920.

Chapter 79. The Making of Peace

DODD, WILLIAM E. *Woodrow Wilson and His Work*.

HARRIS, H. WILSON. *Peace in the Making*, 1920.

KEYNES, JOHN MAYNARD. *The Economic Consequences of the Peace*, 1920.

NOBLE, GEORGE BERNARD. *Policies and Opinions at Paris, 1919*, 1935.

SCOTT, ARTHUR P. *Introduction to the Peace Treaties*, 1920.

SHOTWELL, JAMES T. *At the Paris Peace Conference*, 1937.

Chapter 80. The Russian Revolution

CHAMBERLIN, W. H. *The Russian Revolution, 1917-1921*, 1935.

LAWTON, L. *The Russian Revolution, 1917-1926*, 1927.

MAVOR, J. *The Russian Revolution*, 1928.

PARES, B. *Fall of the Russian Monarchy*, 1939.

VERNADSKY, G. *The Russian Revolution*, 1932.

Part XV: AFTERMATH AND RECONSTRUCTION

General

BUELL, RAYMOND L. *Europe: A History of Ten Years*, 1931.

FORD, GUY STANTON (ed.). *Dictatorship in the Modern World*, 1935.

GATHORNE-HARDY, GEOFFREY M. *A Short History of International Affairs, 1920-1934*, 1934.

HOCKETT, HOMER C., and SCHLESINGER, A. M. *Land of the Free*, 1944.

LANGSAM, WALTER CONSUELO. *The World since 1914*, 1948.

LEE, DWIGHT E. *Ten Years: The World on the Way to War, 1930-1940*, 1942.

MAY, A. J. *Europe and Two World Wars*, 1947.

NICHOLS, JEANNETTE P. *Twentieth Century United States: A History*, 1943.

OAKESHOTT, MICHAEL JOSEPH. *Social and Political Doctrines of Contemporary Europe*, 1942.

ROGERS, LINDSAY. *Crisis Government*, 1934.

SCHMITT, BERNADOTTE E. *From Versailles to Munich*, 1938.

TOYNBEE, ARNOLD J. *Survey of International Affairs* (annually since 1925).

Chapter 81. Fascism in Europe

EBENSTEIN, W. *Fascist Italy*, 1939.

NEUMANN, FRANZ. *Behemoth: The Structure and Practice of National Socialism*, 1944.

STURZO, LUIGI. *Italy and Fascismo*, 1927.

Chapter 82. Democracies and Dictatorships— the Struggle for Security

ELTON, LORD. *Imperial Commonwealth*, 1946.

GRAHAM, MALBONE W. *New Governments of Central Europe*, 1924.

GRAHAM, MALBONE W. *New Governments of Eastern Europe*, 1927.

GUÉRARD, ALBERT L. *France: A Short History*, 1946.

NEVINS, ALLAN, and BREBNER, J. B. *The Making of Modern Britain*, 1943.

SIEGFRIED, ANDRÉ. *France: A Study in Nationality*, 1930.

STEINBERG, S. H. *A Short History of Germany*, 1946.

Chapter 83. The Republican Decade and the New Deal

ALLEN, FREDERICK LEWIS. *Only Yesterday: An Informal History of the Nineteen-Twenties*, 1933.

NEVINS, ALLAN. *Ford: The Times, the Man, the Company*, 1954.

RAUCH, BASIL. *The History of the New Deal*, 1944.

SLOSSON, PRESTON W. *The Great Crusade and After, 1914-1928*, 1931.

Chapter 84. Latin America Between Wars

PARKES, H. B. *History of Mexico*, rev. ed., 1950.

WILLIAMS, MARY W. *The People and Politics of Latin America*, 1938.

WYTHE, GEORGE. *Industry in Latin America*, 1945.

Chapter 85. Events in Africa and the Far East

BLAKESLEE, GEORGE H. *Conflicts of Policy in the Far East*, 1934.

CHIROL, VALENTINE. *The Occident and the Orient,* 1924.

FISCHER, LOUIS. *Mohandas Karamchand Gandhi,* 1950.

HOLCOMBE, ARTHUR N. *The Chinese Revolution,* 1931.

LASKER, BRUNO. *Asia on the Move,* 1945.

MORAES, F. R., and STIMSON, R. *Introduction to India,* 1943.

OSBORN, FAIRFIELD. *The Pacific World,* 1944.

QUIGLEY, HAROLD S. *Japanese Government and Politics,* 1932.

SOKOLSKY, GEORGE E. *The Tinder Box of Asia,* 1933.

TOWNSEND, MARY E., and PEAKE, C. H. *European Colonial Expansion since 1871,* 1941.

VINACKE, H. M. *A History of the Far East in Modern Times,* 5th ed., 1950.

Part XVI: WORLD WAR II AND AFTER

General

CHURCHILL, WINSTON. *The Second World War,* 6 vols., 1953.

COMMAGER, HENRY S. (ed.). *The Story of the Second World War,* 1945.

SCOTT, JOHN. *Europe in Revolution, 1938-1945,* 1945.

SHOTWELL, JAMES T. *On the Rim of the Abyss,* 1936.

SHUGG, ROGER W., and DEWEERD, H. A. *World War II,* 1946.

SPROUT, HAROLD and MARGARET. *Foundations of National Power: Readings on World Politics and American Security,* 1946.

Chapter 86. Munich and the Outbreak of War

HAINES, CHARLES GROVE. *The Origins and Background of the Second World War,* 1944.

SCHUMAN, FREDERICK L. *Night Over Europe: The Diplomacy of Nemesis, 1939-1940,* 1941.

Chapter 87. The War to Pearl Harbor

CLIFFORD, ALEXANDER C. *The Conquest of North Africa, 1940-1943,* 1943.

DRAPER, THEODORE. *The Six Weeks War: France, May 10-June 25, 1940,* 1944.

KERR, WALTER B. *The Russian Army: Its Men, Its Leaders, and Its Battles,* 1944.

LANGER, WILLIAM L. *Our Vichy Gamble,* 1947.

Chapter 88. Destruction of the Axis

CANT, GILBERT. *The Great Pacific Victory,* 1946.

EISENHOWER, DWIGHT D. *Eisenhower's Own Story of the War,* 1946.

KARIG, WALTER, and KELLEY, W. *Battle Report: Pearl Harbor to Coral Sea,* 1944.

MARSHALL, GEORGE C. *The Winning of the War in Europe and the Pacific,* 1945.

MILLIS, WALTER. *The Last Phase: The Allied Victory in Western Europe, June 6, 1944-May 8, 1945,* 1946.

PRATT, FLETCHER. *War for the World,* 1950.

Chapter 89. Postwar Nations

CH'IEN, TUAN-SHENG. *Government and Politics of China,* 1950.

COLE, TAYLOR (ed.). *European Political Systems,* 1953.

JERRÍN, MIGUEL. *Governments of Latin America,* 1953.

KOESTLER, ARTHUR. *Promise and Fulfillment: Palestine, 1917-1949,* 1949.

LENGYEL, EMIL. *World Without End: The Middle East,* 1953.

MILLS, LENNOX A. (ed.). *The New World of Southeast Asia,* 1949.

NEHRU, JAWAHARLAL. *The Discovery of India,* 1946.

NORTH, ROBERT. *Moscow and Chinese Communists,* 1953.

ROSTOW, W. W. *Dynamics of Soviet Society,* 1954.

ROSTOW, W. W., and others. *The Prospects for Communist China,* 1954.

Chapter 90. The World in the Atomic Age

CANHAM, ERWIN D. *et al. Awakening: The World at Mid-Century,* 1951.

DE GRAZIA, ALFRED. *Elements of Political Science,* 1952.

DEWHURST, J. F., and Associates. *America's Needs and Resources,* 1955.

KENNAN, GEORGE. *American Diplomacy, 1900-1950,* 1952.

LEVI, WERNER. *Fundamentals of World Organization,* 1950.

PEFFER, NATHANIEL. *America's Place in the World,* 1945.

POTTER, ROBERT D. *The Atomic Revolution,* 1946.

Index

N

Naboth, 66, 67
Nachtigal, 598
Nagasaki, 417, 697
Naguib, Maj. Gen. Mohammed, 704
Nanking, 676-678
Nantes, 479
Nantes, Edict of, 330, 370, 407
Naples, Belasarius, 201; Frederick, 280; kingdom, 301; Charles VIII, 349; outbreak, 503; unification, 529
Napoleon, vii; Map, 95; Charlemagne, 209; Frederick II, 374; Holland, 417, 426; Bourbon crown, 419; treaty with U. S., 454; Louisiana Purchase, 456; Berlin and Milan Decrees, 457; early life, 481; First Consul and Emperor, 482; empire, 483; growing power, 484; policies, 485; Spain, 486, 488; Russia, 489, 490, 496; Elba, 491; England, 494; Italy, 495, 529; Denmark, 497; Congress of Vienna, 499; armies, 500; nationalism, 501, 502; Louis XVIII, 503; Pius VII, 508; classicism, 510; Brazil, 516; Germany, 530; Bernadotte, 536; Metternich, 539; English industry, 550; Louis Napoleon, 555; German Confederation, 556; Concordat of 1801, 620
Napoleon III (Louis Napoleon), 518, 555, 609
Naram-Sim, 28
Narbada River, 149, 155
Narmer, 18
Narses, 194, 201
Narvaez, 391
Naseby, 365
Nasser, Gamal Abd el, 704
Nast, Thomas, 514
Nathan, 64
National Assembly (France), 473, 474, 556
National Constitutional Assembly (France), 475
National Convention (France), 447, 478, 480
National Guard (France), 474
National Guard (U.S.), 689
National Industrial Recovery Act, 699
National Insurance Act, 553
National Liberation, Committee of, 686
National Republicans, 567
National Revolutionary Party (Mexico), 672, 673
National Road, 562
National Socialists (Nazis), 654-656
Nationalism, After World War II, 701-2; Africa, 704-5; Zionists, 705-6; Iran, 706; Indonesia, 709; China, 710; Indochina, 713

Nationalist Government (China), 710, 714, 715
Nationalities, Council of, 662
NATO, 703
Nausicaa, 97
Nautilus, 719
Navarre, Great Schism, 295; Christian, 341; Charles V, 344; Francis I, 350
Navigation Acts, 521
Nazareth, 47, 66
Nazi, Sphere of influence, 679; Maquis, 686; drive into Russia, 690; defenses in France, 695; Atlantic Charter, 699; treatment of Jews, 700, 706; Yalta, 700; Austria, 702
Near East, Geography, 1, 5; commerce, 4; peoples, 6; pottery, 15; empire, 32; politics, 33; Labarnas, 34; cities, 40; menace, 60; David, 64; language, 70; library, 72; Assyrian, 73; races, 83; neolithic, 84; Crete, 88; Rome, 134; Buddhism, 153; bronze, 163; Church, 188, 242; Mohammed, 204, 205; Moslems, 241, 245; Crusaders, 243; colonies, 384; English policy, 522; English prestige, 523; imperialism, 593; Russia, 600; Europe, 618; exposure in World War II, 688; postwar, 701; new nations, 705
Nebraska, 578
Nebuchadnezzar, 69, 73-76
Necker, 472
Neferbauptah, 25
Nefrititi, 49-51, 53
Nefrure, 43
Negro, Slavery, 393, 412, 468; Hawkins, 401; Africa, 705; civil liberties, 716; desegregation decision, 717
Nehemiah, 81
Nehru, Jawaharlal, 707
Nelson, Lord, 481
Nemi, Lake, 122
Neolithic, Anatolia, 14; culture, 84, 85; Italy, 121; China, 164; Chou, 165, 167
Nepal Hills, 152
Nerchinsk, 418
Nero, Jews, 82; rule, 139; death, 140
Nerva, 140
Nessus, 94, 95
Nestorians, 179
Netherlands, Vesalius, 318; Holy Roman Empire, 324; Charles V, 326, 343, 345; Reformation, 330; Spanish, 340; Hapsburgs, 342; Philip, 246; Burgundy, 348; League of Augsburg, 355; Elizabeth, 362; William III, 367; War of Austrian Succession, 373, 428; contention, 419; revolt, 420; Philip II, 421-423; French Revolution, 426; Austrian Netherlands, 481; Congress of Vienna,

499; Belgium, 535; 19th century, 536; European Coal and Steel Community, 703; NATO, 703; Indonesia, 709-10
Netherlands East Indies, 683, 709
Neuilly-sur-Seine, 644
Neutrality Act of 1935, 670, 688
Nevada, 578
New Amsterdam, 410, 426
New Britain, 691, 697
New Brunswick, 525
New Caledonia, 610
New Deal, 669, 670
New England, Compared with China, 160; Spanish exploration, 388; compared with *Cabildo*, 392; Champlain, 395; compared with Quebec, 399; soil, 406; New Netherlands, 410; landholding, 411; products, 412; education, 413; local government, 414; Sugar Act, 434; Quebec Act, 438; militia, 439, 442; Burgoyne plan, 441; John Adams, 453; Federalists, 454, 456; Embargo Act, 457; War of 1812, 459, 460; transcendentalism, 561
New France, Verrazano, 395; royal province, 396; colonists, 399; De Laval, 400
New Granada, 516
New Guinea, Germany, 610; World War II, 683, 691, 697; western, 710
New Hampshire, Land, 405; settled, 407; Articles of Confederation, 446; Pickering, 454; state churches, 563
New Hebrides, 610
New Jersey, Land, 405; York, 410; Washington, 441; Morristown, 442; Articles of Confederation, 446; Federal Convention, 448; Ratification, 450
New Mexico, Santa Fe, 391; Mexican War, 566; Gadsden Purchase, 567; territorial government, 569; statehood, 578; U. S. expansion, 612
New Netherland, 410
New Orleans, Founded, 398; colonists, 399; French influence, 400; proposed capture, 447; frontiersmen, 456; War of 1812, 459
New Stone Age, 84, 121
New Sweden, 409, 410
New Testament, 197
New World, Spain, 341, 345, 363, 392, 421; Mary, 361; England, 362, 401, 404; Prince Henry, 384; first colony, 387; Americus Vespucius, 388; Christianity, 394; France, 395, 400; struggle for domination, 398; Dutch East India Co., 409; culture, 413; colonial governments, 502; progress, 516
New York, Land, 405; colony, 410; fur trade, 412; settlers, 414,